Margaret Follis

The Catholic Church in Tennessee

The Catholic Church in Tennessee

The Sesquicentennial Story

THOMAS STRITCH

THE CATHOLIC CENTER
Nashville • 1987

Library of Congress Cataloging-in-Publication Data:

Stritch, Thomas.
The Catholic Church in Tennessee.

1. Catholic Church—Tennessee—History.
2. Tennessee—Church history. I. Title.

BX1415.T35S87 1987 282'.768 87-10301

ISBN 0-9618260-0-2

The heraldic arms of the Diocese of Nashville ornament the title page.

To my brother

Father Morris Stritch

Priest of the Diocese of Memphis

Contents

Illustrations

Yellow Fever

A Variety of Churches

Some Hospices

Some Nashville Schools

Four Bishops from Tennessee

Byrne the Builder

Bishop Smith and His Times

The Adrian Years

A Hierarchy of Tennesseans

These Also Served

Miscellany

Acknowledgments

Monsignor John Tracy Ellis, the *fons et origo* of modern American Catholic historical scholarship, has read the manuscript of this book with his usual meticulous care, and saved me from many an error both of matter and style. Two Notre Dame professors of history, Father Marvin O'Connell and Philip Gleason, have been equally generous. I am appalled to think of how much weaker my book would be without the unselfish kindness of these three distinguished scholars, and at a loss to express my gratitude.

Richard Quick, for forty years the administrative stalwart of the Catholic diocese of Nashville, has helped me much with his retentive memory of things past. The late Charles Pool set me straight on west Tennessee facts and figures, and counselled me wisely besides. I learned most of what I have written about the Chattanooga region from the writings of Monsignor George Flanigen, my predecessor as diocesan historian, who was a Chattanooga pastor for many years. My mentor for Knoxville and northeast Tennessee was Laurence V. Gibney, Jr., the most reliable of helpers.

Three Tennessee academic historians have saved me from blunders in secular history. They are Professor Anita Goodstein, of the University of the South; Professor Don H. Doyle, of Vanderbilt University; and Professor Emeritus James Livingood, of the University of Tennessee at Chattanooga. I am grateful to two other Notre Dame professors, Father Thomas Blantz and Fredrick B. Pike, and to Professor James Patrick of the University of Dallas, for assistance in their specialty areas as well as welcome encouragement. Professors Robert E. Corlew and Robert P. Jones, of Middle Tennessee State University, also read the manuscript and cheered me on.

Two pillars of the Tennessee Historical Society provided sensitive and acute criticism. They are James A. Hoobler, its Executive Director, and Walter Durham, its brilliant historian. Another professional historian, the Most Reverend Oscar H. Lipscomb, Archbishop of Mobile, contributed some penetrating insights.

Other helpful readers were Most Reverend Francis Shea, Bishop of Evansville and a native Tennessean; Sister Agnes Geraldine McGann, Archivist of the Sisters of Nazareth, Kentucky; Dominican Sisters Cecilia Lynch and Aloysius Mackin of Aquinas Junior College, Nashville; Father Peter Meaney, O.S.B., of St. Mary's Abbey, Delbarton, New Jersey; Monsignor Charles Williams, former Chancellor of the Diocese of Nashville; Louise Davis, of the *Nashville Tennessean;* Charles Nolan, Associate Archivist of the Archdiocese of New Orleans; and Josiah Brady, of the Memphis Public Library.

Now I come to try to thank the home team, an impossible task, for never have I found more generous and cheerful friends than my fellow workers at the Nashville Catholic Center. Father Owen F. Campion and his staff of *The Tennessee Register,* Anthony J. Spence and Thomas F. Shaughnessy, were totally cooperative. Evelyn Peek did a hundred things well to lighten my work while unselfishly adding to her own. Anne Franz's work on the word processor literally made the book possible; I cannot praise her warm and generous assistance highly enough. Ann Nicholson's assistance has been so invaluable that her name belongs on the title page as co-author. As the first Archivist of the diocese she has brought order to the archival holdings and intelligent service to its clients, myself most notably. It is a joy for me to thank her publicly for helping me in so many different ways.

I owe a great debt to Robert A. McGaw, Secretary Emeritus of Vanderbilt University, who designed this book and accompanied me on every step of its labor. I can imagine no more congenial collaborator than this old friend, who, with his wife Elizabeth, has so immeasurably enriched my life.

But my greatest debts are to two people who had nothing directly to do with putting this book together. Bishop James D. Niedergeses, the chief planner of the diocese's Sesquicentennial celebration, commissioned this book, but, following our initial agreement that it should be, as far as I could make it so, a book Tennessee Catholics would want to read, left me alone, thus proving himself the wisest and kindest of patrons. But I would not have accepted the bishop's invitation to write the book without the hospitality of my sister, Katherine Stritch, who welcomed me into her Nashville home while I wrote. The bishop commissioned the book, but sister Kate victualled it.

Thomas Stritch
Professor Emeritus, American Studies
University of Notre Dame

Introduction

July 28, 1987, marks the 150th Anniversary of the establishment of the Catholic Diocese of Nashville. Natchez and Dubuque were created dioceses at the same time, making a total of sixteen in the United States. Today there are 150.

Nashville is, then, one of the oldest dioceses in the country. It has a long and eventful history and pre-history, beginning with the great explorers DeSoto and LaSalle, and embracing all our great wars and every American presidency. Its nine bishops have known flood and fire, bias and bigotry, tragedy and triumph. It has given the Church eleven bishops who were born in Tennessee or worked in the diocese, four of them living, and countless holy men and women both clerical and lay.

Professor Thomas Stritch, of the faculty of the University of Notre Dame and a member of an old Nashville Catholic family, has written the story of Catholicism in Tennessee for our Sesquicentennial. His eminently readable book serves as a centerpiece in our year-long Sesquicentennial celebration.

It is a centerpiece because it tells us about our rich Catholic heritage. That fascinating past is too little known. I hope this book will make it better known. I found reading it a pleasure. But the book meant more than that to me. It made me prouder than ever to be a Tennessee Catholic. I hope it will strengthen the faith of those who read it, and inspire them to recall and record their own histories for our Bicentennial in Anno Domini 2037.

James D. Niedergeses
Bishop of Nashville

Prologue

The Spanish and the French

To begin with, there were the Spaniards. So saturated are our legends with the English explorations and settlements such as Jamestown and Plymouth Rock that the much earlier Spanish explorations tend to be forgotten. This is especially true of southeastern United States. In the Southwest, of course, the Spanish influence is everywhere, reflected in a thousand place-names and legends. Even so, southwesterners tend to forget the Spanish origins of their own mythology. The origin of the cowboy is Spanish, not American, right down to the names of the tools of the trade, like lariat. But, although Spanish explorers strove mightily in the Southeast, they were, on the whole, failures, and left scarcely a lasting mark upon the land.

Heaven knows they tried hard enough. Again and again they sent out expeditions that floundered and failed. Hernandez de Cordoba lost his fortune and his life fighting Indians in Florida (1517); Francisco de Garay, the first white man to explore the Gulf Coast around Mobile Bay, died challenging the great Cortez in Mexico (1523); the fabled Ponce de Leon made a second attempt to take Florida and was killed by the Indians there (1521); Vasquez de Ayllon died near the mouth of the Savannah River in Georgia in 1526 and his expedition limped back to Santo Domingo in failure; and Panfilio de Narvaez came to the saddest end of all, lost at sea as he tried to save himself while abandoning his men, a remnant of whom fizzled out in Texas. All these expeditions combined cross and crown, Church and State, envisioned the conversion of the Indians as well as their conquest, and derived no small part of their drive from their faith in God as well as in themselves. Indeed, in most, the two were indistinguishable.

By far the best planned, widest ranging, and best led was that of Hernando de Soto, 1538-43. De Soto had retired to Spain, rich from his youthful adventures with Cortez and Pizarro, but — what was it? — a spirit of adventure, an urgent restlessness, a fierce patriotism allied to impregnable Catholic piety, whatever, took him back to the New World to recoup the failures of his predecessors and take possession of southeastern continental United States for the King-Emperor of Spain. He sailed from Spain in the spring of 1538, stopping at Cuba for supplies and re-grouping, and landed near the present Bradenton, on the west coast of Florida, in the spring of 1539.

He brought with him an ample supply of the richest gift of the Spanish to the New World, horses. The horse, plentiful in prehistoric America, had died out, no one knows when or why, since the buffalo, who have the same needs, throve. The Spanish explorers re-populated America, both North and South, with their tough, wiry native beasts, who found the entire New World to their liking. De Soto also brought with him a herd of hogs to butcher along the way for fresh meat. Descended from a hardy Andalusian breed accustomed to foraging for themselves, these hogs were bred on the long exploration and lasted almost until its end.

Disputation about de Soto's route is endless. The United States Congress sought to end it in 1937, when it set up a commission to study the good contemporary accounts and settle the matter once and for all, in preparation for a 1941 Pan-American Exhibition planned for Tampa, which never took place because of World War II. Since then, some archaeologists, assiduously digging in the Indian sites, have thought the findings of the commission erroneous, though not by much.

The commission says that de Soto ranged northward from Tampa to western South Carolina with a force numbering around 500. From here he headed west, and in a formidable performance crossed the Blue Ridge Mountains, pigs and all, from present-day Walhalla, South Carolina, to Highlands, North Carolina (present U.S. Route 64). From here the expedition made the difficult crossing into the valley of East Tennessee south of Etowah, and on June 3, 1540, came to the Tennessee River. This the expedition followed downstream to an area of islands in the neighborhood of present South Pittsburg. They settled on one of these — which, is in scholarly dispute — for almost a month, restoring the energy of their horses on the rich pasture, and swimming and playing games with the Creek Indians.

According to this reckoning, then, most of May and June was spent in Southeast Tennessee, and it's quite certain that Mass was celebrated by the priests who accompanied the expedition. Just how many priests there were by this time isn't clear — eight are named, but there may have been more, some say as many as twelve. It's more than a speculation that these tried to convert their Indian hosts all along the route, but the Indians of the Southeast, all through the colonial period, proved extremely difficult to convert. Yet one can't help wondering what they thought as the priest raised the host at Mass before a silent and worshipful throng of Spanish soldiers.

Not long after this, Mass was said no more. The friendly Creeks of island days inevitably turned hostile for the inevitable reason, Indian women for the Spanish soldiers, and as de Soto continued his quest southward, suspicions and skirmishes turned into real battles. At one of these, Mabila (Mobile), Alabama, the Indians set fire to the supply wagons containing the altar breads and wines. Sticking close to the theology they were taught, the Spanish priests refused to consecrate the cornbread that was daily fare of both the invading Spanish and the native Indians, so from then on only the "Missa Secca", the "dry" Mass was possible — if Mass without the Eucharist can be counted as Mass at all. The tradition of saying the prayers for Mass when priests were not available, in prison, at sea, in heathen lands, was, and is, as old as the Mass itself.

De Soto fought at Mabila, as he had earlier in Florida, only because he was in search of treasure such as he had found in Peru and Mexico. Despite the priests, he was openly and crassly in search of plunder, gold and silver most especially. Of course, he didn't find any; the most he got were some little pearls, so familiar to Tennessee boys searching for mussels along the banks of the streams. After Mabila, the expedition turned north. A worse battle with the Indians on the Tombigbee River followed, but these clashes were exceptional. On the whole, the expedition fared well. In addition to the drove of swine, there was plenty of game along the way, ample wild nuts and fruit — the soldiers were especially fond of the persimmons, which they called medlars — and they rarely lacked for cornmeal and vegetables supplied by the Indians. Eventually, they did lack good clothing as their own wore out, something the Indians obviously couldn't provide.

Working generally westward, de Soto, who edged south from Tennessee, veered north again when he smelled the salt wind off Mobile Bay — perhaps fearful his men would insist on returning to Tampa. He "discovered" the Mississippi, as every grade-schooler mistakenly knows, in May of 1541 — mistakenly, since the river's existence had been known for some years. De Soto was simply the first white man to identify its southern course. That course is so changeable, and so changed, that it is impossible to be definite about where de Soto's expedition crossed it, especially since the upheavals of the earthquakes of 1811-12 which created Reelfoot Lake. So, the 1937 commission says, the expedition probably crossed the great river at some point a few miles south of Memphis in the barges they built for the purpose. De Soto then explored much of Arkansas, but turned back to the river, with which his name is forever associated, to die, on May 21, 1542. No doubt a "Missa Secca" was said for him then. His body was put in a sack, weighted with sand, and dumped in the river for burial near Natchez, for fear that the Indians would desecrate it. Without his leadership, his men headed for Mexico and home. Three hundred eleven of them made it, four years and four months after they had departed. Five priests are said to have been among them.

About twenty-five years later, another Spanish force came into Tennessee. Led by Juan Pardo, a sizable group of Spanish trod much the same path as did de Soto. By this time, however, 1566, the Spanish were more interested in protecting their sea routes and living in peace with the Indians than in non-existent plunder. The able leadership of Pedro Menendez threw the French out of South Carolina and established a base at St. Helena, the present Parris Island Marine Corps Base. Pardo led his force from here, and built a string of forts, one on or near the de Soto campsite on the Tennessee River. It is more than likely that Mass was celebrated again in Tennessee; in his journal Pardo notes there was a priest with him, whom he left for a time with a group of Indians to instruct them in religion. The Pardo expeditions — he returned in 1567 to build more forts — were part of Menendez' plan to occupy the eastern coast of North America. He got as far as Chesapeake Bay, where the Jesuits attempted Indian missions in the 1570s.

In view of the relative success of the missions of the Southwest, the failure of the missions in the Southeast is puzzling. The horses, dogs, and gunpowder that so terrified the natives from Peru to San Francisco had less effect on the Indians of the East Coast, who stoutly resisted both conquest and conversion. First the Jesuits, then the Franciscans, strung missions all through Florida and Georgia, but by the time the English moved in, in the early eighteenth century, these had all but vanished. The Jesuits in the Chesapeake Bay area were murdered, to a man. Only at St. Augustine, founded by Menendez, is there some tangible Spanish memory.

By the end of the century the Spanish on the East Coast were reduced to a meager garrison at St. Augustine, surrounded by unfriendly Indians. The Spanish sun was setting; the costly wars with the English and the Dutch left their leaders no room to maneuver in North America. Although fascinating historically, the Spanish expeditions left no mark on Tennessee's history, religious or secular, not even a place name or a ruin. It was as though the expeditions, with all their hopes of plunder and aspirations to the conversion of the Indians, had been voyages on quicksilver, which leave not even a wake behind. The tragic history of the Indians of southeastern United States seems more poignant, because of this silence, than the equally tragic, but more noisy and turbulent northeastern and southwestern Indian histories. The missionaries of the Southeast were zealous, and their labors were arduous. They rightly complained that the civil authorities frustrated their efforts, but left to themselves they fared little better. The wilderness simply swallowed them up, as it did the silent Indians the white men often saw merge into the landscape as if part of it. To watch them do so without being moved by the message of the Gospel meant sad failure to the hundreds of missionary priests, mostly Jesuits and Franciscans, who sowed so industriously and reaped so little.

The French

The Spanish came north into Tennessee, but the French came from the north. They found a natural waterway from their settlements on the St. Lawrence River through the Great Lakes and into the Mississippi River system, and from various bases they built on this. They thoroughly explored the vast heartland of North America. As Spanish exploration waned, the French waxed, and the Mississippi that de Soto discovered in 1541 was, a century later, being claimed for His Most Christian Majesty, the King of France, by French explorers, many of whom were priests.

The early French settlements on the St. Lawrence became a durable civilization, deeply Catholic and full of missionary zeal. Although several religious orders were involved, expecially the Franciscan Recollects, the Jesuits dominated. The French Jesuits were more assertive than the Spanish missionaries, more independent of civil authority (and often at odds with it), and far more effective in converting the Indians. They were especially successful with the Indians along the shores of the eastern St. Lawrence, until they were caught in the crossfire of Indian tribal warfare. The great French explorer, Samuel Champlain, imprudently committed his support to the Hurons in their eternal wars with their cousin Iroquois, which caused the Iroquois to turn anti-French. They then persecuted the missionaries with fierce zeal, culminating in the martyrdom of the five Jesuits who were canonized by Pope Pius XII in 1930. Champlain's imprudence also contributed materially to the French defeat in the long French and Indian wars.

The missionaries fared better further west. Missions at Sault Sainte Marie, Green Bay, and many other places flourished in the mid-seventeenth century; from one such, Saint Ignace on the straits of Mackinac, Father Jacques Marquette, a French Jesuit, who wished to extend the Jesuit missions to the south, joined Louis Joliet, who had been sent by Count Frontenac, the Governor of New France, to explore the Mississippi. They floated past Tennessee coming and going, in mid-summer 1673, and stopped at the inviting bluffs of Memphis.

The site of Memphis was a very important place to the Indians. The Mound Builders left ample marks of their presence there; their ceremonial center, Chucalissa, was just south of present-day Memphis. In recent years, archaeologists have harvested rich artifacts from these sites, and have reconstructed the culture of the Chickasaw Indians, who succeeded the Mound Builders in the seventeenth century. Many of them believe de Soto came to the site of present-day Memphis, partly because, they argue, he could scarcely ignore so important a place.

It is indeed a striking one. The four Chickasaw bluffs rise from an enormous surrounding country of flatlands and floodlands, deltas and creeks and oxbows, that tell of the meandering river which changes its course and the character of its banks almost year by year, always excepting the mighty bluffs. They, along with some shorter high ground, are unique from St. Louis to Natchez. Father Jean Cavalier, the famous LaSalle's older brother, described them as he saw them in 1687: "We came to some precipices, rising to a height of 80 to 100 feet, all of different colored earths, viz red, yellowish and white, some of which the Indians took for painting themselves. These precipices extend for a league and a half [around four miles], and were on the right of the river going up."

Fourteen years previously, Father Marquette described the Indians themselves, comparing them to the St. Lawrence Indians he had known: "They wear their hair long, and mark their bodies in Iroquois fashion; the head-dress and clothing of their women were like those of Huron squaws." Joliet and Father Marquette found the Indians armed with guns, a tell-tale index of what these explorations were really all about. Joliet was a fur trader, and wished to keep the Mississippi Valley French to monopolize the rich fur trade. The ablest of these French explorers, Robert Cavalier, the Sieur de la Salle, was clear in this purpose. It was his aim to establish a string of forts on the great river to back up the French claim of all "Louisiana" for the King of France, and he established one north of Memphis, in Lauderdale County, in 1682 as part of his plan. He named the fort after one of their own party, Pierre Prud'homme, who was joyfully found after being lost hunting — on this perilous expedition LaSalle lost not a single man. Two priests accompanied the expedition, so it is reasonable to assume that Mass was celebrated here. It is perhaps significant of their presence that a second fort in Memphis proper, at the confluence of the Wolf River and Gayoso Bayou, was named Fort Assumption.

The white man was slowly moving into Tennessee. At about the same time as the first visit of Father Marquette in 1673, the Virginia explorers and traders, James Needham and Gabriel Arthur, were in East Tennessee. A deserter from the first LaSalle expedition, Martin Chartier, married a Shawnee woman and lived for some time in Shawnee settlements on the Cumberland River. And in 1736, Christian Priber, an Alsatian, was discovered living with the Cherokees who were often hospitable to white adoptees. Chartier and his son Peter were influential in bringing the Shawnees under French influence, which made a great deal of trouble during Tennessee's colonization, though it wasn't lasting.

A Frenchman who had less devotion to French interests in the Mississippi Valley was Jean Couture, who switched his allegiance to the English. He was one of the many *coureurs des bois,* French fur traders who traveled everywhere throughout the valley, trading and trapping for furs and skins. They were a strange and fascinating band — a good picture of them is in A. B. Guthrie's novel set in the American West of the 1830s called *The Big Sky.* They fanned out from Quebec and Montreal all over the North American continent, except for the southwestern desert. They lived with the Indians, and often married them, though they were not greatly given to monogamy. They were engaged for more than a century in one of the most booming economic enterprises of their time, and everybody connected with it but them made pots of money. Buffalo and deer skins were in enormous demand in Europe for leather, to make clothing and shoes. The traffic was immense; between 1774 and 1781 peltry valued at 200,000 English pounds a year passed through the port of Montreal, and in 1731 alone 250,000 deer skins were shipped to Europe from Charleston, South Carolina. In 1743 there were 150 trading posts for skins reporting to St. Louis, and the fur merchants of Albany, New York, were rich and numerous enough to form an effective political pressure group. Millions of beaver skins were shipped to Europe for the tall hats made from them — in England, for a time, a man's hat was known as a "beaver". And John Sevier, when he went to Washington as a delegate from Tennessee to the United States Congress, bought a beaver hat there for $7.

Most of the *coureurs des bois* were agents for their government. Their activities were resented by the missionaries, who thought they were working at counter-purposes to their efforts to convert the Indians, and in 1696 the missionaries persuaded the government of Louis XIV of France to order the *coureurs* to settle down to permanent family life and leave the wilderness to the priests and the bureaucrats. As can be readily imagined, this had about as little effect as later edicts to leave the Indians unmolested; its major result was to encourage the trappers to trade with the English, as Couture did. This change of allegiance helped to make Charleston a major port, and weakened the allegiance of the trappers, largely French, to their mother land. However, Charleston was already being serviced by trappers of Anglo-Irish extraction. The earliest of these (1673) were James Needham and Gabriel Arthur. Cornelius Dougherty (1719) was long thought to have been a Catholic, but there is no record of his religion.

An untypical coureur was Jacques-Timothe' Demonbreun, let's call him — to this day his name, difficult for Americans to pronounce, is spelled as variously as it was heard. Demonbreun is frequently called the first white man to settle in Middle Tennessee, though he did not move to Nashville permanently until 1790. He was a "free" trader, that is, in business for himself, not working for the French government like most of the *coureurs*, or, like Daniel Boone, for a land company. Beginning around 1768, he hunted during the season, late fall and early winter, in Western Kentucky and Middle Tennessee. He was attracted to the Nashville area because of the salt-laden earth called a salt lick, left by the evaporation of the sulphur water in the natural sulphur springs in the flatlands north of the hills that became Nashville. Buffalo and deer congregated to lick the salt, so it was a hunter's paradise. The spot was fairly well known; about fifty years before Demonbreun another French trader named Charles Charleville had established a post there.

Demonbreun is a legend in Middle Tennessee. The romantic story is that he lived in a cave in a bluff on the Cumberland River, close to the present Nashville Water Works. In this cave, the legend goes, he set up housekeeping, and one of his children was born here. Since all his children by his first wife were baptized in Kaskaskia, Illinois, this is probably pure legend. How much housekeeping went on is a matter for interesting speculation. It does seem likely that he took refuge in this cave from a storm, and it is certainly true that he was accustomed to rugged outdoor living during his long hunting trips. But he was also accustomed to spending his off seasons in a comparatively comfortable home in Kaskaskia, so the legend of a winter in the cave seems unlikely to the skeptical.

What makes it unlikely is Demonbreun's background, character, and what is known for sure about his life history. This was no ordinary long hunter, like Big Foot Spencer, whose legendary tale is that he spent a winter living in a huge hollow sycamore tree in Sumner County. Demonbreun was a frontier aristocrat, descended from Pierre Boucher, the first Canadian to be elevated to the French nobility. Born in the place named for his ancestor, Boucherville, Quebec, and educated there according to the best standards of the time and place, Demonbreun was anything but crude and illiterate. His letters and published documents make it plain that he was cultivated far beyond the usual frontier standards. He married, in his home city, a girl of his own class. What moved him shortly thereafter, at the age of nineteen, to leave her and home for the Illinois country probably even he didn't know. Was it the same mysterious call to adventure, wealth and fame that moved so many young men during the age of exploration? Perhaps, but throughout most of his life Demonbreun acted with prudence, not romantic recklessness.

He emigrated to Kaskaskia, where he had Boucherville connections. This was a thriving little French town in southern Illinois near the mouth of the river of the same name, then about five miles upstream from its junction with the mighty Mississippi. Here he settled down. He brought his bride to a comfortable home he built for her and their eventual children, and became a leading citizen. From here he left on his highly profitable hunting trips, floating down the Kaskaskia to the Mississippi, thence via the Ohio to the mouth of the Cumberland or the Tennessee. When his hunting season was over he collected his skins, built a large flatboat to transport them, and floated downstream all the way to New Orleans, where he also had Boucherville connections. From there he returned to Kaskaskia, by river, or by horse up the Natchez Trace. Kaskaskia is no more, obliterated by the changing course of the Mississippi, which now flows over its site.

Demonbreun became an officer in the Virginia militia — Illinois was then Virginia country — and when the Revolution came was an enthusiastic supporter of the American cause. He fought under the great George Rogers Clark and earned that able leader's warm respect. In 1783, he was made Lieutenant Governor of the Illinois Country, a post he filled with distinction until 1786. Here was indeed a versatile man of parts.

When he moved to Nashville, in 1790, his first wife simply disappeared — from the eyes of the historians at least. There is no record of her being in Nashville, or anywhere else. Demonbreun prospered in his new city on the Cumberland, near his old hunting grounds. He opened a store and a tavern on what is now Third Avenue North, near Broadway. He built a new home near there for his many children, five by his first wife and three by his common-law second wife, Elizabeth Bennett or Hensly. She eventually married a man named Durrett, or Durand — creative spelling was common in those days. She outlived Demonbreun by thirty years. He died in 1826, leaving a substantial fortune evenly divided among his legitimate and illegitimate children whose descendants are spread all over the South.

Despite this peculiar marriage situation, Demonbreun was by birth and conviction a Catholic, more devout than most. He took a keen interest in church affairs in Kaskaskia, and in Tennessee. His home was a center for Catholic meetings as attested by the following notice which appeared in *The Nashville Gazette* for October 29, 1820: "Request a meeting of the Roman Catholic brethren of the city and vicinity at the house of Timothy Demonbreun, College Street, on Monday the 6th of November for the purpose of taking into consideration the propriety of erecting a church and appointing trustees, signed, A. Redmond, T. Demonbreun."

In this same year of 1820, he sold, for one dollar, a lot just north of the Public Square for a church. The deed, registered February 20, 1821, in the Davidson County Deed Book, says "that Timothy has a desire that a Roman Catholic Church should be erected in the Town of Nashville, where he may worship the deity after the forms of the religion he professes and the religion of his fathers." But the church did not materialize, and in 1825 Demonbreun bought the lot back for $125. (Incidentally, his name is spelled three ways in the deeds.)

During the year following his purchase of the lot, the first Mass ever celebrated by a bishop of the Catholic Church was offered in his house by Bishop Benedict Flaget, of Bardstown, Kentucky. Demonbreun was thus a pioneer in what was to become a pattern for much of the Diocese of Nashville lasting almost to 1900, the sacraments administered by a traveling priest in the homes of the devout. Many elderly Catholics still alive remember hearing their parents, especially if they lived on farms, speak of such occasions.

Demonbreun is a singular figure in Tennessee's history. He has many clones in St. Louis, Dubuque, St. Paul, Detroit, and other places where the French left a mark on the developing American civilization and American Catholicism. Even in those places the mark is a light one, a small thin note in the general English, German-Irish, and Scotch-Irish clamor of early United States. In the South, the French Catholic influence stayed prominent and important only in southern Louisiana and a few isolated spots elsewhere, like Natchitoches. The French influence in Charleston, still faintly discernible, was Huguenot and Protestant. There is little of it in Tennessee, so little that the fascinating Demonbreun story seems exotic, out of key with what was happening around him. But Catholics especially ought not to forget it.

1

Roots of the Present: Maryland and Kentucky

The French influence on the Church in Tennessee came not so much from men like Demonbreun, but from men like the Bishop of Bardstown who celebrated Mass in his home. Flaget was born in France and became a devout priest of the Society of Saint Sulpice, whose main purpose was seminary training. However, his budding career as a theologian was cut short by the closing of his seminary at Angers by the French Revolution. Like hundreds of his fellow clergymen, he chose the missionary fields rather than submit to the atheist and violently anti-church new government, and came to America in 1791 to fulfill his vocation.

What a curious situation it was! The Church in the United States was struggling to get going. Its first Bishop was John Carroll, a native of Maryland, the cradle of so much early American Catholicism. The bishop was a cousin of Charles Carroll, the richest man in America, an early supporter of the American Revolution and a signer of the Declaration of Independence. John Carroll was a Jesuit, educated at the Jesuit seminary in St. Omer, Belgium, who became the first American Catholic bishop (1790) and archbishop (1808). Many of his priests were French emigres. Generally speaking these were, like Flaget, well-educated and cultivated, and they went unwillingly, for the most part, to become clerical *coureurs des bois* on the rough and uncultivated frontiers of Kentucky, Tennessee, and Indiana. For this is what they were, priests on horseback, trying desperately to read their prayers while their beasts poked along the Indian trails leading from one crude settlement of a few Catholic families to another.

The earliest Catholics in the Ohio Valley came from Maryland to north-central Kentucky around 1785, in the area neatly bisected today by the Bluegrass Parkway. Maryland had, of course, been settled early by Catholics, but only a few became rich like the Carrolls, and despite the early Catholic presence and prominence, Maryland was no earthly paradise. The land in St. Mary's County, where the earliest Kentuckians came from, was beginning to be exhausted, and a group of Catholic families there formed the Maryland Colonization League, to settle gradually in the richer virgin soil of Kentucky. These settlers were solidly of English extraction, as a sampling of their family names indicates: Hayden, Lee, Bold, Payne, Brewer, Johnson, Clark, Elliott, Norris, Brown, Bowles, Melton, Spalding, Mattingly, Miles, Peak. These contrast strongly with the names of their priests: Flaget, David, Badin, Fournier, Salmon, Chabrat, de Rohan, Angier. It was an odd situation: a laity but little French, a clergy dominantly so. But briefly. A generation later the clergy became increasingly filled with names like Fenwick, Young, Wilson, and Tennessee's first bishop, Miles. Yet these were formed and taught by a dominantly French clergy who brought to Maryland and Kentucky, Michigan, and Illinois, and many other places, standards of learning and piety of inestimable benefit to the fledgling Church. In the flood of the Irish and German immigrants that followed them, their heroic work is often forgotten.

Heroic is not too strong a word. Forgotten, too, are their hardships, more severe on men of education than on the ordinary unlettered farmers. Learning withers without books, and books were hard to come by on the frontier. A missionary was as wedded to his horse as a cavalryman, and, between books and horses, horses came first. A good horse cost somewhere between $75 and $250, usually complete with saddle and bridle, and these priests were poor folks, very poor. Bishop Flaget had to wait six months after his consecration in Baltimore before he could afford the fare to his new diocese. The roads were so bad that a cart or carriage, so often a necessity when goods had to be transported, was more nuisance than help much of the time, and almost never used when making the rounds of the missions. The primitive cooking was not to their French taste; even worse were the harsh fasting laws of their time which, true to their French austerity, they obeyed to the letter and fretted when their flocks failed to follow their example. The worst of their troubles was pay. They had to struggle hard for what they could get, often as little as $200 a year. Much of their recompense was in farm produce. Their best bet was to have someone work some land given them by the devout, but their hired help, often slaves used to minute direction, was anything but efficient. Because they had so little cash, their clothes were often shabby and hard to replace, although they wore what everyone else wore, and were addressed, by each other as well as the laity, as Mister, not Father.

Their labors were incredible. The foremost among them, the Reverend Stephen Theodore Badin, was the first priest to be ordained in the United States and the first missionary to be sent to Tennessee. He refused ordination at the hands of his Bishop of Orleans, in his native France, because the bishop had failed to stand up to the new Revolutionary government. Badin was finally ordained in May of 1793 by Carroll not long after he arrived in America, and was immediately sent by him as a missionary to Kentucky. Badin didn't want to go, but go he did, in obedience to his bishop's wish, not command. He stayed twenty-five years till a disagreement with Bishop Flaget prompted him to return to France, but in Europe he could not forget the missions, tirelessly collected money for them and was their spokesman in France and at Rome. Eventually he returned, not to Kentucky, but to Indiana and Ohio and Michigan, where he worked among the Indians as well as the settlers and helped found the University of Notre Dame in northern Indiana, where he is buried.

Except for his years in Europe, Badin was the prototype of the peripatetic missionary. From 1793 to 1805 he had the assistance of several priests, some of them admirable, but none with his hardihood; he was the stalwart of the Kentucky missions, ranging from Bardstown to Danville to Frankfort to Louisville and back, with many small places, mostly now slipped off the map, in between. He customarily heard confessions in the morning when he arrived at one of his stations; as he was notoriously scrupulous, this often lasted till Mass was celebrated around noon. Then came baptisms, marriages, and instructions. Then the next station. In addition, since Carroll had named him Vicar General of the area, he had to write long reports on the progress of the Church and of his assistant priests. He went to Baltimore now and again to do this in person, stopping everywhere along the route to preach and try to bring Catholics back to their Church. He made frequent visits to Vincennes, Indiana, part of his charge.

When the Dominicans arrived in Kentucky in 1805, Badin found himself a little more free. It was then he planned his trip to Tennessee. He went to Knoxville because some years earlier, in 1799, John Sevier, the first Governor of Tennessee, had offered him some land for a Catholic settlement, but Badin thought the price too high and the deal fell through. Sevier, like practically everybody else of his time and position, from George Washington on down, was a land speculator, and it is likely he wanted Badin to bring in Catholic settlers as well as to look after such as were already there. Although Sevier's son said his father had no religion, it is clear he had some interest in Catholicism, perhaps because of his friendship with James Dardis, a prominent citizen of Knoxville, then Tennessee's capital, and a devout Catholic. In his journal, Sevier speaks of subscribing to a Washington newspaper for Dardis; a few days later he speaks of attending a "Catholic meeting", the first of several such entries which mention visits to Catholic churches.

Badin's visits to Tennessee were long a-borning. As early as 1800, he wrote Bishop Carroll that he had been in touch with a "French gentleman who lives with Governor Blount", but after the land deal with Sevier fell through he was unable to make the trip because there was no one to replace him in Kentucky. Four years later he wrote of another "one of my countrymen", undoubtedly Demonbreun, who lived in Nashville, but it wasn't until 1808 that, on receiving an invitation from Patrick Campbell of Knoxville, he decided he was able to go. He arrived there in November of 1808 and found only six or seven Irish families. He also preached four times in the State House.

Both these tiny statistics raise interesting speculations. How many Catholics were there in the Tennessee of Badin's time? How many attended the meeting called by Demonbreun and Redmond in Nashville? How many Catholics were there in Bolivar when Valentine Derry Berry so surprisingly in 1832 wrote Bishop Kenrick of Philadelphia requesting a priest to minister to them? Was there more than one John Rogers, "An Irishman and a Catholic", who settled near Brownsville, Tennessee, in the 1820s? It is reasonable to suppose that only the wealthy and prominent got into the local histories, but how many more simple folk clung to their faith without benefit of clergy? In 1823 Catherine Dwyer, later Mrs. Owen Daily, from Franklin, Tennessee, was a student at Nazareth College for Women in Kentucky, the first of many in later years; had these well-off girls deep roots in the past? There is a general feeling, repeated in most Catholic histories of Tennessee, that the woods were full of fallen-away Catholics who might have returned to the Church had there been priests. Some there certainly were, as there always are. But Father Badin's Knoxville experience does not suggest many. He returned to Knoxville twice more, in 1809 and 1810, but his preaching fell on stony ground. Although a notice in the *Knoxville Register* for October 9, 1821, signed by James Dardis, announced an impending visit from Father Robert Abell and Father Guy Chabrat, Badin's successors in Kentucky, the visit seems never to have materialized, and East Tennessee did not see a priest again for thirty years. This is a pity, for some Catholic presence there might have mitigated the strong anti-Catholic feeling that arose later, displacing the piety of a Dardis and the tolerance of a Sevier.

The second statistic, Father Badin's sermons in the "Statehouse", conjures up scenes of the legislators sitting enthralled at his expositions of Catholic doctrine. Wilson's *Knoxville Gazette* for Saturday, November 2, 1810, notes that Stephen T. Badin will preach on Baptism in the courthouse "tomorrow at 3 P.M." But, note that tomorrow was Sunday. The other sermons were also scheduled for Sundays. It is probable that the "Statehouse", also the Courthouse, was the only available public building for such gatherings, and it is clear that going to such sermons was a popular social occasion, like going to the movies today. The journals of the time are filled with accounts of attendance at various religious services of many different denominations.

Had the legislators chosen to listen to Badin they might have been surprised, fascinated even. For he was a most remarkable man, who surely stands with Jogues, de Smet, and a few others as among the foremost missionaries who lived and worked in North America. He had considerable learning, wrote Latin verse with offhand ease, and lots of it. He also wrote the first Catholic book published in the west, *Principles of Roman Catholics,* and other apologetic works, in both English and French. He knew his standard theology forwards and backwards — after all, he had been trained to teach it. He was austerely pious, too much so for the frontier. In some ways he resembled the puritanical Protestant preachers who were following the same Indian trails as he; he thought dancing, for example, plainly immoral. He upheld with stalwart integrity his own high standards, and disdained those who thought them too severe. He was consequently constantly quarreling with his fellow clergy, overbearing toward his far-flung parishioners, and stridently independent toward his superiors. But for this, he would surely have been made a bishop. And but for this, perhaps a good one, for he had the intelligence to see what was going on around him. His 1805 report to Rome puts the matter as well as can be: "All the [Protestant] sects have the same prejudice against the Catholic religion, which they do not know at all: the reading of and the private interpretation of the Bible are the points around which all these sects unite. Nevertheless, the non-Catholics who live among the Catholics are less under the influence of prejudice, and they treat us generally as brothers". The great sense of separation did not come till the floods of immigration from Europe poured in, and while there were never real floods in the South, there were enough to raise the hackles of older settlers — who were, nevertheless, happy to have Irish workers build their railroads and Irish girls toil in their stores.

Father Badin also came to Nashville in June of 1810. "I was cordially received by Mr. Priestly and other acquaintances", he wrote to Bishop Carroll, "but found very few Catholics." There were very few. The state was part of the new Diocese of Bardstown, created in 1808 from the vast Baltimore territory. Bardstown's extent was vast enough: Tennessee, Kentucky, Ohio, Michigan, Indiana, and Illinois. Badin was the first priest to visit Nashville. The first Bishop of Bardstown in 1815 wrote to Rome, "In the neighboring State of Tennessee there are about twenty-five families of Catholics who are deprived of the aids of the Church. Not yet has it been possible for me to call on them." That time came six years later when, in the company of the Reverend Robert A. Abell, one of the earliest native Kentucky missionaries, the bishop visited Nashville and celebrated Mass in the home of Demonbreun.

Father Abell was technically the first "pastor" of Nashville. He came from a distinguished Kentucky family, one of the first to

Benedict Flaget, Bishop of Bardstown, visited middle Tennessee in 1820s and celebrated Mass in the home of pioneer Timothy Demonbreun.

In the 1820s Nashville was a mission on the long circuit of Father Robert Abell, who came as often as he could from his base in central Kentucky.

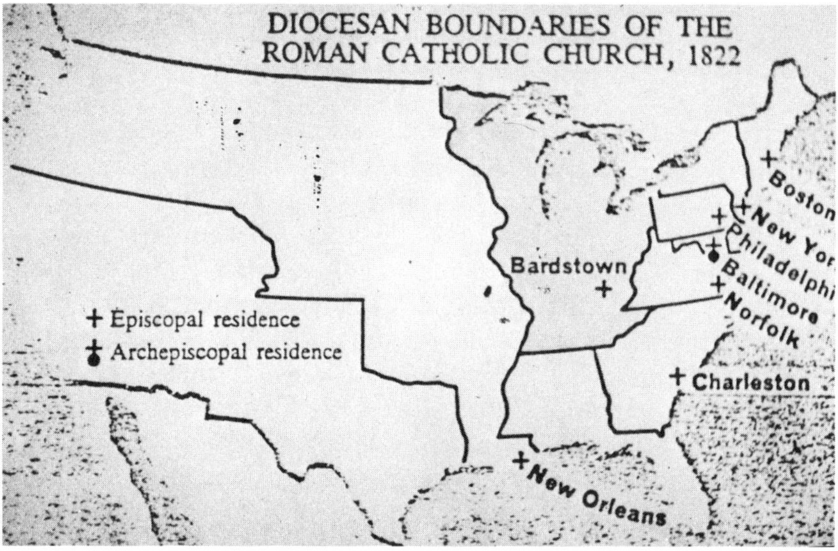

On this 1822 map Tennessee is bare space within the vast Bardstown diocese.

Except where noted otherwise among photographs that follow in this book, all are from official sources in the Diocese of Nashville. Most came from two collections at The Catholic Center: the Diocesan Archives and The Tennessee Register. *A third major collection is the Monsignor George J. Flanigen Papers at Aquinas Junior College. A smaller collection is at the Cathedral of the Incarnation.*

emigrate from Maryland. His father was a member of Kentucky's first constitutional convention. A friend and associate in that body was Felix Grundy, who later emigrated to Tennessee and played a major role in its development. However, the senior Abell died when Robert was only ten years old, and Robert the younger gave his life to the Church as completely as his father gave his to Kentucky. Ordained by Bishop Flaget in 1818, Father Abell was given charge of a missionary area as large as a state. He made his home in its northern sector, in Breckenridge County, and he several times visited Nashville, about 120 miles away. What a parish! And what a pastor! The name of Abell is a distinguished one in Kentucky history to the present day.

The First Church

What brought Father Abell to Nashville for the first time in 1820 was the initial sounding of the keynote to most of the early history of Tennessee Catholicism. This keynote was the call of the Irish Catholic workers for a priest. It resounds again and again in the history of the Church of Tennessee, although sometimes the workers were German, or rarely, another nationality. The Catholic Church is a community affair; its life is lived in parishes. Isolated on individual farms, or kept alive by the intense faith of some lone farmer or merchant, it still lacks nourishment, however pious and loyal these individuals are. The Church embraces these hermits, but they are exceptional; Catholics normally tend to live in communities.

The first Nashville Bridge Company was organized in 1819 to bridge the Cumberland from Main Street in Edgefield to the Public Square. Stacker and Johnson, of Pittsburgh, were the contractors. They brought from Pittsburgh thirty skilled Irish workers, who settled with their families near the site. The bridge cost $75,000; stock was sold to raise the money, so it probably was a toll bridge. It was open to traffic in the midsummer of 1823. Because it was too low for the steamboats of the 1850s, it was replaced about 1855. Some of its masonry was occasionally visible just north of the present Woodland Street Bridge until the Corps of Engineers system of dams steadied the depth of the Cumberland.

When Bishop Flaget responded to the call of the workers by sending Father Abell, they threw up a small frame church at once, in their off-hours, precious few, in the long work days of the time. Abell continued to visit Nashville every few months; the trip normally took about ten days each way. Abell was a good preacher and a ready one; on one occasion in Nashville he tackled a Protestant preacher in the man's own church. Abell chanced to overhear him as he passed the meeting house, slipped in at the back, and challenged the attacks on the Catholic Church by offering to refute them the following evening. He did so admirably, and it is interesting to note that he referred to himself as a "minister of the Catholic religion and an American-born citizen." This was a clear sign of the new era ahead, one in which the French priests were replaced by that dream of every American bishop of a missionary diocese almost to the present: a pious and educated native clergy.

Still, Abell made no dent in Nashville Protestantism. He continued to minister to the Irish bridge workers, who gradually replaced their little frame church with a stouter brick one. This was on Cedar Knob, also called Campbell's Hill, later still Capitol Hill — Nashville did not become the state capital until 1843. The land was donated by Anthony Foster, Grand Master of the Masons, "a benevolent, hospitable and wealthy man." It stood on the northeast slope of the hill; the site is marked by an historical marker, near the tomb of President Polk. The deed,dated October 25, 1821, says that the plot was conveyed to Bishop Benedict Flaget "for and in consideration of the desire said Foster has that a Roman Catholic Church should be erected in the Town of Nashville, where the said society may worship the deity after the form of religion which they profess, and in consideration of one dollar to the said Anthony in hand paid by the said Benedict Flaget, the receipt whereof is hereby acknowledged." On the same day Foster also sold the bishop an adjoining lot for $250.

It was a brave start, but no more than that. Father Abell was transferred to Louisville in 1824. By that time, the bridge was completed, and most of the Irish workers moved on to another project. The little brick Church of the Holy Rosary was left unfinished, and even unblessed; it was used for a while as a preparatory school for Cumberland College. Cumberland College had been preceded by Davidson Academy, the first institution of learning in Middle Tennessee; it became the University of Nashville in 1826 and, in 1878, Peabody College. The Catholics of the Nashville area, like those in the rest of the state, were once more without a pastor, and reverted to their former status of seeing only missionary priests as they happened along.

Early Missionary Priests

The early missionaries were an interesting and often shadowy lot; little is known of them. The earliest of them, ante-dating Fathers Badin and Abell by twenty or so years, was that curious figure, Father William de Rohan, or just plain Rohan, or Roan, or Roane, as Father Badin calls him — the name is spelled as variously as Demonbreun's. What is known of him comes largely from Bishop Martin Spalding's book on the early Catholic missionaries of Kentucky: "In the summer [of 1790] there arrived [in Kentucky], in the company of a caravan of emigrants from North Carolina and East Tennessee the Reverend Wm. de Rohan. He seems to have been born in France, of Irish parentage, and was a reputed Doctor of the Sorbonne. Some chance had thrown him on the American shores; and a few years previous to his arrival in Kentucky, he had received faculties for a mission in Virginia from Bishop Carroll. Shortly afterwards he traveled to Tennessee, where he remained for more than a year."

Father Rohan built the first Catholic church in Kentucky, Holy Cross, in Nelson County, and his Kentucky career is fairly well known. But nothing more than Spalding's laconic remark is known of his year in East Tennessee. It's possible he built some sort of church there, lost to all knowledge and recollection.

Even more shadowy is a Father Sutt(on?), who was mentioned by Bishop Flaget in an 1826 report to the Congregation for the Propagation of the Faith in Rome, as visiting the State of Tennessee twice a year. But there is no Tennessee record of these visits. The lack of priests in Tennessee is poignantly noted in a letter from Dublin, Ireland, in the Charleston, South Carolina, *United States Catholic Miscellany* for March 1, 1828. This letter, perhaps inspired by a letter to Dublin from an Irish emigre to Tennessee, asks that the Charleston diocese send a priest there. Alas, the newspaper responded, Charleston is itself short of priests. "It is painful'', the article went on, ''to reflect on the situation of those Catholics who seek for the Bread of Life, and there are but a few to break it to them. The places mentioned where the aid of a priest is required are Nashville, Franklin, Winchester and Gallatin.''

Shortly after this article appeared, Father James Cosgreve, who had been appointed to Nashville by Bishop Flaget, appeared on the scene in a dramatic way. In the Nashville *Banner* and Nashville *Whig* of March 28, 1828, there was the following announcement: ''ROMAN CATHOLIC CHURCH — on Sunday next, the 30th instant, the Rev. James Cosgreve will celebrate Mass in the Catholic Church and preach from the gospel of the day. The professors and musical amateurs (ladies and gentlemen) have kindly consented to give their aid for the occasion. The Church being yet in an unfinished condition, and from the circumstance of the intention of having a resident clergyman located here, in order to comply with such intentions, the Roman Catholics appeal to the liberality of their fellow citizens, already amply experienced in their generous contributions when building the Church itself, for further means to finish the interior of the building. Mass will commence precisely at 10 A.M.'' However, the weather was bad on the day appointed, and the event did not take place until April 6. It was a considerable success, with Andrew Jackson in attendance, and that same month the enterprising Father Cosgreve held a $10,000 lottery to complete the church. He then disappears from the records. Born in Ireland, he had come to Bardstown in 1827 with his mother, a widowed sister, and her little child. Perhaps he had too many relations for a missionary, perhaps he died. In any case he vanishes; it is an odd story. But he will live in the history of Nashville Catholicism, because it was most likely he who finished the first little church.

The next priest to come to Tennessee has a clear, complete and fascinating history. This was Father William Byrne of Kentucky. From his earliest youth in Ireland he wanted to be a priest, but his family was poor and he had to help out at home, a familiar story to so many Irish families. It wasn't until he immigrated to America at the age of twenty-five that he had the chance to try his vocation, and then he was found inadequately prepared by the Jesuits, to whom he presented himself. But he persevered, went to the seminary at Baltimore, and then to the fledgling one of St.

Thomas in Kentucky. There he was ordained in 1819. Two years later he began the College of St. Mary's for boys, in Marion County, Kentucky, which educated many Tennesseans; their sisters often went to the nearby College of Loretto, or to Nazareth College for Women, a little farther up the pike. St. Mary's lasted for nearly 150 years. Its founder was a simple, good-hearted, pious, indefatigable, humorless, and devotedly single-minded man. He came to Nashville in response to the cry for a priest there. By accident he met one of the Rogan family in Gallatin, and through this was brought to see the touching condition of Tennessee Catholics. He planned to start another St. Mary's here, but died of cholera in 1832 before his plans could be developed.

With the next priest to become "pastor" of Middle Tennessee, we come into the full light of historical record. This was the legendary Elisha Durbin, who, in a manner of speaking, succeeded Father Abell. His headquarters were in Morganfield, Kentucky, somewhat closer than Abell's, but still a long, long way. His commission from his bishop was that he should visit Nashville at least once a year, beginning in 1832.

Father Durbin had some of the characteristics of Father Byrne. His was a simple piety. He was notoriously inept in the pulpit, and quiet and modest of manner. He was anything but humorless, however, and his loyalty and devotion became a by-word for a generation of Kentucky-Tennessee priests. How many miles must he have traveled on horseback during his nearly fifty years of missionary activity! At the age of eighty-three he retired, but two years later, fretting at his inactivity, he asked his bishop (of Louisville) to give him something to do. Since Father Durbin was the priest who made Nashville ready for its first bishop, he will turn up again in these pages shortly.

Father Durbin was exceptional, though. Father D. A. Quinn, who left Tennessee a generation later to become a missionary in Arkansas, thought five years was about all one could take of missionary life — and he traveled as much by rail as by horseback. Father Quinn wrote from Rhode Island, where he spent his later years. This, too, is more typical than the life of Father Durbin. Throughout this period priests come and go, appear and disappear, join an order and leave it, turn up in California and Texas, knowing that wherever they go their lot is loneliness and hardship. If they have homes, they are away from them more than in them; and they rarely have churches. They say their Masses in the homes of the scattered and isolated Catholics they serve. A list of some who visited the home of Hugh Rogan in Sumner County spans nearly fifty years: Fathers Byrne, Durbin, Maguire, Hoste, O'Dowde, Stokes, McAleer, Schacht, Jacquet, Revis, Lyons, Bergrath, Ryan, Meagher, Veale, Orengo, Gazzo, Coughlin, Paulinus, Braun, Graham, Murray, and Tobin. A few older Tennessee Catholics will remember meeting and knowing some of these last.

What an heroic and far-off time it seems! So far, only the bridge workers seem within our grasp. They were technological, they worked for a corporation, they moved about as we do. The priests and their scattered flocks seem too good for us, as well as too much. Here were men and women, both lay and clerical, dedicated above all to freedom. They and their immediate ancestors had come to America and to Kentucky and Tennessee for that, for a new and independent life. They were determined at all costs to make a go of it, to subdue the wilderness, to create a new life for themselves and their children. They saw a doctor as seldom as they did a church service, and were often none the better when they did see one. All but a few died young, and their babies died so readily that the shadow of death was intimately associated with the joy of birth. Perhaps these very uncertainties, these long odds against survival, despite their innate optimism, made them value religion so highly. How these Catholics clung to their faith! James Dardis, who brought Father Badin to Knoxville, ended his days in Winchester, and told a priest who visited him there that he never failed to read the prayers for Mass on Sundays, most of the time without the Mass itself. What enormous powers of faith, hope, charity, and perseverance underlay such loyalty.

Their lives seem legendary, like that of Roland, or the Chevalier Bayard, some medieval crusader or a saner Don Quixote. Take the case of Hugh Rogan, a signer of the Cumberland Compact, the first instrument of government in Middle Tennessee. It is as fascinating as that of Demonbreun. He was born in Ireland, where he became a member of one of the many Irish patriotic societies, "The Irish Defenders". Appalled at the prospect of Irishmen being drafted to put down the American Revolution, so dear to his own heart's desire, he left his wife and infant son to come to America to see what he could do to help. At first he had bad luck. On landing in Philadelphia, shortly after the Battle of Bunker Hill in 1775, he became enmeshed with Tory sympathizers, on whom he had to depend for his livelihood, but, after an abortive effort to serve in the new United States Navy, he escaped to western North Carolina, where he set up in business. He came into Middle Tennessee with the John Donelson party, and took a courageous part in the fights against the Indians. For this he was rewarded with a grant of land near Nashville, which he swapped for the same acreage in Sumner County near Gallatin.

As soon as he could he set out from there to Ireland to bring his wife and son back to his Tennessee land, but on the way he was told that his wife had died, and he returned home with a sad heart. But in 1796 a letter from his wife in Ireland reached him via a kinsmen who was immigrating to America, and he joyfully set out once again. The reunion must have been poignant, after so many years — his son Bernard was now twenty-one years old. They returned to Sumner County after a Sinbad-like voyage which included shipwreck. His second son Francis was born there in 1798. Hugh Rogan died in 1812. He and his family remained true to the Catholic faith, although son Francis did not see a priest till he was thirty years of age, when he was baptized by missionary Father Joseph Alemany, who eventually became the first Archbishop of San Francisco. Hugh Rogan's descendants are still part of Catholicism in Middle Tennessee.

Rogan is remembered because of his romantic history, as well as his stalwart character. So are a few other names, the Derry Berrys of Bolivar, the Hughes of Jackson, the Farrells and Phillips of Nashville. But little is known about these very early Catholics, and nothing of most of their fellow worshippers. The history of Catholicism in Tennessee is largely a history of the missionaries until Nashville got its first bishop.

2

Richard Pius Miles

Nashville became a diocese largely because of geography. Its parent diocese, Bardstown, Kentucky, was a geographical monster. Bardstown had become a diocese in 1808 when Catholics, mostly from Maryland, settled in central Kentucky, creating almost solid Catholic enclaves in numerous towns and districts. This was the heart of the new diocese, this plus the French settlements around Vincennes, Indiana. But the actual physical extent of the diocese was enormous. A missionary priest in 1820 could, and one or two did, travel from Tennessee to Michigan, and still report to one bishop, the ordinary of Bardstown.

Benedict Flaget, Bardstown's first bishop, ruled for nearly forty years, (1810-1850). He was well aware of the impossibility of keeping tabs on all this territory, and all through his long espiscopate kept urging the American bishops in their provincial council meetings at Baltimore, as well as the Holy See, to limit his diocese to the State of Kentucky.

Gradually his hopes were fulfilled. Cincinnati was made a diocese in 1822, and Vincennes (later transferred to Indianapolis) in 1834. In 1837 three new dioceses were created, Dubuque, Natchez, and Nashville. The See of Bardstown itself was transferred to Louisville in 1841. The Catholic Church west of the Alleghenies was beginning to take shape. Bardstown, with its imposing church and neighboring establishments, has itself gradually faded, since the town never embraced industrialism. But it remains proud in the history of the American Catholic Church as the oldest see in the west.

Neither Nashville nor Natchez was a viable diocese except geographically. Natchez had no church and only two priests. One of these soon died, and the other left the diocese. Tennessee had the little church on Capitol Hill, Campbell's Knob, in Nashville, and not a single priest.

For the new bishops, the challenge was formidable. Indeed, the creation of the new dioceses made life harder for the clergy who worked in them, since they were officially cut off from their former home bases. The necessity of supporting a bishop also created difficulties for the laity. And yet, hard as the early years were, it is clear that the creation of the new dioceses was the right step to take. New pride replaced old dependence, new accessibility to real authority replaced old neglect, new hopes replaced old apathy. Nashville and Natchez joined a vibrant and developing set of southeastern dioceses. Both Richmond and Charleston had been created dioceses in 1820. Richmond got off to a bad start, but the administration of the third bishop, John McGill, a native of Bardstown who was a lawyer before he became a priest, brought Catholicism into the good repute it has enjoyed since, despite some rough times.

The first Bishop of Charleston, John England, was one of the most dynamic figures in the history of the Catholic Church in America. His diocese embraced both the Carolinas and all of Georgia, and there was the usual scarcity of priests and resources. Yet this whirlwind of a bishop founded the first Catholic newspaper in the United States, was a prime mover in setting up the provincial councils at Baltimore, and by his preaching and writing brought Catholicism into excellent repute in the country-at-large as well as his region. The first two Bishops of Little Rock, Andrew Byrne and Edward Fitzgerald, were also men of cultivation and ability. Natchez had to wait till 1857 before it found a leader in William Henry Elder, whose outstanding abilities brought him the Archbishopric of Cincinnati in 1880.

These, and many other bishops and priests, gave a distinctly southern touch of courtesy, charm, and cultivation to the Church in the South. The sheer numbers of Catholics in populous northern cities made them clan-conscious ghetto dwellers to a considerable extent. The charm and cultivation of New England, for example, took a long time to help form the Boston Irish Catholics. The South made Catholics southern. No matter that they were born in Ireland and emigrated from Canada, or born in Bavaria and pushed on from Cincinnati, they were too few to create much of an ethnic culture of their own. Some tried, and racial memories stayed alive in families. But the Germantowns and Irish-towns of the South were, until the recent fascination with ethnicity, generally dissolved into southern-ness. This gave the Church in the South a special flavor, a sweetness and grace and courtesy typical of the South at its best. One indication of this is the number of southerners, from John England through James Gibbons, John Keane, John J. Kain, the Spaldings, Denis O'Connell, Samuel Stritch, and Joseph Bernardin, who became influential leaders in the Church. Reflecting in a modest way the great influence of the South in the political formation of the nation, these southerners brought a touch of moderation and accommodation to the conduct of the affairs of the Church, sometimes in contrast to the more belligerent hierarchy of the North.

Richard Pius Miles, the first Bishop of Nashville, belongs to this persuasion. He was born in southern Maryland in 1791, but within a few years his father joined the westward movement of the Maryland Catholics to Kentucky. The move was a good one for the Miles family, whose piety was blessed with some measure of prosperity, and it was natural enough that the youngest son, Richard, should be attracted to the Church. It was equally natural that the attraction should be to the Dominican Order of Preachers.

The Church in the United States owes much to the anti-religious passions of the French Revolution in Europe. An important house of studies for the Dominicans was at Bornheim, in Belgium. This was in the orbit of the persecution of the Church by the French Revolution, and the seminary was temporarily moved to England. Transferring along with the institution was young Edward Fenwick of Maryland, who had been ordained at Bornheim just prior to its forced closing. Although England was more tolerant than Belgium, it was not exactly hospitable; its Catholics still could not attend the major universities or hold public office, and they still felt the intense weight of the old English prejudice against "Romanism" and "Popery", so cleverly aroused by the Whigs and thrust home by the Protestant royal succession. Because of this, Father Fenwick cast his eye toward a Dominican establishment in his native United States, specifically his home state of Maryland. To this end he enlisted the support of three of his colleagues; together they offered their services to the

Diocese of Baltimore. But they ended up in Kentucky, where the need was greater, and there founded the first Catholic college west of the Allegheny Mountains. Dedicated to the first American saint, Rose of Lima, this was a house of studies for aspirants to the priesthood. A college for the laity, St. Thomas, came a few years later. Both colleges were in the neighborhood of Springfield.

One of the first students of St. Rose's was fifteen-year-old Richard Miles, in 1806. He was also one of its most exemplary ones. Young Richard took to the service of the Lord and the rule of St. Dominic, not like a single duck to water, but like one of a covey of ducks swimming happily in the wake of their mother. Miles loved the little community and dedicated himself to it. In 1808, the little covey of postulants to which he belonged were given the black and white habit of St. Dominic. The odd thing about them was that every one was a native American, and all save one a Kentuckian. 1808! That was the year that the Diocese of Bardstown was established, and the year that Father Stephen Badin, the first priest to be ordained in the United States, made his first visit to Knoxville, finding there six or seven Irish Catholic families.

Upon his investiture, Richard Miles, as was the Dominican custom, chose a new name in religion. His choice was Pius, the name of the great Dominican Pope St. Pius V. In the community from then on he was known as Pius, but as bishop this became his middle name. It seems a perfect name for a bishop, though its bearer, still in his teens, probably never thought of such a thing. Dominican priests did not usually become bishops, for one thing. But more importantly, there was nothing in his immediate future to suggest anything more than what he actually did in the ten years following his investiture and preceding his ordination.

This was to work at the Kentucky Dominican establishments of St. Rose and St. Thomas, studying, teaching, and doing whatever else came to hand. There was plenty of this last. Much of it was the sheer physical labor of keeping up the place, farming, repairing, helping the household of the Lord. But for Miles there was something special. He seemed to have an early and innate talent for music, and he became in time organist and choir director for the Dominican convents and churches he was attached to.

The Prior of St. Rose's, Father Samuel Wilson, wrote in 1820 an account of life there to the Office of the Propaganda, the Church's missionary headquarters in Rome, in which he says "Only one of our young men understands the chant well." This was, of course, the ancient Gregorian chant developed by the monks of the west through the long centuries of monasticism, and kept alive in religious houses through all the changing fashions in music. It is easy and pleasant to think the young man was Richard Miles.

Father Wilson's report is filled with other details of life at St. Rose's, a life so different from ours as to seem from another planet. It was not an easy way of life. "No one has a farthing in his own name", the letter goes, "nor does anyone even think of having money here in a country where there are neither books nor any other desirable objects to purchase, . . . since our principal concern is to live without the need of buying, we have all the necessaries in our power; that is, goods and clothing, except the secular dress for the missionaries." On the road, both priests and nuns wore the secular clothes of the time; cassocks and habits were for the convents and the church. American Catholics who were shocked by the reversion to this custom in the wake of Vatican II in the 1960s mistook a minor custom for a major rule. Clerical dress has varied immensely through the long history of the Church. Pious attachment to modes of dress that usually were originally what everybody wore can be a useful part of ecclesiastical discipline and a means to personal sanctity, but in times of persecution, and in places where the climate is searing hot or freezing cold, traditional costumes became merely bad habits.

The diet at St. Rose's was less surprising. They ate what all Kentuckians ate, only less of everything, and particularly meat, which was permitted only three times a week in ordinary time, and not at all in Lent, except on feast days. They ate what would grow, cabbages, turnips, potatoes; chicken, duck, goose, and turkey; and pork in all its varieties. Oddly, they had no fish, according to Father Wilson's letter, but anyone accustomed to the excellent southern river fish must wonder how long this lasted. The corn bread was superior to white bread, until yeast became commercially plentiful. For fruit, Father Wilson mentions only apples and grapes, but there must have been pears and plums, persimmons, and peaches, as well as walnuts, chestnuts, and hazelnuts. He does mention efforts to make beer and wine, mostly unsuccessful, and says there isn't time for making cider, which also must have been shortly remedied. They kept cows and sheep, as well as hogs, but the cows were for milk, butter, and cheese, and the sheep for wool. They shared the strange prejudice against lamb for the table that was true all over most of the South. The really remarkable thing about this diet is that it was standard for the South, Kentucky and Tennessee at least, for over a hundred years in the country, and in the city until refrigerated railroad cars began to be common in the 1880s and 1890s.

Like the vast majority of people in all world history, the convent of St. Rose took its principal meal at midday, or near it. The other two meals were sketchy, a little bread, tea, and perhaps sorghum or butter. The official prayers of the Church for priests were said in common; parts were sung on Sundays and feast days. The general rule was, intellectual work in the mornings, physical in the afternoons. Although Father Wilson does not say so in his letter, the winter dark, with its fitful candle, or, more usually, pork-grease-with-wick illumination, must have been trying. He does say what is still true, that the winter cold could be intense, especially from four to ten in the mornings.

Only a deep and whole-souled spirituality could thrive on such a life. There is no diary, there are no letters, no documents of any sort that tell of the thoughts, doubts, and aspirations of young Miles as he made his ten-year long preparation for the priesthood — the time span is about normal for some religious orders to this day. There is not even a surviving account of his ordination. The most likely year was 1816; this date is repeated so often in the records that a correction, if needed, would surely have been made. But no one knows the day or the place. What an interesting little mystery this is! This was the first ordination of Dominican priests in the first American Dominican priory. Four in all were ordained, almost certainly by Bishop Flaget of Bardstown, and there is frequent mention of the four in the later Dominican records. But the ordination itself may as well have taken place in the catacombs, or the desert, for all we know of it; there was then no Catholic press of any sort, and nothing about the ordination in the secular press.

In a way, this is fitting. For while his ordination surely made a great difference to the inner spiritual life of Father Miles, his outward life changed little. In addition to his teaching and physical work he now became a missionary to the burgeoning Kentucky Catholics near Springfield. The growth of the Catholic population spelled some prosperity for the College of St. Thomas. Miles taught candidates for the priesthood, as well as lay students, and worked in several branches of learning, as was the custom of the time. He was also prefect, counselor, and foster-parent. St. Thomas Springfield began to acquire a reputation. In the year Miles was ordained, young Jefferson Davis was sent by his father to school there. The eight-year-old traveled from his home in Mississippi to be schooled by the Dominicans, making the journey mounted on a pony along with a large party headed north — there was another boy about his age in the group. Davis was, of course, no Catholic, but Catholic schools often had more non-Catholic than Catholic students. Davis's first wife, the daughter of Zachary Taylor, was schooled by the Sisters of Charity of Nazareth, Kentucky; their nieces also went to Nazareth, and their nephews to St. Joseph's College at Bardstown. In a fairly typical year, 1824, the women's college at Nazareth had twenty-four non-Catholic girls as compared with twenty-two Catholic ones. The still-frontier country was hungry for education, and grateful to those who provided it; Jefferson Davis loved St. Thomas, and praised it highly in his autobiography. He must have known Father Miles, but there is no record of it.

Ordination made a big difference to Miles's work. In addition to teaching, he now became a pastor of souls, ministering to the Catholics of the region. In the old Catholic boarding schools, all the priest-teachers fulfilled both offices, but Miles went on the mission trail just about every weekend, to Danville, to Mooresville, wherever there was a Catholic settlement. In these days he formed his pastoral style, and it was an unusual one for the time. To begin with, Miles was an impressive person physically, six feet tall, unusual for his generation, big-boned and stalwart, broad of countenance, with a big nose and a thin firm mouth. One wouldn't say handsome, yet a film director would seize upon him to play the part of a bishop. Of the nine bishops of Nashville, Miles most looks the bishop. He wore his hair to his shoulders, as was the custom of the time, and, unlike most of his contemporaries, he was clean-shaven. Looking at his photographs and paintings, you'd say he looks benign, looks compassionate, a man in control of himself.

And so he was. To judge from several letters written at critical periods of his life, Miles was deeply emotional, yet he rarely displayed this to those who lived with him. He was even-tempered, stable, reassuring. Those who knew him often spoke of his voice, a singer's voice, mellow and resonant, a great advantage to a clergyman. His general health was also, so far as can be told, excellent, but this is a negative judgment — there is simply no early record of illness, and ample mention of his reliability, helpfulness, and spirit of cooperation, none of which is possible without good health.

Such was Richard Pius Miles about 1830, nearing his fortieth birthday, at the peak of his powers in all likelihood, devoted to the short-lived College of St. Thomas, his main work in life, an experienced missionary on weekends and during college vacations. It is quite possible that he was also at the peak of his happiness in this life, for two tremendous changes befell his next decade.

The first was the closing of the little college for lay students, officially called St. Thomas of Aquin. Nearly all of the many Catholic schools which sprung up in central Kentucky had all sorts of ups and downs. Father William Byrne's St. Mary's waxed and waned; the Jesuits took it over for a spell in the 1840s, and the Resurrection Fathers in the 1870s. It closed down for a while after the Civil War, then made a fresh start, lasting till the 1950s. St. Joseph's at Bardstown made a brave start; it, too, suffered many a sea-change, but also lasted into contemporary times. The schools for lay women were more stable, since the convents that ran them also staffed various grade schools throughout the region. Nazareth had a long run, down to our own time, as did Father Nerinckx's Loretto. The Dominican sisters at Springfield were still going in the 1950s, though the name of the school was changed in 1851 from St. Mary Magdalen to St. Catherine of Siena. All these are gone now, and their many and often elaborate buildings — the Dominicans were especially given to lavish architecture — either torn down or lying mostly empty, melancholy reminders of the days of their splendor.

St. Rose's Dominican seminary flourished all through the first half of the nineteenth century. Its final building was monumental, a miniature Escorial. But the St. Thomas school for boys went downhill, no one knows why — nor, indeed, exactly when. The great man of the Kentucky Dominicans, Edward Fenwick, was made first Bishop of Cincinnati in 1822, and his eye was on Ohio rather than Kentucky. However, St. Thomas may have closed before this time; its date of termination is a minor mystery, like the exact date of Miles's ordination. Its brief life spanned a decade or a little more. It was not among Fenwick's top priorities.

There is no question of Fenwick's stature. He was a remarkable man, a strange blend of forcefulness, accomplishment, and almost neurotic modesty. He had on most people he met an instant effect of personal charm, apostolic zeal, and goodness of character. For most of his life he was a leader, a do-er, the man who dreamed up the Dominican presence in the United States, the man who used his family inheritance — the Fenwicks were large Maryland landowners — to build St. Rose. His zeal and optimism kept it going. But practically all administration went against the grain with him. What he wanted to do was to be pastor to the Catholics in the wilderness, to make converts, to recall the fallen-away, to preach, to hear confessions, to build new small churches, not colleges or cathedrals, to be all the missionary he could be. Despite his background, he disclaimed any pretensions to learning.

Following his inner light, he became, in the words of the old lives of the saints, apostle to Ohio. Leaving St. Rose's to what he honestly (but mistakenly) thought better hands, he made his way through the wilderness from Cincinnati north to Somerset County and beyond. Ohio was then what Kentucky had been a generation before; it is often hard to remember that the country stretching directly west from Pittsburgh was settled a good deal later than the country stretching directly west from Richmond. One important reason was the frightening prairie of western Ohio, and much of Indiana and Illinois. A man on horseback would be lost to view in five minutes in the high tossing, blooming, perfumed grass, and without a reliable compass and good maps be lost himself in an hour. When it was finally tamed, the prairie made the greatest farmland perhaps in the history of the world, but the taming had to wait on technology good enough to provide steel plows to cut the deep rich black soil. A second reason, equally important, is that the waterways headed southwest from Pittsburgh. North-south travel between the Great Lakes and the Ohio was difficult. The great national east-west highway, from Baltimore to Centralia, Illinois, was not completed until 1840. But somehow Fenwick made his way through the Ohio country and founded a second Dominican priory, St. Joseph's, in Somerset County, near Zanesville. He wrote, in 1817, "In the State of Ohio, with a population of 500,000, there is not one priest". Here was a challenge for this dedicated missionary. It was nigh to inevitable that he should become the first bishop of this enormous territory. It wasn't as inevitable that he should found St. Joseph's as the second Dominican foundation, and the one destined to endure, for his relations with it after he became a bishop are a strange mixture of scrupulosity and diffidence. In addition to being bishop, Fenwick was also the Dominican superior, appointed for life. Not unnaturally, he could never make up his mind whether he should favor his own community, or give the appearance of doing so, or whether he should be harsh with them to favor the secular clergy. He was bishop for only ten years before the cholera took him in 1832.

It is easy to see, reviewing Fenwick's career, how Father Richard Miles was absorbed into the Ohio missions.

It may be that this first great change was, for Father Richard Miles, a good thing. He was no scholar, and a life in education would not have suited him. While too little is known to do more than speculate, it does seem that his pastoral life in Ohio was more productive than his academic one in Kentucky. His college closed, but his missions throve. He was an admirable chaplain for the Dominican sisters at St. Catherine's in Springfield, Kentucky, whose convent he helped to found, and when the sisters had to borrow money to finish their buildings, Miles personally made himself responsible for repayment. In their many difficulties he was their stalwart sponsor always, and when he went to Ohio as a missionary in 1828, he established a branch of the community there. This is pastoral work at its most productive. Miles knew how important the work of the sisters was, and he gave them what they needed most for the development of their work, male understanding and support.

Leaving Kentucky was a wrench for Father Miles. His family home and his spiritual home were conjoined there, in a small area; he was a product of the soil, so to speak, as at home there as a man could be, at ease amid so many wanderers and travelers and displaced persons, so many priests who had been torn from their roots, including not a few clerical vagabonds. But however bound to Kentucky, Miles took to Zanesville, Ohio, his new headquarters, with his usual zeal, and before long felt this was a good place for him. "I have been in Ohio only a few weeks", he wrote, "and I am beginning to feel I should like to remain here permanently, for I clearly see that the people of Ohio are so well disposed that, if you had sufficient priests, you could make the whole state Catholic." From Zanesville, Miles ranged through Muskingum, Morgan, Noble, Guernsey, and Coshocton counties normally, and often went further. He was continually on horseback. He built churches and schools, most notably the first parochial school in the diocese and perhaps the state. This was truly an apprenticeship for Tennessee.

But it was not for long. On May 1, 1833, he was elected Prior of St. Rose and so went back to Kentucky. Miles was like one of those men voted by his college classmates as most likely to succeed. These are generally neither showy nor brilliant. They are solid and substantial, reliable and trustworthy; their leadership is like that of a father rather than the charismatic hero. They rise through rather than above others, even as leaders still part of the group, still hewers of wood and drawers of water even though tribal chieftains as well.

They are usually fated to suffer with their brethren as well. Miles came back to St. Rose's in Kentucky at the height of one of the many visitations of the cholera plague. It was a sad, hard time. Eighty persons in and around St. Rose's died in fifteen days. Dominican priests, brothers, and sisters tended the sick, buried the dead, and comforted the survivors as best they could. The plague cast a pall over Father Miles's three years as Prior of St. Rose, though he continued his missionary work and planned to reopen the college eventually.

But the great changes of this decade for Miles now waxed cataclysmic. The years 1836 and 1837 were his years of decision, the time of his major transformation. After his term as Prior of St. Rose's expired in 1836, he might have slipped back into his old role of missionary, pastor, perhaps teacher. He might have become a Dominican like many another, praising God and honoring Him in orderly ways, as most did. But he was struck like Paul on his way to Damascus. Something apocalyptic hit him, to his confusion, dismay, terror, and eventual eternal credit.

The first thing that happened was not out of the way. He was made Prior of St. Joseph's in Ohio, his territory a few years past. But within a year he was elected Provincial of the entire Province of St. Joseph, comprising then all of the Dominican places in the United States and Canada. This was on April 22, 1837. On almost the very same day the American bishops, assembled at Baltimore for their Third Provincial Council, petitioned the Holy See to create the See of Nashville and recommended Richard Pius Miles as its first bishop. This was proposed by the coadjutor Bishop of Bardstown, John David. The aged Bishop Flaget, in Europe at the time, still was pushing for the reduction of his enormous diocese, and it was the sense of the council that more dioceses were needed.

Miles's prospective loss was a heavy blow to the Dominicans. They could ill afford to lose their new provincial, and they said so, loud and long. So did Miles himself. He wrote to Fenwick's successor, Bishop John B. Purcell of Cincinnati, "I do not see how I can in conscience accept . . . How could it ever have entered into the mind of anyone to appoint a poor religious, who cannot command one cent in case he accepts, to a See where there is neither a church nor a clergyman, nor any means, that I know of, to procure either. I shall not even have a book except my breviary; and my brethren are not obliged to supply me."

These remonstrances lasted over a year — the mails were slow, of course, but astonishingly reliable; and faced with the direct order of the Pope, Miles, as he had said all along he would if this were truly the wish of the Pope, yielded. It is difficult not to think that Bishop Flaget had something to do with pressuring Rome into its ultimatum. In 1837, he had been Bishop for twenty seven years and was to live for another thirteen, outlasting his two French coadjutors, David and Chabrat. His successor was

Martin John Spalding, a native Kentuckian. Only in Vincennes and New Orleans did the French line last longer.

Miles was consecrated bishop in the cathedral of Bardstown on Sunday, September 16, 1838. Bishop Flaget was still in Europe, and the senior coadjutor, Bishop David, was too aged to take on the taxing cermony, so the next senior bishop in the west, Joseph Rosati of St. Louis, was the consecrating bishop, assisted by junior coadjutor of Bardstown, Guy Chabrat, and the first Bishop of Vincennes, Simon Brute. The first missionary to Tennessee, Father Stephen Badin, was appropriately assistant priest, and the most recent, E. J. Durbin, was deacon. A fellow Dominican, W. E. Clark, was master of ceremonies, and Dominicans S. H. Montgomery and Joseph Haseltine were Miles's chaplains. The sermon was preached by Vincentian Father John Timon, afterwards Bishop of Buffalo. In the church were 130 young ladies from Nazareth Academy, among them perhaps Mary Eliza Winston, of LaGrange, Tennessee, in Fayette County, and Virginia Carr, from Memphis near the Mississippi border. Catherine Dwyer from Franklin, the first Tennessee girl we know of there, was probably gone by then to become Mrs. Owen Daily. It is altogether likely that some boys were also present, students at St. Joseph's, Bardstown, or even from St. Mary's some fourteen miles down the pike towards, eventually, Nashville. But we don't have any names.

Thus was made the first Bishop of Nashville.

3

The Bishop of Nashville, 1838-44

In the Catholic press of late 1983, there appeared a story of an American missionary bishop, who was feared lost in the mountains of troubled Nicaragua. The bishop turned up ultimately, however, explaining that he had been traveling with a party of Indians, bringing the consolations of religion to remote villages. He disclaimed any political connections or motives.

This story is very like what happened to Bishop Miles after his consecration. Although a bishop, a successor of the apostles, he was still basically a missionary on horseback to a vast diocese of 42,000 square miles, running six hundred miles from northeast to southwest, without a single other resident priest, dependent on the charity of the perhaps three hundred Catholics in his diocese for his very bed, literally without purse or scrip. Like the bishop in Nicaragua, he was straight out of, or rather into, the *Acts of the Apostles.* Those stories of the early Church, which fill the liturgy after Easter, are almost literally the stories of Bishop Miles in Nashville. We read of Peter's going to Lydda and Joppa, names which mean little to us; but Miles's visits to Jonesboro in East Tennessee and Ashport on the Mississippi are almost as exotic. St. Paul in the *Acts* is frequently at sea, shipping to such interesting spots as Perga and Iconium. The ordinary mode of transportation for Bishop Miles was horseback, little used by the apostles, but he took to the rivers whenever he could, frequently traveling from Nashville to Memphis by boat, via Paducah and Cairo, and from Cincinnati to the numerous smaller Ohio river ports.

Now and again he went by stagecoach, if there was one available, and when the railroads came he happily used them. Railroads were a-building vigorously during Miles's time in Nashville; as early as 1831 the State legislature issued six railroad charters. But the principal centers for the new roads in Miles's first Nashville years were Knoxville and Memphis, and their grandiose plans were almost transcontinental in scope. As time went on, these plans dissolved down into small roads going short distances; it is a long, fascinating, and complicated story.

But one reads in vain throughout all of its ups and downs, tangles and maneuvers, for any mention of the Irish who came to Tennessee as railroad workers and stayed on to be stalwart citizens. The earliest Irish immigrants did not, however, come as railroaders. They were mostly building trades laborers, and workers on the waterfronts of the river ports. In old ledgers their names are listed for payment. But the numerous histories of Tennessee railroads barely mention the camps of the Irish workers which moved with the tracks. New York newspapers frequently carried ads for railroad workers — "Wanted, 300 laborers!", read one such. Of course immigrants other than the Irish joined in the hard labor of laying track. And not only laying track, but felling trees for ties, quarrying stone for bridges, and moving heavy materials long distances over bad roads with wagon teams.

There were Catholics in Tennessee before the Irish railroaders came, but they were few in number and widely scattered. And, of course, once the early generations of immigrants got a foothold, they brought their kin to join them, and these often found employment a little higher up the social scale. Working for the railroad led readily to construction work as the cities expanded, giving the Irish roots in a stable community rather than lives in the rude temporary railroad camps.

Life in the railroad camps was life at almost its lowest level, except for the comparatively good pay. This enabled the Irish to indulge their notorious fondness for whiskey, and the camps were often the scenes of the most violent sort of drunken brawls, as were Irish enclaves in town. At the same time the most popular, and most prosperous, of all the Irish church societies which flourished everywhere were temperance societies, and much of the energy of the clergy went into founding and fostering these.

Bishop Miles was, of course, not an Irishman. He was descended from Maryland farmers; a horse, not a railroad car, was his natural mode of transportion. His consecration present from St. Rose's was their best horse, but he did not go directly to Nashville on it after his consecration. The indefatigable Father Elisha

Durbin, in whose vast parish Nashville had been, hurried from Bardstown to Nashville to make the church ready for its pastor. The little church, which had been finished by Father Cosgreve, made a modest enough cathedral for the bishop. It had fallen into disrepair, after being used as an educational institution in the absence of priests. With the appointment of Miles as bishop, Father Durbin was released from any responsibility for Nashville, but this is not the way this staunch priest saw it. ''I cannot consider myself released from the place,'' he wrote Bishop Flaget, ''until I see him installed. I have promised to give $200 to help him fix himself there. I hope you will urge others to assist liberally — both priests and people of the different congregations [of the Diocese of Bardstown]''. On his previous visits to Nashville in 1835 and 1837, Father Durbin had said Mass in the homes of the faithful, so dilapidated was the church, but for the first bishop he had the windows, doors, and floor repaired, and put in a temporary altar and pulpit, and some pews.

On Monday, October 8, 1838, Miles left St. Rose's to take possession of his See accompanied by a fellow Dominican, Father Joseph Jarboe, closely associated with Miles in Dominican life and work, younger than he by some fifteen years. Miles was now forty-nine years of age, perhaps a little old for the hardships that lay ahead. He and Jarboe came on horseback, Miles on his new steed, via Franklin, Kentucky, where they spent a day on the threshold of Tennessee and where Miles preached to the Catholic congregation. Arriving in Nashville, they took lodgings in the Washington Hotel on the east side of the Public Square, and there were received by Father Durbin and received in turn visits from Nashville Catholics. On Sunday, October 14, Miles officially took possession of his See.

Father Jarboe wrote about it to *The Catholic Advocate,* published in Louisville, and distributed all through the former territory of the See of Bardstown, as well as into St. Louis territory. ''Although the Sunday was unfavorable, the church was tolerably well filled. The Bishop addressed the congregation before Mass in a most feeling and paternal manner, and assured them of his devoted attachment to those lately committed to his charge. In truth, he seemed almost unearthly. Putting self entirely out of view, he declared that he lived only for them, and that his greatest and only happiness in life and death would be to see them faithful in the practice of all those Christian virtues which our holy religion inculcates on her members . . . After Mass, Rev. Mr. Durbin preached on 'Regeneration', and I must say he did his subject ample justice." The adults of those days went to church expecting, and looking forward to, much preaching.

Miles stopped in Nashville barely long enough to catch his breath. On Monday, October 22, in the experienced and reassuring company of Father Durbin, he set out to visit his diocese. Heading southeast, they first visited Murfreesboro, where they found a Catholic family. Then they went on to McMinnville, where they found another. They were bound for Athens, Tennessee, where they found over a hundred Irish Catholics building the Hiwasee Railroad. Here they spent six days catching these families up in their religious observances.

Now the travelers headed southwest, towards what is now Chattanooga, slipping into Georgia to visit Calhoun and Rossville. Then they went mainly west back into Tennessee, to Winchester and Fayetteville, one wonders how, whether across northern Alabama and up, or taking what is now I-24 to Jasper. They then headed north back to Nashville, via Mount Pleasant and Columbia, the natural route. How many Catholics they found in these places isn't known; Father Durbin complained to the editor of the *The Catholic Advocate,* that it had printed a poor digest of these travels. But *The Advocate* urged strong support for the new bishop. He won't lack the means of subsistence, the editor quoted Father Durbin as saying, since though the Catholics are few they are generous and noble souls. But in all else the bishop is needful. The church is in debt, and unfinished, its roof decayed; the bishop is without a home or a priest to assist him; let better off Kentucky come to his assistance, the paper pleads.

Just how badly off the bishop was is made plain in a letter he wrote shortly thereafter to the Bishop of New Orleans, Anthony Blanc, who had offered to assist him. It is a touching and revealing letter. "I am consoled to find that some of my brethren remember me in my lonely and destitute situation," he wrote, "where I am left entirely alone to perform all the arduous duties of this hitherto cruelly neglected region, and where so much aid is needed . . . to repair the evils that have taken root among my poor, deserted and scattered flock. I find Catholics in almost every part of the state, many of whom have for many years neglected their duties, and in many instances have lost their faith, for the want of someone to stir them up to a sense of religion. And what can a single individual do, now on the verge of fifty, amidst this general desolation?

"My great poverty deprives me of the means of offering a competent salary to a clergyman; and in default of this I am doomed to struggle alone among the frightful difficulties of every species that surround me!"

". . .You were kind enough to say that you would aid me . . . my wants are so numerous that I am ashamed to begin to mention them, lest I should frighten you by their number. . . . I need first of all a good zealous active priest to help me . . . I need money to assist in repairing our church, for vestments, chalices, etc., etc. I should be particularly pleased to get one of those cloth antependiums [to be hung in front of the main altar, changing with the liturgical seasons] which I have seen sent from France. I wish also to get a keg of pure wine for the altar; for which I will pay you . . . in fine, I need everything."

. . ."Should it be in your power to send me any of the above articles, please direct them to the care of Connor and McAlister, Commission Merchants of this place." Connor sounds like an Irish Catholic, McAlister could be.

There is no record in Nashville of how Bishop Blanc responded to this. But there is ample evidence that help was forthcoming, probably most of it from Kentucky. The church roof was repaired, and the building improved. Dear to Bishop Miles's heart was the organ, bought by him after much investigation from a Cincinnati organ builder. Christmas, 1839, was celebrated with liturgical solemnity. On the altar were six large candlesticks donated by a lady from Brooklyn, New York, an indication of how far Miles's appeals for help were broadcast. On this day Miles dedicated his refurbished church to the Holy Mother of God under the title of the Holy Rosary. One hundred years later Nashville's son, Bishop Samuel A. Stritch, also dedicated his new cathedral in Toledo, Ohio, to Our Lady of the Rosary.

But the main need, that of "a good, zealous, active priest" went sadly unheeded. Twice he visited Kentucky seeking priests, the first time directly after his initial trip through the east half of his diocese. On Sunday, December 2, 1838, he preached in the Bardstown cathedral. His appeal for a priest went unanswered. On his second visit, in the summer of 1839, he ordained one Dominican and conferred the subdiaconate on another, but failed to get a fellow Tennessee missionary. Those who volunteered were refused exeats by their superiors. But, as so often happens, help came from an unexpected quarter. One would expect an eager young priest to volunteer. The priest who did come was devoted, but not young and basically not a missionary. He was, of all things, the rector of the seminary in Cincinnati, Father Joseph Stokes.

Father Stokes had been born in Ireland and educated for Bishop England's Diocese of Charleston. He was prepared to teach in the seminary there, but the need for missionaries was more acute, and he spent ten years ranging from Savannah to Portsmouth, Virginia. From Portsmouth he went to Cincinnati to the seminary post he had trained for long before. Of his competence as a theologian it is impossible at this distance to judge, but he was clearly a man on the model of Bishop England, intelligent, energetic, and articulate. His letters to *The Catholic Advocate* mark him as the first historian of the Diocese of Nashville; much of what we know about the Miles early years in Nashville is owing to his somewhat overpious accounts. However, it is easy to see why Bishop England never advanced him. There was more than a little of the vagabond, both physically and intellectually, about Stokes. In 1844 he decided to become a Jesuit, but soon realized he was not cut out for the role. He then went to New York, like so many others who were missionaries in Tennessee, but unlike most moved around still more in the East. It is interesting to note that he ended his days as Vicar General of the Diocese of Hartford, Connecticut, his talents once more to the fore.

The abundant energy and versatility that marked all his work was never more needed than during his early days in Nashville. On his way there, early in the September of 1839, he was met in Franklin, Kentucky, by a messenger urging him to proceed with all speed, since Bishop Miles was very ill. And ill he was, in extremis; for more than a week after Father Stokes arrived, the bishop lay between life and death with what was probably pneumonia. Father Stokes wrote in something like desperation to Bishop Purcell of Cincinnati that Miles had appointed him vicar general and administrator, and that he in turn needed the help of another priest.

But Bishop Miles surmounted the crisis, although the effects of this near-fatal illness stayed with him for long, possibly as long as he lived, certainly for the rest of 1839 and 1840. As soon as he got hold of things again, he dispatched Stokes to revisit the Catholics whose interest he had previously awakened in Franklin, Columbia, Shelbyville, Winchester, and Fayetteville. Still too weak to see for the first time the western part of his diocese, he then sent Father Stokes to Jackson, Ashport, and Memphis in November, 1839. Ashport had a sizable contingent of Irish working to create a port there, up river from Memphis, but the town never materialized. Father Stokes was delighted with his reception in Memphis; he was the first priest of the diocese to visit there. He preached in Eugene Magevney's famous school, and met with the committee soon to erect a church. The bishop did not get to Memphis until shortly before he left for Europe, in the spring of 1840.

But things were looking up. The longed-for clergy began to appear. True, as one might expect, they were of a roving disposition, the adventurous sort — the conventional need not apply to this priestly version of the Foreign Legion. But this very spirit helped to make them excellent missionaries. They rejoiced in hardship, they revelled in the strange, the outre, the groundbreaking "firsts". Miles himself was not of this breed. He was the steady, pastoral, stable type. But Father Stokes certainly was, and so was the next to join the Tennessee clergy, Father William Clancy. He was a nephew of the scapegrace Auxiliary Bishop of Charleston, South Carolina, William Clancy, John England's one great mistake, his biographer declared. Nephew William came to Nashville from the south, perhaps originally from his uncle's Charleston, though he seems to have taught for a spell at Spring Hill College in Mobile. During his brief Tennessee stay, he was useful. He accompanied Bishop Miles on his first trip to Memphis early in 1840, and was assigned there by the bishop. But he stayed less than a year, when he went to join his uncle bishop who had been transferred to Demarara in British Guiana. Here we lose track of him. His uncle was removed from his diocese in the wake of minor scandals and major troubles, returned to Cork in Ireland where the family came from, and died there in 1847. Perhaps the nephew shared his uncle's misfortunes all the way, perhaps he was one of the many Father William Clancys to be found in the clergy rolls of the times elswhere in the United States. But he belongs firmly in the history of the Church in Tennessee, as the first pastor in Memphis, and the first to officiate at a Catholic marriage there, that of Eugene Magevney to Mary Smyth.

The year 1840 is a pivotal year in the diocese's history. Another first was the ordination of Father William Morgan, the first priest to be ordained for the diocese — as well as the first of its clergymen to die. Little more than this is known about Father Morgan. He was born in Ireland and may have received his seminary training in Cincinnati. Ordained in April, 1840, he scarcely had time to complete his "firsts" — Mass, confessions, assignment — before he died of another of the great disease scourges of the day, consumption, in the November of the same year.

Bishop Miles conferred holy orders on Father Morgan in Cincinnati on his way to Europe. The decision to go abroad was a momentous one, and certainly an inevitable one. At bottom, it was based on finances. His own poverty, and that of the diocese, haunted Bishop Miles from the first news of his appointment. What kept him, and many another American missionary bishop afloat, was the Society for the Propagation of the Faith.

Every American Catholic church goer knows that special collections are taken up every year for this organization to help the missions. At these times, they think of Asia and Africa and exotic unknown islands, and they remember the stories told by visiting missionary priests to their parish churches during appeal time. What they don't know is that this Society, in its early days, was of enormous help to the United States Church. Without it, progress would certainly have been much slower. And today's American Catholics most likely don't know that, at the time of the great need of the Church in the United States the Society for the Propagation of the Faith was predominantly French, and indeed known everywhere as La Societe de la Propagation de la Foi.

This was founded in Lyons, France, in 1822, to help Catholic foreign missions. After some faltering at the beginning, the Society expanded with extraordinary rapidity — the foreign missions in the nineteenth century were mostly French in origin, and the Catholic aspect of French nationalism considered itself specially appointed by Providence to spread the Church to the whole world. For this each member of the Society would contribute one sou a week, which would be collected in groups of tens by a member, and then tens of tens on up the ladder. In this way contributions were steady. By 1826 the Society had spread beyond the limits of France, and ten years later was dispersing three-quarters of a million francs a year to missions all over the world. It is still going strong; middle-aged Catholics will remember Bishop Fulton Sheen of television fame as its National United States director. Today about 37 percent of its revenues go to the American Board of Catholic Missions, the remainder to the rest of the world, a handsome repayment for what the Society did for the United States in its beginnings.

In the fall of 1839 Bishop Miles received the first of many donations from the Society, 26,827 francs. It's hard to calculate its value in American currency, but $5,000 is a good guess, and ten times that in today's money. In all, the Church in Tennessee received around 230,000 francs during the twenty years of Bishop Miles's tenure. The diocese also received 18,000 florins, about the same value as francs, from the Austrian Leopoldine Mission Society. Other special donations also came in from time to time, some from Bishop Miles's begging-and-preaching expeditions to other American dioceses, some from Europe.

If there was any hesitation in the mind of the new Bishop of Nashville about the usefulness of a trip to Europe, it must surely have been dispelled by the 1839 windfall from the Propagation de la Foi. Very probably this was the basis of Miles's purchase of his home on Market Street, a place large enough to be residence, office, and small seminary. Trips to Europe in those days couldn't be taken lightly, especially begging expeditions. The European trip that prevented Bishop Flaget from consecrating Miles lasted for four years. Anything under a year simply wasn't worthwhile; Miles was gone eighteen months. Raising money takes time and skill, and there is no doubt that the Diocese of Nashville lived largely on the charity of others in its early days.

Not all this time was budgeted for Europe. Miles left Nashville for his beloved St. Rose's in Kentucky toward the end of March, accompanied by his Vicar General, Father Stokes. They then proceeded to Cincinnati, where Bishop Miles ordained the ill-fated William Morgan, and recruited for Nashville the talented Father Michael McAleer. Father McAleer was born in Ireland and ordained in 1837 by Bishop Purcell. All four proceeded to Miles's other Dominican post, St. Joseph's in Somerset, Ohio. From there the three priests returned to Tennessee, while the bishop continued eastward, to the Fourth Provincial Council of Baltimore, which opened on May 16, 1840. Just before that, Miles ordained another recruit, Father John Maguire, at Emmitsburg, Maryland; Maguire did not come to Nashville, however, until Miles returned from Europe.

When the council closed, Bishop Miles, along with the other Europe-bound bishops, Rosati of St. Louis and Portier of Mobile, was commissioned to present a letter of condolence to the Archbishops of Cologne and Posen, who were being persecuted by the King of Prussia. They also carried the decrees of the council to Rome. But Miles was fearful of Rome's summer heat, and went first to Dominican houses in France, Belgium, and The Netherlands. He wrote an account of his diocese for the Society for the Propagation of the Faith, and very probably received financial and other aid from the Austrian Leopoldine Association. The bishop arrived in Rome for Christmas and spent about two months there. He then resumed his begging expeditions throughout the spring and summer, and got back to New York on August 26, 1841.

The bishop had left his diocese with his first pastoral letter on the subject of the Lenten regulations. He returned to autumnal rejoicing, on October 9, 1841, having halted on his return trip once more at his old Dominican posts in Ohio and Kentucky. Father Stokes, his Vicar while he was abroad, was on hand to greet him, along with Father McAleer, now pastor of Memphis. A Mass of Thanksgiving was sung, the school children marched, the faithful cheered. There was a distinct sense of well-being in the diocese. The bishop brought back with him two excellent priests to work in the diocese, Fathers Louis Hoste and Nicholas Savelli. More importantly, toward the end of the year, the bishop for the first time in Nashville celebrated the sacrament of holy orders. Father

John O'Dowde was raised to the priesthood, and minor orders were conferred on Ivo Schacht and William Howard.

The trend was up. The diocese was beginning to have a life of its own. Miles kept buying more land around his residence, eventually some ten acres, intending to build his cathedral there. And, to crown all, six Sisters of Charity came from their motherhouse in Nazareth, Kentucky, to start an academy for girls, which flowered into almost instant success. These were the first nuns in Tennessee.

Bishop Richard Pius Miles

Father Ivo Schacht was the bishop's ablest assistant in the 1840s.

Father Aloysius Orengo served the longest and built the most churches of any early missionary.

Before photography was invented, an unknown artist drew Nashville's first church and the diocese's first cathedral, Holy Rosary. It was near the present site of President Polk's tomb on Capitol Hill.

In continuous use since dedicated by Bishop Miles in 1842, the oldest Catholic church in Tennessee is St. Michael's, near Cedar Hill, Robertson County.

This early view of St. Mary's Cathedral includes the house next door that architect Adolphus Heiman built for himself, the cupola that he designed for the church, and a corner of the Planters Hotel porch.

Mother Xavier Ross left Nashville and founded a new order, Sisters of Charity of Leavenworth, and a new and wider apostolate.

Philip Olwill was a leading Catholic layman during the era of Bishop Miles.

This view of St. Mary's, seen from the State Capitol grounds, shows the renovations of the 1920-1940 period.

4

The 1840s and the Cathedral

Ever since Bishop Miles came to Nashville he had lived in the old part of the city. This stretched north and south from the Public Square. Demonbreun's home and tavern was on the south side, as was the home of Philip Callaghan, where Miles is said to have lodged for a while, on the corner of Market, now Second Avenue, and Church. Possibly the Washington Hotel became too expensive. But the Bishop needed a home, and as soon as he could he rented a house from a Mr. Dougherty just north of the Square.

This northerly direction may have decided him to stay on that side when, in 1839, with the first money he got from the Society for the Propagation of the Faith (and, perhaps, a little help from the Miles family), he bought a property from James and William Park, a little farther north on Market Street, where the Gas Company now is. Two years later he added the adjacent ten acres to the north. This is where he planned to build his cathedral and the seminary-plus-school for boys he so yearned for, no doubt recalling his early days in Kentucky.

Meanwhile, his home became the center of activities of the diocese. His biographer, Victor O'Daniel, says there was a house on the Park property the bishop adapted to his use, but Dan Barr, in his 1897 souvenir history of the fiftieth anniversary of the old cathedral, says he built a large three-story brick house, "elegantly furnished with all the necessities of a home, and in the basement two rooms were reserved and transformed into richly adorned chapels." Why two, the historian does not say. The little cathedral was some five city-blocks up Campbell's Hill to the west, no great distance, but it is clear that Miles did not envision the hill as the right place for a Catholic Center.

The house on Market Street was the residence not only of the bishop, but for all the priests of the diocese except the resident pastor of Memphis. Of course, these were mostly missionaries, on the road more often than not, but the bishop's house was their headquarters and their home when they were in Nashville. Father Stokes, Miles's vicar general and rector of the cathedral, was in residence most of the time; so was Father John Maguire when he was rector. But the missionaries, Fathers Hoste, Savelli, Alemany, Clancy, Howard, O'Dowde, all came and went, no doubt with news from the missions and adventurous tales to tell. A long-time resident was Father Ivo Schacht, a native of Belgium, ordained by Miles for the diocese, and vigorously useful in it, especially to the growing German Catholic group, whose language he spoke fluently. He, too, became a rector of the cathedral. Father Samuel Montgomery, a Dominican associate of Miles in the old days in Kentucky, came eventually to live with his friend the bishop, and Father John Jacquet came especially to teach the seminarians, who had a dormitory in the house. This was, it was clear, no ordinary bishop's house, but a center on a miniature scale like a Renaissance palace — offices, schools, entertainment, kitchens, and lodging, all under one roof.

But the little enterprise couldn't last. For one thing, the development of Nashville didn't follow the flat land to the north out towards the salt licks, but went instead west, especially following the choice of Nashville as the State Capital in 1843 and the immediate decision of the legislature to build the Capitol on Campbell's Hill. But more importantly the railroads did follow the flat land, and the L & N claimed a right of way which divided the church property, rendering it, in Dan Barr's words, "undesirable either for worship or residence."

To his dismay, Miles was forced to sell, and with the proceeds bought, in March, 1844, at a cost of $4,400 the land for the new cathedral on the southeast corner of Summer and Cedar streets, now Fifth and Charlotte. The seller, ironically, was railroad tycoon V. K. Stevenson. Stevenson's second wife was a Childress, a relative of Mrs. James K. Polk, and a convert to Catholicism during her school days at Nazareth, Kentucky.

Excavation began at once, and the cornerstone of the new church was laid on the feast of Corpus Christi, June 6, 1844. It was quite a ceremony. "Curiosity," wrote Father O'Daniel, "favored by a beautiful day, brought an immense crowd to see a spectacle which was the first of its kind in Nashville.'' Bishop Miles wrote to a friend in Baltimore, ''This is the first time that a Mitre and Crozier have been seen in the streets of Nashville, and they must have produced strange feelings in many.''

They must have indeed. And yet, not necessarily hostile feelings. Across the street from the site of the new church lived a Major Daniel Graham, a former Comptroller of the state and a Presbyterian. With neighborly good feeling, the major not only lent his mansion to the bishop for the occasion, but also permitted a platform to be set up in front of it, from which the rector of the cathedral, John Maguire, gave a long sermon to the assembled throng. After that, the bishop, in his best vestments, proceeded to bless the place and lay the cornerstone, according to the ritual of the Church. The cornerstone contained, as usual, a document which said, in Latin, ''All to the greater glory of God and of the Blessed Virgin Mary. In the year of the Incarnation of our Lord 1844, of the Declaration of American Independence the sixty-ninth; on the sixth day of June, The Feast of Corpus Christi; the Supreme Pontiff Gregory XVI governing the whole Church; John Tyler being President of the United States; James Jones being Governor of Tennessee; P. W. Maxey being Mayor of Nashville; the Right Reverent Pius Miles, the first Bishop of Nashville, with the assistance of the Very Reverend Joseph Alemany, O.P., and the Reverend Rector of the Cathedral, John Maguire, and the clergy of the Episcopal Seminary [Miles's household], solemnly dedicated and laid this cornerstone to the honor of God under the auspices of the Blessed Virgin Mary, and under the invocation of St. Dominic, the Founder of the Order of Friars-Preachers.''

It was a great day for the new Diocese of Nashville.

Major Graham's liberality brings up the vexed question of the anti-Catholic movements which were so strong in the 1840s. It was a peculiar phenomenon, for the side represented by Graham's kindly gesture was widespread. In Nashville, too, there was handsome precedent. More than twenty years previously the Grand Master of the Nashville Masons had given the land for the first little church still standing up the hill, and non-Catholics had contributed generously to its construction.

There was general interest in the Church. Tennessee's first governor and founding father, John Sevier, tried to persuade Father Badin to start a Catholic colony "with a hundred families" in East Tennessee. Of course he was interested in selling the land, but he wasn't afraid to sell it to a colony of Catholics. As noted earlier, Sevier's journal tells of his attending Catholic services several times in Washington. This, too, can be misleading. All sorts of people attended preaching-as-theater on the frontier, just as non-Catholics visiting Rome in the 1840s went with breathless excitement to witness the Catholic rituals in the great churches. College students seem to have gone to various churches much as today's breed go to rock concerts; Nashville's Randal McGavock's journal tells of many such occasions. Neither he nor Dr. Felix Robertson shuddered at Catholics. Robertson's two daughters were taught French by Father Hoste, educated in France, and became Catholics.

There was, of course, during the 1820s anti-Catholic prejudice, but much of it arose out of ignorance; it was a tremor of fear at the unknown, the exotic, which people feel at anything strange and new — the same sort of fear and fascination that early settlers felt upon meeting bands of Indians.

The anti-Catholic passions of the 1840s were more than this. Part of the fierce and unreasonable hatred arose from fear of the waves of Irish immigrants then pouring into the country. In the years between 1846 and 1854 this Irish immigration amounted to one million souls. Americans of Irish descent in the 1980s should remember that fear of their ancestors was well-founded; their forefathers were indeed ignorant, violent, and unmannerly. They had been so unmanned by British oppression that they often seemed like the barbarians at the gates of civilization a thousand years before.

This was the reaction of the older Americans who watched the Irish create the slums of Boston, New York, and Philadelphia, the response of men and women concerned for their security and culture. But, of course, these same men and women were satisfied to see the Irish men build the railroads and dockyards and offices, and welcomed the women into their homes and hotels as maids and nurses and cooks. Yet there was still the uneasiness that follows when differing cultures meet.

Anti-Catholic prejudice in the South was markedly different because there were so few southern Catholics. Most immigrants came to the great northern ports of Philadelphia, New York, Boston, and Montreal. Only a few went to Baltimore, Charleston, and New Orleans. In these places the small increment of immigration found some settled Catholicity which the immigrants did not overwhelm. The infusion, indeed, may have strengthened and vivified Catholic life, since so many distinguished Catholic leaders came from the South.

The most distinguished of these, perhaps the most distinguished Catholic the United States has produced, was John Carroll, the country's first bishop. Carroll came from a rich and distinguished Maryland family; his distant cousin, Charles, was said to be the richest man in America. He was a signer of the Declaration of Independence, and a wise and respected statesman. Cousin John was early destined for the Church, and was educated in Europe for the priesthood. An early leader of the clergy of the United States, he was elected by them to be their first bishop in 1789. His diocese was, of course, the entire thirteen colonies, until he managed to get bishops for New York, Boston, Philadelphia, and other places. Carroll was pleased to be elected; he favored election for all bishops. His thinking on this, and other matters, was thoroughly in harmony with that of the founding fathers of the nation, with whom he was on good terms. He was made the first American Archbishop in 1808.

John England, too, was national in stature. He founded the first Catholic newspaper, the *United States Catholic Miscellany,* was invited to address the Congress of the United States, and was very influential in the bishops' councils. He, too, thought American. He introduced a scheme of democracy in the governance of his diocese. It did not outlive him, but the drive he and Carroll headed toward democratic ways was a harbinger of things to come. For the great Archbishop of Baltimore of the turn of the century, James Cardinal Gibbons, was of the same mind. He and his collaborators, notably Archbishop John Ireland of St. Paul, were decisive in the Americanization of the Catholic Church.

But there was still a mountain of prejudice to erode. Carroll, on revisiting Boston toward the end of his life wrote happily, "It is wonderful to tell what great civilities have been done to me in this town, where a few years ago a Catholic parish priest was thought to be the greatest monster in creation." England, as we shall see, lived to see his humane attitude toward the black race emphatically repudiated by his Charleston neighbors. One might expect impregnable anti-Catholicism from a Protestant clergyman like Lyman Beecher, but one is surprised at the malignant anti-Catholic and anti-Irish remarks tossed off by Emerson and Thoreau. Perhaps the most remarkable specimen of the breed is Samuel F.B. Morse, who wrote and lectured against Catholics with crusading force — despite, or maybe because of, a long residence in Catholic France.

It's a puzzling, see-saw affair. John Mitchell, the famous Protestant Irish patriot, whose amazing career included transportation to Tasmania, escape, and residence in Tennessee near Knoxville, wrote in 1854 of the tolerance he found in the law-abiding South. Yet months later he was threatening to leave the country because of the rapid success of the Know-Nothing Party. The Know-Nothings exploded into being during the 1840s out of alarm over the torrent of immigrants, then mostly Irish. It was basically a secret society whose members, when questioned by outsiders, were instructed to say, "I know nothing". The Know-Nothings were the political expression of the anti-Catholic rioting which disgraced the cities of Boston, New York, Philadelphia, St. Louis, Louisville, and many more. The Protestant clergy and their journals inflamed this lawlessness grievously, creating lurid visions of faceless legions directed by the Pope (the Lord knows where they would come from), invading the United States and subjugating honest Baptists to their fiendish will. The popular literature of the time made Catholics villains with the same easy freedom they damned the Indians.

Tennessee, despite its tiny Catholic population, participated in this ugly scene. There were no large-scale riots, but anti-Catholic feeling boiled over in politics. The Know-Nothing party won a sweeping victory in Memphis in 1855, electing its candidates to every office except that of Governor. Nashville, too, had a Know-Nothing mayor, and Clarksville, Murfreesboro, Loudon, and Lawrenceburg elected Know-Nothing officials. Prominent political leaders, like Edward Cheatham and former Governor Neill S. Brown, joined the bandwagon.

The great Tennessee prophet of anti-Catholicism, however,

lived in Knoxville. He was William Ganaway Brownlow, familiarly known as ''Parson'' Brownlow because for the first ten years of his maturity he was a Methodist preacher riding the rough circuits of Appalachia. But he was basically a journalist of the old-fashioned polemical sort. He founded and edited a variety of papers, none of which survived his proprietorship.

At the outset, Brownlow ignored Catholics, probably because he didn't know any and hadn't encountered them in his reading. His early targets were Presbyterians and Baptists. ''When will this denomination [the Baptists] learn wisdom!'' he exclaimed in 1856, ''When will the hide-bound clerican dolts of that order acquaint themselves with the Scriptures?'' He accused them of ''selfishness, bigotry, and intolerance''.

But the Baptists were angelic compared to the abolitionists. Brownlow defended slavery with all his passion, which was monumental, and all his talent for invective, which was oceanic. ''What an unmitigated generation of hypocrites!'' went one of his milder blasts, ''what despicable cowards!'' This, from the minister of a religion which was generally, before 1850, opposed to slavery, but Brownlow loftily ignored opinions opposed to his, even if they were John Wesley's.

It was inevitable that Brownlow should become engaged with politics, but scarcely inevitable that he should take so odd a position. He was 100 percent in favor of slavery, and a 100 percent unionist. The Confederates of Knoxville slapped him into jail. He proved too hot to handle in jail, and said, if he were released, he would do more for his captors than the Devil had done: he would leave them. He did, and returned when the Federal troops took Knoxville, to enter upon a career in Reconstruction politics that made him twice Governor of Tennessee and, at the end, United States Senator.

In the 1830s Brownlow became infected with Morse's disease, the form of anti-Catholic prejudice that was based on fear of a conspiracy which would turn the United States over to the Pope and his vassals, the Catholic monarchs of Europe.

Especially as it affects the Mississippi Valley, where Catholic France and Catholic Spain had proved incapable of colonization, the conspiracy theory seems remarkably incredible. It is hard to believe that Brownlow could think that Martin van Buren was in cahoots with the Pope to take over the country, or that the Democratic Party was a possible fifth column for the legions of poor Pope Gregory XVI, who could scarcely keep order in his own backward and chaotic little Papal States, let alone threaten a foreign power over three thousand miles away. Brownlow's great adversary was Andrew Johnson, the man who won the governorship in 1855 by sheer force of character. "Show me the dimension of a Know-Nothing and I will show you a huge reptile, upon whose neck the foot of every honest man ought to be placed". With this as his theme, Johnson won in a close race. Brownlow said that his victory came from "foreign and Catholic votes, out to subvert the government!" Catholics were then perhaps two percent of the state's population.

This, then, is the political background against which Bishop Miles was raising his new cathedral. It was immensely complicated by the Mexican War, presided over by Tennessee's own President James K. Polk. The state was immensely preoccuped by the war, so much that *The Tennessee Baptist* complained, in its issue of June 6, 1846, that "our city [Nashville] is converted into a military camp". Since Mexico was a Catholic country, many Protestants thought the Catholic Irish would side with their fellow religionists. But the American Irish fought vigorously for their new country — only mixing up the issue the more by insisting on Catholic chaplains. Polk assented to this, and persuaded Congress to establish dipolomatic relations with the Vatican.

Miles himself was all his life a-political. If he had any political preferences he kept them to himself, like most other Catholic bishops of his time, who took a hand in politics only when the interests of the Church were threatened. Some of his neighbors thought their interests were threatened by the building of the new Catholic cathedral. Miles bore these remonstrances with patient good humor. "We are making preparations for the commencement of our cathedral in the spring," he wrote to his good friend Bishop Spalding of Louisville on February 6, 1840, "which we intend to make the prettiest thing in Nashville...Whilst this has delighted the liberal portion of the community, it has horrified the *saints.* The latter are terribly scandalized at the inroads Popery is making among them, and I am seriously afraid some of them will die of the blues before this cold spell is over, their faces are already as blue as their stockings, which, as you know, are dyed in the wool.'' This was the right man for the times. But he could not help but be hurt by such anti-Catholic bigotry. He was more likely to have been hurt by the cries of protest over the coming of the Sisters of Charity of Nazareth to start a school for girls. Anti-Catholicism of the 1840s hated a convent more than anything else in the Catholic presence.

The slow building of the church, 1844 to 1847, probably owed something to the Mexican War, but more to lack of money. Bishop Miles was by now accustomed to regular contributions from the Society for the Propagation of the Faith, but at just this crucial juncture the Society cut his appropriation in about half. This was probably due to Miles's failure to keep in touch, to make annual reports, to press the claims of the new Church along with the usual missionary needs. In any case it was trouble for the bishop. But he was more than equal to the occasion. He made preaching-and-begging trips through the North, especially to Philadelphia, whose Bishop Kenrick, brother to the Archbishop of St. Louis, was friendly, and thus raised the needed money in his own country. At the same time he reinstated himself in the good graces of the Society, although he never got back to the amount of his allocation for 1842, 28,000 francs, about $10,000, no mean sum for 1842. Ten years later it was running about 18,000 francs.

What is most astonishing about Miles's new cathedral is its handsome and artistically satisfying style. Its facade is simply beautiful, and the interior, with its elegantly coffered ceiling, is charming and ingratiating. It was an era of good building in prospering Nashville, the time of the great homes that dot the area, Belle Meade, Belmont, Two Rivers, Kingsley, Burlington, many more. All of these have been attributed to the genius of William Strickland, the great Philadelphia architect who won the competition for the Tennessee State Capitol in 1845 and came to Nashville that year to supervise its construction. Strickland did indeed design the beautiful Hugh Kirkman house across the street from St. Mary's, perhaps next to, perhaps replacing, Major Graham's home. But there is no documentary evidence of his designing the others. However, until he came to Nashville, Strickland had designed very few houses; he was famous for his brilliant public buildings.

And brilliant they were. Strickland was one of America's foremost architects. A somewhat wayward pupil of the great Benjamin Latrobe, who designed the base of the United States Capitol, Strickland was, in the words of Talbot Hamlin, one of the foremost historians of American architecture, "that extraordinary man William Strickland, engineer and architect, painter and engraver, one of the most interesting personalities, as he was one of the most brilliant and original designers, of the entire Greek Revival movement". Not that Strickland confined himself to the Greek Revival; he did some of his best work in the Egyptian style, and incorporated elements of the Italian baroque as well. When he came to Nashville, Strickland had to his credit a long list of important commissions. Perhaps the foremost was his prize-winning design for the Second Bank of the United States, still standing as a museum in Philadelphia. But equally impressive, and more original, is his Philadelphia Merchants Exchange Building. And there were dozens more.

Of course, the chance to design the Tennessee State Capitol was a wonderful opportunity. Nashville was chosen as the capitol of the state in 1843. The capitol commission approached Strickland the following year, and in 1845 his plans were accepted, along with his provision that he supervise the construction. He was then 55 years old, and did not live to see the capitol completed; he died in 1854, and is buried in the north wall of the building.

Did he or did he not design the cathedral of the Seven Dolors of the Catholic Diocese of Nashville? Until lately, he was everywhere credited with it; he is named its architect on the historical markers erected by the Tennessee Historical Commission in front of both the capitol and the cathedral. Book after book, and article after article on Tennessee architecture, on Strickland, and on the church, name Strickland the cathedral's architect.

Most of these historians note there is no documentary evidence that Strickland designed the church, but believe that the long tradition that names him its architect is authentic. A recent book on Tennessee architecture by James Patrick, however, contends that Strickland almost certainly was not the St. Mary's architect, but rather that the almost equally talented, if not as famous, Adolphus Heiman, probably was. Patrick argues that Strickland did not come to Nashville until St. Mary's was underway, which is true; but he designed the Mints at Charlotte and New Orleans without ever going to those cities, and since Miles was often in Philadelphia it's possible he could have engaged Strickland there. More plausibly, Patrick contends that there is no mention of Strickland in connection with St. Mary's all through the latter half of the nineteenth century and on into the twentieth, when Strickland is off-handedly named as architect by Father Victor O'Daniel, Bishop Miles's biographer, in 1926. Patrick's conclusions are supported by other Nashville historians.

But it is intriguing that the only newspaper reference to the architect is that of the *Nashville Union,* which said, of the 1847 dedication, "It is a neat and chaste specimen of Grecian architecture, which reflects credit upon its architect". But it does not say who the architect was, nor does any other reference to Nashville architecture, until the biography of Bishop Miles names Strickland. But the biographer almost certainly relies on tradition, for he gives no documentation, either because he had none, or much more likely, because he thought none was needed, so well known was the Strickland touch upon the church.

One reason for believing Adolphus Heiman was St. Mary's architect is the beautiful home he designed for himself next door to the church on Summer Street. As old photographs show, the original facade of this home so neatly and beautifully dovetails into the elegant facade of the Church that they seem to be the work of the same classic imagination. To judge from its subsequent history, however, the only good thing about the house may have been its facade. Heiman lived there only five years, building himself a house just as beautiful but in a very different style, more airy and spacious, on Jefferson Street at Ninth Avenue. Heiman had many ties with the Germantown settlement in north Nashville. When he moved into his new house, Bishop Miles moved into the old one, but he never loved it — he referred to it in a letter to his friend Bishop Spalding of Louisville as a "rattrap". Neither did Bishop Feehan, who is listed as living there in the Nashville city directories from the time he came to Nashville in 1868 almost to the time of his departure in 1880. Only one of his successors lived there. The diocesan offices were there until Bishop Byrne built the new Cathedral complex on West End Avenue in the early 1900s, at which time the old Cathedral became St. Mary's Parish, which it remains till now. However, the parish priests mostly did not live in the old house. Never very livable, it would seem, it deteriorated more and more. When Bishop Alphonse J. Smith in the mid-1920s decided to renovate old St. Mary's to save it from collapse, the man he chose to do the job, Father Edward P. Desmond, gave up the house as impossible, and lived in hotels. Finally, in 1929, the house that Heiman built was torn down and a new office-residence erected, with Christian Asmus of Nashville as the architect. This building, the present one, has nothing of the style and charm of Heiman's facade, but it is at least livable.

The present church closely resembles the original. The facade is chaste and simple, pure classicism; it has none of the flamboyance of Strickland's Egyptian Revival Presbyterian Church three city blocks to its south, none of the Italianate baroque grace and luxury of Belmont, which is characteristic of Heiman's later work. The facade of St. Mary's reflects the shallowness of Bishop Miles's exchequer, and may be all the better for it; it has a disarming simplicity and tranquil harmony more lasting and endearing than the Presbyterian church's rich exoticism, striking and splendid though that church is. St. Mary's is a simple building. Its slope to the east contains a big basement for parish meetings, clerical assemblies, classes, and such like, most useful. Its demarcation also adds esthetic interest to the north side of the Church, the heavy stones of the foundation making a pleasant textural contrast to the smooth sides of the nave. The construction is very simple. The main joists are of heavy yellow poplar, hand-cut, impervious through the years to termites. Not so with the smaller runners of floor and ceiling, which are of all kinds of wood and by no means uniform of size, leading to the belief that Miles engaged workmen as he could, until his money ran out, but with no continuity. When the stabilizing pews are removed, the floor of St. Mary's undulates in a slight roller-coaster effect.

The walls are of solid native brick, probably originally plastered on the outside with stucco, a favorite building material of the day, and ordinary wall plaster inside. What is remarkable are the lovely proportions of the facade and the exposed north wall.

The plain pediment is a perfect topping for the beautiful columns, whose original carved wood capitals have been retained through all the renovations. The recessed entrance is both sensible and architecturally effective. To judge from a pre-Civil War sketch, it was originally more elaborate, but it is almost certain that the present handsome proportion of door to wall to facade is the same. A perfect echo to this recess are the two niches, which, along with the elegant quasi-baroque cupola, the documented work of Heiman, afford pleasing relief from the severity of the Greek plainness. The same sort of effect on a less subtle scale is seen in the north wall, whose pilasters, working with the corner pilasters and the lovely window openings, create a handsome rhythm.

The interior has, of course, been much more changed through the years with restorations and renovations, but, to judge from old photographs, retains much the same character. The curved apse, where the main altar stands, is an echo of the basilica style. Tradition has it that originally there was a crucifixion scene painted on the wall by a talented young priest who was stationed at the church in 1863-1866, Father Henry V. Brown. The present free-standing crucifix dates from 1926. It is not very effective, but the sanctuary of the old church never was; no wonder Bishop Byrne, on coming into his cathedral in 1896, concluded it was too small for proper episcopal liturgies. However, the disappointing effect of the sanctuary is compensated for by the charming coffered ceiling. The present coffering is deeper and more pronounced than the original, but it was always there. One wonders how it got there. In an article in the *Tennessee Historical Quarterly* in 1956, Mrs. John Trotwood Moore says, "Theodore Knoch and John Wolfe Schleicher, Sr., painted the ceiling in the Capitol, and also the Crucifixion in St. Mary's". The ceiling helps to give the church the warmth and intimacy which old parishioners speak of. Originally the ceiling had no paintings; the present scenes from the life of Christ date from the restoration of 1895. In the center is The Deposition from the Cross, the only scene of the Seven Dolors of the Blessed Virgin Mary, the church's patroness. In addition, there are paintings in the corners of the four Evangelists.

The church was dedicated in 1847. That was a big occasion, one can't help thinking the most important of Miles's episcopal life. Here, ten hard years after he became Bishop of Nashville, was a cathedral church which would do credit to any small diocese in the world. The *Louisville Catholic Advocate,* describing the dedication ceremonies of November 20, 1847, speaks of an "appropriate group of statuary representing the Most Sorrowful Mother receiving the lifeless body of her dear son when He was taken down from the cross, these principal figures being surrounded by a circle of angels. The figures are composed of what is called *sand-stone paper,* and the whole group was procured in France." This was probably plaster of Paris. As Bishop Miles walked round this and the rest of the church in the ceremony of dedication, Bishop Purcell of Cincinnati explained from the pulpit what was being done. After this, Bishop Portier of Mobile celebrated a solemn high Mass, and the sermon was delivered by the eloquent Bishop of Louisville, afterwards Archbishop of Baltimore, Martin J. Spalding. Spalding was persuaded to remain in Nashville to give more lectures on the Catholic faith, and the day after the dedication Bishop Purcell confirmed a class of twenty-two, fourteen of whom were converts. But the dearest touch of all was the presence in the sanctuary of Father Elisha J. Durbin, who had prepared the predecessor Church of the Holy Rosary for Miles back in 1838.

One month later Bishop Miles wrote to Bishop Purcell, "We are much gratified to see a fine congregation in our new church every Sunday. . . . Sit nomen Domini benedictum [May the name of the Lord be blessed]." Miles had every reason to be satisfied. He had spent upwards of $40,000 on his fine cathedral, a huge sum for those days. But he knew that the church would, as symbol and fact, enormously stimulate the growth of Catholicism in Nashville.

The appurtenances of the church reflected European rather than American taste, as did so many "cathedrals in the wilderness", to use Professor Schauinger's neat term. Missionaries and bishops from America toured Europe on begging trips, and especially when no money was forthcoming, often were given religious articles of exceptional quality. Thus Miles's church had a fine ostensorium, for exposing the Holy Eucharist at Benediction and other devotions, handsome vestments for the church services, paintings, missals, and so on, many of which the bishop and his priests had brought back from Europe. No Miles church would be complete without a good organ, and a new one was installed in the cathedral in 1849 — the church was always known for the excellence of its music. Heiman's charming, almost whimsical cupola with its clocks and bell was added by 1863; the bell became famous — it was the foremost Nashville sound!

By then Nashville and the South were three years into the Civil War, three years of doubt, chaos, and difficulty, but undisturbed by actual fighting. Then came the Battle of Nashville in 1864, and the Federal authorities turned St. Mary's into a hospital. Monsignor Charles M. Williams, Pastor of St. Mary's in the 1970s, gives a day-by-day account of this culled from the daily papers in his sketch of St. Mary's: December 18, 1864 — "The Catholic Church was dismantled yesterday and prepared for the reception of the sick and wounded soldiers. The churches which shelter these heroic men are doubly consecrated in the eyes of God." January 1, 1865 — "The Sisters and orphans were moved from the Cathedral, where they had been for four weeks, and took up quarters in the Reade House on the Franklin Turnpike near the city limits." January 12 — "The Cathedral is being vacated by the medical authorities and will probably be restored this week." January 19 — "The Angelus bell at six o'clock last evening rang out the glad tidings that the Cathedral of Nashville had been evacuated and restored to its legitimate uses." February 11 — "The Cathedral is being fitted up again, carpenters having been busily at work yesterday replacing the pews in their proper positions. It will be completed next week, so far as the carpenter work is concerned." February 15 — "The Choir of the Cathedral proposes giving a grand concert on next Tuesday evening on the 21st inst. The proceeds, we are informed, are to be used to aid in the refitting of the church, which was for some weeks used as a military hospital."

This was the first renovation of St. Mary's. There's no record of the Federal authorities paying for the use of the church, but it is to be supposed they made some sort of recompense, and no doubt the fourteen year episcopacy of Bishop Patrick Feehan (1865-1880) and the ten-year reign of Bishop Joseph Rademacher (1883-1893) saw some changes. But not many. The Nashville Gas Company ran a line up Cedar Street to light the Capitol in 1855.

Since old photographs show enormous gas chandeliers in St. Mary's, it's probable the church was among the earliest to tap the line; electricity came with the first major renovation.

This was the work of the fifth Bishop of Nashville, Thomas S. Byrne. The interior of St. Mary's today is essentially the work of Bishop Byrne. A photograph of the church's interior in pre-Byrne days shows a much more shallow coffering in the ceiling with no paintings visible, but each coffered recess highly decorated, whose motifs are repeated in the recessed ceiling of the main altar's semicircular space. Two angels flank the altar, and the table is supported by a wooden tomb, although Bishop Miles was not buried in it. The wall to the left has a painted memorial to Miles, surmounted by a mitre and crozier; there is a similar one to the right, whose purpose is unknown. Angels with wreaths are painted on each side of the altar space, and a huge gas chandelier hangs squarely in the middle of the photograph.

Byrne retained the altar, but hung a big free-standing crucifix over it. He had the ceiling redone, retaining the coffering but making the coffers deeper, and added the paintings that are still there, though doubtless changed and retouched. He enlarged the twin sacristies on both sides of the altar, and covered the walls of the entire church with a stenciled pattern of small geometrical design. He put in new stained glass windows and ''myriads of electric lights'', says the dedication bulletin. The effect is that of a small church in Rome, Byrne's ideal, which he created more purely in his new cathedral on West End Avenue.

When Byrne moved to the new cathedral complex in 1908, St. Mary's fell into a decline that continued until Bishop Alphonse J. Smith appointed Father Edward P. Desmond to shore up the old church's sagging foundations, and refurbish it thoroughly, inside and out. Byrne had not touched the exterior, but Father Desmond put new brick on the sides, and finished off the facade with the pressed stone-bit blocks that are there today. Father Desmond also put up the useful and tasteful cast iron gates and fences. A new altar was installed, and the interior cleaned and brightened — the original moulding was picked up with bolder colors, and still is one of the best features of the church. The rubber tile flooring he added was handsome, but did not wear well. The steel girders that were later put in the basement to prop up the wood joists have no doubt contributed to the long life of the church; the basement itself reverted to its original usefulness, becoming a chapel during World War II. No major changes have been done since the Desmond extensive remodeling, but new lighting, carpeting, and such like have been necessary from time to time by various rectors. Monsignor John M. Mogan removed some of the old lighting. Father George L. Donovan completely redecorated the church interior and once again replaced the floor. Father Thomas P. Duffy renovated and redecorated the interior, and redesigned the basement. At that time the organ was augmented and largely replaced. Monsignor Charles M. Williams redecorated and constantly improved the building during his pastorate. And finally, Father Richard G. Buchignani did some remodeling and recarpeted the church. Some major repairs have recently been done on the roof and cupola.

5

The Early Church in Memphis

In some ways the Catholic Church in Memphis was a separate diocese almost from the beginning, so different is its story from that of the See city of Nashville, or those of Knoxville, Chattanooga, Clarksville, and other early Catholic one-church centers.

However, "the beginning" is very like Nashville's, only a generation later. An early missionary, Father Joseph Stokes, the Rector of the seminary of Cincinnati who came to help Miles out, plays the part played in Nashville by Father Robert Abell. The part of Demonbreun goes to the Irish Eugene Magevney, in whose Adams Street home Memphis's first Mass was celebrated by Stokes.

The first Mass was celebrated in 1839. In 1840 the same house was the scene of the marriage of Eugene Magevney to Mary Smythe, the fiancee who had to wait twelve years in her native Ireland before Eugene could send for her. Their first child was baptized in this house in 1841.

So the records go. But it is difficult to believe that there were not other and earlier priests and Eucharists. Memphis was laid out as a town in 1819, by Nashville's John Overton, and there was much river traffic from St. Louis to the north and New Orleans to the south, both rich in early Catholicism. But there is no record till Eugene Magevney built his historic house on Adams Street.

That house is now a museum of the City of Memphis, excellently restored with the furniture and furnishings of its 1833 period. It was a pioneering period. The rooms are small, the handiwork apparent everywhere, from the child's nightdress on the bed to the heavy timbers of the house's framing. Everything here speaks of small-scale life, of family intimacy and homeliness, of simple elegance and plain good style. And yet, only ten years later, there came the Gothic sophistication of St. Peter's Church,

The pioneer Catholic family of Memphis, Mr. and Mrs. Eugene Magevney, and their two daughters. Their historic home is now a city museum.

Immaculate Conception Church became Cathedral in 1970 when a new diocese was created.

Dominican priests have staffed St. Peter's Church since it was built in 1843. *Diocese of Memphis photos.*

Altar of St. Mary's, 1874. *Diocese of Memphis photo.*

Interior of St. Paul's, 1946. *Diocese of Memphis photo.*

Christian Brothers College in Memphis is one of two Catholic institutions of higher learning in Tennessee.

The Christian Brothers throve under leadership of Brother Maurelian Sheel, F.S.C.

St. Agnes Convent on Vance Avenue was a Dominican landmark for many years.

Some of the children in St. Peter's Orphanage, in Memphis, during the era of the first World War.

The congregation stood in a circle for the blessing of the outdoor shrine at the Church of Our Lady of Perpetual Help, Germantown.

Diocese of Memphis photo.

next door.

Eugene Magevney is a fascinating and by no means unique type of Irish immigrant, before the flood of the 1840s. He was poor, but he was not illiterate; his excellent classical education had resulted in cultivated taste and high ideals. It was also the foundation of his substantial fortune. Starting a private school for boys, he prospered because he often took land for payment in lieu of his fees, and as land values soared, so did the Magevney wealth. Shortly after his marriage he abandoned the schoolroom for real estate, going into partnership with his brother Michael, who was a building contractor. They both became wealthy. But Eugene never lost his interest in education. Elected an alderman, he became the father of the Memphis public schools system, one of the earliest in the South.

Nothing could be farther from the career of Nashville's first prominent Catholic, Timothy Demonbreun. The similarity lies in their hosting the first Masses in their homes, and their public and proud Catholicity. Father Michael McAleer, the first Catholic pastor of Memphis, was also different from Father Robert Abell, the Kentuckian who was Nashville's first "pastor". Born in Ireland, McAleer immigrated with his parents to Maryland as a child, studied at Mount Saint Mary's Seminary in Emmitsburg, Maryland, and was ordained for the western missions in Cincinnati the year Nashville became a diocese, 1837. He immediately embarked on the arduous missionary travels of the times, first in Ohio, then after 1840 in Tennessee. He probably visited Memphis as early as 1840; the earliest baptismal records are signed by him early in 1841 at St. Peter's Church. He began St. Peter's that same year, and was made its permanent pastor in 1842. But McAleer wearied of the missionary life. He had learning and eloquence unsatisfied in it, and moved to a place more suited to his talents, when he became official theologian to the first Bishop of Dubuque, the well-known Matthias Loras, at the sixth Provincial Council of Baltimore, in 1846. Here he met the dynamic Bishop of New York, John Hughes, who induced him to come to his diocese, where he became pastor of St. Columba's Church, a post he held for nearly forty years.

The pattern of similarity between Nashville and Memphis continues with the building of the first church in Memphis. In

Nashville the land for the first church had been donated by the Grand Master of the Masons. In Memphis, the church lot was also donated, by anonymous non-Catholics. The church itself, the first St. Peter's, was a plain brick building seventy by thirty feet; as with the first church in Nashville we have nothing but an imagined sketch to tell us what it looked like. Photography didn't become commonplace until after the Civil War.

However, at this point, the Nashville comparison disappears, and Memphis Catholicism begins to take shape. The 1840s and 1850s were a time of prosperity for Memphis. In 1850 it was catching up to Nashville in population, 8,000 plus to Nashville's 10,000 plus. By 1860 it had passed Nashville by the same margin, with 22,000 to Nashville's 12,000 plus. The building of the expanded Memphis was done in good part by the Irish immigrants. Whether it was the Navy Yard, or the water-front, or the office buildings, whatever, much of the heavy labor of brick-laying, stone cutting and carpentry was done by the Irish. Late in the 1840s the Germans came in considerable numbers. Many of them labored with the Irish, but more came with a little something in hand, and tended to go into trade. The Italians did not immigrate to Memphis, or elsewhere in the United States in numbers, until after the Civil War. But, as early as 1847, and from then on, there were more Catholics in Memphis than in Nashville. In 1868 there was even talk of moving the See city from Nashville to Memphis.

St. Peter's became the leading parish of the diocese. But Bishop Miles had great difficulty staffing it. Shortly after Father McAleer departed, Father John Maguire, the Rector of the Cathedral in Nashville, also left to teach and help run St. Mary's College in Kentucky. Then Fathers John O'Dowde and William Howard, who had been ordained for the diocese by Bishop Miles, followed Father McAleer into the Diocese of New York.

These defections left Bishop Miles very short-handed. Small wonder that he looked for stability at St. Peter's. He found it, not unnaturally, in his own Dominican community, by persuading them to take over St. Peter's. So it was that Father McAleer was succeeded by a Dominican priest, Father Joseph Sadoc Alemany, a Spaniard by birth.

But Father Alemany's stay was brief. He was made Provincial of the Dominicans after two years, and after two more his successor in Memphis, Father James Clarkson, died of the cholera. For a while it seemed that St. Peter's also was doomed to swift turnovers in pastors. But then came Father Thomas L. Grace, who gave the parish the stability it needed. He loved Memphis, and was loved by Memphis. He remained for ten years of solid achievement.

He built the splendid church which still stands, engaging the soon-to-be celebrated Patrick Keely to be its architect. Keely was to design dozens of Catholic churches around the country, among them the cathedrals of Charleston and Dubuque, and became the favorite architect of the Dominican Order. St. Peter's was one of his first churches. It is a remarkable building for so small a Catholic population, a clear mark of the prosperity of the Church in Memphis, as well of Father Grace's distinguished leadership.

The church stands with Nashville's old cathedral of St. Mary's as the most distinguished of the state's older Catholic churches. These two, indeed, are little architectural masterpieces, ranking with any of their time and purpose. They are wholly different. Nashville St. Mary's is pure classicism, formal and elegant and tranquil. Memphis St. Peter's is Gothic, romantic, lush, ardent, heavily decorated, bursting inside with arches and statues and lunettes and trefoils and tall lancet windows busy with dramatic stained glass scenes. The exterior is bold and fascinating, with its twin crenellated towers and beautifully proportioned central facade, basic brick covered with stucco lined to resemble stone. Each tower is pierced with charmingly varied openings, constrasting nicely with the big window of the center, under which is the small but emphatic entrance. The nave is plain, and the transept, with its long windows which echo that of the facade, is perhaps a little thin to match up to the rambunctious and imaginative facade.

The interior, now being restored to its pristine elegance, is in tune with the exterior, but perhaps a little showy, the taste of the times. It has been renovated often, not always to advantage. During World War I a new altar was installed, and the new stained glass windows included a World War I memorial. However, the present restorations, projected over a period of years, aim at bringing the splendid old church to its 1850-1860 style.

The church is handsomely complemented by its rectory, built

in 1873, and designed by the well-known Memphis firm of Jones & Baldwin, who also designed the first St. Agnes Academy on Vance Street, and most of the Memphis public schools of the time. Here the Victorian taste for ornament, restrained in the church's exterior, exuberantly swarms all over the rectory, a little much for some tastes, perhaps, but full of period charm. There is a delightful little court between the rectory and the church.

All this sounds as if St. Peter's were the bon-ton church of Memphis Catholicism, as indeed for many years it was; it was the first church in the diocese to have air conditioning. Although the city has long since moved away from its location, it is still cherished by old-time Catholics. Historically it was predominantly Irish, but never exclusively so, as a partial list of early pew holders suggests: P. J. Carrol (sic), Thomas McKeon, Thomas Williamson, Thomas Rice, J. J. Murphy, Mrs. Daniel, William English, Mrs. Hogan, H. Metter, Mrs. Thurstan, Mr. Gandolpho, Mr. Bolwis, Mr. Milton, and Mr. Boro, from 1847 to 1851.

So grateful was Bishop Miles to his fellow Dominicans for their success at St. Peter's that he made over to them title to the church and its properties. The actual title is in the name of St. Peter's Literary Society, a misnomer for the parish organization that looked after widows and orphans in the early days, and helped newcomers to get going. It is the only church in the state whose title is not in the name of the Bishop, an interesting tribute to the Dominican Fathers who have staffed it so long and so lovingly, and who are still its pastors.

Father Grace, who was responsible for so much of the St. Peter tradition, was named the second Bishop of St. Paul in 1859. Most reluctantly he left his beloved Memphis and went upriver just about as far as one can, on the steamship *Memphis Belle,* to his new home. The City of Memphis gave him a rousing sendoff, including a touching testimonial signed by Edward Tighe, John Lilly, Michael Magevney, Jr., L. Collins, T. O'Donnell, and Edward O'Neil, all leading members of the parish. Grace responded in kind: "It is no small alleviation of the pain of separation", he wrote his Memphis friends, "from a place which I had begun to regard as a permanent home, and in which there is so much to endear me, that my leaving has given occasion to an expression of feeling toward me by the Protestant as well as the

Catholic community of Memphis, which I could hardly imagine to have existed.''

The second Catholic church of Memphis followed much the same pattern. As in Nashville, Germans followed the Irish. Not until 1852 were there enough German families to demand their own parish. But it took a long time for the parish to get going. In 1852 the ''St. Boniface Building Society'' was formed, and a lot purchased for the church. Father Wenceslaus Reapis came to preach to and confess the Germans in their native tongue, the dearest wish of their spiritual lives. But, like Father McAleer at St. Peter's, he departed after a year, and when his successor, Father Cornelius Thoma, got around to the problem of building the church the lot the St. Boniface Society had chosen was deemed unsuitable because it was marshy.

The Civil War delayed building, and it wasn't until 1864 that a little frame structure was built on the site of the present church, Third and Market streets. But that was never completed, and Mass was celebrated in the little school building adjoining. Until 1870 the situation was full of doubts and uncertainties; perhaps firm leadership was lacking. In any case St. Mary's, as the church was named, did not acquire stability until, again as with St. Peter's, a religious order undertook its charge. This time it was the Franciscans of the mid-west Province of the Sacred Heart. They at once set about building a church, securing the services of one of the foremost architects of the South, James B. Cook, whose rich background included work in his native England on Joseph Paxton's Crystal Palace in London.

Cook's church is tasteful and elegant, a worthy companion to St. Peter's in every way. Like St. Peter's, it is Gothic in style, but plainer and more elegant, especially the nave. The tower is beautifully proportioned, and its windows help make it graceful and imposing. The interior, with its handsome wooden altars carved by itinerant Franciscan brothers, is similar to the other Catholic churches of its period, St. Peter's and Nashville's Assumption, but lighter and more elegant than either. But it is a question of taste, whether the power and stability of St. Peter's seem more effective than the lightness and grace of St. Mary's. Both are superb.

St. Mary's was a long time a-building, and the time saw many changes. The sanctuary was not added until 1874, and the steeple remained incomplete until 1901. Only a few years ago the steeple had to be removed because of termites, which made the church revert back to its early appearance. In the early 1900s, the brick exterior was covered with stucco, but this was happily removed in 1972, again bringing the church back to its excellent initial appearance.

During the 1860s the Germans brought to Memphis a taste for the arts, and aspirations toward learning, education, and the life of the mind that, says Gerald Capers, Jr., in his fascinating book on Memphis, greatly enhanced the cultural life of the city. Although few in number compared to the Irish, the Germans were proud and high-minded. Too much so, indeed, for the smooth progress of the church.

For, with the stabilization of St. Mary's, Catholicism in Memphis takes on its own distinctive character. It is, or rather was, unlike that of the rest of the state, but very like Catholicism in the rest of the United States in the middle of the nineteenth century. What made it so was the rise, and almost the domination, of the "national," or "ethnic" parish. Historically, most parishes were territorial, founded by and for a certain neighborhood, often as small as a few city blocks, sometimes as large as a county. As envisioned by the Council of Trent in the sixteenth century, these parishes would naturally be mostly ethnically homogenous; one wouldn't expect many Spaniards, for example, in a parish in northern Italy. And if there were, for some special reason, they would normally set up a church of their own, which would be locally known as the Spanish church, just as today, Santa Susannah is known in Rome as the "American" church. But this would be very special. The typical parish in Ireland was composed of Irish, in Bavaria, of Bavarians, in Poland, of Poles. The Church, in short, had not thought about the large-scale immigration to the United States, both Catholic and non-Catholic.

That immigration put Polish churches in Buffalo, Chicago, and Toledo, side by side with Bavarian and Irish ones. There was nothing territorial about it. It was not — is not, in places where inner cities remain viable — uncommon to see an Irish church, a Polish church, and a German or Belgian one, scarcely a block apart. In Memphis, German St. Mary's is only three city blocks from Irish St. Peter's.

The Irish, in Memphis and everywhere else, because their language was English, and because they got there first, were top dogs. Within the American Church most bishops were Irish or of Irish extraction. There was a tense struggle within the Irish ranks. American Irish, mostly Catholic, with bitter memories of English oppression in their homeland, tried to raise regiments to invade Canada and eventually land in Ireland to fight for Irish freedom. Supplies of all sorts were sent to Ireland to help its underground opposition groups, as well as its new and powerful presence in the English Parliament. It is tragically ironic to reflect that today the Irish question is still unsolved.

To their everlasting credit, the American hierarchy of Irish birth or parentage stood aloof from these shenanigans. Most of the bishops recognized the emotional extremism of the Irish patriots and shied away from such positions as opposing the appointment of American bishops who, although of Irish extraction, were not of Irish birth. These extremists wanted Ireland-in-America, although how they thought this possible seems to us beyond imagining. However, they were no different from the extremists among the Poles and the Germans, and even to some extent the Italians, not to mention the Lithuanians, the Slovenes, Croatians, Hungarians, and many other smaller national groups. All these had extremists who wanted their Church as it had been in the old country, with sermons and confessions in the old tongue, and schools conducted in German, Polish, or whatever.

But also within the Irish spectrum, for they were by far the most numerous of the immigrant groups, was an "Americanist" position, led by Bishop John J. Keane, Archbishop John Ireland, and, more cautiously and prudently, James Cardinal Gibbons. Gibbons, the second American to become a Cardinal, was the most influential churchman of his time. His long episcopate in Baltimore, from 1877 to 1921, saw him grow steadily in stature, influence, and wisdom. He was the friend and advisor of three Presidents and many other non-Catholic leaders, and he did more than any other man to make Catholicism respectable to non-Catholic Americans. John F. Kennedy is unthinkable without him.

This little group of bishops wanted the United States' Catholics to be American, not German or Irish or Italian. And they wanted them to be democratic. The perceptive Alexis deTocqueville, in his famous book *Democracy in America,* predicted in the 1830s that Catholicism would prosper in the United States: "These Catholics," he wrote, "are very loyal in the practice of their religion . . . Nevertheless, they form the most republican and democratic of all classes in the United States . . . I think one is wrong in regarding the Catholic religion as a natural enemy of democracy." So much for the nativism that poisoned the American atmosphere for Catholicism during the 1840s and 1850s.

All this applies to Memphis far more than to any other Catholic group in Tennessee. The Memphis Irish resented the blacks, both slave and free, with whom they competed for the jobs at the lowest rung of the economic ladder. And when the Federal Government in 1866 foolishly brought in a regiment of black soldiers for their release from the Army, it didn't take much to spark a terrible three-day riot during which the Irish, to their shame, killed forty-four blacks, wounded around seventy more, and burned ninety-one black houses, four black churches, and twelve black schools. There was, to be sure, nothing Catholic about this terrible episode, except that most of the Irish who led the rioting were Catholics. This was the side of the Irish that the older Americans justly feared.

Merely pathetic was the wrangling among the Catholics of different nationalities. In Memphis the German and Italian immigrants were intransigent. Once the Franciscans were safely ensconced at St. Mary's, the parish sailed along happily enough internally, but more German than the Americanists wanted to see. The unfortunate precedent of the title of St. Peter's being vested in the Dominican Order led the parishioners and their pastors at St. Mary's to believe they, and not the bishop, "owned" the church and its institutions. When, in 1900, Bishop Byrne sought to draw parish lines he was vigorously opposed by them; the Franciscans even withdrew for a time till the matter was settled, largely on the bishop's terms. But the bishop was forced to withdraw a pastor of Irish extraction he appointed to St. Mary's; it was an imprudent move on his part.

It was the same story with St. Joseph's. This parish, founded in 1878, came to be *the* Italian parish for Memphis, although actually the Memphis Italians were scattered throughout the city. But under the leadership of Father Anthony Luiselli, St. Joseph's became home base for those who spoke Italian, especially those who spoke little else, and Memphis Italians, whatever their home parish, belonged to one of the numerous Italian clubs that flourished around St. Joseph's. Father Luiselli was one of the few who lived through yellow fever, which he caught working night and day to ease his fellow sufferers. But when Luiselli died in 1901 there was no Italian priest in Memphis to take over. Nashville's Father Eugene Gazzo filled in for nearly fourteen years, but his long length of service to his fellow Italians in Memphis failed to dim his affection for the Nashville parish of the Holy Name with which he was so long identified. When he returned to Nashville in 1915, he was replaced at St. Joseph's by a succession of non-Italian pastors, and the St. Mary's scenario was replayed. The Italians wanted a national parish and an Italian priest to be its pastor; the bishop could supply neither. In the early 1920s the pastor was locked out of his own church by the volatile Italians, but they eventually learned to live with non-Italian pastors. At one point, the bishop rounded up an Italian priest from Italy to be the new Father Luiselli, but he failed in the opposite direction — he spoke no English, and couldn't accommodate to American ways.

Of course the bishops were dead right. Admittedly, it was hard on the old Germans and Italians; some wrote pathetically to the bishops mourning the loss of the old hymns and prayers, perhaps the only remaining link for most to their childhood. Others wrote more boldly, and took legal steps; there are thick folders of briefs and lawyers' letters in the diocesan archives, along with many yellowed newspaper clippings. There are also petitions with pencilled signatures, which bespeak the pressure of the intense upon the indifferent. It was a small minority of the intense that forced the issues; the fact that most were only mildly concerned is shown in the subsequent parish histories of easy accommodation to the norms of the American Church. The key word here is "American." Father Luiselli himself did not wish St. Joseph's to be a national parish, and second generation Germans and Italians overwhelmingly opted for the English language in church and school, along with American culture in work and leisure. One trouble with St. Joseph's was the continuing new immigration, going on until the 1920s. The early Italians came from Liguria, but by the turn of the century the new arrivals came from Sicily and the Piedmont, plus a small influx from Lucca. The older families were thoroughly assimilated; it was the new immigrants, still unschooled in English, who wanted the national parish.

The bishops, who couldn't have supplied the national parishes with priests even if they had wanted national parishes, were models of tact and patience, to judge from their letters and other communications. But they were firm. Parishes must be territorial, not ethnic; only in very special cases were national parishes to be tolerated. This was as American as our system of congressional representation; to this day, it is the general arrangement for American Catholic parishes — the European models vary so as to make comparison virtually impossible.

Looking back on the question of the national parish, one wonders, as with so much else, what all the shouting was about. But, although it is difficult to feel the same passions and excitements and resentments the immigrants felt, the storms remind us of the hard times our grandparents faced in assimilation into the America of their dreams. They generally got the freedom they wanted so desperately, and generally prospered in it, but it was hard-won. What is really remarkable is the vitality of the Catholics and their Church. Think of all the national churches that didn't prosper, think of the innumerable sects that came and went among the Protestants, think most of all of the dissident Puritans from England who founded the Yankee half of the original American colonies, all their drive, all their theological ardor, all their revolutionary zeal, sunk with scarcely a trace. Many a Catholic also fell by the wayside, some from neglect and mistreatment by the Church. Add to this the prejudices and anti-Catholic myths and persecutions, and one can only marvel at the enduring vitality of the Church in America.

Particularly in Memphis has the Church prospered through its trials. The ethnic parishes are the heart of its history; the other parishes are spin-offs from the old ethnic downtown churches. The long Memphis careers of two of it best-known pastors tell a large part of the story. Monsignor Dennis J. Murphy, long-time Vicar General of the diocese under Bishop Byrne, first went to

Memphis as an assistant at St. Patrick's in 1903. In 1911 he was made pastor of St. Patrick's, after a stint in Nashville, and in 1922 pastor of Immaculate Conception, which he founded, as old St. Patrick's faded.

Monsignor James P. Whitfield, younger than Murphy by six years, moved eastward in the city even more often. He was at St. Patrick's most of the time from 1912 to 1917, when he was made pastor of St. Brigid's. Like St. Patrick's, St. Brigid's also faded, this time completely off the cityscape; its site is now a vacant lot. Before this happened, Monsignor Whitfield developed yet another spin-off, Little Flower Parish; in its turn Little Flower spun off St. James.

Central to both these careers, and to the growth of the Memphis Church, is old St. Patrick's, founded just after the Civil War in 1866. In a way, St. Patrick's is a spin-off from St. Peter's. Memphis had a phenomenal growth of population during the Civil War, as did Nashville; the numerous Irish among them settled largely in South Memphis, south of Union Avenue. St. Peter's and St. Mary's were a long way uptown for these folks, and Bishop Feehan laid the cornerstone of a church for them at Fourth and Linden on November 18, 1866. The *Memphis Daily Avalanche* reported the event in full detail, brass band and all, and noted that the bishop was accoutred "with crook and mitre."

The first pastor, who orchestrated all this, was Father Martin Riordan, an Irish-born priest ordained for the Archdiocese of St. Louis. Nashville's third Bishop, Patrick Feehan, brought Riordan to Memphis, made him Vicar General of the diocese, and Riordan responded with resounding success.

The first St. Patrick's was plain. It is described in *The Catholic Advocate*, the Louisville paper which served as the organ for all this part of the Catholic world, for August 11, 1869: "The building is a handsome frame, one hundred feet long and fifty feet wide. The exterior is plain, the only attempt at ornamentation being at the main entrance, which is surmounted by a cross and has something of the Gothic style about it. The interior has a neat and chaste appearance, the walls being painted white, and the pews, wainscoting and other woodwork tastefully grained. The roof is supported by two lines of pillars that add to the beauty of the edifice. The sanctuary is separated from the body of the church by a handsome railing that is really beautiful, and is a credit to the workman who executed it. Six rows of pews have been erected which, it is estimated, will seat about seven hundred people. Immediately over the main entrance is a gallery for the choir. The congregation numbers some two or three thousand souls.'' The church was lighted by gas and heated by coal grates. A well on the back of the lot furnished water.

The Advocate's correspondent probably exaggerated the number of Catholics in the congregation, but the vitality and spirit of the new parish could scarcely be exaggerated. St. Patrick's from roughly 1870 to 1920 was *the* parish of the ordinary, workaday, unpretentious Irish, who knew everybody who was Irish and wished to know, except when the melancholy came upon them, no one else. From St. Patrick's the Irish marched in Paddy's Day parades, which ended with High Mass — and the saloon across the street. They soon wanted a finer church, and got it in 1905, a large, ambitious, baroque Roman building, whose architect was clearly the Right Reverend Thomas S. Byrne, the Bishop of Nashville, whose hand is plainly seen in most of the churches built during his episcopacy. St. Patrick's seems like a study for the later Cathedral of the Incarnation in Nashville. The two churches are very similar, but St. Patrick's by comparison seems sketchy. The exterior has some style, but it is a little too busy for the size of the church, and the campanile is disappointing. The round arches of the interior were covered with the imitation marble which was the worst flaw of the Nashville Cathedral, and the other similarities to the Nashville church are almost as unfortunate — the angels at the sides of the chancel arch, the main altar, and the decoration of the capitals and the ceilings, the glory of the Nashville church, are here thinned and cheapened. Still, the effect in 1904 must have been rich indeed, and must have gladdened the heart of the bishop, who wanted all the churches in his diocese to look like urban Rome. The more modest churches, like Blessed Sacrament in Memphis and Holy Name in Nashville, come off rather better than the more pretentious Memphis ones, St. Patrick's and Immaculate Conception.

Scarcely had the new St. Patrick's been dedicated than St. Thomas' in South Memphis was spun off it, and later on Immaculate Conception. But the parish most like St. Patrick's was its contemporary, St. Brigid's. Or was it? St. Brigid's has an odd history. Its opening decade, 1870-1880, is largely the story of the yellow fever, in which St. Brigid's pastors, Fathers Martin and William Walsh, played heroic roles. Their successor, Father Moening, a Franciscan, was mainly pastor of St. Mary's, and was therefore a German Franciscan, an odd choice for Irish at St. Brigid's. But how Irish was the congregation? Among the first communicants were such names as Smiddy and Zapf, in a list of Foleys, Griffins, and such like. In the pastorate of Father John Larkin, St. Brigid's was constantly embroiled in skirmishes with the other parishes, as well as making plans for improving and rebuilding its own plant. When Father Larkin resigned, in 1907, his successors struggled with debt, a dreadful flood, and such extra duties as the orphanage. When Father Whitfield came in 1917, things got a little better. The old church was remodeled, and as the parish faded away Father Whitfield embarked on his long career of developing new ones.

This account ignores the most important historical event in the history of Memphis, and especially of the Catholic Church of Memphis, the yellow fever epidemics of the 1870s. Because of these the city suffered grievous declines in population, wealth, culture, and destiny. The Church suffered enormous losses of good men and women, mostly Irish, and the priests, brothers and nuns who tended them in their illness and died with them. All sorts of values were depressed by the terrible scourge of the fever. A good illustration is the cemetery which Father Riordan bought, and which still serves the Memphis Catholics. At $40,000, Calvary Cemetery was a great bargain. But the Church had difficulty paying the purchase price when land value prices plummeted after the fever depopulated the city. The story of the Church's role in the fever deserves and gets a separate chapter.

6

Taking Care of the Young

Bishop Miles was just plain unlucky. His character was stalwart, his disposition even, his devotion to duty nonpareil. But he was plagued by the ill luck with which, as St. Teresa said, the Lord visits his best friends. Too many of his priests defected to other dioceses — or, on two occasions, became unwilling bishops, like himself; his European missionary funds dried up; the coming of the railroads aborted his building plans for Nashville. But nowhere was he more unlucky than in the wreck of his dearest hopes, education.

The bishop invited likely young student aspirants to the priesthood into his home for study, yet sometime during the late 1840s that miniature seminary, named for St. Athanasius, evaporated. Its directors were able men, Fathers Morgan, Hoste, Alemany, and Jacquet in that order — Jacquet was recruited for the purpose. Three excellent priests were ordained from it, Fathers Howard, O'Dowde, and Schacht. Some who started in Nashville went elsewhere, and were ordained for other dioceses. But it was not a record of great success, and must have sorely disappointed Miles, who wanted above all a zealous native clergy.

Mixed in with the aspirants to the priesthood were secular male students. One of Miles's unluckiest endeavors was trying to secure a religious order of men to take over this school. Early on he tried the Jesuits without success. He then, in 1844, tried the Brothers of Holy Cross, then called Brothers of St. Joseph, from Notre Dame, but their Superior seems to have decided that the field was not a fertile one. Meanwhile, the bishop hired secular teachers from time to time, and finally decided to organize a teaching order of his own, called the Brothers of St. Patrick, which disbanded for want of vocations, not students, after a few years. In 1854, Miles wrote his friend Bishop Spalding of Louisville, urging him to share with Nashville the Xaverian Brothers who had recently come to Louisville. But none could be spared. However, the Nashville school went on till the Civil War came.

The Bishop had better luck, though still laced and broken by strains of ill fortune, with the religious orders of women. Almost from his arrival in Nashville he sought the help of the Dominican sisters in Kentucky, for whom he had done so much. But the first community to lend a sympathetic ear to his appeal was the Sisters of Charity of Nazareth, near Bardstown, Kentucky. This thriving community had been founded in 1812 by Catherine Spalding, its first Superior, yet another distinguished member of Kentucky's foremost Catholic family. Six sisters from Nazareth arrived in Nashville on August 25, 1842, staying at first with one of the Nazareth former students, Mrs. V. K. Stevenson. Before long, however, they rented a house on the brow of what was soon to become Capitol Hill, and here opened their school, St. Mary's Female Academy, in time for the fall term.

Despite opposition from rabid anti-Catholics, the school flourished from the beginning, numbering, as usual with convent schools, many non-Catholic girls among its students. In two years it had an enrollment of nearly one hundred. A roving correspondent from the *Catholic Advocate* of Louisville described its 1845 commencement exercises as follows: "I was present at the annual exhibition of St. Mary's Female Academy conducted by the Sisters of Charity. I was kindly received by Sister Serena, the Superior. Their neat, clean and beautiful house charmed me. Its location is a delightful one; it is one of the best furnished houses of the city. I met with many of the elite of the city, accompanied by their blooming daughters full of hope and anxious to display the knowledge acquired during the scholastic year." Note that "commencement" was then "exhibition", that is, oral examinations often conducted by outsiders, and specimens of student work on display. This was the standard year's-end exercise of the time; assembly halls were often called exhibition halls, since a sizable part of the exhibitions at male academies was the interminable and highly rhetorical bouts of oratory, the main sport of the time. The female seminaries were more given to music, plain and fancy needlework, and versification by the yard.

Clearly, the sisters had struck a responsive chord in Nashville; the following year the main speaker at the annual "exhibition" was Governor Aaron V. Brown. Success meant expansion. After the opening of the new cathedral, Bishop Miles decided to turn the old one into a hospital, also under the care of the sisters from Nazareth. He asked the new Rector of the Cathedral, the man he had ordained four years before, Father Ivo Schacht, to oversee the changeover, which he did, enthusiastically, as he did everything. He turned the entrance to the building around, so that it faced North High Street, just below where the tomb of President Polk is today. The hospital came just in time to fight the Asiatic cholera epidemic of 1848, during which the sisters closed their school and did faithful service as nurses.

The Church in the United States was now growing rapidly, and sisters were in great demand by schools, hospitals, and orphanages. Conflict with the bishops was inevitable. The convents wanted autonomy, the bishops wanted them under their authority. The situation came to a head in New York, whose dynamic leader, Bishop John Hughes, persuaded the Mother Seton Sisters of Charity, after long and rueful dickering, to set up a New York motherhouse under his control.

Other bishops were quick to follow Hughes's lead, Bishop Miles among them. He began to make demands of the Nazareth sisters that Mother Catherine did not wish to meet. She came to Nashville in 1851 and after amicable but unbudging conferences with Bishop Miles decided to withdraw her community from Nashville. However, six of its members wanted to stay in Nashville. With the cooperation of Mother Catherine, the bishop, and Father Schacht, they became an independent community. The sisters who adhered to Nazareth were sent home, and the Capitol Hill property advertised for sale. Although St. Mary's Academy on Vine Street was lost, the new little community persevered through many difficulties and hardships and eventually attained some degree of success. The hospital, of course, was the property of the diocese, and some went to live and work there. The former home of Dr. William Cheatham near the cathedral was bought for the new St. Mary's Academy, and a small building the doctor had used for an office made into a novitiate. Father Schacht was appointed by the bishop ecclesiastical superior of the little community, and took his duties very much to heart. He steeped himself in the rule of St. Vincent de Paul, which the community, like that of St. Elizabeth Seton, had adapted for its own use, and when he made a trip to Europe in 1855 he studied the European convents, and brought back several books on their rule, as well as quantities of vestments, linens, and so on. It was on this very successful begging trip that Schacht raised enough money to pay off the remaining debt on the cathedral.

On his return to Nashville, Father Schacht bought a farm for a boys' orphanage, three miles out from town on the White's Creek Turnpike, near the W. D. Phillips place. Here the sisters spent summers working as farm hands along with the boys; here they and their director, Father Schacht, decided to expand. A brick house was erected, and plans made for an academy and motherhouse.

This was the undoing of the whole enterprise. In 1857 Schacht quarrelled with the bishop. It isn't wholly clear what the quarrel was about; Schacht seems to have used an ordinary glass for a chalice at Mass instead of the metal one the rubrics then called for. But this seems too slight a matter, and one too easily compromised, for a breach so severe that the bishop, usually so mild and accommodating, and Schacht, usually so zealous and responsible, that both of them became unyielding and bitter. From this distance it seems likely that Schacht, who had been given such a free hand by the bishop, may have gone too far in acting on his own, and it is even more likely that Bishop Miles may have become petulant and arbitrary as he approached the end of his days. In any case, Father Schacht was suspended from his priestly functions in the Diocese of Nashville, and had no choice but to leave it. He went first to Kansas, then a territory, but ended his career in Kentucky, as ever a popular and beloved pastor, at Lebanon, Paducah, and Owensboro, dying at the last place in 1874.

Father Schacht's departure left the little independent community holding the bag, and an empty bag it was. To expand the farm place, Schacht had borrowed money. When he was dismissed from the area, the creditors became uneasy, and began to demand their money. The bishop refused to assume the debts, Schacht was gone, the sisters were stony broke. They decided they had to sell to pay off their loans, and sell they did, nearly everything, down to the furniture and curtains. The orphans were returned to their families and relatives, or found homes.

The sisters themselves were homeless. But they were a sturdy and loyal set of women, full of faith in God and His Blessed Mother, and little inclined to self-pity. They decided, as a body, to send their superior, Mother Xavier Ross, a convert of remarkable abilities and deep faith, to the Provincial Council at St. Louis in 1858. There Mother Xavier was directed by the legendary Father deSmet to Bishop John B. Miege, a Jesuit who had been Vicar of the vast Kansas territory since 1851, and who was anxious to secure the services of sisters. In Bishop Miege, Mother Xavier, who had been disowned by her family when she became a Catholic, found a faithful friend and pastor. And in Leavenworth, Kansas, the community found a new home and new hope. They prospered mightily as a community, far more than they could have done in Tennessee, spreading all over the northwest and west, as far as Wyoming and California. It is good to note that they never blamed Father Schacht for their debacle in Nashville. He remained their good friend, visiting them from time to time after they settled in Leavenworth.

Mother Xavier's story is a remarkable one. To become a nun she alienated, at the age of sixteen, her family, and to become one of the great women of the American Church she left home and bishop and struck west, like the pioneers of her time. Following her was a sizeable group of Nashville women who were fired by her enthusiasm, among them the first woman in Tennessee to become a nun, Sister Julie Voorvoart. A native of Holland, she joined the Sisters of Charity of Leavenworth in 1854, and pioneered their hospital mission in Helena, Montana. Mother Xavier lived into her eighties to see her community one of the foremost in the United States.

Meanwhile, in Memphis . . .

The spirit of St. Dominic hovered over the development of Catholicism in Memphis even more than it did in Nashville. Bishop Miles had failed to get Dominican Sisters for Nashville, but fellow Dominican Father Thomas Grace was more fortunate. He secured the services of six Dominican sisters, three from St. Catherine of Siena in Kentucky and three from St. Mary's, Somerset, Ohio. Accompanied by Dominican Father Francis Cubero, they arrived in Memphis by steamboat rather dramatically at midnight, January 1, 1851. As with most such new foundations, at first a house large enough to provide rooms for a beginning school, to be called St. Agnes, was rented. From the outset the school prospered. A charming ad for it in the *Memphis City Directory* for 1855 reads in part: ". . . delightfully situated in a beautiful and retired part of the City of Memphis . . . the buildings stand in the center of extensive and highly improved grounds . . . with a view to prevent extravagance, and promote habits of economy, the following uniform has been selected: Winter, to consist of a slate colored merino dress with cape of same, plain white collar, black silk dress apron and white sun-bonnet. Summer uniform to consist of blue gingham, muslin or calico (solid colors) to be made with long sleeves to fit close to the neck, with small white collar, black silk apron and white sun-bonnet . . . This institution is Catholic, but as its object is to afford educational advantages, irrespective of religious creeds, no influence beyond that object will be exercised. Discipline and order only will require attendance at divine services on Sundays."

"This Institution" was located for many years at 697 Vance Avenue, where it was rebuilt after a bad fire in 1878. Its growth is typical of such convents, which generally were established for just such genteel education of young women as described in the ad. But, as in Nashville, it wasn't long before the need for an orphanage became urgent, and St. Peter's Church founded St. Peter's Orphanage, under the care of the sisters. At first housed on Vance, it was later moved to Gracewood Farm, but that location proved too far from the convent and had, moreover, no chapel. Eventually, in 1862, a property was bought on Henry Street, but that, too, proved too small, and in the 1880s a large plot was bought on Poplar Street. This was large enough for St. Peter's Cemetery as well as the orphanage, and today is the site of a day care center, high-rise apartments for the elderly, and St. Peter's Villa, a nursing home. St. Agnes was little troubled by the Civil War. Once, when a drunken soldier frightened the sisters, General Vitch, of the Federal occupation troops, gave them a well-behaved armed guard. In 1863, at the request of Bishop Whelan, they acted as volunteer nurses in the City Hospital. However, their school remained open throughout the war, and grew as the city did during it. In 1864 a house on Adams Street was set up exclusively for day students, moving the following year to Third Street between Poplar and Washington. This was named "Our Lady of LaSalette," a French place of pilgrimage somewhat like Lourdes of the next generation.

And so it went, the extraordinary progress of an extraordinary body of nuns. In 1858 they took on St. Peter's Parochial School, the first of a long list. They set up a school in Jackson, Tennessee, in 1869. They were the first to have a school for blacks in Memphis in 1880. They played an heroic part of their work in the yellow fever decade of the 1870s in Memphis. But that belongs to another chapter.

Back in Nashville . . .

When the Sisters of Charity departed, there was no school for young women left in Nashville. The need was still strong, the prospects good. Miles's successor, Bishop James Whelan, handpicked by Miles and like himself, a Dominican, found an answer. Whelan, a former Provincial Superior of the Dominicans, was, of course, close to the Dominican sisters in Somerset, Ohio, and these sisters were able to provide Nashville with the nucleus of a convent. A little band of four pioneering sisters reached Nashville on August 17, 1860. They spent their first days with the Sisters of Charity, who still operated St. John's Hospital, but within days moved to the location that is still their home, the hill on Clay Street in north Nashville then called Mount Vernon, which Bishop Whelan had purchased for them. It came complete with a good-sized, two-story house with double porches.

Soon the sisters were setting the house in order for a school for young women. They decided to call it Saint Cecilia Academy, after the patroness of music. On October 4, 1860, the first students were enrolled. The school prospered; applications flowed in, the schoolhouse was filled to bursting, and new sisters had to be sent from Ohio. Civil War or no, Bishop Whelan decided to build at once. The new academy building was three stories plus a full basement, and included all the necessary dormitory and boarding facilities.

Despite the nearby Federal defense works, St. Cecilia scarcely felt the war until 1864. New students kept on enrolling in the academy, the community grew, though anxiety replaced the confidence growth engenders when Bishop Whelan was forced to resign his office. He had been the sisters' good patron, and while another Dominican, Father Joseph Kelly, took over as Administrator, things weren't the same. Moreover, in 1864 the war came to Nashville, and the city was a chaos of rumor, near-by battles with their horrors of the dead and wounded, broken transportation lines, rioting by the mobs of hangers-on, and, of course, loss of students and the business of the school disrupted.

The smoke of battle had scarcely cleared away when the new Bishop of Nashville arrived, the able and intelligent Patrick A. Feehan. He helped out St. Cecilia with a number of small loans, but could not manage the large sums that were owed. The Superior and the Bishop put their minds to work on the problem of keeping St. Cecilia from being another casualty of the war, and came up with an ingenious solution. The academy and its grounds were advertised for sale to pay off the creditors, just as the Sisters of Charity had been forced to, but at the auction, Bishop Feehan himself bought the property for the sisters. The ad in the Nashville papers for the sale of personal property is of interest: "Two horses, two express wagons and harness, one barouche and harness, two cows, three large cooking stoves, twenty heating stoves; all the china, crockeryware, cutlery and table furniture; glassware and kitchen utensils and kitchen furniture; five tables, three bureaus, six clocks, forty school desks, with benches and all school furniture; 200 bedsteads, 130 beds, 150 sheets, 125 chairs; carpets, center tables, sofas, lamps, etc.; 35 oil paintings, 100 engravings, 700 volumes of books; two large harps, nine pianos, and three guitars." Thank heaven, nobody wanted to furnish a school at just that time, and Bishop Feehan had no trouble buying it in. Wealthy Catholic laymen rallied round the bishop to help him pay the notes as they came due, in particular Mr. and Mrs. Michael Burns, he a railroad magnate with many other business interests as well. The less wealthy also helped out; a faithful old employee who had lent the academy $1800 tore up his note to help the sisters survive.

St. Cecilia Academy reopened in the fall of 1867, but times

were much harder than they had been in 1860. Southerners impoverished by the war could not pay the tuition, much as they wished to, and the place struggled mightily and at times almost despairingly. The sisters were tempted to pack up and go elsewhere, as the Sisters of Charity had done, but what was lacking in that case was happily present for St. Cecilia's: the intelligent and devoted interest of the bishop. Gradually things improved all round; times got better, the sisterhood grew in number and took on the direction of parochial schools. It is interesting to note that the sisters, like other Catholic leaders in the south, went on begging trips to Mexico, Cuba, and South America. What a difference a hundred years makes!

By the time Bishop Rademacher arrived, in 1883, St. Cecilia was once more thriving, with its splendid new building, still standing, just completed. The Nashville orphanage was also managed by Dominican sisters.

Now that orphanages are virtually anachronistic, it is hard for today's young people to imagine how very important they were to religious groups of all sorts throughout American history until the very recent past. Taking care of the parentless young, and the young whose parents were unable to take care of their offspring, was the very hallmark of Christian spirit. No appeal to a Christian community was as successful as one for the orphans, and none needed less hype.

Orphanages in Nashville and Memphis were at first appendages of other institutions. In 1848, when the Sisters of Charity in Nashville converted the first church on Campbell's Hill into a hospital, the orphanage was part of the work of the hospital. Similarly, in Memphis, the orphans were looked after in St. Agnes Academy at first, beginning in 1851.

But the real beginning of St. Mary's Orphanage in Nashville came in the unlikely year of 1864. Actually, the plans were made a year earlier, in the very middle of the war, when, in the words of the first chronicler of St. Mary's, Father I.A. Bergrath, the Catholics of Nashville "could not rest satisfied until they, too, should be able to take rank among the first of their brethren elsewhere as founders and supporters of an asylum, where charity, the first-born of heaven's first daughters, might reign supreme, and fill a mother's place to the motherless and fatherless of the earth."

Thus, on November 18, 1863, twenty Catholic laymen formed the St. Mary's Orphanage Association. The guiding spirit among them was Philip Olwill, whom Bishop John B. Morris of Little Rock, in his sermon on the centenary of the Nashville Diocese, called "saintly." Olwill was elected president of the association. The vice-presidents were Michael McCormick and Thomas Connor, the secretary, E. E. Jones. Pending the arrival of the new bishop, Father J. A. Kelly, the Administrator of the diocese, to whom the association owed complete support and encouragement, was named treasurer. The other members were: J. Cunningham, W. Winter, P. Tyrrell, J. Curran, J. Lyons, J. Doyle, P. Hearn, P. Ryan, J. Dolan, H. S. Thatcher, P. McGovern, T. Farrell, F. H. Cunningham, P. Prendergast, B. Ecklecamp, D. N. Burke, P. McShane, W. Keegan, M. Hayes, T. Pantony, M. McKeon, P. C. Hanson, T. Reilly, M. Drury, H. Preston, M. Kane, M. Corcoran, and C. H. Sanders.

An eight acre plot in south Nashville was purchased as a site, close to where Trevecca College now stands. The land had a substantial brick house, of typical middle Tennessee architecture, quite handsome. Three Dominican sisters from Somerset, Ohio, at the request of Father Kelly, came to run the asylum, and the first orphan was placed there on May 17, 1864, by Governor Andrew Johnson. Fourteen children in all, ranging in age from three to seventeen, filled the place, whose early days were anything but auspicious. Some of the children were sick, and one of the sisters died on July 7. But soon things brightened. Two more sisters came from St. Catherine's in Somerset, and local fund raising went on apace to give the asylum enough resources.

Then really dark days descended, as the War Between the States came to Nashville with all its dislocations. The Murfreesboro Pike was a main highway of the armies, and a Federal officer came to warn the sisters that they, so near to it, had better get out of the way. They were almost caught between the contending forces when Father Kelly and some friends arrived in wagons, to take them out of danger. But where to go? The only place anyone could think of was the basement of the cathedral. There they stayed for several weeks, cramped and miserable, but at least safe. Their orphanage was almost entirely destroyed by the Federal artillery. But, after a miserable interlude in a rented house on the Franklin Road, the Federal government rebuilt the old orphanage, and its occupants thankfully returned to their old-new home, which was now enhanced with a handsome cupola surmounted by a cross, the gift of William Simmons.

A time of equal anxiety came during the yellow fever epidemic in Memphis in 1878. Bishop Feehan was eager to remove the orphans there to a place of greater safety, and decided that the best thing to do was get them to St. Mary's in Nashville. But that was easier said than done. On September 3, 1878, Bishop Feehan wrote Father Kelly, the former Administrator of the diocese, then pastor of St. Peter's in Memphis: "Our asylum is overcrowded; we have 81 children there. I have spent two days trying to rent a place and offered to pay anything required, but nobody here will rent a house. They are so much afraid of contagion. The only thing I could do is build a temporary house on our asylum grounds . . ." Then on September 9, "We are hard at work — ready in a few days." And on September 13, "Send them on Monday. Let them bring no luggage or clothing but what they wear. We will provide everything. P. A. Feehan."

Sixty children came to Nashville. Two became ill shortly thereafter, and one died, but that was all. After eight weeks, the Memphis orphans returned home, and St. Mary's was happy to have the new extra building. Even so, it was overcrowded, and remained so until Bishop Byrne removed it to west Nashville in 1903. The old building needed constant repair, and the land surrounding it was too small to enable the asylum to be at least partially selfsustaining. So the bishop moved cautiously. First, he got young lawyer Mike Smith to negotiate for new property, having discovered that direct negotiations prompted alarming increases in prices. The property Byrne wanted was on Harding Road, with a long entrance drive from it until White Bridge Road was built in 1915. Here the bishop, with the assistance of his building consultant on the cathedral project, Father Thomas J. Plunkett, planned and erected a limestone building of conventional appearance, with the exception of the same red tile roof he used for the cathedral. Byrne found the land unsuitable for farming, and traded it off for better.

Although the entire diocese except for Memphis, which had an orphanage, was supposed to contribute to the upkeep of St.

Mary's, and indeed to some extent did so, the main burden fell on Nashville, and old-timers around the city will remember the annual Fourth of July picnic there not only as a major fund-raiser for the orphanage, but a major social event for the Nashville Catholics. Help also came from gifts and bequests. With many a sea-change through the years, the orphanage continued to be a major diocesan institution until the 1960s, when the great changes along White Bridge Road were initiated by the completely new cottage-type orphanage which replaced the old building, and a whole new world took over what used to be rural Bosley Springs.

7

Catholic Life in the Miles Era

There is no clear-cut pattern to the settlement of Catholics in Tennessee. There was a Catholic family here and there, and occasionally a little knot of four or five families, as in Sumner County. But there is no reason to think there were very many. Catholics numerous enough to sustain a priest did not arrive until the Irish influx of the 1820s and the German immigration of the 1840s.

Nor was the majority of those who settled early Tennessee Scots-Irish. These non-Catholic Irish, settled in northern Ireland by the English as part of the Catholic repression, did immigrate to the United States in considerable numbers. But there were fewer than is ordinarily thought — in fact, if the legend were half-true, the Scots-Irish would have flooded the entire country. The people who settled Tennessee were mostly of English descent, with the Scots-Irish probably next most numerous, but well behind the English. The early settlers of Tennessee came from Virginia, the Carolinas, and Georgia, and the same people who settled those older colonies settled Tennessee.

Another myth that needs questioning is the social status of the Irish Catholic immigrants. Most, to be sure, were illiterate and barbarous; steady economic exploitation and cultural deprivation by the English for centuries created perhaps the sorriest peasantry in Europe. But not all the early Irish immigrants were as pauperized as most of those driven out by the great famine of 1845-1849. All during the nineteenth century there was ceaseless political agitation for Irish amelioration, at home and abroad. This was the period of the great Irish emancipator, Daniel O'Connell. Many Irish immigrated to the United States for fear of being jailed for their participation in this fight. Many more left to find freedom in the new country. Among these were some educated schoolmasters, journalists, tradesmen, and other middle-class types, most with a little money in their pockets for the start in the New World. But neither these nor the famine victims were headed for the farm. They had seen enough farm poverty in the mother country. The Irish wanted to be city people.

The first sizeable groups of Irish Catholics that Bishop Miles and the early missionary groups met were workers on the railroads, and no doubt many of these settled in the towns permanently. But there were others. Consider the cases of Thomas Farrell and Michael Burns.

Farrell came to Nashville in 1832 when he was twenty-seven years of age, bringing with him his wife and five-year-old son. What else he brought isn't known, whether of education or money or connections, but he was probably not destitute. In any case, within ten years he was a successful businessman, dealing in "Queensware", that is, Wedgwood china and accessories imported from England.

Farrell is an excellent example of the devout Catholic layman, a type which played so large a part in the development of the Church in the United States. Although elected Alderman in 1841, he did not pursue further political ambitions. He devoted himself to his business, out of which he made a considerable fortune, and retired from it to live with his beloved wife in the fine new house he built for himself in north Nashville, at Monroe and Vine, after previous residence in east Nashville. Their last decade was saddened by the death of their son James, Nashville's first altar boy, who died in 1867 at the age of forty, of consumption contracted while a Confederate soldier.

Farrell's was the helping hand in many Catholic works. He passed the hat, and put a lot in it himself, for Bishop Miles when he first came. While living in east Nashville, he played a prominent role in building St. John's Church, the first in Edgefield; he also contributed to the building of the cathedral and the orphanage. He supported to the hilt the work of the Sisters of Charity in Nashville; when they moved to Kansas, his wife Margaret went with them, and Thomas paid the freight, as he did to help place the orphans the sisters were forced to leave behind them. Mrs. Farrell died within a week of her husband, in 1882, and is buried alongside him in one of the first lots in Calvary Cemetery, which they helped to create. There were many good people like the Farrells in Nashville, devout and good-hearted Catholics who were widely known and respected in the community, like the DeMovilles, the Olwills, the Callaghans, the Ottenvilles, and the Philipses, to name just a few of the earliest.

The respect these early Catholics enjoyed is nicely shown in the *Nashville Whig* account of the celebration of St. Patrick's Day in 1838. General Jackson sent a note of congratulations; William Carroll expressed his good wishes, while Philip Lindsley, President of the University of Nashville, testified his respect "for Ireland and especially for her enterprising, virtuous, gallant sons who have found a happy home in America and who have contributed so essentially to the prosperity of the land of their adoption."

Michael Burns was the prime example of Irish Catholic enterprise. He was a wheeler-dealer, a mover and a shaker, a maker and a fixer. He came to Nashville from his native Ireland via Canada in 1836, having emigrated as an apprentice along with his master, a saddler. It was in this trade that he established himself in Nashville, and rapidly became successful. But Burns was not content with successful business. Like a modern entrepreneur he moved into banking, railroads, insurance, and politics. In all of them he was a winner. He was mentioned prominently for Governor, was elected State Senator, played a most important part in the development of the railroads in Middle Tennessee, and was a notably successful banker.

Burns's career illustrates nicely the anomolous position of so many Nashvillians during the Civil War. Some historians say outright that he was a "Union man"; certainly he was close to Governor Andrew Johnson, and a great admirer of Abraham Lincoln, whom he visited in Washington. But according to Woolridge's history of Nashville, he also helped the southern cause, getting pardons, staying executions, doing favors of all sorts; Burns's Confederate Light Artillery was named for him. The plain fact was that Nashville was occupied by Federal troops. Life must go on, and men like Burns made it go. He worked with the powers that were. What a comparison there is with the sad career of Bishop Whelan, who was blamed for his Union sympathies. Incidentally, in 1860 Burns owned seven slaves, the bishop four.

There is a curious gap between these prominent Irish Catholics, and others who were following in their footsteps up the American ladder to success, and their clergy. The lay men and women wanted stability, prosperity, roots. Most of the clergy had to be rootless; they had been uprooted from their birthplaces, in Ireland, Italy, France, Maryland, or New York, and they stayed uprooted because of their missionary vocations. It is a wonder they got along as well as they did with the laity. Perhaps the element of romance, and association with far away places and tongues, added to their aura of specialness as clergy, giving them an air of visitors, if not precisely from heaven, at least from another planet. This was true even of second generation Irish, who were fascinated by the brogues of the Irish-born clergy, a fascination which continued almost to our time, since older readers will remember the rich brogues of Fathers Plunkett and O'Hanlon.

Take the case of Father James Aloysius Orengo. He was a seminarian in the Dominican seminary in Viterbo, Italy, when Bishop Miles visited there in 1841. The bishop inspired him with the desire to serve in the American missions, and he came to the United States with a little band of Dominicans which included Fathers Grace and D'Arco, who also worked in Tennessee. But nobody worked as long, as hard, and as productively as Father Orengo. He and the earlier Father Elisha Durbin are the protomissionaries of Tennessee, the most heroic of that heroic band.

Father Orengo worked for twenty-five years in the Diocese of Nashville, from 1848 to 1873. He then returned to Italy, where he lived for another thirty-five years — his longevity suggests the extraordinary energy he must have been endowed with. His labors in Tennessee were Herculean. He went everywhere, knew everybody, and everybody seemed to know him. His accomplishments were astounding. He built churches at Franklin, McEwen, Columbia, Pulaski, Edgefield Junction, Tracy City, Gallatin, Humboldt, Brownsville, Grand Junction, Covington, and Jackson, some abandoned as the towns declined. He extricated the churches of Clarksville and Shelbyville from their heavy debts, and bought the land for churches at Trenton, Fayetteville, and Union City.

The church at McEwen is an interesting example of the work of Father Orengo. It has been well-known for over a century in Tennessee as that rare thing, an Irish Catholic farm area, the original home of many Nashville Catholic families and a place of pilgrimage for Irish Catholics of the area. Yet the sparkplug of all this was no Irishman, but Italian Father Orengo. As he made his mission rounds between 1842 and 1844, he came upon a group of Irish sheep herders in Humphreys County. These had come, the poorest of the poor, to staff a ranch owned by a New Orleans physician named Knapp. Orengo persuaded these Irish families to build a little church about two miles from the present one. This encouraged other Irish to settle in the area, and by 1855 there were enough to build a church on the present site. But, as usual, it was the railroad that made the place — indeed, its very name is from the railroad. McEwen was one of the railroad engineers, and often visited the town planning the road. Building the railroad brought other Irish to the area, and by the end of the Civil War the place was known as "Little Ireland." Both town and church prospered mildly to the present. But not until Father Orengo went back to Italy did Little Ireland have an Irish pastor. The clamor of ethnic groups for one of their own as their pastor is refreshingly absent from the early McEwen story. Until a native clergy could be developed, most Catholics in Tennessee were happy to welcome good priests from wherever. In his centenary sermon, Bishop Morris spoke of having been baptized by Father Orengo, served Father Joseph Jarboe as an altar boy, and learned much of the diocesan history he so happily preserved from Father Eugene Gazzo — not one of these Irish. Jarboe was a native of Kentucky. Orengo and Gazzo were Italian born.

Father Gazzo himself is another fine illustration of this multinationalism. He came from a distinguished Genoese family, and, like so many high-minded Europeans, decided to devote his life to the American missions. He is most closely identified with Holy Name parish in Nashville, but he was the effective pastor of the Italians of St. Joseph's in Memphis for many years as well. Many still alive will remember him, with his dignified and sensitive Italian countenance and his charming accented English.

Bishop Miles also interested some French priests in his diocese, a natural turn for him in view of his acquaintance with them in Kentucky. During his 1841 trip to Europe, Miles inspired a young French priest, Father Louis Hoste, to become a missionary in Tennessee. He arrived here in 1841, and began a career quite different from that of Father Orengo. The latter was above all on the go; Hoste had the instinct to settle down. He became the pastor of the oldest Catholic church in continuous use in Tennessee, St. Michael's near Cedar Hill in Robertson County, which was dedicated by Bishop Miles in May of 1842. He then began, with the bishop's hearty blessing, a boarding school.

St. Michael's was twin to the church at Clarksville. Both were missionary stations for the generous Father Stokes. Stokes left the following November, to resume his academic career, and Schacht took over, to build a church in Clarksville two years later. Meanwhile, Hoste became resident pastor at St. Michael's, buzzing with plans for his school. He brought with him a cultivated French gentleman, Gustave Bouchard, who became the intellectual stalwart of "St. Michael's Male and Female Academy", as the 1849 announcement read, "Near Turnersville, Robertson County, Tennessee. Under the patronage of the Rt. Rev. R. P. Miles, D.D., Bishop of Nashville." The handbill says that this school is established for the not-so-wealthy, and aims to improve the pupils in "Religion, Morals, Good Breeding, and Health". Board, including bed and bedding, was $30 a session in cash, $35 in produce. Tuition ran around $5 or $6, depending on the course — plain sewing at no extra charge. As usual with Catholic schools, especially in those days but continuing to the present, the announcement ended with the statement that, although the school is run by Catholics, "there will be no interference whatsoever with the religious feelings of the pupils who do not belong to the Church". The Academy was located in Caleb's Creek about a mile from the church. It operated until 1855, when, to the great regret of Bishop Miles and its proprietors, it had to close for lack of funds. But even that short run is testimony to the determination and courage of its founders. Its enrollment could never have been large, and luck did not favor it — Turnersville did not prosper, and was by-passed by the railroad.

The other French priest who came to Nashville also had bad luck with his school. This was Father John M. Jacquet, a priest of the Diocese of Lyons, France, who may have been recruited by Bishop Miles to head his seminary in Nashville; this was his first post, and he its last rector. The seminary disappeared within a year or two after Jacquet was placed in charge of it, but he remained in the diocese, becoming a vigorous and successful missionary mostly around Chattanooga. After eight years of this, he went to do similar work in Ohio. In both places his constituency was mainly composed of Irish laborers on the railroads and in construction.

Father Jacquet's career is a paradigm of what was happening, and was to happen, in Tennessee Catholicism. The school faded away, but the coal mines expanded, the furnaces grew larger, the railroads spread. The core of the Catholic Church throughout the United States, as well as in Tennessee, was the employment this new industrialism offered to the Irish immigrants.

German immigration was a different matter. Less numerous, they were also better off; they farmed, went into trade, were better organized and, through various welfare societies, better shielded against misfortune. The Irish were more desperate. They had to work at whatever came to hand, and for most of them, those 407 listed as laborers in Nashville's 1860 census, this was the hard work of digging ditches, laying rails, moving cargo, mining coal and iron, the necessary bedrock of labor on which the new industrialism was built.

The railroads were at the heart of the new industrialism. And, generally speaking, where the railroads were projected, the Irish followed, building them as they went. This is history made simple, but there is truth in its simple description despite the many exceptions. There is scarcely a Catholic center in Tennessee not made, or confirmed, by the railroads. The original towns were, of course, built on waterways. But the waterways had to be confirmed by railroads. If the railroads couldn't, or wouldn't, get in, the town's growth usually stopped. Not all the railroad towns prospered, of course, but scarcely a one prospered without the iron horses.

The railroad fever hit Knoxville and Memphis harder than it did Nashville at first. Nashville's early growth and prosperity was based on river traffic, to a much greater extent than Knoxville's. Memphis was, of course, mainly a river port, but its leading citizens, unlike those of Nashville, were early railroad enthusiasts and ambitious projects were begun. Some Memphis historians hold that if the Civil War had not broken out, Memphis would have become what Chicago finally did become, the great internal city of the United States. Of course, this became just an impossible dream after the war, but even so, Memphis grew faster than any other Tennessee city, and completed by 1857 a railroad link with the Atlantic. Other links to the north and south were also in use. Nashville, too, was the center of no fewer than five railroad lines, mostly unfinished. But Knoxville, originally the most enthusiastic railroad town, had only one main line north and one south. However, Chattanooga, with lines radiating in all directions, was the most important junction town in the state.

Practically every Catholic parish in Tennessee, from the Civil War to the present, was on a railroad line, and in every case railroad workers increased the Catholic population substantially. Many, of course, had a Catholic population before the railroads came; it will be recalled that Bishop Miles's first journeys through the state took him south, through Franklin, Columbia, Pulaski, and Shelbyville. All of these became railroad towns, but the largest of them, Columbia, was never much of a Catholic town. In 1887, to pick a year just after the railroad systems became stabilized, there were still Catholic missions in the now unfamiliar towns of Alpine, Etna, Wartburg, Erin, Iron Furnace, and Purdy, while the missions at the railroad towns that still survive contain well-known names like Gallatin, Murfreesboro, Shelbyville, Tullahoma, Winchester, Cleveland, Union City, Lawrenceburg, and Jonesboro. Most of the places in the first group still survive, but they are not familiar except to their residents and neighbors, and they do not survive as Catholic parishes or missions.

That word, mission, is somewhat misleading in Tennessee history. Almost as old as Nashville's old St. Mary's and St. Peter's of Memphis were the missions at Franklin, Columbia, and Clarksville. But Columbia did not have a church till 1867, nor Franklin till 1871; liturgies were held before this in private homes. Clarksville's first church was built in 1845. In all of these places, and many others — Winchester, Shelbyville, Murfreesboro, Bolivar, Brownsville, Rogersville, Jonesboro, — there were a few Catholic families. Of these, only Shelbyville had a church, a converted Presbyterian one, in 1857. There were small Catholic enclaves here and there — in Sumner County, at what later became McEwen, in Jackson, but in none of these enough for a church. The plain fact is that the churches came with the railroads.

This is nicely borne out by Chattanooga's history. Bishop Miles visited the site before it got its present name, but it is significant that the only sizable group of Catholics the first bishop encountered were railroad men camping near Athens. This was in 1839. In the summer of 1841 Father John Maguire, the second priest ordained for the Nashville Diocese, made a tour of the East Tennessee missions, and chose Chattanooga as his headquarters. He wrote an account of this to the vicar-general, Father Stokes, the bishop then being in Europe. Here are some excerpts: "I arrived on the first of June at Chattanooga, and on the second I visited the men who are employed on the Western and Atlantic Railroad. There are 100 Catholics among them, with whom I remained for the last six weeks. [These are the same Bishop Miles had visited.] . . . They received me with joy, and immediately erected a temporary church in the forest. I heard that there were many Catholics in Bradley, McMinn, Meigs, and Monroe Counties. I set out to visit these on June 10. . . . I performed several marriages, administered Baptism to 14 children and admitted to Holy Communion nearly 50 persons. I returned to the railroad on the 10th of July after this arduous but consoling mission."

The "temporary church in the forest" was the first church ever erected by Catholics in East Tennessee. But it was not till 1847 that Chattanooga country again had a semi-permanent missionary. This was the redoubtable Father John Jacquet, who administered the first baptisms of record in Hamilton County on May 19, to Helen Deady, Thomas McNaly and, conditionally, to Mary Sullivan. But this was just one station among many. His itinerary gives some notion of the life he led in 1847: "Feb. 15, baptized four at Gallatin; April 27, near Murfreesboro; May 19, near Chattanooga; May 23, Bayer's Settlement in Polk County; May 26, Cleveland; May 31, Battle Creek Valley; June 3, back at Murfreesboro; June 23, at Rogan's; Sept. 28, back east in Coffee County; Oct. 7, in the Sequatchie Valley; Oct. 15, Tellico; Oct. 20, Hillsboro."

One of the most curious places Father Jacquet visited was Vineland, a settlement which was the project of a wealthy New York family named Parmentier. They bought fifty-thousand acres in the mountains northeast of Chattanooga, around what is now the Cherokee National Forest in Polk County, and persuaded a colony of mixed French and Germans to settle there. Later immigration became predominantly German, but the colony petered out, as so many did, and in 1897 Rosine Parmentier gave or sold the land to those living on or near it. A little earlier Bishop Miles had joined in sponsoring a similar, though more modest, settlement in Morgan County, which also fizzled, as did the ambitious Rugby in the same county later. The woods were full of colonies, but all that worked was the railroad and, occasionally, attendant industries.

Catholicism became really visible in Chattanooga in 1852, with the pastorate of Father Henry Vincent Brown. This priest is yet another of the fascinating characters who made the history of the Church in Tennessee colorful. He was born in upper New York State, into a Puritan family to whom Catholicism was as abhorrent as the bubonic plague. Young Henry naturally adopted the prejudice, which lasted throughout his early life and good education. He had a natural affinity for the arts, and came to Kentucky as a young man to teach drawing. He found a post at the Dominican college of St. Catherine, in Springfield, and there his prejudice gradually abated. He became interested in the Church, was instructed by Father Jarboe, and baptized by Bishop Miles. He was disinherited by his family, but his was a thorough conversion; he felt a call to the priesthood, and, after studies at St. Joseph's in Bardstown, was sent to Rome in 1844 by Bishop Miles. He was ordained there in 1848, and came to Nashville to begin his ministry. He devoted his spare time to the decoration of the still unfinished cathedral (the bell tower was not completed till 1863), and painted on the wall behind the high altar a crucifixion scene which was the wonder of its day, now long gone.

In 1851 Bishop Miles sent Father Brown to Chattanooga, releasing Father Jacquet entirely to the missions. Chattanooga was ready. Its Catholic population, linked mostly to the new railroads and railroad supplies, had grown with the rest of the town, and Brown began to plan a church large enough for them. Thus began the Catholic settlement on the hill later known as "Irish Hill", where the church buildings still stand. Reserving the best site for the church, Brown sold the rest of the land at cost to his parishioners, to encourage them to live nearby. In line with this family theme, the first building he built was a rectory for himself, a charming Victorian Gothic home in the fashionable architectural style popularized by Andrew Jackson Downing of New York. Until 1916 it was one of Chattanooga's showplaces, and it is a great pity it was pulled down to make way for the present tasteless rectory.

The church was not built till 1857, a plain but serviceable House of the Lord which served the city till 1888, when the present church was built in much more elaborate form than it is today, dripping with Gothic decoration inside and outside, and prinked up with enamelled glass windows imported from France. All very grand, but without Father Brown's elegant touch.

The war hit Chattanooga harder than it did any other Tennessee town. Its importance as a railroad center, and its strategic geographical position, made it a center of logistics, and eventually of fighting — the fighting around the city in the fall of 1863 was among the fiercest of the war. In a minor way, this is nicely illustrated by the story of Dan Hogan, a devout member of the Catholic congregation and a stone mason by trade. When the war broke out, Hogan had assembled piles of cut stone and marble for the new church. But so great was their need the Federal troops filched these for their own use, setting the new church back some years. It was not completed until 1888. The claim for $27,000 that Father Brown filed for his lost building materials was finally settled at about the same time, well after Brown had departed, for $18,729, no little help toward the building fund.

Brown was not only the founder of the first permanent church in Chattanooga, but also that of Knoxville; he was indeed the apostle of East Tennessee, shaping the second phase of Catholic life there following the pioneering missionaries. Prior to these missionaries there is no documented Catholicity in the area. In colonial times, the western Carolinas were full of hunters and traders, a picturesque band, intermediaries between the Cherokee Indians and the colonial government in Charleston, South Carolina. Because many of these white traders had Irish names such as McCormick, Fitzgerald, and Callahan, some historians have thought one or more might be Catholic. The man most often mentioned in legend is Cornelius Dougherty, an engaging figure, who made and lost a good deal of money in peltry, and claimed to be one hundred and twenty years old. This may be more likely than his Catholicism.

Not so with the Dardis family nearly a century later. Theirs is a fascinating story, somewhat reminiscent of the Rogans of Middle Tennessee. The three Dardis brothers, James, Thomas, and Edward, fled Ireland as fugitives around 1790. The best-known of them is James, the friend of John Sevier and lodger of the William Blounts, host to Father Badin, prominent in the life of East Tennessee for many years before he moved to Winchester, where, toward the end of his life, he welcomed with joy Father Stokes. He was one of the first Aldermen of the City of Knoxville, and an early landowner. His Catholicism was proud and open. Father Badin speaks of a ''French gentleman'' as ''the principal Catholic of the place.'' He almost certainly means James Dardis, who was no Frenchman, though his unusual name may suggest it. But for an unfortunate duel which resulted in his early death in 1809, his brother Thomas might well have joined James in prominence. Nothing is known of the third brother, Edward.

The careers of the Dardis brothers show that there was little prejudice against Catholics in the early frontier days of Tennessee, none that merit and character could not readily overcome. There was always some Catholicism at Winchester after James Dardis settled there, and it became a Catholic center of a sort toward the end of the nineteenth century, when the Paulist Fathers came there, largely because one of their own priests was born in Winchester. The unfortunate thing about the Knoxville story is that Catholicism almost ceased after the Dardis era.

It is more than a little strange that Knoxville seems to have had no Catholic tradition to preserve. James Dardis did not move to Winchester until 1829. The following year there came the first wave of Irish railroad workers. Although Knoxville was a center of railroad planning and direction, the potential congregation for the new church was scattered along the railroad right of way. It was only when many of these workers settled in Knoxville, finding employment there on the railroads or allied industries, that the parish was possible. By 1853, the Catholics were joining together to celebrate Mass, frequently in the home of the Lyons family at the foot of Summit Hill, on the site of the present TVA towers. In February 1855 land was purchased on the crest of the hill, and construction began.

Two important matters affected the fledgling Church. One was intensely Catholic. The declaration of the doctrine of the Immaculate Conception took place in 1854. This assertion by the Church of Mary's unique sinlessness electrified the Catholic world, especially the United States, which placed itself under the special patronage of the Mother of God under that title. So, there was no question of what the new church in Knoxville was to be called. Like the church of the same period at Clarksville, it became, happily, the Church of the Immaculate Conception. It still is.

The other was purely American, and violently anti-Catholic. It was the Know-Nothing movement, which was especially virulent in Knoxville. Led by the fanatically anti-Catholic (he was a fanatic in all his beliefs) William Brownlow, its program included opposition to the Church and to Catholics doing anything. But, although the Catholics felt they had to place guards around the site of the new church, the opposition was mostly vocal, and the church went up despite it. By the fall of 1855 it was ready for use. It would serve the Knoxville community for the next thirty-one years. As early as 1857 it spawned a parochial school taught by laymen for twenty years.

In yet another way was the Catholic body different from most of the Knoxville area. Brownlow, and the large majority, were strongly pro-Union. The situation in the Tennessee of the 1860s was strange. Memphis, and especially Nashville, were prime targets of Union armies, which occupied both early in the war. The Union forces, however, ignored Knoxville, rightly thinking it of little strategic importance, so Confederate forces held the city. But, their grip was uncertain and loose, since the prevailing opinion went against them, and they had a hard time managing to keep order, let alone marshal support for their side. There is a telling drawing of the time showing Union forces recruiting at one end of Knoxville's main street, and the Confederates at the other. However, the Irish Catholics were solidly pro-Confederate, and it is an interesting irony that Father Abram J. Ryan wrote his most famous poem, "The Conquered Banner", in Knoxville, the least Confederate town of the entire Confederacy. But Ryan, for all his whole-souled devotion to the cause of the South, preached reconciliation and healing, and large crowds overflowed the church into the streets to hear his eloquent Sunday sermons.

Father Brown's good taste did not desert him in Knoxville. The old church was a thing of beauty, done in a simple Gothic style, with a beautiful stone texture, dark grey picked up by occasional white stones, with cut stone trim around the handsome thin windows modulated by a wide broad entrance. It was torn down in 1886 when the larger new church was built, itself not without a certain style, but nothing like as fine as the older building. The architectural taste of the pre-war South was, simply, better than that of the late Victorian era.

Even before Knoxville's Immaculate Conception came the Church of St. Mary at Clarksville. Clarksville is an old town, going back to 1784, just a little later than Nashville, and several Catholic families are reported living there as early as 1839. Mass was said by the missionaries at first, in private homes, later in the brick church erected by the energetic Father Ivo Schacht in 1844 and dedicated in December of that year by Bishop Miles. No picture or sketch of this church has come down to us, nor did it have a steady resident pastor. The priest's schedule, according to the *Metropolitan Catholic Almanac and Laity's Directory,* was as follows: ''First Sunday of every month, Clarksville. Second Sunday, St. Michael's, Robertson County; Third Sunday, Gallatin; Fourth Sunday (if last) St. Dominic's, near Waverly, in Humphreys County. St. Dominic's is a new plantation, comprising a large tract of good and cheap land, sixty miles from Nashville near the Tennessee River and on the stage road between Nashville and Memphis.'' As the name suggests, St. Dominic's was another pet project of Bishop Miles. Here, and at Gallatin, there were log chapels. Hoste succeeded Schacht, and was resident at Clarksville 1846-48, 1855-58, and 1862-64. The famous Orengo made Clarksville his headquarters from 1848 to 1855, and returned there briefly in 1858. The railroad came late to Clarksville, but, in the 1860s when it was being built, it brought the usual complement of Irish workers to the city, swelling the ranks of the Catholics there.

The railroad, however, had nothing to do with the founding of the Church of the Assumption and its parish. It was, from the beginning and for long after, a church of and for the German Catholic population of Nashville, which settled largely in North Nashville. The pioneer family was the John F. Buddekes, who arrived in the 1830s. They first lived on the Lebanon Pike, but after Mr. Buddeke prospered in the grocery and whiskey business they built a large and handsome house in north Nashville, on the southeast corner of Vine and Monroe, still standing. Mrs. Buddeke's maiden name was Ratterman, and she persuaded her brother to come to Nashville. They too, prospered, and built a fine house on Summer Street. In time they were joined by many other German Catholic families.

Of course they wanted a church of their own — Mass was celebrated at the Buddeke house, and there is a tradition that Bishop Miles lived for a time with the Buddekes. But the hoped-for church was a long time coming. It was 1857 before the building bricks were laid by. In that year, Bishop Miles, foreseeing that the State of Tennessee was going to demand all the land on Capitol Hill eventually, sold the first cathedral's site, later the site of St. John's Hospital, to the State. He moved the bricks to north Nashville, where they eventually became the north wall of the German Church of the Assumption.

The land for the church was the gift of David McGavock, who owned most of north Nashville, on the condition that the Bishop, to whom the lot was deeded, erect a church within eighteen months. The new church made the deadline narrowly, and was dedicated on the eve of the Feast of the Assumption, August 14, 1859. Its exterior is Gothic, with three entrances, surmounted by a charming little tower and, eventually, a graceful steeple. The interior has been changed so often that only the original lines are discernible, but they are relatively clean Gothic lines, without much ornamentation. Some of the builders weren't paid, and two months later, the pastor, Father John Vogel, and Bishop Miles, were sued to collect a mechanic's lien. Another well-known German Catholic, George Wessel, came to the rescue, and laid out more than $2,500 to clear the building of some of these debts, though the larger one of $7,000 went unpaid for some years.

Father Vogel had come on as pastor after the departure of Ivo Schacht, that dynamo of the Church in Nashville of the 1850s.

Schacht is the father of Assumption Church. Naturally, he was a great favorite with the Germans, since he spoke German and had special services for the German Catholics in their native tongue for some years. Very possibly Father "Scat", as he was universally known, along with Jacob Geiger, the builder, designed the church. If so, it is a great tribute to them.

These German Catholics were very different from their Irish co-religionists. They were not laborers; they went, often straightaway, into their own businesses. Butchering and processing meat was one of their specialities — Neuhoff, Petre, Baltz, and Lahart were among the prosperous meat dealers. The Wessels were bakers, the Thusses originally ran a grocery but became photographers. The Floershes were cigar makers, the Brackmans skilled mechanics, the Strobels musicians, and so on. Their north Nashville neighbors, mostly German, were of the same stamp, and the few Irish who filtered in, like the Farrells, the Stritches, the Doyles, and the Cains were also white collar types. North Nashville had a sturdy little sub-culture of its own, but it grew into southern-American gradually. Intermarriage diluted its German style; by World War I Assumption pastors had become mostly Irish. The expansion of the black community, the loss of local color like the Sulphur Dell baseball park and the sulphur waters of Morgan Park, and above all the growth of the West End, sparked by the opening of Vanderbilt University in 1875 and the Tennessee Centennial Exposition of 1897 contributed to the decline of Germantown.

The East Nashville parish was the old story all over again. Because of the lay of the land, Edgefield, just over the toll bridge from old Nashville, was the terminus of three railroads; as a matter of fact, had it not been for the unusual situation of the river being frozen over when the settlers first came to Nashville, the lay of the land might well have dictated it, rather than the bluffs, as the more important settlement, though in the earliest days the bluffs provided good defense. But when the railroads did come, Edgefield grew into importance, and the Irish came with them, as usual.

The same priest who planned Assumption planned the first church in Edgefield, St. John's. This was Father Schacht, and in this case his energy overtook his prudence. The growing Edgefield community had been attending Mass at the home of William D. Phillips, on Brick Church Pike, but this was a good ways out of town, and too small. So, after the Cathedral Midnight Mass on the Christmas of 1854, a group of Edgefield Catholics presented Bishop Miles with their petition for a new church. But the bishop did not have a priest to spare for the work of planning and building. His able missionary, Father Louis Hoste, selected a lot at Bass and Fifth, but it was three years before Father Schacht began to build there. The cornerstone was laid on November 8, 1857, and a month later the church was dedicated. When Schacht got going, things happened.

The new church, dedicated to St. John the Evangelist, was a neat simple structure, barely Gothic so straightforward was its style. It seated one hundred. Only one photograph survives, showing a side. Trouble set in almost at once — the history of the East Nashville parishes is an almost incredible avalanche of disaster. Father Schacht had failed to get a clear title before he built, and the owner of the land threatened to hold him up for many times its worth. Finally Thomas Farrell settled the matter, and bought the land for Schacht. St. John's was the third church in Nashville and the tenth in the diocese.

These two Nashville churches were the last dedicated by Bishop Miles. He barely managed to get through the ceremony at Assumption on August 27, 1859. The sermon on that occasion was delivered by his longed-for new coadjutor, Bishop James Whelan, who had taken up his duties only three months before. Miles was now sixty-nine years old, and had been bishop for twenty-two years. It was fitting he should die before the Civil War; he belonged to an earlier age. What did he think of, in his twilight days? What did he remember best?

Was it the two ordinations he administered early on, in 1841 and 1843? He could see the promising young men in memory, Fathers O'Dowde, Howard, and Schacht, the first two long gone to the Diocese of New York, and the third, so zealous, so energetic, so impulsive, so — arrogant?

The bishop could remember writing indignantly about him to his close friend Bishop Spalding of Louisville, and this may have set him thinking about his colleagues. Spalding and Francis Patrick Kenrick of Philadelplhia, these were close friends. Also

Blanc of New Orleans, and Portier of Mobile, his close contemporary. Had he cut the right sort of figure in the hierarchy? What did it matter? At least he survived, more than could be said for his colleague at Natchez, poor van de Velde, who asked to be transferred there from troubled Chicago. Perhaps Miles grinned inwardly when he recalled his quip at the time, "It seems the northern climate is too hot for him!"

Musing about ordination, the old bishop could have smiled at the recollection of another which took place in 1844. This was Tennessee's first priest, Father John F. Aiken, a member of an East Tennessee family especially dear to Miles. Migrants from Virginia, they lived in Washington County, far removed from Catholic influence. And yet somehow they became converts, the whole family. Father Aiken went to Georgetown as a student, and joined the Jesuits who ran his beloved Alma Mater. Miles kept in touch with him, but more with his brother Robert and sister Mary, to whom he wrote often and affectionately. He went out of his way to confirm them at Jonesboro in 1844.

That might have set him musing about other confirmations, so many. Nashville's first, in 1842; Memphis's first, in 1843; Chattanooga's and Knoxville's firsts, both in 1856. Many in Kentucky for old Bishops Flaget and Chabrat.

And the baptisms! "Ego baptizavi . . .", how often that appears in the records. Garvin, Frensley, Boyle, Allen, Buddeke, Ratterman, O'Neil, Armstrong, Farrell, Hughes, Flanagan, Murray, Dildy, Quinlan, Kutman, Woods, names, names, names, crowding the memory, names he cherished, for these holy words of baptism and the people they redeemed, this was why he was here.

If only he had been able to sustain them with the proper Catholic schooling and training! Oh yes, he had been at the First Plenary Council in Baltimore in 1852 when the Catholic Church of America made the startling commitment to parochial grade schools, one he shared to the hilt. Perhaps the saddest of his recollections was the closing of so many schools he had sponsored. His last act as a bishop was to reopen the seminary in Nashville, shortly before he died.

He did not take a long time a-dying. He had been ill from time to time; he was subject to colds and had bouts with bronchitis. He simply did not recover from one of these, early in 1860, and died on the afternoon of February 21. At sixty-nine he was the oldest man in the American hierarchy.

Since the bishop died the day before Ash Wednesday, the Lenten funeral was an in-house affair. The Nashville *Republican Banner* said, "Owing to the suddenness of the demise of Bishop Miles, and its occurring in the season of Lent, when all the bishops are engaged in their own dioceses, the oration was postponed until some future time." That time never came, however, and Miles was mourned only by the members of his episcopal household. Bishop Whelan pontificated and preached.

Miles was buried in a specially prepared brick tomb underneath the basement of the church, as near to being under the main altar as the solid brick understructure would permit. His remains lay there for over a hundred years until, in 1969, the then chancellor of the diocese, Monsignor Charles Williams, discovered it. The discovery excited keen interest among Catholics and non-Catholics. Miles had been buried in a cast-iron coffin mummy-shaped, with a wide head space which sloped down to a narrow end. Set into the top was a glass plate which enabled Williams and his group to see the face of the dead prelate, and to find it, to their astonishment, well-preserved. By contrast the miter on top of the casket was almost disintegrated, though retaining its shape.

After much discussion among the bishop of the time, Joseph Durick, and his curia, it was decided to move Miles's remains to a specially prepared chapel in the cathedral he built. It has become a place of pilgrimage and prayer.

8

Catholic Attitudes toward Slavery

The mood of the American people for the last twenty-five years makes it difficult for them to see the peculiar institution of slavery as it appeared to the vast majority of southerners throughout most of the nineteenth century. The movement toward racial equality, the crusade of Martin Luther King, Jr., the political and legal successes of blacks, the popularity of *Roots* , as strong in the South as anywhere, all these and many more signs suggest a new temper, a different mood from the one held by the average person in the South straight along, from the sad day that the first black slave ship touched Jamestown, Virginia, in 1619, on down to, and often much beyond, the Civil War.

This attitude was like that toward the high rate of infant mortality, or slow transportation over bad roads, or corporal punishment of children, to name three other institutions then accepted as part of the natural conditions of life. Slavery was there, it was a fact, it was incorporated into the Constitution and the laws of the land, it was part of the culture, like vote-less women and vegetable-less winters. Even in the South it was no direct concern of most people, for most didn't own slaves, and often didn't aspire to. Tennessee in particular had a sizeable slave population only in its western third. Perhaps 40 percent of the population of West Tennessee was black in 1860, compared to 25 percent in Middle Tennessee, and 8 percent in East Tennessee. Incidentally, these figures still roughly hold good.

Nor was the big plantation, Tara-style, the rule in Tennessee. Most slave owners owned just one slave. Those who owned from four to six were next most numerous. Most slaves worked and often lived next to and with their masters. There developed between slave and masters those relations which older Tennesseans are so familiar with even now. It is hard to describe, this bond between white and black. It is not based on equality, heaven knows, but it is not based on exploitation either. It is full of affection and tolerance and mutual understanding and humor and ease and of looking out for one another.

Thinking southerners, and especially intelligent sensitive ones, were deeply concerned about this relationship. The churches and their most devout ministers also were deeply concerned, the Methodists perhaps outstandingly so. In conference after conference they agonized over the problem. Many contended it was one's Christian duty to own slaves so as to instruct them in Christianity. For these, as for everyone who thought about it, the central problem was, what would become of the blacks if and when slavery were abolished? Northern abolitionists could airily dismiss this as no problem compared to the ruinous fact of enslavement itself, but southerners, especially those who had lived with a sizeable free black population, as in Nashville, knew that the lot of the free black was often worse than that of his slave brother.

In 1820 such questions were constantly debated, in church circles, in legislatures, in college debating societies, and in families. By 1835 the ring was tightening; the Vesey conspiracy and the Nat Turner slave revolt in 1822 and 1831 frightened southern whites into greater severity and more security. Slowly the menace of conflict grew; both the Methodists and the Baptists split off from their northern co-religionists in 1844 and 1845. And as they did so, their leaders and preachers became more and more defenders of slavery, with fewer and fewer reservations and qualifications.

Catholics were too few in number to make any difference to the general environment, but they followed this same pattern. The great Bishop of Charleston, South Carolina, John England, took a keen interest in the problem of Negro religion, and himself often led their Sunday afternoon instruction classes. He founded a school for free blacks, like his Methodist counterparts, the Mood family, but Charleston was becoming intolerant of programs to help the blacks. Accused of abolitionism, and threatened with the destruction of his cathedral and rectory, as well as assault on his own person, England soon saw that he was faced with moderating his interest in black welfare or surrendering the development of the entire Catholic Church. This was literally true throughout the South, so little presence did Catholics manage. Only in Louisiana would the general welfare of the state be affected by Catholics — and Louisiana Catholics were perhaps more deeply committed to slavery than any other similar body in all the South.

In any case, by 1840 Bishop England was writing to clear the Catholics of the charge of being abolitionists. In 1839 the then Pope, Gregory XVI, issued a letter condemning the slave trade; it was but one more document among many deploring slavery that Rome had published to a world which largely ignored them. But it roused a wave of anti-Catholicism among defenders of slavery. England forcefully showed that the Pope's condemnation of the slave trade did not condemn the existing institution. But, his courage still strong, he added, "Am I friendly to the existence of the continuity of slavery? I am not — but I also see the impossibility of abolishing it here. When it can and ought to be abolished is a question for the legislature and not for me." Shortly before he died, in 1842, he added, "On this question it may be laid down as a maxim, that no greater moral evil could be brought upon a country than the introduction of slavery; but it is a very different question, whether in a state which has the misfortune of having been, for a long series of years, under the infliction of such a calamity, an immediate or indiscriminate emancipation would be safe, practicable, or beneficial."

It's likely this was the prevailing Catholic opinion, North and South. The influential Archbishop of New York, John Hughes, during the years immediately preceding the Civil War, wrote: "The Catholic Church considers, and has so taught, that naturally all men are free — and that it is a crime for one man to reduce another, both being equally free, into bondage and slavery. Hence she has ever set her face against what has, in modern times, been called the slave trade. But when slaves have been introduced into a country she does not require of her members that they be restored to their primitive condition, which would be oftentimes worse than the one in which they are placed. She would require in such cases that the master should treat the slave with all humanity and Christian care and protection. And that the slave finding himself in such a condition should bear with his lot and be faithful to his master."

Throughout its history in the United States, the Catholic Church has as far as possible tried to keep its official self and its ministers out of politics. They were constantly being drawn into politics by their enemies, who to this day accuse them of subservience to a foreign power(s), and it is one of the themes of American Catholic history to try to stay away from politics to demonstrate that this isn't true. But there was no escaping the political implications of slavery, abolitionism, and the Civil War.

From the beginning the Church owned slaves. The Jesuits acquired big tracts of land in Maryland and employed slaves to make the crops; there were three thousand Catholic slaves in the state at the end of the Revolution. There were probably more in Louisiana, then under French rule. Long experience of slavery in the Caribbean Islands had led the French to develop a "Code Noir", a set of rules for the governance of slaves which included religious instruction, Sundays and holidays free from work, no separation of families, and such like humane regulations. However, Catholic missionaries frequently complained that these were too often ignored by the plantation owners. It would be interesting to be able to compare the treatment of their slaves as between Catholic and non-Catholic owners. The thin evidence generally suggests there was little if any difference.

The institution of slavery was deeply ingrained in southern life. Postulants at the convent of Carmel in Maryland sometimes brought slaves as part of their dowries. The practice continued when Maryland settlers moved into Kentucky. The Sisters of Charity of Nazareth, Kentucky, which gave Nashville its first convent and school for girls, had slaves. So did their Tennessee schools and convents, as did most all of the ecclesiastical establishments that could afford them. At the same time many began schools for the religious instruction of blacks, and often went further. In that seed-bed of southern Catholicism, central Kentucky, Father Charles Nerinckx, who founded the Sisters of Loretto, attempted to incorporate a black women's group in the convent, but found no support from the bishop and gave up on the idea. Bishop Miles had instruction for blacks in both Nashville and Memphis, and the Sisters of Charity conducted religious instruction in the basement of the cathedral.

So far as can be ascertained, Bishop Miles made no public pronouncement on the subject of slavery. Apparently, he took the peculiar institution for granted; his father owned nine slaves in 1790, probably more later. Miles died, of course, before the war blazed out, and had been ill for some time before, so his silence is understandable. The other southern bishops were varied, but it is likely that most of them were basically pro-southern, if not entirely pro-slavery.

Miles's good friend, Bishop Martin Spalding of Louisville, was openly pro-southern. Bishop Patrick Lynch, of Charleston, was so devoted to the southern cause that he became an official Confederate commissioner in Rome. Bishop William Elder, of Natchez, was briefly detained for refusal to cooperate with the Union Army. Bishop John Quinlan of Mobile spoke for the majority of southern Catholics, lay and clerical: "While regretting the dismemberment of this great republic, — and heaven knows we would do all we could legitimately to preserve it — we would not purchase union at the expense of justice."

Better publicized were the views of Bishop Augustin Verot of St. Augustine and Savannah, who had a knack of getting publicity both at this time and later in the first Vatican Council in Rome. In a famous sermon preached in St. Augustine in January, 1861, and later widely distributed throughout the country, Verot stated what most Catholic southerners held. This is, put simply, that slavery was not necessarily evil, was not opposed to natural or divine law. The Catholic doctrine, he said, was one of toleration, until the time when slavery could be replaced by a better arrangement. Verot emphasized the duty of masters to treat their slaves humanely, and to instruct them in religion, and secure "their social, moral, and religious improvement".

This position, which was also the position of many Catholic bishops in the North, was buttressed especially there by two important facts of Catholic life. The first was that the abolitionists linked Catholicism to slavery, greatly to the outrage of Northern Catholic leaders. Again and again Protestant abolitionist preachers coupled Catholicism and slavery, as "natural allies in every warfare against liberty and enlightenment". The vindictiveness of these preachers, much of the Protestant press, and other abolitionists, is nigh incredible; their rhetoric of hatred and vilification betrays an irrational anti-Catholic prejudice. No wonder such northern Catholic leaders as Archbishop Hughes of New York wanted no part of them; no wonder their savage attacks made other Catholics, who were opposed to slavery on moral grounds, neutral. There were many such, including Catholic Chief Justice of the United States Supreme Court, Roger B. Taney, who wrote the Dred Scott decision which did so much to whet the antagonism between North and South, but who freed his own slaves.

The other fact of Catholic life which made many Catholics think twice about the South was the low position of the immigrants, especially those from Ireland, on the social scale. Many Protestant preachers rated the Irish below blacks; many employers, both northern and southern, engaged the Irish to do the dirty work which they withheld from their valuable Negro slaves. This did not endear the blacks to the illiterate Irish immigrants, but it did make them despise more and more those who rated them below the blacks. The Irish might well wonder why there was no abolitionist society to free them from their low-wage slavery. They had plenty of reason to envy some blacks, slavery notwithstanding.

In the North, this feeling persisted right through the Civil War. An outstanding Catholic newspaper of the time, *The Freeman's Journal,* of New York, steadfastly defended the southern position throughout the war years; its scrappy and outspoken editor, James A. McMaster, was jailed for some months because of his partisanship of the South. Much more temperate was the *New York Metropolitan Record,* but it too, defended the South's constitutional argument for secession. Heavily Irish Boston, through its newspaper, *The Pilot,* took a natural strong stand against abolitionism. As late as 1862, the influential Courtney Jenkins wrote in the *Catholic Mirror* of Baltimore that emancipation would be fatal to the country. More typical of northern feeling however, was the view of New York's Archbishop Hughes, who agonized over the war, saw much merit in the southern position, resented more deeply and more outspokenly than anyone the slurs of the abolitionists against Irish Catholics, yet ultimately supported the preservation of the Union. The ablest Catholic intellectual of the time, the famous convert Orestes Brownson, was whole-heartedly pro-union; so was the Archbishop of Cincinnati, John Purcell, whose brother, Father Edward, ran the pro-union Cincinnati Catholic newspaper, *The Telegraph*. And there was other spotty Catholic support for the Union cause.

But of course the North was nearly untouched by fighting. The war was fought mostly in the South, and southern emotions, southern patriotism, southern commitment, ran much higher than in the North. As always, when the band played "Dixie" and the Confederate flags fluttered in the wind as the neighbor boys went off to fight, theories and arguments went down the drain as hearts were caught up in fierce loyalty to their own place.

Both Nashville and Memphis were supply centers for the Confederate armies. Memphis never saw any fighting to speak of, Nashville none till toward the war's end in 1864, and even then the Battle of Nashville took place well outside the city limits. The lives of the two cities, however, did not proceed quite as normal, although the two Dominican girls' schools, St. Agnes in Memphis and St. Cecilia in Nashville, stayed precariously open till the war's end. Memphis was the center of the smuggling of goods to the Confederate armies on an enormous scale. The Union forces in Nashville were more efficient, and the city suffered greatly from the confusion, uncertainties, shortages, and the rest of the grim consequences of war. Yet both cities grew fast during the war. Because of the number of transients — Memphis is said to have had 19,000 such in 1864 — population figures are unreliable and not significant of real growth, but there was plenty of that.

Bishop Miles saw little of this, of course, since his death occurred before the war. He was succeeded by James Whelan, like himself a Dominican. Whelan was born in Ireland and brought to New York in infancy by his family. As a boy he attracted the attention of the intelligent and capable Father Andrew Byrne, also Irish-born, who was the pastor of St. James Church in New York City and later the first Bishop of Little Rock, Arkansas. Byrne introduced young Whelan to Father N. D. Young, of Miles's St. Rose Priory in Kentucky, and Whelan followed Young back the long miles to Kentucky, where he was professed a Dominican at St. Rose's. He went to St. Joseph's in Ohio for his advanced studies, and was ordained there in 1846 by Bishop Purcell of Cincinnati. Three years later he was made president of St. Joseph's, a fair indication of his extraordinary abilities. He seems to have been an ideal Dominican, keenly interested in philosophy and theology, a successful teacher, but above all a splendid performer in the pulpit, a real "Preacher". In addition, Whelan seems to have had an engaging and companionable personality.

In 1854, he was made Provincial of his Order of Preachers, continuing the while his teaching. No doubt his preaching made him well known, for he was named a likely future bishop all through the 1850s. He was third on a list of candidates sent by Bishop Miles to Rome for the selection of his coadjutor. Why he and not one of the first two was chosen is not known; perhaps they declined, perhaps Whelan's friendship with influential Archbishop Purcell was decisive. In any case he was named Coadjutor Bishop of Nashville with the right of succession, and was consecrated in St. Louis on May 8, 1859, by the Archbishop of that city, Peter Kenrick, Nashville's Metropolitan. Bishop Miles was too ill to attend, and much too infirm to have planned a consecration for Nashville. The new bishop came directly to Nashville, but Bishop Miles was still too ill to install him officially for three weeks. This finally took place on May 29. In tremulous tones Bishop Miles introduced to the cathedral audience his coadjutor, to whom, he said, "I cheerfully surrender the labors, cares, responsibilities of the episcopacy. I give up to him all but my title and my chair, which I am not at liberty to relinquish while I live." Bishop Whelan's reply was, to judge from contemporary accounts, all one could expect of a renowned preacher. From the city directories of the time it appears he came to live with Bishop Miles in the house on Summer Street next to the cathedral.

"It is difficult", says Father Reginald Coffey, the excellent historian of the Dominicans of the United States, "to estimate the effectiveness of Father Whelan's administration" as the young Provincial of the Dominicans. It is even more difficult to estimate his Nashville episcopate. Whelan gave an account of his administration in a document entitled "Report of the Diocese of Nashville by the Rt. Rev. James Whelan, O.P., D.D., Second Bishop of Nashville", dated June 30, 1863, and "Respectfully submitted" — to whom? His successor? Archbishop Kenrick? The Propaganda? All these? There is a copy of this report in the Manuscript Collection of the University of Notre Dame, and another in the State Library and Archives in Nashville. It gives a seemingly sensible and straightforward account of the finances of the diocese, and of the various concerns of the Church the bishop dealt with — finishing up the cathedral, St. Cecilia's, the German church in Memphis, the boys' school, Assumption, St. John's, Edgefield, and so on. It sounds reasonable and level-headed.

But by this date Whelan was just about through as Bishop of Nashville. As early as May, 1862, Archbishop Kenrick is writing about his "discreditable conduct" to the Propaganda; Kenrick has already asked for Whelan's resignation. Other area bishops wrote to Rome in support of Kenrick's position. This opposition reached a climax in the spring of 1863, when The Holy Father directed Whelan to resign and authorized Bishop Kenrick to appoint an Administrator.

Even more telling is a letter in the Notre Dame collection from Father Januarius D'Arco, a Dominican who was Whelan's chancellor at the time, and well acquainted with the diocese, to Bishop Lefevere of Detroit. It is worth quoting:

"It seems that he [Whelan] was never satisfied to stay here, though he has done a great deal of good since he came here, he was never fit for this place, as intelligent as he is, he had very little to occupy his intellect. No business here, a priest is enough here, hence the blunder, and knowing the consequences his mind occasionally was troubled and he gave way to d . . . Those, whom he offered the hospitality of his table, have been partially the cause of his downfall . . . he is young, and I hope this will be a good lesson for him for the future . . ."

Alas for Father D'Arco's hope, Whelan's future was already decided. But the D'Arco letter is tantalizing. It concedes that the principal allegation of the bishops against Whelan, insobriety, was at least occasionally true, but notes that a "blunder" of another sort, apparently, was more important. What this was can only be guessed at. There was a sermon Whelan preached just before the Union Army arrived in Nashville that badly backfired. He told his flock that, come what may, they must put their trust in God and not forget their religion — a pious and harmless sentiment, one would think, but the sermon was thought by many to be pro-Union.

It does seem likely that Whelan was pro-Union. Monsignor George Flanigen, the foremost historian of Tennessee Catholicism, said he was. Whelan's friendship with the general of the invading Federal Army, William Rosecrans, is well documented. Rosecrans was a devout Catholic who wore a crucifix in plain view over his uniform, and carried a rosary in his pocket. His brother became the first Bishop of Columbus, Ohio. He surrounded himself with devout Catholics as far as possible; his adjutant-general, Julius Garesche, came from a well-known Cincinnati Catholic family, one of whom, Father Edward Garesche, was a well-known Jesuit writer of the 1920s. Julius was killed in a bizarre mischance when his head was blown off by a stray cannon ball as he rode with General Rosecrans near Murfreesboro. When his body was recovered he was found clutching a copy of *The Imitation of Christ* by Thomas a' Kempis. Not even the Confederate General, Episcopal Bishop Leonidas Polk, was as conspicuously religious.

And yet, the picture never becomes quite clear. In one of his letters home, Father Peter Paul Cooney, a Holy Cross priest from Notre Dame, chaplain to the 35th Indiana Regiment, tells of journeying from Bowling Green, Kentucky, with Bishop Whelan, along with the Union Army, in March, 1862. After arriving in Nashville Father Cooney said Sunday Mass in the Nashville cathedral. His opposite number, Father Henry Brown, chaplain of the Irish Confederate Regiment of Nashville, preached. What a beautiful illustration of Catholic unity, Bishop Whelan remarked, to see a chaplain of the Union Army singing Mass, a chaplain of the Confederate Army in the pulpit, before a rebel congregation. This incident tells us that the bishop went where he wanted to go, and that chaplains moved around with similar freedom. But it does not tell us why Whelan's Union sympathies isolated him. The most prominent Catholic in Whelan's See city, Michael Burns, was pro-Union; so was prominent non-Catholic Judge John M. Lea, and others. Nashville women of good family were being courted by, and eventually marrying, Union soldiers. What went wrong with Whelan? He had brought his mother down from New York to live with him in Nashville; did she muddy the waters for him? Was it because of her that he held on in Nashville nearly a year after he had resigned? Not until early in 1864 did he send her back to New York, and he himself retire finally to his old convent in Ohio, where he lived on till 1878, writing learned treatises in Latin on theological subjects and helping out in Dominican parishes.

It is hard to blame Whelan. Of all the southern Catholic bishops, only he had to deal with a Union Army quartered in a hostile pro-Confederate environment. If, as seems likely, he was a strong Union man himself, his position was perilous, for most of his clergy were pro-Confederate. As Father D'Arco says, he was the wrong man in the wrong place at the wrong time. It was a sad fate for one as talented as Whelan. What was needed was someone just to keep things going, and hold the diocese together. That was provided by his successor, Father Joseph Kelly, another Dominican of high distinction in the annals of the Order of Preachers of the United States. Nashville necessarily almost ceased to be a functioning diocese from 1861 to 1865. It was James Whelan's unhappy fate to be the captain of a non-existent ship. It is a poignant irony that part of his time in retirement was taken up in the invention of a new method of embalming, for which he received a patent. This is more suggestive than any other explanation of his failure. He was an oddball, and oddballs don't make good administrators.

James Whelan, the second bishop, resigned in 1863 during troubles of war.

Bishop Patrick Feehan was an organizer and builder, first in Nashville from 1865 to 1880, then as Chicago's first Archbishop.

The poetry of Father Abram Ryan has touched the hearts of southerners for more than a hundred years.

Father Emmeran Bliemel, pastor of Assumption Church, became a chaplain and was killed while administering last rites to a Confederate soldier.

The Tennessee State Capitol stands on the horizon of this wartime photograph, with Assumption Church directly below it and the Buddeke house on the left. *Tennessee State Library photo.*

The Buddeke house, later acquired by the parish and used as a school, gym, and parish hall, stands yet across the street from the church.

Two of Nashville's oldest Catholic families united when Felix Demoville married Helen Philips and built this house. Castner-Knott is on its site. *Tennessee State Library photo.*

Andrew Johnson and his Catholic daughter contributed to the building of old St. Patrick's in Greeneville, his home town.

School and convent of the Dominican sisters of St. Cecilia are longtime landmarks on a hill in north Nashville. Mother Frances Walsh kept St. Cecilia going in its difficult early days.

9

Civil War Chaplains and Nurses

The Tennessee story of the participation of priests and nuns in the Civil War is dominated by the fame and fascination of Father Abram J. Ryan. Nothing about his story is typical; he was never an official chaplain, never attached to a staff or a regiment, and never received a cent of pay. Nor is he, of course, best known and remembered as a chaplain. He became nationally famous as a poet, and before that was locally famous as an orator. No one knows why he was in love with the South, but no one knows why anyone is in love. His attachment to the South was not based on a stake in its welfare. He came from no planter family, from no cousinship or connection with the old South. He was far more Irish than southern in background and temperament. But, like the vast majority of southern Irish, who had no more stake in the cotton economy than he did, he was romantically attached to the cause of the South. Ryan was first and foremost a priest. In all his printed works the cause of religion, and the devotion of his heart to God and his Blessed Mother, came first. But his devotion to the South was a strong second.

Geographically, Father Ryan was a fringe southerner. He was baptized on the fringe, in Hagerstown, Maryland, in 1838. His boyhood was spent in Norfolk, Virginia, but his formative years and schooling took place in St. Louis, a city to this day with a split North-South character. His seminary training took place in Niagara Falls, New York, in an atmosphere determinedly hostile to clerical participation in the Civil War. And yet Ryan never wavered in his conviction of the justice of the cause of the South. He defied and ignored his ecclesiastical superiors in becoming an unofficial chaplain to the Confederate Armies, and, a born orator and writer, preached and promoted the glorious righteousness of the Confederacy wherever and whenever he could.

The romantic Irish make good romantic southerners. Ryan came close to being born in that most typical of Irish places, Tipperary, and in the United States his family followed the usual path of trying first this, then that, place to live. But this meant little to Abram. He dwelt in no earthly spot. He lived in the depths of his romantic imagination, the dreamy mini-mystic unmapped country of emotions. Like most dwellers in this dream land, Ryan tended to melancholy, and his upward spirals soared toward ecstacy and sublimity, rather than jollity and camaraderie. In public Ryan was a spellbinder, like William Jennings Bryan or Fulton Sheen; in private, though much courted by those who had heard him and read him, he liked solitude, loved the midnight hours, cherished the picturesque and the romantic, including his personal appearance — in his photographs he looks like an ampler version of the famous violinist, Paganini, or a poet of the 1800s. Like the typical Irishman, he found success pleasant but couldn't build upon it or even live with it very well; when he had it he tempted it with the usual results of failure, banishment, or some sort of boomerang indirection. He did not have the typical Irish fondness for strong drink, but in his language, his piety, his love of travel, his journalism, his friendships, almost everything else, he was as intemperate as any other Irish poet and as fanciful and moody.

Romantic, maverick, independent, peripatetic, all these, yes; but first and foremost Ryan was a priest. His vocation came to him, as it does to most, in mid-adolescence, and he embraced it with all the fervor of his passionate soul. "I wish I were the little (tabernacle) key", begins his poem called "A Child's Wish", "That locks Love's Captive in/ And lets Him out to go and free/ A sinful heart from sin". And the child then wishes he were the bell, the chalice, and the altar. Nor did the grown man waver. The first poem in his Collected *Father Ryan's Poems,* "The Song of the Mystic", begins, "I walk down the valley of Silence/ Down that dim distant valley alone", and develops the idea that this valley is "my trysting place with the Divine". But the melancholy that is always the reverse of the romantic turns up at the poem's end; the valley "lieth afar between mountains . . . And one is the dark mount of Sorrow/ And one the bright mountain of prayer". Again and again his poems celebrate his vocation, his devotion to the altar, his love of Our Lady and the saints. Father Ryan's best known poems are about the cause of the South in the Civil War, but of the more than a hundred poems in the famous volume of his collected works, more than seventy-five are directly or in part religious verses.

After his vocation, his central loyalty was to the South. Since during the poet's adolescence the Ryan family lived in St. Louis, it was natural enough, in that stronghold of the Vincentian Fathers, for the young man to turn to them for the fulfillment of his vocation. He was ordained a Vincentian in 1860. The offical Vincentian policy was hands-off the North-South issue. Result: Ryan left the Vincentians, and became, for the rest of his life, a free-wheeling secular priest, tolerated by three of his nominal bishops and fired by one. Never an official chaplain, he circulated among the Confederate armies, mostly in southeastern Tennessee, partly, perhaps, in penitential mourning for his beloved brother David, a Confederate soldier who was killed in a skirmish in Kentucky.

Father Ryan was in Tennessee for only a few years, from 1862 to 1866 or 1867, the first year as informal chaplain, the second at the cathedral in Nashville, the third as pastor of the Catholic church in Clarksville, and the fourth in the same capacity in Knoxville. Nearly every event in Ryan's life is in dispute, from his birthplace to the reasons for his peregrinations, so it isn't entirely clear when he left Tennessee or where he wrote his most famous poem, the one that first brought him to national attention, in Nashville, Clarksville, or Knoxville. This was "The Conquered Banner", with its famous refrain of "Furl that Banner". "The Conquered Banner" was brought to national attention in 1866 when it was published in the well-known Catholic paper, the *New York Freeman's Journal*.

In Augusta, Georgia, Father Ryan began a career as an editor which lasted until 1873. Editor Ryan was the oddest Ryan of all. Augusta was a city well known for its integration of Catholics into the community. Its war-time mayor, Robert H. May, had been baptized by Ryan. Yet here of all places Ryan constantly lashed out against Protestantism in all its forms. Ryan also took on his own bishop, Augustin Verot, an outspoken and determined opponent of defining papal infallibility during Vatican Council I in

1870. Ryan's paper, *The Banner of the South,* plumped strongly in its favor. This may have been a reason why the bishop fired him in 1870, though no one really knows. It's likely that both Ryan and Verot were too independent and strong-minded to get on for very long.

But, for the two years of Ryan's editorship, *The Banner of the South* really made a splash. Already widely known, in the South especially, for his poems, which were published in various magazines and newspapers, Ryan now began to be known as well for his continuing devotion to the Confederacy. The deliberate mimicry of his famous poem in the name of his paper, *The Banner of the South,* made his purpose clear. He ignored local news in favor of building up the legend of the romantic South. He aimed at national circulation, and had northern correspondents, but his editorship was too brief for a fair trial in the North. He was successful in the South; in a poll taken in Nashville in 1868 the *Banner* led all other southern publications in circulation.

From Savannah Ryan escaped to Mobile, where he lived longest, from 1873 to 1886. But this is misleading. After a fling at editing the New Orleans Catholic paper, which lasted less than a year, he was beginning to be more and more famous. By 1873 he had traveled to Europe, and begun the lecture tours which took him all over the eastern half of the United States until his death in 1886 at the age of forty-eight. To the television generation the taste of their grandparents for Ryan's sort of emotional and flamboyant preaching seems almost incredible. A ninety-minute sermon, or political oration, seemed disappointingly brief to many of them. Oratory and sermons were theater, social occasions, celebrations, all at once. Ryan was a master at this sort of thing. His letters show that he was half-pleased, half-fretful about his success. All his life Ryan was a great letter-writer; many survive, in many places, his beautiful handwriting in appropriate accord with his highly praised character. For all his romantic appearance and manner, Ryan's was a manly and on occasion convivial personality. He was attractive to children, and fond of their company, liked visiting pleasant normal families, but also maintained a copious correspondence with intellectuals like the Brownsons as well as with cloistered nuns.

Father Ryan's name did not become a household word in the

South until the publication in 1879 of his collected verses, entitled *Father Ryan's Poems*. During the next thirty years this went through forty editions; southerners of all religions placed this volume on their parlor tables along with the Bible and the family photograph albums. It was a rare and backward child who didn't know some of his poems, or parts of them, for they tended to length, by heart, and in the days when "Lines for Committing to Memory" were part of ordinary schooling, Father Ryan's name came alongside that of Sidney Lanier and Edgar Allen Poe.

His fame was, in the 1880s and 1890s and for long thereafter, nearly as widespread as that of Robert E. Lee or Stonewall Jackson. He was, in the South, what Bishop Fulton Sheen was to the country during the days of his television fame. Southern Catholics especially doted on him; a fair index of their devotion can be seen in the given name of one of Tennessee's most popular priests from 1920 to his death in 1980, Monsignor Merlin F. Kearney. This name came from a character in a long Ryan poem, "Their Story Runneth Thus." Kearney's mother had become a Ryan devotee, one of the thousands who read his frequent articles and poems in Catholic journals, and attended his sermons and retreats.

Ryan was indeed a fascinating phenomenon among priests, but not unique. His near contemporary, Father John Bannister Tabb, enjoyed a similar fame as a poet; his devotion to the South is less well-known. The two poet-priests have fascinating similarities, and sharply contrasting differences. Ryan, the fringe southerner, came from a poor immigrant family, while Tabb was to the manor born, the son of a wealthy plantation family of early settlement in Virginia. Ryan was twenty-four years old when his devotion to the cause of the South crystallized into his activity as an informal chaplain; Tabb was only sixteen when, debarred by his weak eyesight from soldiering — he eventually became stone-blind — he enlisted as a blockade runner. Captured by a Yankee ship, he spent the last year of the war in prison at Point Lookout, Maryland, in the company of another famous southern poet, Sidney Lanier, who became his lifelong friend. Lifelong also was his devotion to the southern cause, in one way at least stricter than Ryan's, for Tabb steadfastly refused to set foot north of the Mason-Dixon line. What a strange coincidence, that the only two poet-priests in the history of the Church of the United States who achieved wide popularity were devoted southerners and rough contemporaries.

Here the resemblance ends, however. Ryan was a cradle Catholic, Tabb so rootedly Episcopalian that his family never forgave him for his conversion to Catholicism. Deeply disturbed by a critical time in his spiritual life directly following the war, Tabb found a sympathetic and helpful advisor in Father Alfred Curtis, an Episcopal priest going through the same turmoil. Curtis shortly became a Catholic, and eventually the Bishop of Wilmington, Delaware. Tabb followed, and in 1872 received on the same day four sacraments from his Catholic spiritual adviser, instructor, and eventual good friend, James Gibbons, then the Bishop of Richmond. Some years later Gibbons added a fifth, Holy Orders.

Even more marked is the contrast between the personalities of Ryan and Tabb. Although he loved long periods of solitude, Ryan alternated with bouts of furious activism, fulminating against his and the South's enemies, preaching to packed churches, travelling constantly. Tabb spent most of his life teaching English at St. Charles College, then near Ellicott City, Maryland. He was very shy and reserved, the archetype of the scholar-poet, shying away from new encounters, writing and re-writing his brief lyrics, while Ryan tore off his poems in flat-out sprints, letting the length run as long as his inspiration lasted. Tabb received the attention of serious students of English poetry, Ryan almost never; in his introduction to the thirteenth edition of Ryan's volume of poetry, the Catholic historian, novelist, and editor, John Talbot Smith, complains of this inattention. And yet, the two can sound remarkably alike. Tabb's verses are counter-part to Ryan's "A Child's Wish" in this little Christmas poem: "A little boy of heavenly birth/ But far from home today,/ Came down to find his ball, the earth,/ That sin had cast away./ Oh comrades, let us one and all/ Join in to get Him back His ball."

Tabb had, of course, nothing to do with Tennessee. He may have met Ryan when the latter visited his college, and they certainly knew each other's verses — and worth. Neither is much read these days, Tabb especially. The name of Father Ryan lives on in Tennessee in the Catholic high school named for him in

Nashville. He is also commemorated in the Confederate Museum in New Orleans, and with a full-length portrait statue in Mobile, Alabama, erected by the pennies of the school children of that diocese in 1913.

Father Ryan was a chaplain, so to speak, by divine right. Like the Old Testament prophets, he would have been one though all the world said no. He simply adopted the Confederate Army. In this he was not unique; other Confederate chaplains were volunteers, some briefly, some for the duration.

The subject of chaplains in the Confederate Army might have been as complicated as that subject in the Army of the United States had it not been for one important difference: the piety of Stonewall Jackson. James Madison, the most important single figure in the making of the American Constitution, was very touchy about whether chaplains had any place at all in the American Army, on the principle of the separation of church and state. Although George Washington insisted on chaplains during the Revolutionary War, little support for them was forthcoming from Congress thereafter. From 1818 to 1838 there was exactly one chaplain in the Army of the United States, and he was a professor at West Point with his chaplaincy as additional, and no doubt, not very burdensome duty. New legislation in 1838 established twenty Army chaplaincies, all Protestant, which led to a revolt by Catholic troops during the Mexican War when they were forced to attend Protestant services. Hastily President Polk, after consultation with some Catholic bishops, appointed a couple of Catholic chaplains, the forerunners of thousands in later history.

Jefferson Davis and Confederate Secretary of War, James Seddon, were indifferent about making chaplains an integral part of the Confederate Army, and in fact they never were. The most nearly typical arrangement was that made in Nashville by the Governor of Tennessee, who confirmed the election of Charles T. Quintard as Chaplain in the First Tennessee Regiment. Election by his fellow soldiers was a common way of becoming a Confederate chaplain, although not for Catholics. The Catholic chaplains, elected or not, needed the sponsorship of a bishop.

Such was the experience of Tennessee's most famous Catholic chaplain, after Father Ryan. This was Father Emmeran Bliemel, a

Benedictine priest who was pastor of the new Church of the Assumption in north Nashville, a natural post for a young Bavarian missionary who immigrated to the United States to serve God and his fellow German immigrants as best he could. A friend introduced him to St. Vincent Abbey in Latrobe, Pennsylvania, and following his studies there he was ordained a priest in 1856. He then ministered to German-speaking congregations in western Pennsylvania and Ohio, a time of missionary wandering. But in 1860 he heard the call of the new Bishop of Nashville, James Whelan, for priests, came to Tennessee in the fall of 1860, and was immediately made pastor of Assumption Church in north Nashville, whose parishioners were mostly German and mostly spoke German. Why Bliemel's passionate devotion to the cause of the South? We know nothing of its origin or nature, just the stubborn fact.

Stubborn it was, though the young pastor had two years in which it grew to maturity. These two years, from 1860 to 1862, were times of wild fluctuation in Nashville. At first the city boomed, becoming a center for the collection and transshipment of Confederate supplies. At the same time, however, the young men disappeared into the army, family ties became looser, and church attendance everywhere went down. All this worsened when the city became open to Federal occupation in the spring of 1862. By the time General William Rosecrans, commanding the Federal Army of the Cumberland, set up his headquarters in Nashville in October, 1862, the city was booming again, unwilling host to an occupation army of 45,000, many billetted in the city, plus the usual collection of army followers, provisioners, railroad men, horse traders, wheelers and dealers of all sorts, drifters, prostitutes, riff-raff. Life in the city was disorganized, messy, troubled.

For Catholics, it was wildly mixed, part liberating, part terrifying, and deeply clouded. The records of the time are few and cryptic, so the fate of the Nashville Catholics, perhaps four or five thousand of the state's estimated twelve thousand in 1860, can only be guessed at. It is generally described as distressed and confused, because of the resignation of Bishop Whelan, but this is not the whole of the matter. For one thing, the Catholics in trade, and they generally were or wanted to be, prospered. The merchants, like Farrell, Buddeke, Olwill, Callaghan, Ratterman, Smith, and Wessel, did well, and rose in the social scheme of things. For these, as for all Catholics, it is likely that parish life was less vital than before, and it must have been somewhat difficult for them to accept the Catholic Union soldiers who, surely, must have come to church occasionally. But life goes on, war or no war, as the large number of marriages between southern women and Union soldiers attests. Many of the unionists settled permanently in Nashville, thirteen high Federal officers among them, and swiftly became part of the city's business and social life, without rancor or prejudice for the most part.

Complicating life for the Nashville Catholics to a degree one can only guess at was the fact that General Rosecrans was not only a Catholic, but a deeply dedicated and devout one, who proclaimed his Catholicism from tent and home. Rosecrans was a martinet, exacting from friend and foe strict obedience to his commands. After he had confiscated horses from the region, he said, to a deprived owner seeking the return of his property, "No, sir, the Government needs your horses and will pay for them. I cannot restore them to you; I could not restore those of my old friend Bishop Whelan, the Catholic Bishop of Nashville, nor can I yours."

However, the Rosecrans connection did do Father Bliemel some good. He was allowed to pass with immunity wherever he wished to go, and this led him to smuggle medicines and other contraband to the Confederate forces. Learning of this, Rosecrans wrote to Bliemel's Benedictine superior, the Abbot at Latrobe, asking him to recall the Nashville priest, but nothing happened, no one knows why. Meanwhile, Father Bliemel went to live with Bishop Whelan at the cathedral rectory, and blithely continued his smuggling. Apprehended, he was let off with a stern rebuke by Rosecrans.

After the General departed to fight first at Murfreesboro and later at Chickamauga, Nashville became a refuge for the ill and wounded. Both the Cathedral and the Assumption church were converted briefly into hospitals. Early in March, 1863, five black-cap Sisters of Charity from Cincinnati, headed by Father Tracey, sometime chaplain to Rosecrans, came to Nashville to nurse at the hospital on College Hill in south Nashville. Another contingent of

Sisters of Charity from Emmitsburg, Maryland, spent some months in Nashville nursing.

Meanwhile, Bliemel besieged Whelan with applications for permission to join the 10th Tennessee Confederate Infantry, called, by a pleasant ironic twist, the Irish Brigade, whose chaplain he had been elected. By the time permission was given, Bishop Whelan had resigned his bishopric, and Bliemel's passport was a letter from Father Henry Brown, the stalwart of the cathedral staff, which simply said Bliemel was off to the Tennessee missions. This served him to get into Confederate territory, where he was swiftly commissioned chaplain by Bishop Verot of Savannah. This adventure came to a sad end on August 31, 1864, when Father Bliemel was killed at the Battle of Jonesboro, Georgia, while administering the last rites to a soldier. He was the only Catholic chaplain killed in the War Between the States.

It is doubtful that Father Bliemel could have made such a career but for the example of Stonewall Jackson, whose famous dedication of his army before battle to the Lord's mercy in prayer became as well known as his fabulous success. Robert E. Lee was also a devout Christian, though less flamboyant than his treasured Jackson, and their combined example may have forced a reluctant Confederate bureaucracy to create chaplains. The Confederate armies were generally not eager to have chaplains at first, but as the weary war wore on — "Neither party expected for the war the magnitude or the duration which it has already attained", said Lincoln in his second Inaugural address — they began to cherish them. Yankee witnesses were astonished at the esteem southern chaplains enjoyed; there was little like it in the Union forces. Even Jefferson Davis came to appreciate their worth, and began signing commissions for them.

Oddly, Father Bliemel was the second Catholic chaplain of the Tennessee Tenth. Its first was the redoubtable Father Henry V. Brown, the easterner who had been converted by Father Jarboe. Brown served when the regiment was formed, but after the fall of Fort Henry his name disappears from the records. Since his devotion to the southern cause was well known, it is almost certain that he felt he should not travel with the army. He was made a diocesan consultor in 1861, and one of its Vicars General shortly thereafter, was the stalwart of the cathedral for all the war years during Bishop Whelan's unpopularity, somehow managing to retain the loyalty and affection of both Whelan and his restive clergy. As his work as the virtual founder of Catholicism in both Chattanooga and Knoxville demonstrates, this does not seem impossible to this remarkable man.

Only Fathers Abram Ryan and Bliemel were Confederate chaplains from Tennessee in any meaningful sense of the word. Another Father Ryan, Patrick, is listed as chaplain to the Eighth Tennessee Regiment, but there is no trace of him in the archives; a Father Patrick Ryan was a victim of the yellow fever scourge in Memphis in 1873, but he was not ordained until 1869. Two Dominican fathers, James Daly and John Nealis, are sometimes named as chaplains, but it seems they did no more than attend the Catholic troops both Confederate and Union stationed where they happened to be. Father Nealis's is a sad and strange story. In 1862 he was shot through the body by some anonymous ruffian, and for long it was thought he would not survive the brutal and gratuitous assault. When he did, he became subject to fainting spells, and in one of these, apparently, he fell from the second story window of the cathedral rectory and was killed.

But finally there is Father Joseph Jarboe, the Dominican who accompanied Bishop Miles to Nashville when Miles first occupied his See. Father Jarboe was chaplain to the Second Regiment of Tennessee Volunteers beginning in 1861, and went with them to the fierce and bloody battle of Shiloh, April 6-7, 1862. Like many of his fellow Dominicans, Jarboe had a little printer's ink in his veins, and a year after Shiloh, wrote a long letter to the editor of the *Freeman's Journal* about his war experiences.

He says he was in Zanesville, Ohio, when the war broke out, but when Bishop Whelan wrote his superior there asking for a chaplain, he answered the call. The soldiers "did not go through the ceremony of electing me Chaplain", he wrote, "but . . . in my whole life I never received such marks of respect and friendship as while I was with the Confederate forces." There follows an interesting adventure at Shiloh:

"On the first day of battle, two Federal surgeons, with perhaps forty of their wounded, were captured, and brought as prisoners to our Division Hospital. After I had rendered what help I could to our wounded, for both soul and body, I felt anxious about the wounded of the faith in the Federal camp; and as I did not know whether they had a priest among them, I wished to go to their aid. Three Confederate surgeons, and the two Federals, concurred in the belief that, as I was not a military man, but a minister of peace and charity, my appearance among them would give no offense."

"On Saturday after the battle, taking in my pocket a paper written by our head surgeon, and signed by all three, and by one of the Federal surgeons, I went, under the flag of truce, which came to take back their wounded." But when Father Jarboe got to the hospital, the wounded had been moved some distance away, too far for him to go, and he headed back to his own regiment. "When I reached the pickets, they took me to their Colonel," with whom there was an acrimonious dispute about religion, but no safe conduct back to his own lines. Instead, the Colonel sent him to a General Nelson, who met him with a volley of oaths and curses, and threw him in jail. "They left me from Sunday to Wednesday," Father Jarboe goes on, "lying on the cold ground, getting a dirty tin cup of coffee, sometimes sweetened, sometimes not, all the time surrounded by a brutal soldier pouring out oaths and imprecations on me day and night."

"Wednesday, I was ordered to report to Halleck's headquarters . . . and fortunately was delivered over to Major John J. Key, Provost Marshall of the Post. He did not know me personally, though he knew me by character, and after asking me many questions about persons and places in Kentucky he satisfied himself that I was not someone else who had stolen my name, he turned to the other officers and said, 'Gentlemen, this is one of the best men in the country, and the best of you might be proud to have his name!' He treated me most kindly, and gave me permission to exercise my ministry in their camp."

However, subsequent events led Father Jarboe to believe there was still great, if baseless, feeling against him, and at the first opportunity he escaped on a boat to Cairo and back to Kentucky. Such was the life of a Confederate chaplain.

It was not until a year or so later — there is no record of the actual date — that Father Jarboe became officially a member of the Nashville clergy. Appointed Vicar General by Bishop Feehan, who became Nashville's third bishop in 1865, Jarboe also had the spiritual direction of the Sisters at St. Cecilia and St. Mary's Orphanage, both run by the Dominican sisters. After nearly twenty years in Nashville, he retired to St. Joseph's Dominican Priory in Ohio, where in 1887 he died, aged eighty-one. On close terms with death since his birth, a lifelong invalid, Jarboe, like so many other invalids, lived a long and useful life.

It is difficult to estimate the contribution of the Diocese of Nashville to the Confederate ministry. Since there were only fifteen Catholic chaplains in all the Confederate forces, the Nashville contribution seems to be about what might be expected, or something more than that. But the whole story cannot be neatly told. Many a priest visited camps and battlefields near his church without becoming official chaplains; many a confession and consolation cheered a lonely soldier on leave or camped near a church. This is clear from the number of priests reputed to be chaplains in Tennessee, but who don't appear on the official rolls.

The Catholic nuns who were nurses are better documented. Bishop Whelan asked the Dominican sisters of Memphis to help staff the Memphis City Hospital, which they did with great efficiency and charity. Other communities not based in Tennessee sent sister-nurses to work in the state, among them the Sisters of Mercy of Chicago and Cincinnati, the Holy Cross Sisters of Notre Dame, and the Sisters of Charity of Cincinnati. The early histories of the Civil War are full of praises for these noble women, many of whom lost their own healths and lives tending the sick and wounded. The Catholic sisterhoods who nursed both sides during the war are the subject of a detailed account of their labors, including names, by Congressman Ambrose Kennedy, of Rhode Island, in the *Congressional Record* of March 18, 1918.

The last of the Dominicans to govern the Diocese of Nashville is, perhaps, the most attractive. He was the Reverend Joseph Augustine Kelly, the only Dominican Provincial of the area who was elected at an age younger than Whelan's. Both were thirty-one, but Kelly the younger by five months. Like Whelan, Kelly was born in Ireland, but his widowed father brought him when he was ten years old to Louisville, and sent him to St. Mary's College, then conducted by the Jesuits. But before graduating from St. Mary's he had been schooled by the Dominicans, and it was to them he took his vocation to the priesthood. Within a few months after his ordination he was elected Prior, then President of St. Joseph's College, then Provincial, all within eight years.

In 1863 Father Kelly was made pastor of St. Peter's, Memphis, but shortly thereafter was removed to Nashville when he was made Administrator of the diocese upon Bishop Whelan's resignation. The work for which he is best remembered as Administrator is the founding and sustaining of St. Mary's Orphanage in Nashville. He was also a loyal friend to St. Cecilia's. The early tenure of his administration must have been made uncomfortable by the continued presence of Whelan, who did not leave Nashville until mid-1864. Kelly was expected to succeed Whelan at Nashville, but the appointment went to Father Patrick Feehan, another Irish-born but secular priest of the Archdiocese of St. Louis, who compounded Father Kelly's ambiguities by delaying a year before accepting his miter. But Kelly loyally did what he had been appointed to do, and went with faithful devotion to Feehan's consecration in St. Louis on November 1, 1865. He then accompanied the bishop to Nashville, and saw him properly installed in the episcopal residence next to the cathedral on Summer Street in Nashville, before returning to St. Rose's Priory in Kentucky.

Father Kelly eventually returned to Memphis, where he distinguished himself by his courage and devotion during the yellow fever plagues. His long career finally came to an end in 1885, when he died in Memphis, and was buried under the high altar of St. Peter's, a distinction usually reserved for bishops but worthily given to this great man. Both the historians of the Dominicans in the United States, Father Victor O'Daniel and Father Reginald Coffey, call him a great man. Thus ended the influence of the sons of St. Dominic on the bishopric of Nashville. To be sure, they kept St. Peter's in Memphis. The St. Cecilia Dominican sisters gradually extended their teaching, fanning over the state except in its northeast corner. But a Dominican presence again made itself felt there when, beginning in 1916, Dominican priests were established at Johnson City and its missions, where they still minister. But the direction of the diocese went to and stayed with the secular clergy.

What was the character of these Dominican priests? From this distance, it seems full of flaws. They were independent to an almost lordly degree, despite their basic conventual way of life. Influenced no doubt by the missionary nature of their work, they moved about with footloose abandon. Since their schools fared ill in Ohio and Kentucky, they were forced into parish work — at one time two of their number, carefully educated in Rome to teach in their seminaries, were both in Tennessee. One, Father Thomas Grace, was pastor of St. Peter's in Memphis, and eventually became second Bishop of St. Paul. The other, Father Raymond Young, whose free-wheeling career is almost a parody of Dominican independence, flatly refused to teach. He came to Nashville to give a retreat for Bishop Miles, and liked life at the cathedral so well that he decided to stay on, as a guest of the bishop, along with Miles's permanent guest, Father Samuel Louis Montgomery, who lived at the cathedral for the last twelve years of his life.

Neither of these was trained to be a missionary, nor felt it a call, as did Fathers Orengo and Jarboe, the great Dominican missionaries of Tennessee. Not so Father Joseph Sadoc Alemany, a Spaniard who came to the United States from his studentship in Italy especially to serve Bishop Miles, and who went on to become Dominican Provincial and eventually first Archbishop of San Francisco. Other Dominicans who served in Tennessee were the ill-fated Father John Nealis, a native of New York; Father Januarius D'Arco, another Italian, who accompanied Bishop Whelan to Nashville; Father Moses Fortune, who came to help Father Kelly during the latter's administration; Father Sydney Clarkson, who was pastor of St. Peter's, Memphis, during the Civil War; and Father John H. Lynch, who served briefly under Bishop Miles. It's a pity these men are not better known to Tennessee Catholics. They were the pioneers of the Church, worthy companions and successors to the pioneering Fenwick of Ohio. They set the tone for Catholicism in the middle South.

What the Dominicans seem to have had in abundance was *style*. Even at their most individualistic behavior, they spoke, wrote, and acted with touches of elegance and grace; there was little that was rough-cut or uncouth about them. Wherever they went they built beautiful churches, astonishing structures often rising almost dream-like in a wilderness. The foremost Catholic architect of his time, Patrick C. Keeley, designed three of their churches, but scarcely any are dull. The churches are decorated in good taste, and their music was frequently among the best to be heard in Catholic circles. It is probably fanciful to attribute to the Dominican style something that is special to Tennessee Catholicism, some extra grace and charm. Yet some touch may still linger.

In his sermon on the centenary of the diocese, Bishop John B. Morris, himself a native Tennessean who became the ordinary of Little Rock, says that at least ten native Tennesseans became members of the Dominican order. He named Fathers Michael Lilly, Hugh Lilly, Rumaggio, Shea, Arnoult, Mulvin, Grant, and Perry from Memphis, and Daniel Kennedy and his nephew John from Knoxville. Of these, Fathers Michael Lilly and Daniel Kennedy served with high distinction. Bishop Morris continued, "One cannot speak of the Diocese of Nashville without speaking of the Dominicans, because they were for a long time almost the only missionaries in the state, and the diocese is more indebted to the Fathers of St. Dominic for its Catholic life than to any other source whatever." Amen to that.

10

After the War

The situation of the Catholics in Nashville was fairly typical of the decade following the war in Tennessee. Lost in the battle of Nashville was the orphanage, but it was rebuilt fairly soon. Assumption church and the cathedral had both been turned into hospitals, but they were soon restored, repaired, and again in use. St. Cecilia's was in dire trouble, but rescue was imminent. Times were hard. Nobody had any money, except perhaps a shoe box full of Confederate notes to stare at ruefully from time to time. And yet, in some ways things were upbeat.

After the war the four principal cities of Tennessee emerged as real centers of trade and culture, all showing big gains in population and industrial know-how. The transition from agrarian to industrial ways of life was hard. The vast improvements in industrialism in the North were built on the solid foundation of the cheap labor of immigrants from Europe. Relatively few of these immigrants came to the South. The leaders of southern industrialism tried hard to woo them, but the trickle did not increase to a waterfall. City growth in Tennessee, as elsewhere in the South, came from southern rural areas, not from immigration. Wasted in the air were the thousands of advertisements and millions of pamphlets put out by the chambers of commerce and the railroads to lure the children of Europe to the South. Neither these inducements, nor the often elaborate schemes of colonization, had much effect.

But there was an internal effect, made of the homespun of southern stuff. Memphis throve after the war. Knoxville, too, had a prosperous air. Nashville, the most diversified of the cities, did well. Chattanooga did best of all, until the Birmingham area surpassed it as an industrial center. This was no runaway prosperity, no boom time. It was simply a modest little doing pretty well, with many ups and downs. It trembled mightily during the panic of 1873, and somewhat during that of 1893. Only for brief periods did agriculture prosper — the cities and towns grew, the countryside fared less well.

Into this milieu came the third Bishop of Nashville, Patrick Augustine Feehan. He represents something new in the diocese. For one thing, he was a secular priest, not a member of a religious order. Perhaps more significantly, he was a typical Catholic bishop of the United States. Born in Ireland, as so many of them were, he was, again like so many of them, an organizer, a good business man, highly prelatical, a real churchman. As such, he moved from place to place easily — Ireland to St. Louis to Nashville and finally to Chicago, whose first Archbishop he became in 1880. It was a solid, satisfactory career of real achievement. Feehan was an able man, a man right for his time. He had a great fund of good common sense. He kept a low profile, but when he did move he moved decisively. He met crises coolly and courageously, whether the yellow fever epidemics in Tennessee or the excesses of the immigrants in Chicago. Although he was a devoted Irishman, he never mixed in Irish politics; but neither was he an ardent American, after the pattern of Cardinal Gibbons and Archbishop Ireland.

Most of the priests and bishops of Irish descent who were attached to the Diocese of Nashville came from families of some education and cultivation. This was true of the Feehan family. The bishop's father was a classical scholar; in addition he spoke fluent French. He lived on a farm near Tipperary where he supervised the early education of his gifted son until the boy was about sixteen, when he was sent to the well-known school at Knock. Two years later he went to St. Patrick's College, the principal Irish seminary at Maynooth, where he studied for five years.

The story of his coming to the United States has a familiar ring. One of the most astonishing turn-arounds in the history of the Catholic Church occurred after the anti-religious convulsions of the French Revolution. In France there was, beginning around 1820, a return to religion, a tremendous wave of piety and religious fervor reminiscent of the great days of the Counter-reformation in the sixteenth century. This wave swept into some seminaries in other European Catholic countries. The Catholic youth of Europe dreamed of being missionaries, as centuries before they had dreamed of being crusaders. They saw themselves in India, in China, in Africa, bringing the Gospel to the world, now that the world was accessible. When bishops and priests from the missionary countries visited schools and seminaries the students were often fired to enlist as their helpers then and there.

Just this happened to young Feehan, aged twenty-two. There came to Maynooth in 1852 the first Archbishop of St. Louis, Peter Richard Kenrick, himself of Irish birth and destined to be a dominating presence in the Catholic Church of the Mississippi Valley for over forty years, as his brother Francis, Archbishop of Baltimore, was in the east. Feehan resolved to answer Kenrick's call for recruits. He attended for a few months Kenrick's new seminary in St. Louis, and was ordained by its founder November 1, 1852. He stayed on to teach in the seminary.

His family had immigrated to St. Louis two years before. By the time young Feehan made his move his mother was an invalid, looked after by a daughter, one of two who were devoted to their priest brother. The well-educated young priest was badly needed. In two years he was superior of the seminary at Carondelet, and also doing duty in parishes. During the Civil War he established a hospital for wounded soldiers who came up the river from various battles. It is hard to think of a better preparation for being a bishop.

Nevertheless, when the call to Nashville came, Feehan refused because of the illness of his mother. But Rome was willing to wait, and on November 1, 1865, the thirteenth anniversary of his ordination, the new Bishop of Nashville was consecrated in the St. Louis Cathedral by the archbishop, who also accompanied his young protege to Nashville, where they arrived on November 9.

The new bishop's diocese was no plum. Within a month or so after his consecration Feehan reported to the Propaganda in Rome that he presided over twelve priests and thirty sisters running three schools. Some of the priests are easy to spot: the administrator until the new Bishop arrived, Father Joseph A. Kelly, O.P., plus six other Dominicans, Fathers Joseph T. Jarboe, James A. Orengo, Sydney A. Clarkson, James V. Edelen, Thomas R. Fallon, and Bartholomew V. Carey. There were two diocesan priests, Fathers Henry V. Brown and Innocent Bergrath. And there are many questions. Was Father Cornelius Thoma then at St. Mary's in Memphis? Where was Wencelaus or Wentworth J. Repis? Was Father Abram Ryan included among the twelve? No doubt the two priests Feehan brought with him from St. Louis, Fathers Martin Riordan and Martin Walsh, were numbered among them. By contrast, when Feehan left in 1880 there were fourteen diocesan priests and fourteen priests who belonged to religious orders. Among these latter were only five Dominicans — plus seven Precious Blood fathers and two Franciscans.

The diocesan situation posed the usual Reconstruction dilemma. Father Vincent McMurry's essay on the Catholic Church in the South during Reconstruction says "A morally and financially deplorable condition greeted Feehan when he arrived in Nashville, where he found almost every mission burdened with a crushing debt and a scattered flock." Yet McMurry finished this paragraph by noting that Nashville was well supplied with institutions. It depended on where one looked.

Whatever the condition, signs of growth, of mild prosperity even, began to appear. One of Feehan's first acts was the organization in Nashville of the St. Vincent de Paul Society, to which he had been devoted in St. Louis. From the first this flourished like the biblical bay tree, as it still does; in six months its charter ninety-four members had made 2,648 visits to the poor and spent $1,172 for relief for needy families. Equally close to the bishop's charitable heart was the care of the orphans, who had been removed to the cathedral basement during the Battle of Nashville, living catch as catch can. Feehan oversaw the rebuilding of the south Nashville orphanage and saw it grow and prosper under the wing of the Dominican sisters from St. Cecilia's.

At the other end of the human spectrum the bishop bought what is now Calvary Cemetery on the Lebanon Pike close to Nashville. Its dedication, on November 29, 1868, was a grand affair. The procession of carriages was preceded by a band and twenty "neatly uniformed policemen," said the newspaper account. Then came the bishop's carriage, with four priests accompanying him. There then followed carriages containing members of the St. Vincent de Paul Society, the Society of the St. Mary's Orphan Asylum, the St. Joseph's Total Abstinence Society, the school children from the Sisters of Mercy School, and "carriages containing citizens." The line of carriages was so long that "there was no point along the route from which the entire procession could be viewed at one time." At the new cemetery, Bishop Feehan preached to "from 3,000 to 4,000 people," and, "in the gorgeous robes of his sacred office," made the circuit of the cemetery as prescribed in the ritual while the Children of Mary sang processional hymns. The forty-seven acres cost the diocese $15,000, a great bargain. Many Catholic families removed to it the bones of their ancestors from the old Nashville Catholic Cemetery on Cherry Street, now Fourth Avenue South. This portion of the city cemetery had been purchased in 1849, but the railroad appropriated most of the Catholic part, which lay to the west.

The growth continued. The church at Winchester was finished toward the end of 1868, and early in 1869 the indefatigable Father Orengo began one in Jackson. At Jackson too, the Dominican sisters tried a short-lived boarding school for girls, named Immaculate Conception Academy. The German Catholic Homestead Association was formed in Cincinnati to set up a settlement in Lawrence County, Tennessee. This was typically a German way of doing things. Many German Catholic settlements came to the United States sponsored by colonization societies in their homeland. Outstanding among these was the St. Raphael's Society, which not only financed immigration and helped to finance settlement, but raised sand complaining that the Church in America wasn't nearly receptive or charitable enough to their German immigrant brothers.

The Cincinnati society sought to find homes for new immigrants to Ohio who couldn't find work, mostly German-speaking but including a few Poles. It bought 65,000 acres of land for next to nothing, partly because it wasn't very good land, partly because the state was eager to see it settled. Settled it was, split into small lots and farms, forming a rare mostly Catholic farming enclave in Tennessee. These were, and are, common all through western Ohio and eastern Indiana, southern Wisconsin, eastern Iowa, and elsewhere, including, surprisingly, parts of eastern Texas. But in Tennessee the only prior instance was the Irish of McEwen who settled on farms. Even so, neither Lawrenceburg nor McEwen became stable till the railroads reached the former in

1881, the latter during the Civil War.

Agents from the Cincinnati Society visited Lawrence County in the winter of 1869-70. Father Henry Huesser, pastor of a German church in Cincinnati, was one of these, and he stayed on in Lawrenceburg to arrange the purchase of the land and organize the settlement. In the spring of 1870 he moved to Loretto. In both places he built simple church and school buildings. Within two months fifty families settled in the area, and others followed in the next two years. Oddly, few had experience of farming. Most were mechanics and tradesmen. Interestingly, some Catholic families from Chicago came to settle in the area after the great Chicago fire of 1871.

What brought stability to the area's Catholicity was the coming of the Fathers of the Precious Blood. This largely German order had immigrated to Cincinnati in the 1840s at the invitation of Archbishop John B. Purcell, and flourished then and now in the rich agricultural lands of western Ohio and eastern Indiana. They came to Lawrenceburg, along with some Precious Blood sisters, in 1872, greatly to Feehan's satisfacton. They also staffed Nashville's Assumption church and school.

The Lawrenceburg settlements are unique in Tennessee's Catholicism. No fewer than six churches were eventually built in the area, of which three fine specimens survive: Sacred Heart at Lawrenceburg, Sacred Heart at Loretto, and St. Joseph's. The Lawrenceburg church in particular is lavish with interior decoration, but all the churches exhibit the high level of craftsmanship of the German community.

In Memphis, too, there was steady growth. The new St. Patrick's Church was going up, the Christian Brothers had come to develop a school and a college for boys, the new St. Peter's rectory was near completion, and St. Mary's was thriving under the Franciscan fathers and sisters.

The biggest boom in the state, however, was in Chattanooga. Shortly after the Civil War, British capital and technological skill began to exploit the apparently excellent coal and iron resources of the nearby area. A new town, South Pittsburg, sprang up, named in the pious hope it would imitate the astonishing growth of the great Pennsylvania city. The boom had for its barker the loud and energetic voice of Adolph Ochs and his newspaper, the

Chattanooga Times. Scarcely more than a village before the war, Chattanooga now began to turn into a real city. The boom, in the end, came to little enough, especially with the discovery of better natural resources around Birmingham, and it fizzled out, with its chief orchestrator, Ochs, departing for greater glory with the *New York Times.* But the groundwork had been laid, and Chattanooga prospered, a center for tourism as well as industry.

Chattanooga Catholics were part of this new prosperity and ambitious growth. The little frame church which Father Brown had built became too small for the growing congregation, and had to be enlarged. But in the mid-1870s, the pastor, Father Patrick Ryan, ably assisted by Fathers William Walsh and later B. J. McNally, developed the institutions which were to serve the Catholics of the city until the 1930s. These included the new church, rectory, and convent for the Dominican sisters from Nashville, who sent its first foundation to Chattanooga in 1876. They established there a select school for girls, on the model of Nashville's St. Cecilia, named Notre Dame de Lourdes. This was the forerunner of the parochial and high school which have acquired such outstanding reputations through the years.

Where did Feehan get the money for all this? In good part, of course, from the pockets of the faithful. But the bishop spent far more than they could give. The diocese was still receiving yearly donations from the French Society for the Propagation of the Faith, donations which continued into the twentieth century, though getting smaller by the year. In 1876, for example, Feehan received only 5,000 francs, the smallest amount since the diocese was founded.

But the bishop had a reputation for money-raising. In his sermon on the centenary of the old Cathedral of St. Mary's in Nashville in 1947, Samuel Cardinal Stritch, himself a Tennessee native and a Nashville diocesan priest for ten years, said that Feehan collected funds from other places. And Vincent McMurry adds, in his work on Reconstruction, "Feehan sought to relieve the strain by seeking financial aid throughout the United States and in Europe, to rebuild churches and set up chapels, and he invited priests and religious to his mission territory." The details would be fascinating, but this is all that's known. In December 1869 Feehan went to Rome in company with most of the American bishops for the First Vatican Council. He did not stay the course, returning home in February of 1870. He returned to Rome for a somewhat longer stay in June of 1873. Again, no details are recorded, but there is little doubt he did some effective fund raising on both these trips. Incidentally, Feehan is said to have favored, along with most American bishops, less emphasis in the First Vatican Council on infallibility and more on such pragmatic problems as the authority of the bishops.

But, unlike other southern bishops such as Augustin Verot of Savannah, Edward Fitzgerald of Little Rock, and most emphatic of all, his patron, Archbishop Peter Kenrick, all of whom vigorously opposed defining infallibility, he made no waves that reach us through the years.

Certainly pragmatic problems were what Feehan faced in Tennessee. But he was, like the rest of the state, doing fairly well. The *Nashville Republican Banner* of July 12, 1872, said that the Roman Catholic church of Nashville had purchased about $70,000 worth of property since the end of the Civil War, and added, "That's doing remarkably well for one congregation." It was indeed, and a great tribute to the remarkable man who did so remarkably well.

More is known, and still more can be inferred, about parish life in the Feehan era. In May 1868 a two-week mission at the Nashville cathedral was held. It was conducted by Father James Hennessey, Feehan's successor as rector of the St. Louis Seminary, and a much admired preacher of the time. It was a big success. Over four thousand communions were distributed. Missions, so popular in the Catholic Church from almost the earliest days of American Catholicism, were copied from the European model. They are less popular now, partially because the four thousand communions would not today be noteworthy — few today go to Mass without receiving Holy Communion, a once or twice a year occasion for most of our grandparents. Daily Mass, even occasionally, was simply out of the question for workers who toiled a ten to twelve hour day six days a week. And in any case you had to live pretty close to the church to get to daily Mass, since most city dwellers had to walk or use the streetcars for transportation. Only in rural areas were horse-and-wagons familiar sights in the churchyard.

The social side of parish life, however, has changed much less. Then as now societies of all sorts flourished, some nationwide, but most peculiar to a parish or area. Card parties, theatricals, school "exhibitions" and picnics abounded — the 1871 Nashville *Banner* carried a notice which said, "At Weitmuller's Garden, near the Barracks, picnic festivities for the Church of the Assumption. Street cars will carry pleasure-seekers thither, and a Bohemian band will furnish the music." This was a Germantown gala, but the Irish and Italian parishes also had ethnic festivities, culminating in the feasts of the patron saints. And Midnight Mass on Christmas Eve was so popular it had, in the interests of temperance, to be abolished in favor of the Mass at dawn for practically all of the first half of this century. Just about everything connected with the parish and convent schools had a social side, from spelling bees on through Christmas and May processions to such tremendously important occasions as First Communion and Confirmation.

Perhaps the most important attraction was both social and religious. This was preaching. The liturgy was in mysterious Latin, but after the reading of the gospel everyone at Sunday Mass settled down for at least a half hour of pulpit oratory. After Mass the congregation talked about the preaching with interest and excitement in direct proportion to the preacher's talents. The ladies cherished quotations to pass along to their friends and relatives in other parishes and their Protestant neighbors, the men compared this preacher to others they had heard and to the political orators they relished. They had heard plenty. Politics was even more given to oratory than was religion. The appetite in those days for listening to oratory was enormous, and is almost incomprehensible to us, trained as we are to the informal short takes of radio and television. Most people read little and had little to read; authors thrilled the few, orators the many. No one in religion or politics could be successful without competence in public address. In schools, especially high schools and colleges, debating was, between 1865 and 1915, what sports like football became after that. Going to a liberal arts college meant above all learning to speak well.

All this was the stuff of the Feehan era. It was an era of opening new schools, of going to church more regularly, of evolving urban ways of living, of emphasis on rule and regulation and authority, yet with growing awareness of the need for compassion and charity. It was also a time when the problems of intemperance in the use of alcohol were insistent. In Tennessee, this was perhaps the central theme in political life for a generation before the Volstead Act, and nobody knows how much this was due to the puritanism of both Catholics and Protestants, and how much to human stress and need in the face of adjusting to city life. It was a time of the formation of the Catholic press, especially the magazine press. And it was a time when Catholics of various ethnic strains were trying to find out what it means to be a Catholic in the great American democracy.

This last was of paramount importance. What part was the Church to play in the Americanization of all those immigrants? That process seemed often to go counter to what the Church wanted — not just the Roman officials, but the American hierarchy as well. Take the case of the secret societies that flourished all through the latter half of the nineteenth century, and into the present. Rome was very much against Catholics belonging to such societies. Their history in Europe was associated with anti-religion — anti-clericalism, rationalism, deism: Free-masonry is the perfect example. However, Rome left the matter up to the American hierarchy, and the American bishops and archbishops went slowly. They were generally very cautious and cautioning about societies like the Knights of Pythias, the Oddfellows, and others.

Such ideas may have coursed through the mind of Feehan on a Lenten Sunday in 1877 when he mounted the cathedral pulpit to warn his parishioners of the dangers to their faith from the secret societies. Although nothing could seem to people today more innocent than the rituals of the lodges, the Church a hundred years ago saw in them attempts to be substitutes for religion. No one, of course, knows today exactly what Feehan said, but he impressed one member of his congregation, James J. McLoughlin, so strongly that he resigned from the Knights of Honor, a popular fraternity of the time, in which he had been quite active. McLoughlin was an energetic and enthusiastic organizer. Why not, he thought, start a Catholic organization, open only to Catholic men, similar to the Knights of Honor? He had no trouble interesting some of his fellow Cathedral parishioners in the project, and soon the new lodge was on its way.

These lodges, or societies, or whatever, were very important in the Americanization process. They gave their members a sense of belonging to this strange new world, the country they had dreamed of but were only now coming to experience. The newly-made citizens reinforced one another by their membership. Moreover, most of the societies had insurance features, and insurance was a new American idea, just then taking hold of the American people. But the insurance of the secret societies was something special, for along with the real money benefits there went the fellowship of their peers, the help they counted on from one another in time of trouble, the confirmation of their identity as American, for the "peers" were all sizes and conditions. McLoughlin himself was a master tailor by occupation.

Contemporary Catholics often think of the Knights of Columbus as the Church's answer to this problem, and so it was, ten years later. But there were, and are, many others, among them the Catholic Order of Foresters, and the Nashville-born society McLoughlin and his friends worked up, the Catholic Knights of America, both still going strong. The Nashville #1 branch was followed in quick succession by many others; in a dozen years the membership grew to seventeen thousand. Feehan was chaplain of the Nashville branch, and afterwards national chaplain, till he went to Chicago. His sponsorship, his recommendations to his fellow bishops, and his guidance were helpful in getting the society underway.

However, the society that apparently meant the most to Tennessee men was not the Knights but the St. Joseph Total Abstinence Society. This was organized at the Nashville cathedral in 1868, early in the Feehan episcopate, with Father M. A. Coyle as its first president, and the pledge administered by Father Jarboe. Two years later a similar chapter was organized in Memphis, under the presidency of Father Antonio Luiselli. The Nashville organization flourished. It acquired a library, and outfitted a cornet band, which was a feature of Catholic celebrations for years. It had permanent headquarters in one or more of the downtown halls in Nashville which housed dozens of such organizations. More than the St. Vincent de Paul group, more than the much older Hibernian Society, more even than the supporters of the orphanage, the Total Abstinence Society caught the imagination of Irish Catholics. Until the Knights of Columbus came along, the teetotalling sons of St. Joseph made up the most active lay society.

There is no record of a women's Catholic temperance society in Tennessee, though many existed elsewhere. The association between men's fraternal societies and the temperance movement was no accident. Forbidden the mysteries of the secular lodges by Church rule, the Catholic working man often found in the saloon his chapel of ease, his political clubhouse, his employment office, and occasionally his bank. The laborer who did not aspire to rise to a higher station was content enough with this club. Temperance was a middle-class virtue, and until the Irish Catholics, in Tennessee and elsewhere, attained middle-class status, the demon rum continued demonic.

This was more emphatically the case in Memphis and Chattanooga than in Nashville or Knoxville. Memphis especially had a proletariat of Irish Catholics in the famous "Pinch" district. Memphis also had, far more than the other cities, a large influx of blacks into the city after emancipation. Few blacks lived in their own homes in the cities before the Civil War; there was no race problem. All the cities had to face this new problem of a large black population, but Memphis had the worst case in the state of trying to educate and police both Irish and blacks. What might have happened if the yellow fever epidemics had not occurred is a fascinating speculation.

For Memphis was growing and developing faster than the other Tennessee cities. There was talk of transferring the see from Nashville to Memphis. Archbishop Spalding of Baltimore wrote to Archbishop Purcell of Cincinnati in 1868 that the deed was done. The Dominicans thought it was. Feehan wrote plaintively that he certainly would like to know, so he could plan. Nothing more than these straws in the wind have turned up, yet the subject is endlessly interesting. Would Feehan have been in favor of the shift? Memphis was much closer to Kenrick and St. Louis. Or was it all mere rumor? In 1883 the Diocese of Nashville was shifted to the Metropolitan Province of Cincinnati, where, but for West Tennessee, it belonged. But speculation remains: had the see been transferred to Memphis, with its insistent problem of the blacks, would there have been more serious missionary efforts among the blacks?

For what was happening in the Church during the second half of the nineteenth century, it is now fairly clear, was the gradual evolution of the pioneer church, with its catch-all collection of brave and adventurous missionary priests, mostly of foreign birth and education, into the basic Catholic Church of the last hundred years. This is the parish organization pattern. It, too, began in pioneering ethnicity. In most cities there were the Irish church, the German church, the Italian church, the Polish (or Serbian or Hungarian or Lithuanian or whatever), often within a few city blocks of one another, with their liturgies and, often, schools conducted in foreign tongues, clinging to the old countries in religion and social customs while uneasily shifting into the American culture, itself in the making. The Jews and the German Lutherans were, among others, going through the same strange and wonderful process. It is the real story of the United States of America, by no means the melting pot it was often caricatured as, but pluralism, built on the basic principle of freedom, the free man creating his own destiny, but not, as in the classic American representation, alone. This is simply impossible for most. Even the frontiersmen were clubbable when they met at the trading centers. But most men wanted something immeasurably better than the primitive desires of the half-wild frontiersmen. They wanted the society of their own kind, along with the upward social and financial mobility they so eagerly sought. To an incredible extent, they got these things in the United States, with all the faults and troubles and cross-purposes of daily life. And to the same incredible extent the Catholic Church grew and prospered in its ideal: first the school, then the church: religion and education, one and inseparable.

At its best, this was a wonderfully satisfactory, useful and happy way of life. Other denominations shared it; the Methodists, Baptists and Presbyterians all had similar patterns of integrating church and home, minus, of course, the schools. It is a pity that these looked upon one another with something less than fraternal Christian benevolence. The Catholics, especially, were suspect as being un-American. But the fact is that Catholic leadership of the kind that Feehan provided in Nashville was more

American in spirit and aim than that of many Protestant denominations. Whatever the ideal of theologians, practically all American Catholic leaders, both lay and clerical, abhorred the union of church and state, and believed that the American system was the way the Catholic Church of the future should go in much, if not most, of the rest of the world, but certainly in the United States of America. Not all American Catholics were united in this view. The more recent immigrants were often as suspicious of the Americanism of the older Irish-descended bishops as they were of the intentions of the Protestant ascendency in politics.

Feehan was not a reflective man, to judge from the few records of his life and work. But what he did shows him very strongly of this basic persuasion. He loved Ireland, the land of his birth, and he loved the Church. But he was not an Italian nor was he an Irishman. He was an American.

11

Education and Clerical Growth in the Feehan Era

It frequently startles American Catholics to discover there is nothing comparable to their parochial schools anywhere else in the Catholic world. True, there are Catholic schools everywhere, but, compared to the American scene, foreign Catholic grade and high schools are few, far between, and elitist. Above all, they are not *parochial,* not usually attached to and supported by a parish, and supervised by a bishop and his staff.

The bishops of the United States made this commitment to education almost from the beginning. In 1829, eight years before Nashville became a diocese, the First Provincial Council met at Baltimore, and announced that the assembled American bishops judged it ''absolutely necessary'' that schools should be established in which the young ''may be taught the principles of faith and morality, while being instructed in letters''. But this was an ideal. The bishops knew well that their hope for education was something to plan for and work for, not easy of realization. Then as now, the bishops and many other priests and religious hoped for state aid to Catholic education, but generally speaking this never materialized. In New York State, the zealous and combative Bishop Hughes gave up on it by 1842. Archbishop Ireland proposed a complex plan for education-cum-religion in the 1890s, but this met with strong opposition from Catholics and non-Catholics alike, and never had a chance. In some rural areas, where the population was almost entirely Catholic, the Catholic parochial schools were the public schools until well into this century, but these local arrangements have been shot down by increasingly rigorous Supreme Court decisions. The United States plainly does not wish to follow the common European pattern of some state support for church schools, however much some of their supporters may yearn for it. Despite a continuous history of setbacks, the yearning continues.

The Catholic bishops of the United States never wavered in their ideal of every Catholic child in a Catholic elementary school, however costly and impractical as this frequently was. The Third Plenary Council of Baltimore in 1884 shifted, as Philip Gleason writes, "from the language of exhortation to that of command" in backing Catholic education. Indeed, Rome had to act as a brake on this command, for Catholic schooling could never be made a law universal, whatever some United States bishops may have thought and hoped.

By this time Nashville's Bishop Feehan was Archbishop of Chicago and among the leaders in the hierarchy in promoting Catholic schooling. He was no less so in Nashville. Here is a letter he wrote to the French Society for the Propagation of the Faith shortly after his arrival in Nashville.

4th December 1865

Dear Sir,

[this was Monsieur Certes, the Secretary of the Society, in Paris]

I beg leave to inform you that having been appointed and consecrated Bishop of Nashville, Tennessee, I arrived here toward the end of last month. I have learned that my predecessors, and also the Very Reverend Father Kelly, lately administrator, have received through you annually certain sums of money from the "Society for the Propagation of the Faith". May I ask, through you, that this favor be continued to me. I find here much distress and desolation caused by the late war, and a great want of priests and churches and schools. The Catholic population is rapidly increasing in the state; where a few years ago there were hundreds, now there are thousands. I have but six secular priests, while I would need at least twenty. Churches are required in a great many places, and schools everywhere. In this city, for example, there are two churches, one for the Germans, and one, the Cathedral, not very large, for at least ten thousand English-speaking Catholics. There is no school for the children.

Besides, the people of this country are now most favorably disposed towards the Catholic Church, and if there were a sufficient number of priests and churches, great good could be effected amongst them.

Without schools for the children, the young generation cannot be saved to religion.

> To meet so many demands, I find very little means here. I can rely on the people to some extent, they will, I think, cheerfully do what they can, but though numerous they are nearly all poor, the working classes.

Bishop Feehan ended with the hope that the Society will continue its help to the Diocese of Nashville, although surely he overestimated the Catholic population. The Society did help in steady fashion. Here are the figures:

1860	16,000 francs	1866	20,000	1871	10,000
1861	12,000	1867	20,000	1872	10,000
1862	15,000	1868	16,000	1873	8,000
1863	15,000	1869	16,000	1874	6,000
1864	15,000	1870	Franco-Prussian War	1875	6,000
1865	20,000			1876	5,000

Since Bishop Whelan estimated his entire expenses for missions for 1862 at 24,000 francs, and Feehan 46,000 for 1872, it will be seen the Society was quite a help. The franc of those days fluctuated, of course, but was around five to the dollar, and the purchasing power of the dollar of 1870 was roughly twenty times what it is today. In addition to the support from the French Society of the Propagation of the Faith, there was support as well from the Austrian Leopoldine Society.

The decline reflected in the table of support to the United States missions shows, of course, the growing abilities of the United States Catholics to take care of themselves, as well as the growing demands of missions elsewhere, notably in the Far East, where French missionaries were very active.

There are no records of how the money from abroad was spent. What is significant is that Feehan urged the claims of education to a European society which had no parochial schools. A second letter, written in 1874, cited the many conversions his priests, now numbering thirty, were making. They had twenty-seven churches, and these formed centers around which the bishop believed that congregations would gradually grow. (In this belief, and its confirmation by history, the bishops have not changed at all: Bishop James Niedergeses said the same thing in 1985 about certain new churches he was starting in rural areas of the Diocese of Nashville.)

But the main burden of this 1874 progress report concerned the schools. Feehan boasted of the new Christian Brothers College in Memphis, the two academies for young women conducted by the Dominicans there, and various other girls' academies and parochial schools taught by the Sisters of St. Joseph, the Sisters of Mercy, and the Sisters of the Most Precious Blood. In rural areas too small for religious orders, schools were taught, he said, by "good lay persons". The letter spoke of educating orphans, and laid out prospective expenses for education for 1874 of 24,000 francs. The bishop stated he had raised 9,000 from friends in various places, plus the 8,000 from the Society, leaving him a deficit of 7,000 francs, which he would try to pay by the first of 1875, since he anticipated expenses for the new year would be about the same. The future of religion, he maintained, depended mainly on the Catholic schools. It was a theme to which he returned again and again, very likely the main theme of his twenty-seven years as a bishop.

Something for the Boys

One of the peculiar aspects of the history of education in the Diocese of Nashville is the availability of secondary education for women rather than men. This was most likely sheer accident; there were religious orders of women willing to undertake schools for adolescent girls, but only the Christian Brothers of Memphis were found to do similar work for boys. Moreover, there was a history of the cultivation of the feminine graces through women's schools in the South; the Ursuline Convent in New Orleans is the second oldest, after Georgetown, in the country. However, Kentucky Catholicism set out to educate both sexes. It is rather puzzling that the see city of Nashville had no adequate Catholic high school for boys until the mid-1920's. It was not for lack of effort: half a dozen religious communities of men were approached through the years, the Xaverian Brothers, the Jesuits, the Brothers of Holy Cross, the Brothers of Mary among them. All evinced some interest, but none ever came to Nashville.

The Brothers of the Christian Schools came to Memphis, but this through one of those strange accidents that shape history more than do the wills of determined men and women, however strong. The accident was the great Chicago fire of 1871. The

Christian Brothers had been wooed by Memphis Catholics as far back as 1864, and Bishop Feehan enthusiastically supported the suit when he came to Tennessee. But that dreadful curse of the lower South, the yellow fever, striking New Orleans, carried off eleven of the brothers there and in Galveston, and the Memphis project had to be postponed.

But Memphis persisted, and tried to entice the brothers by buying the abandoned Memphis Female College on Adams Street as a site for the brothers' school. This boomeranged to some extent, for the Brothers, who would have to pay most of the $35,000 price tag, thought the deal too costly. But then, on October 4 came the fire that destroyed a great part of the city of Chicago. Like so many disasters, this one had some good effects — in fact, it may be said to have made possible the city's greatness. Out of the wilderness of cheap wood with which the early city had been built there emerged the new fire-resistant American city of steel and brick; out of formlessness there came modern architecture. And Chicago's misfortune became Memphis's good fortune. The Chicago brothers' school was destroyed in the fire, freeing three brothers to come to Memphis. They opened their school on November 19, 1871, in the former Female College building, with helpful financing from many quarters.

But it was their leader who made the difference, and he came not from Chicago, but directly from an overly-ambitious attempt at establishing a college in Pass Christian, Mississippi. A native of Pennsylvania, Brother Maurelian Sheel had spent the war years in and around New Orleans, where his sterling leadership qualities were observed. Sent as superior of the Memphis establishment, Maurelian never looked back. He led the college and its companion high school through all sorts of early financial and other troubles, and became a leading figure in civic, diocesan, and even national affairs. He chaired Catholic exhibitions at the great New Orleans Exhibition of 1885, the Chicago World's Fair in 1893, and the Tennessee Centennial Exhibition in Nashville in 1897. He was instrumental in persuading the City of Memphis and the Federal Government to set up an effective system of quarantine against yellow fever and other epidemics. He was, in short, a great man, and his spirit, intelligence, and vision made the Christian Brothers' Memphis enterprises not merely successful, but a source of Catholic life commanding and winning the respect of the entire area.

The success of the Christian Brothers in Memphis only underscores the lack of such an institution in Nashville. There was some schooling for older boys, which most likely took place in the basement of the Cathedral. "The English and Classical School for Boys, John D. Smith, Principal", is listed in the *Catholic Almanacs* for both 1869 and 1870. In 1871 a Mr. Leonard had replaced Mr. Smith as principal, and he continued until 1874. There is no listing for the next three years, but Smiths reappear in 1878 and 1879, this time with the initials P.M. and P.A. The Smiths and Leonard are listed in the Nashville city directories of the 1870s.

It seems fairly clear that this boys' high school did not get enough support to make it a success. Probably Feehan's interest and help kept it going as long as it did. Its career shows how useful to such schools a religious community is, especially in the early years. There are no records or relics of the Smith school. It would be interesting to know who some of the students were and what they studied — the name "English and Classical" tells us little more than the natural sciences were not stressed. After Feehan departed for Chicago, the school disappeared from the directories, and Nashville Catholic boys who went beyond elementary school attended the public high school, or went, as many of the more affluent did, to Catholic boarding schools in Kentucky, Ohio, Kansas, Washington, D.C., and elsewhere.

Something More for the Girls

No such mystery attends the coming of the Mercy Sisters to the diocese. Indeed, there is little mystery about that splendid community itself. If ever there was a community of religious suited to the times of its foundation, this was it. The Mercies were an Irish order, founded by a wealthy Dubliner in 1831, as if designed by Providence for the great diaspora of the Irish into the New World. The founder, Mother Catherine McAuley (1778-1841), worked hand in glove with the Archbishop of Dublin, which was just what the bishops of the New World wanted. It will be remembered that the first community of religious women to come to Nashville left in disagreement with Bishop Miles, but the new Mercy sisters wanted from the beginning to work closely with the bishops.

One of the strongest needs for the Diocese of Nashville that Bishop Feehan experienced upon his arrival was for a religious community of women associated with his cathedral. Attracted to the Sisters of Mercy, he visited their second United States foundation in Providence, Rhode Island, in the first summer of his episcopate, 1866, and applied for a Mercy foundation in Nashville. That fall six sisters came, escorted by Father Martin Walsh, the pastor of the cathedral. With them came the rich presence of the Sisters of Mercy in Tennessee. ''Associated with his Cathedral'' meant, for the moment to Patrick Feehan, right across the street, and it was there, in the beautiful old home designed for Hugh Kirkman by William Strickland, that the Mercies settled in.

Their school was an instant success, but into the limited quarters of the Kirkman home were jammed the select day students, the working-girl night students, and the nuns, augmented now by eight new postulants, including the bishop's sister, Alice Feehan. This necessitated a new school building, the famous St. Mary's Parochial School on Vine Street, built, said a contemporary account, ''in the latest style of architecture'', at a cost of $47,000. It opened in the fall of 1867. Oldsters around Nashville can still remember the way it looked, for, worn by many different uses, it was not razed till the 1930s. After it ceased to be used for classes, it was turned into a gymnasium, and used by the Father Ryan High School in the 1920s until Ryan's own gym was completed. The Mercy Sisters may be better remembered through this school than any other of the great works of charity and education they undertook. A large number of Nashville Catholics went to school there and loved it, and Catholic life took on a new and much needed social dimension through the school. The sisters' domestic life was transformed, too, when the bishop bought the former Campbell-Brown home, across Cedar Street from the Capitol, for their residence. They moved there in 1868 and there the girls' select school, St. Bernard's Academy, was born.

More schooling than this was described in the *Catholic Almanac* of 1867. This annual volume, the forerunner of the present Official Catholic Directory, printed a statistical summary of each diocese in the country, furnished, generally, by the diocese itself. Nothing could more graphically illustrate the tie-in of Catholic beginnings and Catholic growth with the development of the railroads than the organization of the 1867 report of the Diocese of Nashville. It is broken down by railroads, as follows:

Nashville and Northwestern Railroad:
Newsom Station, with school
Pegram Station, with school
Sneedville Station, with school
Gillens Station, with school
McEwen, with school

Tennessee and Alabama Railroad:
Brentwood, (no notice of a school)
Franklin, "Church being erected"
Thompson Station
Carter's Creek, Maury County
Columbia, Church being erected

Nashville and Chattanooga Railroad:
Antioch
Smyrna
Murphreesboro (sic), with school
Tracy City
Winchester

Here the organization by railroad ceases, and the account is rounded off thus:

Chattanooga, no priest, with school
Knoxville, Rev. Abram J. Ryan, school
Memphis, schools at Sts. Peter and Paul, St. Mary and St. Patrick

The "school" attached to the shanty towns was probably no more than a young girl who attempted to teach the younger ones their letters and figures in one of the shanties. These shantytowns were familiar sights along the railroads of Tennessee; Nashvillians will remember how long the ones at Vaughn's Gap persisted. A missionary priest visited these settlements whenever possible, and many of the railroad workers stayed on, moving to nearby cities and towns rather than continue their nomadic existence with the railroads.

Following is a list of institutions begun in Feehan's time.

Bishop Feehan's Administration, 1865-1880

New Institutions

Nashville: St. Bernard's Academy, 1866
St. Mary's Parochial School, 1867
Memphis: Christian Brothers College, 1871
Good Shepherd Convent, 1875
Chattanooga: Notre Dame de Lourdes Academy, 1876
Lawrence County: Convent, Schools and Orphanage, 1873
Nashville: Calvary Cemetery, 1868
Memphis: Calvary Cemetery, 1866

Religious Orders Introduced

Sisters of Mercy, Nashville, 1866
Good Shepherd Sisters, Memphis, 1875
Sisters of Charity of Nazareth, Memphis, 1871; Clarksville, 1876
Precious Blood Sisters, Lawrence County, 1873
Sisters of St. Joseph, Memphis, 1870
Christian Brothers, Memphis, 1871
Precious Blood Fathers, Lawrence County, 1872
Franciscan Fathers, Memphis, 1870

New Churches Built

Memphis, St. Patrick, St. Brigid, St. Joseph
Columbia, St. Dominic
Winchester, St. Martin
State Line, St. Patrick
Greeneville, St. Patrick
Jackson, St. Mary
Grand Junction, St. Catherine
Brownsville, St. Rose
Gallatin, St. Peter
Pulaski, St. Augustine
Franklin, St. Philip
Humboldt, St. Louis
McEwen, St. Patrick
Clarksville, Immaculate Conception
Lawrenceburg, Sacred Heart
Loretto, Sacred Heart
St. Joseph, St. Joseph
St. Mary, St. Mary
New Einsiedeln, St. Henry
Holy Trinity, Holy Trinity
Edgefield Junction, St. Patrick
Nashville, St. Columba

New Parochial School Buildings
Nashville, St. Mary's, Assumption
Girls' Academy Building
Memphis, St. Agnes

This list foreshadows Feehan's creation of an unbelievable 140 parishes during his twenty-two years in Chicago. Considering the resources, the Nashville achievement is almost as impressive. Along with the new churches and institutions came a new look in the clergy. The Dominican presence diminished. It is odd that after a great initial spurt of them in north central Kentucky, vocations to the Dominicans ebbed away. The women's convents prospered, but the priests stayed at hold until they established centers in New York and Chicago as their apostolate shifted northward. They continued to man St. Peter's Church in Memphis, as they still do, and such Tennessee stalwarts as Fathers Joseph Kelly and Joseph Jarboe lasted into Feehan's episcopate. It is a pity they left so few records. The little Jarboe left is fascinating. Orengo's memoirs, contrasting the Tennessee missions with his native Liguria in Italy, would have made an important contribution to history, but he wrote nothing of the sort.

The new diocesan clergy was developing nicely, however. In the 1870s Feehan ordained five for the diocese, two of whom became legends, Father Timothy C. Abbott and Father Patrick Gleeson. A third, Francis Marron, contracted a debilitating illness not long after his ordination, and little beyond the bare fact of his ordination is known about Father J. A. Coughlin. The promising Patrick Ryan, ordained by the bishop in Nashville in 1869, died of the yellow fever in Chattanooga, being given the last rites of the Church by his younger brother, Father Michael Ryan, who was visiting in Chattanooga.

Father Patrick Ryan's lively and useful career, brief as it was, suggests the general pattern of Patrick Feehan's recruitment of priests. Ryan was born in Ireland, but came with his parents to the United States as a child. The family lived in Cape Girardeau, Missouri, down river from St. Louis. Ireland, and the American Irish, were the twin pillars of the Feehan establishment. Father Richard Scannell, later a bishop, was ordained in Ireland, as were John Veale and Edward Doyle, the latter a yellow fever victim. Father Michael Meagher, a friend of Feehan's from his seminary days in Ireland, and a sometime Jesuit, did yeoman work for his bishop friend and was also felled by the yellow fever, as were John Fahey and John Francis Walsh, both ordained in Ireland for Nashville. Of somewhat later vintage were B. J. McNally and John Gavin.

Shades of Bishop Miles, who would have gone into orbit at the very thought of such a train of good priests. And mark the fulfillment of his prophecy: "with some good zealous priests much good can be done in Tennessee", Miles had written. Feehan was unmistakably about his Father's business. Nor did all his priests come from Ireland. Two splendid Italian priests who served long and well in the diocese came to him, Anthony Luiselli and Eugene Gazzo. Two more priests of Italian descent served with distinction for briefer periods, Anthony Vaghi and John Bertuzzi.

The coming of the Fathers and Sisters of the Precious Blood to Lawrence County and to Nashville, to take care of the German-speaking Catholics in those places, takes the scene sharply away from Ireland. St. Mary's Memphis had for some years been looked after by German Franciscans from Illinois. When they said they couldn't handle the new German settlements in Lawrence County, Feehan turned to the German Catholic settlements in southern Ohio, where the Precious Blood Fathers, a relatively new community, whose headquarters were, and are still, in Carthagena, Ohio, to undertake the charge. It was a happy thought. These splendid religious moved into Germantown in north Nashville as well, and for twenty-five years brought stability to both these parts of the diocese. The great movement toward Americanization had not yet begun, and these first and second generation immigrants wanted as much of the liturgy as they could get in their native tongues. They had been looked after for a while by Father Innocent Bergrath, a native German who spent most of the 1860s in East Tennessee, dividing his time between Chattanooga and Knoxville. In Knoxville he was succeeded by his good friend Abram J. Ryan, and, like Ryan, ended up on the Gulf of Mexico. Other departures of the early Feehan years included Frank O'-Brien, P. F. Coyle, James Malloy, J. W. Gavin, and the evanescent Wentworth Repis, who changed his name to Revis. There are not enough records on any of these priests to even guess why they left, or indeed why they came in the first place. Even more shadowy are a few other priests whose names simply turn up now and then on baptismal registers. Such were the times.

All twenty-one priests who died in the yellow fever epidemics of Memphis in the 1870s are buried around this monument to them in Calvary Cemetery. *Diocese of Memphis photo.*

12

The Yellow Fever in Memphis

The nineteenth century abounded in epidemics, troublesome diseases of all kinds so contagious they spread like forest fires over entire cities and sometimes over their surrounding regions. Generally speaking, plagues were urban, not rural, and can be understood only as the tragic concomitant of city life. Plague abatement waited on science, to be sure, but much more on such simple matters as a good water supply, good drainage, good sewers, vermin control, and all the other aspects of good management cities gradually had to learn throughout the century.

Situation had more than a little to do with the plagues. Memphis was built on the Chickasaw bluffs, but the surrounding countryside is swampy and inundated with Nile-like regularity by the Mississippi River floods. All through the nineteenth century it was notoriously unhealthy, challenged for this unfortunate lack of distinction only by New Orleans, whose situation was even worse. And, indeed, Memphis owed something of its unhealthiness to New Orleans, for from that port came upriver to Memphis diseases brought by ships from foreign lands in addition to the rampant native ailments.

In the 1870s, sanitary conditions in Memphis were deplorable. The water supply was full of contamination, milk went uninspected, but above all, filth and detritus of all kinds were allowed to accumulate in the streets and alleys. Garbage and refuse littered front and back yards, and dead animals were a serious problem — contemporary environmentalists fretting about automobile exhaust should contemplate for a moment the nineteenth century difficulties presented by the horses that were the only means of intra-city transportation. Every American city of any size had trouble cleaning up after horses and disposing of dead ones. But Memphis was worse than most; its own newspapers pointed out in the 1870s that experienced travelers usually acclaimed it the dirtiest city in the country.

Memphis had known plagues before the devastating series of epidemics of yellow fever in the 1870s; scarcely a year went by without cholera or smallpox taking their tolls of fear and death. But these were slight compared to the horrors of the decade of the 70s. In 1873, the yellow fever took 2,000 lives; in 1878, 5,150; in 1879, 600. These came in a population which fluctuated violently because of the disease, but around 40,000 Memphians in 1870 had slipped, in a decade of general growth, to 30,000 — when, in the normal expectations, it should have increased ten or fifteen thousand.

What is yellow fever, or yellow jack, its nickname? Most people have never heard of it, yet it still pops up now and then in the tropics where it came from. Its germ is violent and peculiar. The victims turn yellow in most cases. Also, in most cases, it is accompanied by violent digestive disturbance, often accompanied by vomiting black bile. The course of the disease is swift. It begins with chills, along with severe pains in the head and back. Then, in a few hours, or four or five days at the most, comes the crisis, usually with the tell-tale vomiting — that's how the disease was identified. Then death — the mortality rate was usually around 50 percent — or slow recovery.

Nobody then knew anything much about the disease. Many witnesses thought that the doctors' treatments usually made it worse, and the best thing to do was to leave the sad victims alone, feeding them as little as possible. In fact the best defense against the disease was the one taken in Memphis, with disastrous results for the city: flight. To get away, to seek the highlands, to find a refuge where no one had seen the dread yellow skin, this possessed the minds and hearts of the Memphians who could afford flight. The most efficient recovery for those who couldn't flee were the camps around fifteen miles east of Memphis, organized by relief organizations.

The reason why flight was the only effective defense was not known until 1900, when Major Walter Reed, a doctor in the United States Army Medical Corps, demonstrated that the fever was carried by the bite of the female of the species of mosquito known as *aedes aegypti*. As Reed proved during the building of the

Panama Canal, which but for him could never have been accomplished, get rid of the mosquito and you get rid of the yellow fever. Since mosquitoes range only a few hundred yards from their breeding places, it's easy to see why Memphis, with its surrounding swamps and unsanitary conditions, encouraged their breeding, and why firm land and good sanitation discouraged it. Of course, today the disease might be checked by low-flying aircraft spraying the swamps and tank-wagons doing the same in the cities. But even so, scientists are still carrying on the war against malaria, spread exactly in the same way by the female hump-backed mosquito, the *aedes anopheles*.

Many of the Memphians who fled the disease returned when the plagues subsided, but many did not, and they, of course, the brightest and best-off. The Irish Catholics were the worst off, and they couldn't afford to leave town. They were by far the most numerous victims of the yellow jack in 1873 — for some unknown reason, it did not get much foothold among the blacks until 1878. Its way with the Irish was calamitous. The fever began with them. Early in August 1873, a steamer from New Orleans brought it to Happy Hollow, a community under the bluffs inhabited entirely by the Irish. From there it spread to Pinch, also largely Irish. When the word of the fever got around, the City of Memphis dropped from a population of 40,000 to one of only 15,000 in a month, a nigh-incredible exodus. Of these 15,000, 5,000 caught the fever. Two thousand of them died, at least half of them Irish Catholics.

It is understandable that many, perhaps most, of the Protestant clergy fled the city with their congregations, although they were castigated by the local newspapers for doing so. But it is hard to see why the clergy should have stayed when their congregations had gone. Still, their behavior, however justifiable, cannot help being seen in sharp contrast with the Catholic clergy and the sisters who ran the schools and the orphanage. These heroic souls remained at their posts, nursing the fever victims, bringing them the last rites of the Church, dispensing the help that the departed Memphians, as well as other cities and the United States governmental agencies generously gave, and being the bright light of witness to the gospel that all Christians are supposed to be. Not only that, but priests from other parts of the diocese came to take the places of the fallen ones, and many more volunteered. And considering all this, perhaps the most heroic of all was Bishop Feehan, who could have ordered most of the priests elsewhere, and besought the sisters to return to their mother houses. From his correspondence it is clear that he tried to encourage the religious not to volunteer recklessly, but that he applauded and assisted those whose duty kept them at their posts. It must have been a difficult decision, as it was a heart-rending task, to orchestrate a tragedy so hopeless and so desolate.

When the plague of 1873 broke out, the pioneer Catholic churches of Memphis, four in all, were in flourishing condition. The oldest, St. Peter's, had been Dominican since 1846. It had a staff of four. Father Joseph A. Kelly, the former Administrator of the diocese, was the pastor. He was assisted by brother Dominican priests, J. R. Daily, B. V. Cary, and D. A. O'Brien, all around forty years of age, all to die of the fever. Another Dominican priest, J. D. Sheehy, died a few days after he was sent to help out after the assistants' deaths. What a pastoral mission! The saintly Father Kelly also caught the fever, but recovered and lived through the second and more horrible plague and on until his death in 1885.

German St. Mary's was staffed by Father Lucius Buckholst as pastor and Father Aloysius Wiewer as assistant. Wiewer became one of the authentic heroes of the plagues. He contracted the fever himself in 1873, but recovered, and devoted his thin frame and superhuman humility to the assistance of the stricken. The only listed victim, however, of the plague from St. Mary's in 1873 was Father Leo Rinklake.

The other churches fared better. St. Patrick's had the vicar general, Martin Riordan, as its pastor, and Patrick McNamara and Anthony Luiselli as assistants. All performed prodigies of charity, but all escaped the disease in 1873. The pastor of St. Brigid's was the charming and beloved friend and associate of Riordan, Father Martin Walsh, and his assistant was the man who later wrote the most nearly complete history of the plagues, Father D. A. Quinn, both heroes of the noblest charity. Never did an event call forth the best in the priesthood as these dreadful plagues.

No less heroic were the sisters. In 1873 there were five religious orders of Catholic women in Memphis: the Dominicans in charge of St. Agnes' Academy, St. Peter's School, and the Orphanage; the Franciscans, in charge of St. Joseph's Hospital and St. Mary's School; the Sisters of St. Joseph, who also conducted an academy for young women as well as a grade school; the Sisters of the Good Shepherd, who conducted a school for unfortunate girls; and the Sisters of Charity of Nazareth, Kentucky, who conducted grade schools. It is impossible to estimate how many sisters in all there were in Memphis during the 1870s; but fifty are said to have died of the plague. Twenty-one priests died, a well-nigh incredible number, considering there were only twenty-five in all in 1880. The priests newly incardinated into the diocese in the 1870s just about equalled those who died of the fever.

After the plague of 1873 many Memphians who had fled it seeped back into the city. But many did not, and the place was never the same. All the indices of growth and prosperity fell, and the bright promise Memphis had given in 1869 and 1870 as a rival to St. Louis and Chicago faded forever. But the ill-fated city had more horrors to suffer. In the July of 1878 the yellow jack struck again. Another mad exodus from the city took place. It is estimated that 25,000 left town, by rail, water, on foot, in wagons, any way they could. Another 5,000 took refuge in the camps on the high ground east of the city. These camps were set up by various relief organizations.

One of the best known was the Catholic camp named after Father Theobald Mathew, the Irish priest who was the apostle of the temperance movement among the Irish, in the mother country, in Great Britain, and in the United States. This camp was organized by Father William Walsh, who had watched his predecessor at St. Brigid's Church die of the fever. This fixed his determination to prevent more deaths if he could, and he gathered all he could from his and the other Memphis parishes and established the camp. Not a single life was lost at it during the three months of its life, and many a tale is told of its charity and spirituality.

Memphis had shrunk to a population of 19,000, 14,000 of whom were blacks, no longer immune to the yellow fever. Most of the rest were Irish. Their condition was like that of the plague-ridden towns of Europe in the fourteenth century, forlorn, terror-stricken, living with death as one normally does with breath.

"Deaths to date 2250", read a telegram from the excellent Central Relief Committee to its New York supporters on September 20, 1878, "Number now sick about 3,000; average deaths, 60% of the sick. We are feeding some 10,000 persons, sick and destitute . . . 15 volunteer physicians have died, 20 others are sick, and a great many nurses have died." The Central Relief Committee, the Howard Association, and the Catholic Church carried most of the enormous and horrible burden of care. The plague pursued its terrible course till the frost killed the larvae of the mosquitoes in the middle of October. Yellow fever is not contagious, person to person.

Sixteen priests and brothers and around thirty nuns died during the '78 plague. Five of the sixteen priests were Dominicans, Fathers J. A. Bokel, aged 29; J. R. McGarvey, aged 33; their relief, P. J. Scanlon, aged 30; D. E. Reville, aged 39; and V. B. Vantroostenberg, aged 35. The Franciscans included Father Maternus Mallman and Brothers Wendelin Kummer, Erasmus Hesse, and Amandus Yung, plus Father Chrysostom Beineke in 1879.

The remainder were secular priests of the diocese. The most prominent of these was the vicar general, Father Martin Riordan, a man of outstanding ability and charity, who had accompanied Bishop Feehan from St. Louis. When the plague re-appeared in 1878, he was in the east recuperating from an illness, but insisted on returning to Memphis when he heard the news. Soon he himself became a victim, along with his assistant, Patrick McNamara. Father Quinn of St. Brigid's survived, but his pastor, Martin Walsh, died in September. Michael Meagher, who built the church in Edgefield in Nashville, was a cousin of Walsh, and died within hours of him after doing all he could as a volunteer visitor. Edward Doyle succeeded Riordan as vicar general, perhaps intended by Bishop Feehan to establish himself at Camp Father Mathew, as Father Willliam Walsh urged him to do. But Doyle would have no part of that, and went boldly into the jaws of stricken Memphis. He survived the '78 plague, but died in its whiplash in 1879. Within two days, his assistant, John Fahey, was dead as well. The final priest victim, John J. Mooney, had been transferred to Nashville before the return of the epidemic, but the scarcity of priests was so acute Feehan felt obliged to order him back to Memphis. He returned with a presentiment of his death, which occurred almost at once upon his return. All the priests who died of the yellow fever are buried around the priests' monument in Calvary Cemetery in Memphis.

The sisters' deaths are less well documented, so much so that the records must be questioned. D. A. Quinn, one of the authentic heroes among the priests who served during the epidemics, is the authority for saying fifty sisters perished in the plagues. His book, *Heroes and Heroines of Memphis*, is praised by the other historians of the plagues, and hence his estimate of the number of sisters who died must be taken seriously. Franciscan Father Leo Kalmer says in his book, *Stronger than Death*, that he has been able to identify twenty-eight of the sisters who perished. Writing in 1957, Monsignor Flanigen, the respected historian of the diocese, gives the following account, based on a close study of the previous histories and some material that came to light subsequently.

> The Dominican Sisters of St. Agnes, who had been in Memphis since 1850, conducted two academies (St. Agnes' and LaSalette) and one parish school (St. Peter's) and one orphanage. They nursed the sick in all three epidemics. Three of these sisters died in 1873; eight died in 1878, and two in 1879.
>
> The Sisters of St. Francis of Mary Immaculate of Joliet, Ill., had six nuns teaching in St. Mary's and St. Bridget's Schools when the fever broke out. Two of these sisters died and the four who survived were recalled after the plague of 1879.
>
> The Sisters of St. Mary of the Third Order of St. Francis sent eight nuns to Memphis in 1878. Four of them died and the other four returned to St. Louis after the plague was over.
>
> The Sisters of St. Francis, Daughters of the Sacred Heart of Jesus and Mary, in 1878 sent four nuns to Memphis. They nursed the sick, were attacked by the fever, recovered, and returned to the mother house at St. Louis.
>
> The Dominican Sisters of St. Cecilia, Nashville, sent two of their community to Memphis during the epidemics, but no records exist of their work there.
>
> The Sisters of Charity, Emmitsburg, according to some historians, sent sisters to Memphis during the epidemics, but no records exist of their work there.
>
> The Good Shepherd Nuns established their convent in Memphis in 1875. One nun (Mother Alphonsa?) died in 1878.

Within two days (Sept. 4-6, 1878) the St. Agnes community lost four sisters. Sister Rose died Sept. 4; Sister Josepha, Sept. 5; and Sister Dolores and Sister Alphonsa, Sept. 6. The latter two died within 15 minutes of each other. Three funerals were held that afternoon.

Four Franciscan Sisters of St. Mary who arrived in Memphis August 31 were all dead by September 12. Four others survived.

Sister Irene of the Sisters of St. Joseph took the fever shortly after she arrived in Memphis. She sank into a coma, and both the doctors and priests thought that she was dead and she was almost buried alive! She recovered and lived until 1917. The Sisters of St. Joseph went through all three plagues without suffering a casualty.

Of Sister Antoinette Father Quinn writes as follows: "Men of every persuasion regarded her as a saint. She consoled broken-hearted widows; fed and sheltered abandoned orphans; she not only sat with the sick and dying but she saw they were decently shrouded and buried. She saw more yellow fever victims that any other person."

It is a pity that the names of all these martyr-nuns have not come down to us, but their names are written in the book of life. Strangely enough, Keating, in his list of yellow fever victims, lists only two nuns. The monument to the religious in Calvary Cemetery has inscribed on it the names of seven sisters and three brothers. Father Kalmer gives the names of 22 nuns who died. The *History of St. Agnes'* says that at least 20 Dominican Sisters there passed away in the yellow fever epidemics, but it gives the names of only 13. Father Quinn names 15 sisters who were victims of the plague and says there were "some 35 others".

The following is a list of the sisters who died of the yellow fever in Memphis whose names have been preserved. Obviously it is incomplete, and possibly as many more sisters died whose names have not been recorded. It contains the names of two nuns who did not die during the epidemic but did die of yellow fever (Sister Agnes Ray in 1867 and Sister Mary of Nazareth in 1872). Five died in the epidemic of 1873, 13 died in 1878, and two in 1879. Fourteen were Dominican Sisters, four were Franciscans of Joliet, one was a Good Shepherd Nun, and one a Josephine Sister.

SISTERS WHO DIED OF YELLOW FEVER IN MEMPHIS

Dominican Sisters of St. Agnes:

Sister Agnes Ray, October 30, 1867.
Sister M. Joseph McKernan, October 3, 1873 (on loan from St. Cecilia, Nashville).

Sister Martha Quarry, October 13, 1873.
Sister Magdalen McKernan, October 14, 1873.
Sister Veronica Gloss, aged 19, August 28, 1878.
Sister Bernadine Dalton, aged 40, September 1, 1878.
Sister Rose Callahan, aged 30, September 4, 1878.
Sister Josepha McCary, aged 44, September 5, 1878.
Sister Dolores Gloss, aged 24, September 6, 1878.
Sister Alphonsa Yakel, aged 34, September 6, 1878.
Sister Catherine Kintz, September 1878.
Sister Laurentia Yakel, October 14, 1878.
Sister Imelda Spangler, September 5, 1879.
Sister Domeni Fitzpatrick, September 6, 1879.

Sisters of St. Mary, Third Order of St. Francis (St. Louis)

Sister Wilhelmina Brinker, aged 30, September 10, 1878.
Sister Stanislaus Dickman, aged 21, September 11, 1878.
Sister Vincentia Hickey, aged 22, September 11, 1878.
Sister Gertrude Hentscher, aged 28, September 12, 1878.

Sisters of St. Francis of Mary Immaculate (Joliet)

Sister Gabriel Butzen, September 30, 1873.
Sister Bonaventura Erdmann, September 29, 1873.

Good Shepherd Nuns (St. Louis)

Mother Alphonsa, aged 34, September 1878.

Sisters of St. Joseph (St. Louis)

Sister Mary of Nazareth, June 7, 1872.

In addition to these Father Quinn names a Sister Winkelman and the following without giving family names, orders and dates of death: Sister Frances, Sister Catherine, Sister Veronica, and Sister Regina. He then adds "there were some 35 others."

Other Tennessee cities suffered bad epidemics, not only of yellow fever, but of cholera, dengue fever, and other diseases. But the story of Memphis is truly tragic. It did not come to be the most populous city in the state until the Civil War. Less hurt by the war than any other major city of the Confederacy, by 1870 it was on the way to becoming a great metropolis, the capital of the cotton and lumber trades, the commercial headquarters of the rich delta of the Mississippi. Although it continued to grow after the decade of the yellow fever, its growth and prosperity never had the rich fulfillment of its early promise.

The Church, too, was part of this picture. Since the Civil War

Memphis has always been the most Catholic city in the state, but its Catholicity never attained the influence and rootedness of a Richmond or a Louisville. Rumored in 1868 to be the new see city of Catholic Tennessee, it did not finally become a diocese until 1971. The heroism of its Catholic leaders during the 1870s gives the Diocese of Memphis a magnificent history, albeit a tragic one.

13

The Rademacher Interlude

After Feehan left for Chicago in 1880, Nashville was left without a bishop for three years. No one knows why. A possible guess is the confused situation in St. Louis, to whose Metropolitan Province the See of Nashville belonged in 1880. St. Louis Archbishop Peter Richard Kenrick, under a cloud for his opposition to the definition of papal infallibility in the Vatican I Council, was in virtual retirement. His coadjutor bishop, Patrick J. Ryan, performed the usual episcopal functions, but apparently refrained from nominating, and soliciting nominations, for vacant dioceses. But this is only a guess. In 1883 Nashville was shifted to the Metropolitan Province of Cincinnati, and in 1884 Patrick Ryan was named Archbishop of Philadelphia. Both these events took place after Nashville had a new bishop.

This was Joseph Rademacher, who, if he had a middle name, seems never to have used it, following in this respect the example of his great friend, patron and bishop, Joseph Dwenger, of Fort Wayne, Indiana. In character and personality, however, the two Josephs were decidedly different. Dwenger was forceful and articulate, full of opinions and advice about a great many ecclesiastical matters. Much in the limelight, he was naturally the subject of much controversy, though many of his fellow bishops adopted the workable school system he devised for Fort Wayne.

Joseph Rademacher was a different sort altogether. "Rademacher" means "wheelwright" in German, and there was about Nashville's fourth bishop a solid steadiness that the name connotes. Although not dynamic or charismatic, he was considerate and responsible. But Rademacher was no plodding unimaginative dullard. On the contrary, he had a touch of artistic temperament in him. He was fond of poetry, and contributed to a fund for the publication of a translation of Dante by a Notre Dame professor. He loved history, especially Church history, and knew an astonishing lot of it. Odd by-ways and nearly forgotten incidents especially intrigued him. He must have been fun to talk to, and there are intimations of this in the stiff official sketches of his life. Better evidence, however, comes from his letters. In 1889 he led, along with the Bishop of Newark, New Jersey, a pilgrimage to the Holy Land, no small undertaking in those days. He wrote an account of the last part of the journey to his vicar, Father Patrick Gleeson, which survives. Here are some excerpts:

> [After leaving Jerusalem] For miles and miles, whether we go east or west, north or south, there is nothing but a wilderness, barren hills and valleys, the beds of dried-up streams, with barely a human habitation worthy of the name. Thus an indescribable melancholy broods over the historic city of Jerusalem and its environs . . . These features of the countryside do not change until we come to Samaria. There we find bleak mountains, it is true, but also fertile valleys, in which the eye is greeted and gratified by magnificent groves of olive and fig trees . . . [some biblical place names follow,] then we come to Nazareth. This last place made a more agreeable impression on us than any other in the Holy Land.
>
> [After listing with some small comments other biblical places] we led, in general, a life not altogether in keeping with our advanced ideas of comfort and civilization. However, I enjoyed it very much. It was so different from the luxurious, but "unpoetical" way of locomotion to which we were accustomed. [The party had traveled by horse and camel back, and slept in tents]. It furnishes the "romantic" element, which has well-night disappeared from the modern "civilized" life of Europe and America. . . . I am almost as brown as an Arab, but my health has never been better.

This charming letter is almost boyish in its feeling for adventure, but it is also sensitive, lively, and by no means "unpoetical".

Rademacher was born in Westphalia, Michigan, a small German settlement near Lansing, on December 3, 1840. His parents sent him to St. Vincent's Abbey and College, at Latrobe, Pennsylvania, conducted by the Benedictine Fathers, where Father Bergrath had studied. After completing his classical and philosophical courses there, he moved on to the seminary of the Diocese of Pittsburgh, where he did his theology. He was ordained for the Diocese of Fort Wayne by the first bishop of that new diocese, J. H. Luers, on August 21, 1863. It was mission time in the Diocese of Fort Wayne as well as Nashville in 1863, and young Father Rademacher went on the mission trails for six years, headquartering in Attica, Indiana, twenty-five miles southeast of Lafayette.

He then went to the pastorate of Columbia City, and in 1877 to the see city of Fort Wayne, where he was named chancellor as well as pastor of a parish. Shortly thereafter he was named pastor of the largest and wealthiest parish of the diocese, St. Mary's, Lafayette.

The brief and sketchy biographies of him always speak of his kindness and gentleness, and the affection he inspired in his people. His career speaks for itself. It is no wonder that he was thought episcopal timber by his influential boss, Bishop Dwenger, and was appointed to the See of Nashville. He decided to be consecrated in his new see city, and there he was made fourth Bishop of Catholic Tennessee on June 24, 1883, in the cathedral Bishop Miles had built twenty-five years earlier. Archbishop Feehan returned to his former see as principal consecrator, assisted by Bishop Dwenger and Bishop Watterson of Columbus, Ohio. The Metropolitan, Cincinnati's Archbishop Elder, preached.

Rademacher's decade in Nashville was indeed an interlude. The time was not yet ripe for the changes wrought by his successor, Bishop Byrne, and in any case it is doubtful whether Rademacher had the stomach for the storms such changes arouse. He certainly did not feel he had the support. This touching letter, written when the priests of Fort Wayne, upon the death of Bishop Dwenger early in 1893, unanimously voted for Rademacher as Dwenger's successor, makes this plain. It is addressed to Archbishop Elder.

Most Rev. Dear Archbishop:

It may be well, in view of the efforts which my old Fort Wayne friends are about to make, to have me appointed successor to the late lamented Bishop Dwenger, to define my position as plainly as possible in this important matter.

I would accept this transfer cheerfully if it would meet the views of the Right Reverend Bishops of the Province, and of yours above all, and if it be the unanimous request of the priests of the Fort Wayne diocese, for the following reasons:

> My appointment to this Diocese of Nashville seemed to me from the very moment that it came to my knowledge *a mistake*, because I am German — a German-American, to be precise, but in the eyes of the public, in the estimation of my own people, a German pure and simple. As such I felt when I learned of my appointment that I could not suit — would not be acceptable — to the *large majority* of Catholics of this diocese, who are principally of Irish descent. This fear I mentioned to you and to Bishop Dwenger, and I was for that reason especially determined not to accept the proffered dignity. But I found that my objection was not heeded: that Bishop Dwenger in particular was quite positive that my refusal to accept the mitre would not be listened to at Rome, and as he was on the point of going to Rome, where his word, would, of course, have had more weight than mine, I yielded with many misgivings to what appeared to me inevitable. Since then I have had, time and again, ample opportunity to realize how well my fears were grounded, though I must also acknowledge that I have found many true and loyal hearts, truly Catholic and far above the prejudice of narrow national feelings. Still there is no doubt that these feelings exist here as well as elsewhere, and that they, I have good reason to believe, interfere very materially with the exercise of my ministry, rendering it more difficult and less effective than it would likely be in the Diocese of Fort Wayne, where there are a great many Germans, and where priests and people have known me for more than twenty years.

The letter goes on to note that its author would be content to remain in Nashville if it were best for the Church. What Rademacher says is, as he notes, true of his time, and especially true of Catholicism. It is what Cardinal Gibbons, Archbishop Ireland, and their supporters fought so hard against. Feehan did not fight it very hard in Chicago, and he was probably right — the time was not yet ripe. His German-descended successor, Cardinal Mundelein, did make the fight, and his success was probably his best achievement.

What about Nashville? Rademacher seems very sure of his ground, and, while he may have magnified the Irish-mind-set, what he said was likely true. Bishop Morris, though himself of Irish descent, deplored Irish clannishness, and spoke of Rademacher's kindness — though he knew him only one year, he was his constant attendant as his secretary. The Irish of Nashville gave Rademacher "the finest buggy and set of harness that adorns this city", said the newspaper account. Father D. A. Quinn, the chronicler of the yellow fever in Memphis, wrote glowingly of Rademacher's abilities as well as his amiable nature. So not every Irish face was turned against him, and no doubt the Germans welcomed him as one of their own. Yet there is an odd lack of warmth about these tributes. The atmosphere of the diocese seems to have been one of tepid tolerance. A good man, yes, the dominant Irish seem to have said, but well, you know, not our sort.

Yet this may have been more the times than the man. The times were interlude times. Rademacher's predecessor, Feehan, lived through stirring and dramatic events. The war's aftermath, the first Vatican Council, the yellow fever, the new schools and religious orders and their institutions, made his episcopate eventful. Rademacher's successor, Thomas S. Byrne, had to deal with ethnic intransigence, as dramatic growth made new parish lines necessary. He also had to deal with the rapid expansions of the cities made possible by electricity. But these were not pressing in the 1880s. It may be significant that Byrne never lived in the damp and dismal rectory next to the Cathedral, but Rademacher stayed on there. Feehan had bought a house on Belmont Street just before he was transferred to Chicago, but the tradition is that he sold this as his own property — there is no record of it in the Nashville courthouse. The 1880s seem a time of quiet, of getting used to the new industrialism in the north and middle west, while the far west opened up and the south groped for a new identity.

It isn't as though nothing happened. Bishop Rademacher built thirteen churches and five schools. He opened two cemeteries and helped to establish three hospitals. Some of the churches were major building projects: the new big Saints Peter and Paul in Chattanooga and the fine Immaculate Conception in Knoxville, both still doing downtown duty. He brought the Franciscan Sisters from his former home town of Lafayette, Indiana, to operate St. Joseph's Hospital in Memphis, and, briefly, St. Margaret's in Nashville. He persuaded the Sisters of Charity of Nazareth to open St. Vincent's Hospital in Chattanooga. He built schools for St. Patrick's and St. Mary's in Memphis, Notre Dame in Chattanooga, and St. Genevieve's in Dayton. He also started a school for blacks in Memphis, and saw St. Cecilia's in Nashville and the

Christian Brothers' School in Memphis enlarged. The cathedral was renovated. Perhaps the oddest thing of this sort that happened in Rademacher's time was the strange fate of a building lot on Charlotte Avenue in West Nashville. The developers of that new residential area, to encourage settlers, gave the diocese a lot for a church with an excellent location facing the park. The diocese accepted, but somehow the church was never built, and the lot reverted to the developers. This may indicate a lack of feeling for city expansion. Not until 1921 did West Nashville get its St. Ann's parish.

Perhaps the most significant building project that Bishop Rademacher engaged in was St. Joseph's Church in Nashville. Other churches went up, in Knoxville, Chattanooga, Lawrenceburg, Bellevue, Dayton, Wartburg, Columbia, Union City, Winchester, and Paradise Ridge. Some, like Paradise Ridge, have a long and fascinating history. Others, like Dayton, have brief but equally fascinating periods. But St. Joseph's in Nashville became a kind of symbol of the dominant Irish.

In its prime, St. Joseph's was said to be the "best" parish in the South. It was certainly large and lively. As the railroads developed, more and more Irish, children of the originals as well as newcomers, worked for them. The new Nashville depot, opened on October 9, 1900, symbolized the growth of the railroads, as its recent dilapidation symbolized their decline. The St. Joseph's Church that looked at it across the tracks is now gone altogether, its site occupied by the offices of the Nashville Electric Service. The tracks themselves are still there, but deserted most of the day and night, and those who work on them few and getting fewer.

Practically everybody saw that Nashville needed a new church on the west side of the tracks, yet not so far out as to make walking to downtown impractical. So many Irish had already settled there that the area was referred to as "Little Ireland" when, in 1885, Bishop Rademacher bought a block of the old Hynes plantation, bounded by Morgan, McNairy, Hynes, and Church streets. The price was $24,000, including the Hynes home, which was to become the rectory. Since this new church was designed to replace St. Mary's as the cathedral, the bishop paid one-third of this amount, $8,000. He entrusted the new parish to Father

A rectory replaced the old school next to Immaculate Conception Church in Knoxville. A new Holy Ghost Church let old one above become parish hall.

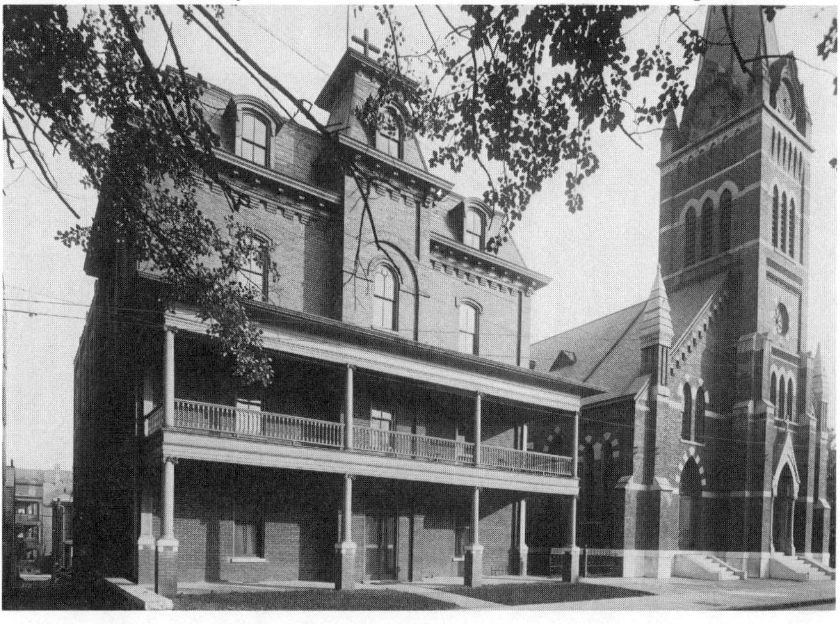

In 1880s German immigrants built Lawrenceburg's Sacred Heart Church.

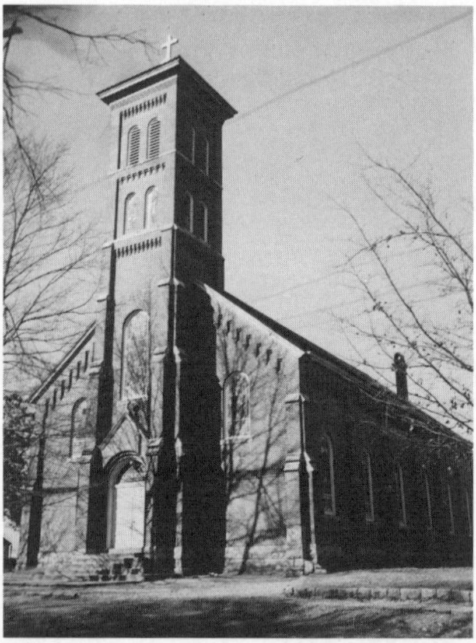

Loretto's Sacred Heart Church is also part of Lawrence County's settlement by German Catholics. Below, laying of the cornerstone of the church at Loretto.

The McEwen parish dates from 1855, oldest of these three churches. McEwen and Camden are in Memphis diocese since 1970 division.

In northwest end of the state, Union City's Church of the Immaculate Conception, built in 1891.

In northeastern Tennessee, Johnson City's first Catholic church, school, and convent all began in this house.

Twin towers are at their original full height in this photo of Chattanooga's mother church, built in 1888 and named for Saints Peter and Paul. The present interior is shown in the photo below.

Nashville's Assumption Church in the early 1900s had this graceful steeple.

Another tall spire graces Church of Immaculate Conception, Clarksville.

Parishioners pour out of Nashville's old St. Joseph's on a sunny Sunday in early 1900s. Its site was at Church Street and Twelfth Avenue.

Land in New Tazewell has been bought for church to replace this store-front.
Chattanooga's St. Francis Church sponsored trailer mission pictured below.

Knoxville's St. Mary's Hospital is conducted by the Sisters of Mercy.

This was first building of St. Thomas Hospital, then on Hayes Street.

New site of St. Thomas is on Harding Road next to the campus of Aquinas Junior College.

Staff and residents of Little Sisters of the Poor Home on Main Street, a few years before it was destroyed in the East Nashville fire of 1916. Below is the old St. Mary's Orphanage, whose site is now occupied by St. Mary's Villa.

Among the pupils in this 1897 Assumption School picture are the future Cardinal Samuel Stritch (sixth from left in first row) and the future Archbishop John Floersh (fifth in third row). Father Peter Shirack was the pastor.

Lone boy in tenth grade graduation picture of St. Joseph's School is the future Father Thomas Nenon. In 1920, when this photo was made, Irish Catholic boys did not commonly go to school beyond the eighth grade.

A class at Nashville's old Immaculate Mother Academy, before boys were admitted.

The first building of St. Bernard's Academy and convent on Hillsboro Road, 1905.

Mother Clare McMahon founded St. Bernard's, mother house of Sisters of Mercy in Nashville.

Joe Horton photo, collection of Elizabeth Baltz.

A layman's retreat at Father Ryan High School, Palm Sunday 1952. The aerial view below shows Aquinas Junior College on the left, elementary and secondary schools on right, Dominican sisters' convent in mansion between.

Richard Scannell, who had been born in Ireland and recruited for the Nashville diocese by that old Irelander, Bishop Feehan. Scannell's abilities were as obvious as the need for the new church. He was chosen to administer the diocese during the long interregnum between Feehan and Rademacher, doing so as rector of the cathedral. As a reward for this, and to help his failing health, he was given a couple of years leave of absence, for travel and recuperation. Back home, he went to work on the new parish with vigor, and started a school almost at once, with the Sisters of Mercy in charge.

The building went up rapidly, and on February 7, 1886, was dedicated with a Pontifical High Mass celebrated by Rademacher. The dedication ceremonies were performed by his good friend, Bishop Watterson, of Columbus, Ohio, who also preached the sermon.

The building was a combination church-school, a popular style since the sharp enforcement of the school requirement. The school was on the first floor, the church on the second. It was a solid building of mixed architectural styles, with some Gothic pointed arches and some round Romanesque ones, along with a firm Romanesque tower. These elements didn't harmonize well. The whole building seemed somewhat heavy and disjointed.

But it had its charms. The grounds were ample, something rare in city parish schools — Assumption's was little more than an alley, the Memphis ones little better. The St. Joseph children could, and did, play on a baseball diamond worthy of the name. The church seated nearly six hundred, which made it the largest in the city, though even so not large enough; the school soon enrolled almost enough children to fill it, four hundred. Unlike St. Mary's, the sanctuary was large enough to move around in. The original decoration is unknown, but many old-timers will remember the ornate renovation Father Maurath installed in 1934.

Most of all it was church and club for the Irish. Connors and McGoverns, Ahearns and Howingtons, Nenons and McDonalds, Brews and Ryans and hundreds more Irish names made up the majority of the parish roster. The pastor, Father Scannell, was too brief in the post to become the legend his successor became. This was Patrick Joseph Gleeson, a Feehan recruit from Tipperary, who became pastor in 1887 and stayed there till his death in 1919, with a brief interval of absence in 1900-1901. With his rich Irish brogue Gleeson was the legendary soggarth, warm, genial, humorous, yet staunchly firm in matters of principle. He presided over his little Irish enclave with style and affection, and when, in an abortive attempt to turn the church into the cathedral, Bishop Byrne removed him, the parish rose up as one in support of their beloved pastor, and welcomed him back with cheers and joy.

The Irish of the period from 1880 to 1920 loved St. Joseph's and its setting as one loves his home place. It was there they became more prosperous, there they emerged more American than Irish, there they met and married one another. More even than Notre Dame in Chattanooga or St. Patrick's in Memphis, Nashville St. Joseph's became a symbol. The Irish loved it even as they moved away from it, for its decline was as dramatic as its rise. The new cathedral took most of its parishioners in time, as the city moved steadily westward and southward. As early as 1925 the place began to look seedy and abandoned, although the school stayed on till 1936 when, the enrollment having dropped to 40, Bishop Adrian finally closed it. From then on it was a matter of looking for a buyer, as the old place went through various changes. The Knights of Columbus used it during World War II. The Franciscan Fathers then tried to rejuvenate the parish, but it was doomed, as so many inner city parishes were. The property was finally sold to Frank B. Welch Realty Company in September 1944 for Nashville Electric Service.

St. Joseph's had a quasi-cathedral status. The cost of the church was paid entirely by parish subscription, but one-third of the cost of the land was paid for by Bishop Rademacher, since he envisioned St. Joseph's as a possible new cathedral. The Bishop acted as if it were a cathedral. Not long after the church was dedicated, Father Scannell was named the new Bishop of Concordia, Kansas (later Omaha). He was consecrated in St. Joseph's on December 1, 1887. When Rademacher was transferred to Fort Wayne, the farewell Mass and reception were held at St. Joseph's. Rademacher's successor in Nashville, Bishop Thomas S. Byrne, was consecrated in St. Joseph's on July 25, 1894.

Quite possibly on this very occasion Bishop Byrne decided that he would make St. Joseph's the official cathedral. He had good reasons. The old Cathedral of St. Mary's was dwindling as a parish; St. Joseph's was what St. Mary's had been. St. Mary's had always been too small for episcopal functions. The sanctuary couldn't accommodate a proper retinue. And compared to St. Joseph's, the income was minuscule.

But for five years Byrne pussy-footed around the problem, which was the pastor, Father Gleeson. Gleeson was in solidly with his people. He was an irremovable rector, and he was determined to stay on. As with two boxers, there was a good deal of feinting and clinching in the early years. Byrne tried to conciliate Gleeson by making him vicar general, but it didn't work. The plain fact was that here were two hard-headed Irishmen. There was going to be a fight.

There was, and Gleeson won. Byrne shifted him to Knoxville. He obeyed but appealed to Rome, and Rome told Byrne that he could not change the cathedral to St. Joseph's, and, that he must return Gleeson to St. Joseph's if Gleeson wished it. Gleeson did wish it. He returned to St. Joseph's for the rest of his life. He died there in 1919.

But Bishop Byrne didn't lose all. In fact, the squalid fight aside, not getting St. Joseph's as his cathdral was lucky for him in the long run. Almost at once he began to plan a new cathedral, which he situated about a mile and a quarter further west. That site is still viable. The beautiful cathedral he built there still stands, as it almost certainly would not had it been built on the St. Joseph's site. Moreover, Byrne made his reputation by building the new cathedral. It was he, not Gleeson or St. Joseph's, that became the new and enduring legend.

Rademacher went to Fort Wayne as its third bishop in July 1893. No doubt he felt at home in that strongly German area. Certainly the priests of the diocese, who had voted unanimously for his appointment, were satisfied. But he had less than seven years of ministry in northern Indiana. He died in Fort Wayne on January 12, 1900.

The Rademacher interlude was not a bad time for the Church in Nashville. Poised between two forceful administrations, it was a time of growing up and catching up. For a long period the diocese was free of war and pestilence, perhaps for the first time. And its bishop left a memory of a kind and good man, a true Christian, a man of charity and compassion.

14

Four Catholic Bishops from Tennessee

The story of the Diocese of Nashville, and to some extent of every other Catholic diocese in the United States during the nineteenth century, is interwoven with the efforts to develop a native clergy. But Nashville lost four of her native sons during this period to wider service to the Church. Four bishops, born between 1855 and 1887, were consecrated to the apostolic succession from 1906 to 1924. What an amazing happenstance, that so tiny a Catholic population should nurture so many bishops! This may suggest something of the high quality of Tennessee Catholicism.

All four bishops were very different from one another, and their paths crossed many times. Two were born within a year of one another in the same parish, Nashville Assumption, and went to the same parochial schools. These were Samuel Cardinal Stritch, Archbishop of Chicago, and John A. Floersh, Archbishop of Louisville. They served as altar boys to John B. Morris, later Bishop of Little Rock, who was also their friend, guide, and helper. Morris in his turn had been greatly helped and encouraged by John P. Farrelly, later Bishop of Cleveland, his senior by ten years. Farrelly and Morris went to the same college, St. Mary's, Kentucky, and also were alumni of the North American College in Rome. Stritch, too, was ordained from the North American College. But Floersh was ordained from a different college in Rome, the Urban College of the Propaganda. This rather set him apart from the other three, though their relations were always warm and friendly. Morris and Stritch were both parish priests before becoming administrators, and this colored their work and thought. Farrelly and Floersh both were ecclesiastical bureaucrats, working but briefly as parish priests — indeed, Floersh scarcely at all, spending only a few months at Memphis's St. Patrick's after his ordination. Farrelly spent five years at the

John P. Farrelly

John A. Floersh

John B. Morris

Samuel Stritch

Nashville cathedral, as parish priest, rector, and chancellor of the diocese, before he was recalled to Rome to represent the interests of the American Church there.

Farrelly, Morris, and Stritch, however, were like a family, intimate, sharing, teasing, in constant touch. Floersh was not a member of this family. Deeply respected by Morris and Stritch — his relationship with Farrelly was slight — he was never very close to either. Indeed, he is not known to have been close to anyone outside his own family; he was reticent and reserved.

Not so the other three. Farrelly and Morris were as close as brothers — in his centenary sermon Bishop Morris said of Farrelly, "I was probably his most intimate friend." How interesting, that the first native secular priest of the diocese, Farrelly, should have been the "most intimate friend" of the first to be consecrated a bishop, Morris. Morris was the executor of the Farrelly estates. The two traveled together, visited one another, and helped one another. In 1887, Farrelly, bound for his new post in Rome, escorted young John Morris there to complete his studies for the priesthood. It was the year Samuel Stritch was born. Ordained a priest in 1892, Father Morris returned to Nashville's cathedral just as little Sam Stritch was beginning his schooling at Assumption School in north Nashville. Morris had him transferred to his own Cathedral School on Capitol Hill; young Sam became his altar boy and protege. In ten years' time Morris passed him along to Farrelly in Rome where, as Spiritual Director of the North American College, Farrelly was the agent of several American bishops. The year after Stritch was ordained in Rome in 1909 his oldest brother, Tom, married Morris's younger sister, Ellen. Family, indeed.

Like most Southerners, Farrelly, Morris, and Stritch were devoted to their large families; there was much visiting back and forth, and letter writing, and sense of one another. Yet Farrelly and Stritch lived but little in the South. Farrelly spent twenty-two years in Rome on top of the nine years he was abroad as a student. For the last twelve years of his life he was Bishop of Cleveland, Ohio, 1909-1921. Stritch spent almost exactly these twelve years as a priest in the Diocese of Nashville. He then became Bishop of Toledo, Ohio, from 1921 to 1930; Archbishop of Milwaukee from 1930 to 1940; and Archbishop of Chicago from 1940 till his death in 1958, being created a cardinal in 1946. Only Morris lived in the South after his Roman studies. He was consecrated a bishop in 1906, took over the Diocese of Little Rock, Arkansas, the following year, and ruled it for forty years till his death in 1946.

Of the three, only Farrelly was a genuine southern aristocrat. John Morris, the bishop's father, was a farmer and road contractor in Hendersonville, Tennessee, and Cardinal Stritch's father was an official in the Sycamore Powder Company, a DuPont subsidiary with a Nashville office and a plant on Sycamore Creek in Cheatham County. But Farrelly came from a very rich family of Arkansas cotton planters. His mother, Martha Clay Moore, was a middle Tennessean with Kentucky relations; as her middle name suggests, she was a connection of the great Henry as well as kin to the well-known Louisville journalist, Henry Watterson. But it was the bishop's grandfather, Terence Farrelly, who is the most striking.

Terence was born in Ireland, and brought to the United States by his father as a child. The family settled in western Pennsylvania, where father and son John became well-off and distinguished in public service. Son Terence, however, set out for the frontier. He landed in Arkansas, where he married a rich widow, Mrs. Mary Mosley. While looking after her extensive cotton plantation, Terence also read law and developed into a distinguished public servant. He became a general of the militia, a member of the Arkansas Territorial legislature from 1821 to 1836 and an influential member of its Judiciary Committee, a County Judge, twice Speaker of the Territorial legislature, and a member of the first State Constitutional Convention in 1836. During these years he was the political boss of Arkansas County, and he could no doubt have gone on in public service, but he retired from the field after Arkansas became a state.

Terence Farrelly raised a family of four boys and three girls, and with them lived the life of a frontier planter, so often described in fiction and history. He died in 1860. His will is full of solicitude for his children and slaves, its maker happily unaware that most of his wealth was about to disappear in the aftermath of the Civil War.

Long before this the Farrellys had made connections with the

Moore family of Middle Tennessee. Robert I. Moore (1791-1848), of Moorelands, near Brentwood, Tennessee, had prospered on land that originally came to the family by a Revolutionary War grant. He married three times, the first to Isabella Harlan, by whom he had two children, Sarah and James; and the second to Martha Clay, by whom he had only one surviving child, Martha Clay Moore. By his third wife, Jane Belle Walker, he had six children; in all, a sizeable clan.

Like many other well-off Tennesseans in the boom times resulting from the settling of the delta of the Mississippi, Robert Moore invested in plantation land. He seems to have bought into the Farrelly holdings, and become a partner of Terence. He sent his oldest son, James, to look after this land. It was a fortunate stroke, for James married Terence Farrelly's daughter, Adeline, in 1848, and eventually the Farrelly plantation became the Moore plantation. James and Adeline built on it an elegant home which survived till the 1930s. They named it "Mound Grove," and it served as a base for both Farrellys and Moores, who frequently visited it from Middle Tennessee. In this way Terence Farrelly's son John Patrick met Martha Clay Moore, and married her on March 28, 1855, in Nashville, at the home of Robert Lusk at the south foot of Capitol Hill.

John Patrick Farrelly, Jr., the future bishop, was born the following March in Memphis, where his father had a law office. But, according to Arkansas historian John Hallum, he practiced little law. He was, says Hallum, "a man of quaint humor and luxurious ease," "educated at the best institutions in the land, and supplied with a great abundance of cash without knowing its value — a great and injurious mistake made by too many of our southern planters."

At some point along the way Martha Farrelly became interested in the Catholic Church, and she and her son were baptized Catholics in the convent of the Sisters of Mercy in Little Rock, probably in 1868 or 1869. By this time John P., Sr. was dead, and the plantation and wealth gone with the wind. Mrs. Farrelly, however, had an ample fortune of her own inherited from the Moores, mostly in Nashville real estate, and she apparently moved back to Nashville. She made no permanent home there, however, living in hotels and boarding houses, while devotedly superintending the education of her only child. The future bishop went to school at St. Mary's in Kentucky, (in ten years' time the future Bishop Morris would follow him there), then to Georgetown, then to the College of Notre Dame de la Paix in Namur, Belgium, then to the North American College in Rome. His mother did not join him in Rome until he had been there about two years. After his ordination they traveled together in the Near East for a couple of years, and then returned to Nashville where Father Farrelly settled down in the cathedral rectory, soon to be its rector. He also became chancellor to Nashville's new Bishop Rademacher.

But his Nashville interlude was brief. Farrelly was fluent in Italian, knew French well, and could get along in two or three other languages. In addition he was very good at ecclesiastical Latin. Intelligent and discreet, he was a natural for the post of agent for some of the American bishops. The chief agent was the energetic and intriguing Denis O'Connell, the intimate of Cardinal Gibbons and Archbishop Ireland. Farrelly was O'Connell's assistant. Their official residence and positions were as staff for the North American College, and it was for that establishment that Farrelly set out in the October of 1887, with young John B. Morris in tow. Two years after Morris' ordination Farrelly was named Spiritual Director of the American College, where he lived for twenty-two years.

His mother went once again to Rome in about a year's time. She never returned to her native land. Farrelly established her on the Via Tutino, and they traveled in Europe when he was free. She died in Rome in 1902, and is buried in St. Lawrence's Cemetery there. Two years later a cousin of hers, twenty-four year old Ruth Brooks, also died in Rome while visiting Farrelly; he buried her in the same tomb with his mother and reserved a place in it for himself. But, although Mrs. Farrelly never returned to Nashville, her son did, with considerable regularity, every two or three years. He visited his relations, kept in touch with the Tennessee Historical Society, to which he presented a rare Hebrew Bible and a Rome-done portrait of its longtime (1884-1903) president, Judge John M. Lea, and visited the many Nashvillians he had assisted in Rome. Morris said that Farrelly had always wanted, throughout his long years in Rome, to return to the United States.

He finally did return, in some state, as Bishop of Cleveland, Ohio, in 1909. He was consecrated in Rome by Cardinal Girolamo Gotti. Bishop Morris came from Little Rock as one co-consecrator; the other was the Rector of the North American College, Bishop Kennedy. Farrelly proved to be a surprisingly effective bishop of Cleveland, but, as he had done in Rome, he kept a low profile in the American hierarcy. He stayed in touch with some of his Farrelly-Moore connections in Kentucky and Tennessee; he died on one of his numerous visits to them, at the home of the Alexander Bonnymans, in Knoxville, on February 12, 1921.

Then came the celebrated will case. Bishop Farrelly left two wills, one an official one as bishop, leaving the ecclesiastical property in his name to his successor, according to the law of the Church. But he was incredibly negligent with the will disposing of his personal fortune, which his mother had left him. She had made a will in Rome in 1896 in which she left her property to her son, and went on to say that "if he should die without a will" she wished her property to go to the City of Nashville "for the purpose of founding an Asylum for nursing poor sick children who cannot be properly cared for at home." In case the city should refuse this bequest the estate was to go to "Rev. Father John Morris, Catholic Priest of Nashville, Tennessee, for the purpose of building a new parish church."

Both wills were probated at the same time, after the bishop's death in 1921. The City of Nashville passed a special ordinance accepting Mrs. Farrelly's bequest. But her Moore kin, headed by her half-brother Hugh, contested the will. The stakes were considerable: around a quarter of a million 1920 dollars.

The heart of the argument made by Nashville lawyer K. T. McConnico, who did all of the trial work for the Moores, lies in the legal phrase *incorporation by reference*. That is, could Bishop Farrelly in his will implement his mother's will merely by referring to it? The law held that he could not, that a holographic will — both wills were in longhand — must, by Tennessee law, be entirely in the handwriting of the deceased. Hence the Farrelly intentions were thwarted by the bishop's failure to copy out his mother's will. But there were other considerations, too. A holographic will is not valid in Ohio, and if the bishop were indeed domiciled in Cleveland, as he appeared to have been, then the whole will was invalid. The question of domicile for a clergyman dedicated to obey his superiors and go where he is told to go is indeed a peculiar one. McConnico made an insistent, if rather unconvincing, case of Farrelly's true domicile being Rome, since he had reserved a place for himself in his mother's tomb there; the defense lawyers contended that home is where the heart is, and Farrelly's had always been in Tennessee, where a holographic will is valid.

The Tennessee law requiring a holographic will to be entirely in the handwriting of the deceased derives from a similar North Carolina one, as does so much of the state's law and usage. Hence precedents are few; most other states admit incorporation by reference, though cases involving such are rare. But none of this troubled the succession of Tennessee judges who heard the case. To a man they ruled in favor of the plaintiffs. The key decision was the long one in the Court of Appeals; the Supreme Court merely affirmed it in a line. So, in 1932, the Moores and the lawyers finally got the money, which had, of course, been Moore money to begin with.

The case is a famous one in the legal history of Tennessee, the subject of many articles and much discussion. It dragged on for ten years. It formed a sad conclusion to Farrelly's life — the man who, said Bishop Morris in his funeral sermon, did more to dispel anti-Catholic prejudice in Tennessee than any other person. What Morris meant by this, however, applies only to prejudice among cultivated and well-born non-Catholics. With these Farrelly moved comfortably. He extended to them the courtesies of the city when they visited Rome, and when he came to Nashville they called on him. "Father Farrelly of Rome is at the Duncan Hotel," said the Nashville *Banner* in 1894. "He is kindly remembered by tourists for his courtesies." More than this, he was the confidant of such converts as Miss Mary Fogg, and did his best to help Florence Drouillard when her marriage to a French nobleman faltered. This was his natural milieu.

He introduced Bishop Morris to it, and Morris was successful in it. He, too, was something of a linguist — in fact, he made a hobby of learning new languages. Morris also was fond of the romantic literature of the generation before his, Sir Walter Scott,

Bulwer-Lytton, and such like two-volume novelists. But Morris was a farm boy, and remained a farmer all his life. One of his first acts, on succeeding to the See of Little Rock in 1907, was to found an orphanage. Characteristically, he placed it on a farm north of the city, and reserved for himself a small acreage on it. Here he grew his own fruits and vegetables, and experimented with grafts and hybrids, not without some success. He corresponded with the celebrated naturalist of his time, Luther Burbank, about some of his hybrids, which he tended with meticulous care. He visited his farm every day he was in Little Rock, which meant most of the days between 1906 and 1946, for he traveled little. He was, then, like so many southerners, part aristocrat, part dirt farmer, and part horse trader.

Many of these traits he inherited from his father, who came to Nashville as a soldier in the Union Army. Like so many other Union soldiers, he liked the place, and after the war brought his bride and her mother to a farm near Hendersonville. But he made more money by building roads, which trade he had learned as a young immigrant from Ireland in western Virginia, soon to become West Virginia, which helps to account for his soldiering in the Union Army. Both his wife and her mother died the year the future bishop went to Rome, 1887, and life on the farm became disjointed. When Father Morris returned from Europe in 1892 he moved them all to the city, where his numerous brothers and sisters lived only a block or so from the cathedral on Summer Street.

In 1906 Morris, in his fortieth year, was named Titular Bishop of Acmonia and Coadjutor Bishop of Little Rock, Arkansas. Bishop Byrne was his consecrator, and Bishop Edward P. Allen of Mobile and Bishop Nicholas Gallagher of Galveston came to Nashville to be his co-consecrators. Morris was made coadjutor to Bishop Edward Fitzgerald, a remarkable man who gained fame for his stand against defining the doctrine of papal infallibility during the First Vatican Council in 1870. Fitzgerald, the second Bishop of Little Rock — there were only three in over a hundred years — had been an intelligent and vigorous leader, but he was now old and ill; Morris succeeded him within a year.

The Diocese of Little Rock included all Arkansas. The Catholic population was very small, and mostly clustered in small ethnic centers. But thanks to Fitzgerald's business acumen — Morris, too, was an excellent man of business — it was not poverty-stricken, and very early Morris set in motion the realization of the dominant ambition of his episcopate. This was the goal of a devoted native clergy, trained in its own region. In 1908 he started Little Rock College, and in 1911 St. John's Home Missions Seminary. Morris was sure Arkansans couldn't be converted to Catholicism by street corner preaching. If it were to be done at all, it must be done, for this highly systematized and doctrinally subtle religion, through education and the influence of the educated. Neither the college nor the seminary has survived, but the native clergy came, in surprising number and quality. Arkansas is a long way from being converted to Catholicism today, but its increasing Catholic population, and its greater tolerance by non-Catholics, owes a great deal to John B. Morris.

Samuel Alphonsus Stritch was also devoted to the cause of a native clergy in the South, so much so that his entire life was lived against the grain. In intellect, temperament, and preferred mode of life Stritch was a scholar, not an administrator. Upon his ordination — he had to get a special papal indult to be ordained at the early age of twenty-two — he wished to teach philosophy. He could easily have done so, with his brilliant academic record and reputation, and he had a couple of inquiries rather than offers. But he turned these feelers down, firmly but with deep regret. He felt obligated to return to the Diocese of Nashville which had underwritten his education, and which badly needed priests, especially well-educated ones. So back he went, and served for six years as pastor of St. Patrick's Church in Memphis. He then came to Nashville to be secretary to Bishop Byrne, and rapidly became Superintendent of Schools and chancellor of the diocese as well. But he never forgot the cause of the native clergy, nor the needs of the poor dioceses of the South and the West. Nothing gave him more satisfaction than helping them after he became the Chancellor of the Catholic Church Extension Society of America.

Stritch's brilliant career in the Church was a triumph of intelligence and devotion. His was not a natural talent for leadership, bold and innovative; he was nothing of an Ignatius, nor even of those patron saints of his, Charles Borromeo and Alphonsus Ligouri. In manner he was quiet and gentle; unlike Byrne and Morris he was never stormy and very rarely showed even the slightest sign of impatience or irritation. He was nearly always kind and — there is only one word for it — sweet, with only enough eccentricity (like his passion for junk foods, hot tamales, ground ham sandwiches, popcorn, and stick candy) to give a pleasant flavor to his personality. He had real style and excellent taste; these combined with his intelligence, learning, piety, and gentle ways made him stand out. There was nothing like him in the American hierarchy. He was admirable and lovable, and he was admired and loved.

His rare intelligence probably came from his father, Garrett Stritch. Talk of Garrett, in the family and in public, usually concerned his learning, education, and devotion to the Irish cause. To quote again from Bishop Morris's centennial sermon, "Mr. Stritch was a scholar in every sense of the word. He was likewise a devoted Irish patriot, one who never forgot his native land nor the causes that compelled him to leave it. As a student in Dublin he became connected with the Fenian movement, and was there an associate of the famous American-Irish poet, John Boyle O'Reilly, in the same movement. To avoid the consequences of being connected with this company of Irish patriots he had to hasten his leave from Ireland."

Stritch came from a family of teachers and clergymen. The family history in Ireland is a distinguished one, remarkable for its religious vocations and school-masters. The future cardinal's father would likely have followed his scholarly bent but for his hurried departure from his native land, in 1869 or 1870. Once in this country, he headed for Louisville, where he had relations. There he met and married Katherine Agnes Malley, who was born in Madison, Indiana, but whose family settled in Louisville. Stritch worked for the railroad, but his superior intelligence and education took him to the white-collar side of railroad construction, and he eventually formed a connection with the well-known Nashville railroad builder, Major Eugene W. Lewis, who headed the Sycamore Powder Company, which manufactured the dynamite used for blasting the roadbed through the southern hills. The family moved to Sycamore, Tennessee, near Ashland City, where the narrows of Sycamore Creek provided power for the company. But they moved on to Nashville in a couple of years, as the business prospered. After a brief stay in south Nashville, Garrett Stritch bought a house at 1121 Summer Street, a few blocks north of the eventual Morris home, in about 1882. Their fifth child was born there in 1885 and promptly christened Eugene Lewis Stritch.

At fourteen young Samuel Stritch was sent to St. Gregory's Preparatory Seminary in Cincinnati, at sixteen to the North American College in Rome. As with his father before him, everyone who knew him remarked on his brilliant mental abilities. But, though he read widely and reviewed books for a couple of ecclesiastical journals, he plunged deeply into the pastoral work of an ordinary southern parish. This, plus his experience after he was moved to Nashville in administration, served him well as a bishop.

When, at the age of thirty-four, Stritch was consecrated the second Bishop of Toledo, Ohio, it was the beginning of a brilliant ecclesiastical career. Stritch has a firm place in the history of the Catholic Church in the United States. A good biography of him has yet to be written. It would be a difficult life to write; it was neither eventful nor dramatic. Its significance lies in the two-way direction his thought and acts took: backward toward re-emphasizing the collegiality the United States Church had known in the nineteenth century, and forward towards some aspects of the Second Vatican Council.

Stritch was neither a liberal nor a conservative; he was a mixture of both. But when you start to reckon on that basis, what he did looks much more liberal than the way he sounded. For example, he pioneered in Catholic high school co-education, first in Toledo and then in Milwaukee, mixing different religious communities as teachers. In Milwaukee and Chicago he reorganized the Catholic diocesan newspapers, urging the appointment of professional laymen to key posts. He supported efforts to deal with the tough racial problems migration brought to Chicago during World War II, and inaugurated others, like the Catholic Interracial Council and the Council on Working Life. Although he tangled with his spendthrift auxiliary Bishop Bernard Sheil over the Catholic Youth Organization in Chicago, he supported the organization as far as he thought he could, and had founded a similar one earlier in Milwaukee. He supported the Cana and Pre-Cana Conference movement and the Christian Family movement. From his earliest days in Nashville he had supported better education; he welcomed state laws requiring religious to take education courses, and was the greatly admired advisor of a dozen or two mother superiors of religious orders of women upon whom he urged the best possible education for their bright young sisters. He was a pioneer in the ungraded school rooms program and in care of retarded children.

To Stritch, these were simply things that needed to be done. He did not do other things urged on him. He was not a proponent of liturgical reform, and he was cool to ecumenism. Most of the "liberal" things he did were administrative; intellectually, he was conservative.

His greatest administrative achievement was his leadership in bringing the American Church back to collegiality. The bishops of the early American Church, led by John Carroll and John England, deeply believed in working together as a group. They met in provincial councils with great regularity, and three times in plenary councils. But after the third Plenary Council in 1884 the impulse to speak with one voice slipped away. Divided by the Americanist controversy and other heady issues, the bishops tended to withdraw into their own bailiwicks. The spokesmen of the American Church in the early part of the twentieth century after Cardinal Gibbons, who died in 1921, were men like Cardinal O'Connell of Boston and Cardinal Mundelein, Stritch's predecessor in Chicago, seemingly not much interested in working with other bishops. Neither took much part in developing the National Catholic Welfare Conference during World War I, which eventually metamorphosed into the present National Conference of Catholic Bishops and its Secretariat, the United States Catholic Conference.

In this development, Stritch gradually assumed leadership. Working closely with Edward Cardinal Mooney in Detroit and Archbishop John T. McNicholas of Cincinnati, he focused attention on the annual meetings of the bishops in Washington, and it was he more than anyone else who made the annual statements of the bishops central in American Catholic policy. To do this without promoting rancor and resentment took a great deal of skill at managing men and ideas, and Stritch was at his best doing just this. It took a fearful toll, of course. Sensitive and delicate, he was a bundle of tensions. He ate too little and thought and worried too much.

On March 1, 1958, Pope Pius XII appointed Cardinal Stritch Pro-Prefect of the Congregation for the Propagation of the Faith, with headquarters in Rome — "Pro-Prefect" because the incumbent, Cardinal Fumasoni-Biondi, was almost ninety years old and nearly blind. It was a puzzling appointment to this day; nobody knows what the Pope had in mind. The main question was, would Stritch also be Archbishop of Chicago? No one will ever know. Cardinal Stritch, ill all that spring, died in Rome before he ever had any conversation with the Pope. Not long afterward the Pope himself died, and not long after that Fumasoni-Biondi died. In some ways it seems a pity that Stritch did not live to greet Vatican Council II, since so much that he did culminated in the work of that body. But he would have been greatly saddened by many developments in the post-Vatican II Church, and at his age would have had great difficulty adjusting to them.

His contemporary, Archbishop John A. Floersh, did adjust to them, with seeming ease. Floersh did everything with seeming ease. He was a quiet and reserved person, of great dignity and utter simplicity of bearing. Much taller and thinner than Stritch, he had, in age, a faint facial resemblance to him.

Floersh was a proper North Nashvillian, a true member of the Catholic Germantown group. His father, who immigrated from Germany at about the same time the elder Stritch immigrated from Ireland, settled in Nashville to his trade of cigar-maker. He became fairly prosperous, and raised his family of eight children in an atmosphere of piety and affection. Like Morris and Stritch, Archbishop Floersh was devoted to his family. His parents lived to celebrate their golden wedding anniversary. When his father died shortly thereafter, in 1931, Bishop Morris came from Little Rock to preach the funeral sermon. His mother lived on till 1943, dying with the archbishop at her bedside. After her death he took his sister Lula to live with him in Louisville.

Floersh's childhood was much like Stritch's. He went first to Assumption School, but in a year or two, under Morris's wing, to Cathedral School. Like Stritch he was outstandingly bright; like him, never had any doubts of his vocation. But Stritch had preceded him to Rome, and enjoyed at the North American College a burse, that is, a scholarship which paid his main expenses. None was available for Floersh, and he went instead to the College of the Propaganda where a burse was available. This was a lucky break for him. The Rector of the Propaganda in 1904 was John Bonzano. Young Floersh caught his eye, and Bonzano became his patron. When, as Archbishop Bonzano, he came to the United States as Apostolic Delegate in 1912, he immediately sought out Father Floersh as his assistant. As Bonzano well knew, Floersh was as gifted at languages as Farrelly had been. With his orderly mind, an immense fund of prudence and infinite patience, Floersh was a sure candidate for episcopal honors. And when Bonzano returned to Rome and was made cardinal, he backed Floersh for a bishopric. The protege became, in 1924, coadjutor to the aging Bishop of Louisville, Denis O'Donaghue, who died a year later.

Floersh was the most reticent of men, and so nothing is known of his personal responses to these events. Little, indeed, is known of his personal life even as Bishop and Archbishop of Louisville. He ruled that See for forty-four years, retiring in 1966 at the age of eighty. He died a year later.

It is a charming twist for this narrative that Floersh of Nashville went to the Diocese of Bardstown-Louisville nearly a hundred years after Bardstown had befriended the new Diocese of Nashville. Nashville, it will be recalled, was fashioned out of the vast expanse of the pioneer Diocese of Bardstown. The first bishop to visit Nashville was the first Bishop of Bardstown, Benedict Flaget, who, like Floersh, was a bishop for forty years; he was head of the diocese when the See was transferred from little Bardstown to big Louisville. Similarly, Floersh became Louisville's first Archbishop when the See was made a metropolitan one in 1937, the same year that the Nashville diocese celebrated its centenary and Bishop Morris preached his magisterial historical sermon at old St. Mary's in Nashville with both Stritch and Floersh in the audience.

Floersh's long years in Louisville were years of great growth. New parishes, new high schools, new administrative organizations, a new college, a new orphanage, the list goes on and on. Floersh ordained an astonishing 459 priests. But he wanted no praise for his work. He was as ascetic in abjuring fame and honor as he was in private life. He ate little, was extremely frugal, disliked show and tinsel, was agonizingly slow about making decisions and filling vacancies, in short as far from flamboyant as one could get.

Farrelly, Morris, Floersh and Stritch — how different they were, how very individual and personal. And yet, they were much alike in some ways. Two stayed in the South, two did not. But the two who didn't never lost their southern heritage. In manners, in style, in dignity, bearing and ease, they all remained southerners. As such, they brought to the Church they served so devotedly a touch of southern charm and grace. It was a happy touch.

15

Legendary Bishop Byrne and Other Legends

Thomas Sebastian Byrne, the fifth Bishop of Nashville, is a fascinating study. His episcopate of nearly thirty years was Nashville's second longest, and it is still the one which left the most lasting mark on the diocese. Byrne had the reputation of being an intellectual. He wrote and translated a half dozen books, and was chosen by Archbishop Elder of Cincinnati to be his theologian at the Third Plenary Council of Baltimore in 1884. Yet in Tennessee he is best remembered as an activist, a builder so close to his projects that he seems both architect and mason, and a rigorous and demanding leader.

Byrne's background is unusual. Born in 1841 and left fatherless as an infant, he grew up in a pious household in his native Hamilton, Ohio, in the devoted care of his mother and grandmother. Hamilton was and is a sort of workshop for the metropolis of Cincinnati, a center of heavy industry. Money was short in the Byrne home, and so young Tom worked as a machinist in local factories. This threw him a few years behind in his studies for the priesthood, but it also gave him useful habits of hard work and manliness, as a balance to a rather priggish native temperament.

Byrne seems from the start to have fixed upon the priesthood as a career. His mother's home was open to visiting clergy, and he served one such prophetically, elderly Father Stephen Badin, as an altar boy. Badin, it will be remembered, was Tennessee's first missionary priest. Out of his wages, and with some help probably from the diocese, Byrne went to St. Thomas Seminary in Bardstown, Kentucky, a favorite proving ground for Cincinnati aspirants to the priesthood. From there he went for higher studies to the Cincinnati seminary, Mount St. Mary's of the West. Older and brighter than most of his fellow students, he was then chosen for final studies at the North American College in Rome.

Thus early in life his two lode-stars were fixed, Cincinnati and Rome. He plainly felt at home in Cincinnati, as he did nowhere else; in Nashville he was a long-time visitor rather than a permanent resident. The deepest affection of his religious life was the Sisters of Charity of Cincinnati; he is buried in the cemetery of their motherhouse, Mount St. Joseph. He fell in love with Rome at first sight, and his intellectual and devotional life was modelled on his Roman experience.

But Rome was in many ways unkind to him, beginning with the climate. He fell ill of the damp winters there, and was sent home to Cincinnati to finish his studies. His reputation was so bright that Archbishop Purcell had him teaching before his ordination in 1869. From then on, till he came to Nashville in 1893, he continued to teach in the seminary, and work in parishes. At first he lived in the parish rectories, but soon fixed his residence at Mount St. Joseph. This was in part owing to his increasing interest in the seminary. He taught all sorts of subjects there, science surprisingly, physics, chemistry, and geology. He augmented his reputation for scholarship by translating, with another seminary professor who knew German, Father Francis Pabisch, Alzog's *Universal Church History*. The project took six years to complete — Byrne was to tackle another such long translation in Nashville.

He impressed his ordinary, Archbishop William E. Elder, who was transferred from Natchez to Cincinnati in 1883, so deeply that Elder took Byrne with him as his official theologian for the Third Plenary Council. It was there that Byrne came to the attention of the hierarchy. Let him tell how, in a letter he wrote over thirty years after the event in 1917 to Sister Mary Agnes McCann of his favorite Cincinnati Sisters of Charity. Because of the length of time since the event, Byrne's details may be inaccurate, but the main outline was known to all present.

> . . .[The Catholic University of America] would not have been a reality . . . had it not been for my courage in replying to a speech by Father Fulton, S.J. [during the deliberations of the council, which set up the Catholic University] . . . Father F. . . . made a violent attack on [the idea of the University], saying that it would be foolish to attempt it; that universities were not created so but grew out of small beginnings . . . that the diocesan clergy were not meant to be

> an educated body, but ordained to do the ordinary work of a parish and that the proper custodians and representatives of learning in the Church were the religious orders to whom alone universities should be entrusted. He interspersed his remarks with biting sarcasm and ridicule . . .
>
> When he came down from the rostrum I said to myself, I will not let that go by — if no one else replies to him, I shall.
>
> Cardinal Gibbons, who was presiding, waited for a few moments, evidently waiting for someone to answer. Finally he said — If no one else wishes to speak on this subject, we shall take up other business. At this point I rose and asked leave to say a word in reply to the Rev'd Gentleman. Leave was promptly granted, and I ascended the rostrum and took up his speech point by point and proved in a matter of fact historically he was incorrect in nearly every statement and certainly in every essential one . . . I also showed how it was feasible to begin a university at once and called upon the Fathers of the Council there assembled to take the work in hand. I fear I was quite as scornful and contemptuous in my remarks as he was and I knew I had the better of the argument . . .

This rare and revealing insight into the deliberations of the Council is also indicative of the best and worst of Byrne's character. The best is plain to see: knowledge, confidence, learning, leadership, optimism, and belief in learning and education in the Church. The worst is almost as clear: arrogance, biting sarcasm and even abuse, self-righteousness, intolerance of other views, and assertiveness. Byrne was human enough, however, to be touched by the commendation of old Archbishop Grace of St. Paul, the former pastor of St. Peter's in Memphis, who met him with warm assent as he came down from the rostrum.

The financial tangle the Archdiocese of Cincinnati got into under the Purcells (the Archbishop and his brother, who set up a bank owned by the Archdiocese which failed), caused the seminary to be closed for lack of funds in 1879. When it reopened in 1887 Byrne was named Rector, which post he held until he came to Nashville. An old history of the seminary called him "an able administrator and a stern disciplinarian". Too strict, indeed — the history notes that the seminary was a better place after Byrne departed.

The invitations to his consecration as Bishop of Nashville, which took place in Nashville on July 25, 1894, read "at the Cathedral of St. Mary of the Seven Dolors'', but the ceremony was transferred to St. Joseph's, no doubt to accommodate more guests. There was much opposition to the move, however — how like Byrne to enter upon his new duties to the tune of controversy. Archbishop Elder was the principal consecrator, assisted by Bishops Watterson of Columbus and Bishop Camillus Maes of Covington, Kentucky. Archbishop Feehan preached.

Byrne had reason to be dismayed at his condition as bishop. He disdained the cathedral rectory as much as he did the cathedral itself, calling it an ''unlivable'' home. He never lived there, taking a house at 1515 Hayes Street at first. He then moved to 607 Capitol Boulevard, where he lived until he took possession of his new cathedral rectory on West End Avenue in 1908. The Hayes Street address is significant; it was near St. Joseph's. Byrne can scarcely be blamed for wanting to make St. Joseph's his cathedral; Bishop Rademacher clearly intended it as such when he subscribed $8,000 to its building. The long and unedifying tangle with the pastor of St. Joseph's, who successfuly resisted the bid to turn his church into the cathedral, took up a lot of Byrne's time and energy. But he had plenty of that. He plunged into building plans for institutions all over the diocese, and kept on with his translations. His biggest project was to turn into English five volumes of sermons by the Right Reverend Jeremias Bonomelli, the Bishop of Cremona, Italy. Bonomelli was a prolific writer on all sorts of subjects, and a politically-minded liberal — an odd choice for conservative Byrne. The volumes of sermons were useful to busy priests, and they sold fairly well as they appeared one after the other between 1900 and 1912, but his best seller was a small volume entitled *Jesus Living in the Priest* (1901), by Father Jacques Millet, which he translated from the French. All his books were published by Benziger, and brought him substantial royalties all through the early 1900s, sometimes amounting to over $1,000 a year but usually less, till his death in 1923.

Writing and publishing, however, helped to sustain the great friendship of his life. This was with the wealthy Collier publishing family. Peter F. Collier is the hero of one of those fantastic American success stories. Born in Ireland, he emigrated with his family as a child to Dayton, Ohio, from where he went to the seminary in Cincinnati, a near-contemporary of Byrne. But he decided he wasn't cut out to be a priest and, with $500 capital, set out to be a publisher. He did well from the outset, with mostly Catholic devotional books sold house-to-house or by subscription. He then turned to publishing all sorts of literary classics and made with them a huge success, selling by subscription. An even greater success came with his encyclopedia. His son Robert, also a devoted fan of Byrne, took over his father's magazine, *Once a Week*, later re-named *Collier's Weekly*, and made it the flagship of the Collier empire.

Peter Collier had apparently kept in touch with Byrne straight along, although their friendship, begun in the seminary, did not become intimate until Peter had become a solid success, married, and produced Robert. But well before Byrne became a bishop he was vacationing with the Colliers. The elder Collier constantly consulted Byrne about his business problems — no doubt Byrne, with his experience as an author, was knowledgeable. They also discussed politics, their illnesses, all the normal give and take of adult friendship. But their over-arching concern was the Catholic Church. A minor theme was the education of Robert, a steady topic until it was plain that well-educated Robert was as sharp a businessman as his father. Father was very generous to his friend the bishop. He gave him trips as far as Europe, he sent him all the books he published, and gave him considerable sums of money — between 1906 and 1908, when Byrne was embarking on the new cathedral, $24,000. Byrne was no doubt grateful, but the friendship was founded on genuine mutual interests and affection, and not on gratitude.

The Colliers introduced Byrne to a wide circle of their elegant friends, but, except for one or two devout Catholics among them, they didn't impress Byrne very much. Still, the bishop no doubt became used to eastern high society, the highest the country had — Collier was friendly with the Goulds, and wrote of lunching with the Baron de Castellane, the French nobleman who married Jay Gould's daughter and her $17,000,000 dowry. Byrne moved at ease in such of Nashville's society as he needed to; he was on good terms with his senators and congressmen, and with other public officials. But he was no salon priest, a genre he would have despised. He thought woman's place was in the home, and there mostly in the kitchen. Yet he was the kind and gentle friend of several women with whom he corresponded.

What a strange bundle of contradictory traits! Intimate with the Colliers, frequenter of summer resorts at fashionable Southhampton in Long Island, the Adirondack Mountains, and various mineral springs (he suffered from rheumatism), yet cold and remote to most of his priests and people. Although sternly opposed to the use of alcohol by priests, he enjoyed tobacco in more forms than one, especially a good cigar. Spiritual adviser of devout and devoted women, including many nuns, he was overcensorious about their conduct. No nun could ever go out at night, nor in the day without a companion, and special privilege for any reason was unthinkable. He was almost as opposed as Father Badin to dancing. The rules for fasting, abstinence, marriage, and above all schooling were rigorously applied, down to refusing communion at the altar to parents who didn't send their children to Catholic schools. Practically everyone was afraid of him. He shifted his priests around with an imperious hand and voice; his letters of appointment usually ran to two terse sentences. He was by no means deferential to his fellow bishops, lecturing them on occasion. He disapproved of the leader of the American hierarchy, Cardinal Gibbons, to the point of rudeness. And yet, along with this Irish Jansenism, Byrne had the seeds of greatness in him. He was as hard on himself as he was on others, an indefatigable worker and shoulderer of responsibility.

Like so many successful bishops, Byrne seemed to gain strength as he went along. At first he aroused hostility right and left. Although Father Gleeson was by no means universally popular among his fellow priests, he was at least well known to them, and Byrne seemed like an imperious impostor, driving and demanding. But as time went on Byrne's devotion to duty, his clear concern for the welfare of the Church, and his dignified and cultivated presence impressed priests and people. In 1905, nearly ten years after he came to Nashville, he convened the first synod of the diocesan priests. Thirty-four of them were present. Although many of the regulations they agreed on and published were more hopes than attainable goals, at least all the priests knew what they were, and could not help feeling more a part of a corporative body.

By 1905 Byrne was in the thick of his efforts to establish city parishes on geographical lines rather than ethnic ones. This was, in Nashville and elsewhere, an epic struggle, and a very important one. It involved the shaping of the Church in the United States. Until about 1900 it was probably a good thing for each city of any size to have "the German Church", "the Irish Church", "the Italian Church", "the Polish Church", and so on. These churches were reassuring and helpful centers for the bewildered newly arrived immigrants. Very often their pastors were the only educated men in the neighborhood, and advised their people on everything, how to get a job, how to open a bank account, how to buy on credit, how to mail a letter, very often ones the pastor had written for them. The church and the school were social centers for these people, and served as powerful agents in getting them going in the new country.

But, like so many useful agencies, they outlived their usefulness, and became a drag on Americanization and the growth of the Church. Geography meant nothing in the ethnic parish structure; often three churches were scarcely three city blocks apart. But by 1900 city expansion, made possible by electricity and, by 1925, the automobile, was beginning to leave these older neighborhoods behind. The bishops were concerned about the new ones. They, and their councils and synods, could see no other way in the United States but geographical parishes with strict boundaries, and they studied, conferred, and quarrelled about the boundaries for a quarter of a century or more, roughly from 1900 to 1925.

There was more at stake than the comforts of ethnicity. New parishes meant loss of revenue to the parent parish. In a diocese like Nashville, with its small Catholic population now beginning to be scattered, this meant hard times for both parent and child. Yet the bishop rightly saw that division, expansion, new parishes, were essential to growth. Pastors could afford the narrow view, but a bishop had to take a longer one.

With a forceful leader like Byrne, the battle lines were clearly drawn. In the see city of Nashville, the bishop himself was in the position of the pastor who sees his constituency cut off by a new church, when St. Joseph's took over most of the cathedral's parishioners. The bishop lost the early rounds of that battle, but won by setting up the parish of the new Cathedral of the Incarnation, which drained off most of the St. Joseph families. Elsewhere in Nashville, there was no trouble. East Nashville and north Nashville had parishes, and for the time being needed no more. South Nashville was an Irish enclave quite a bit smaller than the new Cathedral's. The surprising thing about its parish of St. Patrick's is that its church came so late, 1890.

Memphis was where the real war took place. The Dominicans fought the erection of new parishes as if St. Peter's were forever to be the only church in the city. Yet St. Patrick's and St. Brigid's were clearly needed as the city grew so swiftly directly following the Civil War, and the opposition of the Dominicans amounted to little. The rougher battles came over ethnicity. St. Mary's insisted that Germans belonged to their parish no matter where they lived, and they fought Byrne with petitions, with protest meetings, with innumerable letters and telegrams, and in the courts with injunctions. The Franciscans actually left the parish for a while in protest, but returned in a few months. The Italians of St. Joseph's, for their part, insisted on an Italian pastor whether one was available or not.

In smaller Chattanooga the fight was just as rough, indeed in some ways rougher. So fiercely opposed to a new church was the pastor of the existing one, Father Thomas V. Tobin, that he resigned and went to another diocese. Although Byrne had bought land for a new church, and the foundations were already laid, he was thwarted there. The foundations remained starkly unused, and Chattanooga remained a one parish city until 1937. The situation in Knoxville was similar, but here the bishop won. Despite the strong opposition of the premier Church of the Immaculate Conception, a second church was established in 1908 dedicated to the Holy Ghost.

The ethnic struggle lasted as long as Byrne did, although the 1918 *Revised Code of Canon Law* proscribed ethnic parishes. As the automobile revolutionized the American city, everyone saw that the new neighborhoods and suburbs demanded new parishes, and that the old ethnicity bore but little on the problem. Still, it wasn't until 1924 that Byrne's successor, Bishop Alphonse J. Smith, created firm geographical boundaries for Tennessee Catholic parishes.

Under Byrne, and underneath all this clamor, the diocese was becoming thoroughly Americanized — and southernized. Byrne was deeply patriotic, and promptly and publicly supported the United States in the Spanish-American war. He saw to it that anti-Catholic prejudice, which subsided some in his time, could find nothing to fault in his leadership. But little to praise, either. There was no hint of ecumenism in Byrne. His Catholic flock willy-nilly interacted with their Protestant neighbors, for whom they worked, from whom they bought, and next to whom they lived. The Church frowned on marriages between Catholics and non-Catholics, and Byrne frowned harder. But there were just too few Tennessee Catholics to build more than small and fleeting ghettos. As time went on, Germantowns and Little Irelands disappeared in all the Tennessee cities. Certainly their bishop cared nothing for them. He wanted educated but docile Catholics. Of Irish descent himself, he made no point of it.

The clergy was undergoing the same evolution. Bishop Byrne ordained a number of native priests — Fathers Emmanuel Callahan, John Hardeman, Francis D. Grady, John M. Mogan, to name a few. Many of these had grown up in Nashville, Chattanooga, or Memphis. The priest was no longer an exotic. He was young John Mogan, whom south Nashville had known as a boy, or he was Johnny Nolan, a boy from Chattanooga. Moreover, priests from elsewhere soon seemed almost home-grown. Fathers James P. Whitfield, and Alphonsus B. Parker, and Edward P. Desmond, from other places, soon became as southern as their new friends and associates. The United States of Grant and Hayes was yielding to that of Teddy Roosevelt and William H. Taft; Grant and Hayes, as Presidents, may never officially have met a Catholic, Roosevelt and Taft were friendly with many. And the South of Ben Tillman and Tom Watson was being infiltrated by the tolerance of John Sharp Williams and Joseph T. Robinson. Prominent Nashville Catholic Thomas J. Tyne even made a stab at the governor's office in 1912. He didn't make it, and religious prejudice undoubtedly had something to do with his failure. But the fact that he could even try suggests much about the Byrne era. Knoxville elected a Catholic mayor, Martin J. Condon, as early as 1888, and John Paul Murphy was briefly its mayor in 1904. Both Murphy and Condon were first city councilmen, and Murphy also was elected to two terms in the state legislature. And Memphis did elect a Catholic mayor, Francis J. Monteverde, in 1918.

Much else points to the new temper of the twentieth century. The metamorphosis of the Notre Dame Academy in Chattanooga from a girls' finishing school into a coeducational parish school offered a good example. The organization of the Knights of Columbus all over the state was another. No other Catholic organization, lay or clerical, did as much to emphasize Americanization and American ideals, as did the Knights. The purchase of the Hundred Oaks estate in Winchester, Tennessee, by the Paulist Fathers meant a new sophistication in mission work in the rural areas of the state; they pioneered the trailer chapel and other new approaches to the home missions. The opening in 1900 of Holy Family Church and school for black people in Nashville bespeaks the new century more than anything else. Bishop Byrne was deeply convinced of the necessity of bringing the gospel to the blacks, and his work with Mother Katharine Drexel and her Blessed Sacrament Sisters, and Father Thomas J. Plunkett and his brother Josephite Fathers, a community founded to work with the blacks, were among his noblest endeavors.

Byrne wanted his institutions to be up-to-date. Each major city today has a splendid medical center that was started or encouraged by Byrne. New buildings for the Memphis and Nashville orphanages looked to improving care of the young, while the Little Sisters of the Poor in Nashville made care of the aged available. There was a lot going on. Memphis, with the largest Catholic population, began in 1916 to plan a Catholic Club, a down-town social center with facilities for everything from ping-pong to large meetings. It was not dedicated till 1923, the year Byrne died, but it was a symbol of the new status of city Catholics.

In rural areas, things were different. Catholics in the small railroad towns fluctuated as the towns did. Fairly typical was Edgefield Junction, near present-day Amqui, in northeast Nashville. Here two north-bound railroads crossed. The crews may have changed here, and the station had a little importance because of the shifting of mail and freight. As long as this kept on, roughly till World War I, there were some Catholics here, and occasional Catholic liturgies. The same is true of Grand Junction, in southwestern Tennessee, somewhat southeast of Bolivar and hard upon the Mississippi border, where north-south and east-west railroad lines crossed. There were a few other such places, like Tracy City, on the east side of Monteagle Mountain, Union City, and Covington.

These were railroad settlements pure and simple. Some towns were more. Pulaski, for example, is an old town and a county seat, but the Catholic presence there is entirely owing to the railroad. The same is true of older and more prominent Columbia along the same railroad line farther north. Columbia has a long history of being visited by missionaries, including a bishop even before Bishop Miles came there. This was Bishop Flaget of Bardstown, tradition says, who came to Middle Tennessee in 1821. But even when the railroad came, Columbia Catholicism flourished little.

Franklin, only eighteen miles from Nashville, also had a pre-railroad Catholic history; the ground for St. Philip's Church there was donated to Bishop Miles in 1843. But the church was not completed until 1871. Shelbyville, Winchester, Gallatin, Goodlettsville, and Murfreesboro in Middle Tennessee have similar histories.

Besides the railroad settlements there were mining settlements, impermanent by definition. Irish worked the mines at Erin and a settlement town named "Iron Works", both near Clarksville. Etna, South Pittsburg, and Dayton, all near Chattanooga, were boom towns in the 1880s. Dayton was the largest and had the most active Catholicity, owing in good part to the interest and drive of George Jamme, the general manager of the Dayton Coal and Iron Company. St. Genevieve's Church there was the headquarters of the missions later assigned to Harriman. There were schools for both black and white children, all on land donated to Bishop Rademacher. But the prosperity of these mining enterprises was short-lived. The discovery of better deposits of iron ore and coal around Birmingham, and the rapid growth of that city as an industrial center, caused the abandonment of the mining settlements in southeast Tennessee.

So settlements came and went. When the foundry at LaFollette, in East Tennessee near the Kentucky border, was going at full tilt, there was a sizable congregation of Italian immigrants there who built an attractive Italianate stone church. But when the foundry closed, the congregation perforce moved on. The most unusual such group was a Polish settlement at Deer Lodge in East Tennessee in the early part of the century. This was an agricultural community similar to the German one at Lawrenceburg, but much smaller. In that area of poor land it never had a chance.

In West Tennessee, Humboldt was in the Byrne era a mission headquarters. It had a good brick church and a rectory, whose rector ranged over nine counties with no more than one hundred Catholic families scattered throughout them. But there were ups and downs here, too. Both Paris and Dyersburg at one time had more Catholics than Humboldt, as the railroads opened shops in those places.

The archetype of these missions in West Tennessee, however, was Jackson. Originally a station served from Memphis, the town grew faster than other West Tennessee places, owing to the decision of the Illinois Central Railroad to make it a major facility. Early prosperity encouraged the Dominican Sisters to open an academy, but that faltered and died. However, the parish of St. Mary's flourished and grew as Jackson itself became more diversified.

The missions of East Tennessee are of more recent origin, and owe much to the zeal and talents of Father Francis Thomas Marron. For a quarter of a century, from 1872 to 1899, he *was* the Catholic Church in Knoxville, teacher, pastor, counselor, and most of all friend of most Knoxville Catholics. The conspicuous success of Knoxville Catholics in politics owes much to Marron. Even more do the missionary activities of East Tennessee. He was the mentor of the remarkable Father Emmanuel Callahan.

Callahan was a fascinating figure. He had come from a well-to-do Knoxville family, and had the Great Smoky Mountains in his bones, so to speak. After his ordination at Mount Saint Mary's in Cincinnati, he became a missionary to the mountain stations in East Tennessee almost at once. On horseback, he ran down Catholic families who hadn't seen a priest in years, brought the sacraments regularly to small stations who seldom saw a priest, and in the 1900s brought back the days of the roaming missionaries of Miles's time. To Callahan this was poetry, it was music, it was the good life. He rejoiced in the mountains, loved them as no priest in the diocese's history ever had, loved the rough camper's life, loved his horse ''Rebel'', knew and loved the incredible variety of trees and birds, loved the streams and their mists,. Above all he loved the people, their dialect talk, their hospitality, most everything about them, and loved bringing God to them.

Of course he romanticized it. He was a romantic, something of an anachronism. He was very intelligent and talented, quite conscious of who he was and what he was doing. He became a great friend of the Benedictine monks of Belmont Abbey, those courageous pioneers in western North Carolina, where Catholics were as rare as albinos — it's always a little startling to remember that North Carolina had no Catholic diocese until 1925. These monks were obviously kindred spirits to Father Callahan, and he often stayed with them. The Abbey Press published a dozen or so of his poems and pamphlets. A sampling of them shows that with practice he might have become an accomplished writer. In time he would have found his own voice, and rid himself of the echoes of Father Ryan. Actually, he sounded more like that unlikely but firm friend of Bishop Byrne, Will Allen Dromgoole, the well-known Nashville woman poet of the 1910s and 1920s.

Where Owlets Keen

I left the village at the noon,
To wander by the river's sweep —
    By gorge and cliff
    Up crag and fell -
O'er mighty hills, where torrents leap.
    Till sunset's ray
    In splendor lay
On hill and vale and fluted steep.
Soon comes the peaceful twilight scene —
    Waking voices
    Of the e'en.
Night follows fast the fading flow,
    The owlets keen
    The whispering green
And the whipporwills all chanting low
Greet the silvery hunting moon.

O Ferryman

O Ferryman, Over the river!
Ferryman, ferryman, over the river!
Over the river friends beckon to me
To speak to them of the God of love,
Of a better life in a better land,
Of grace and truth and a faith above,
There duty waits and life's work calls
Ferryman, over the river!

O Ferryman, over the river!
Thus shall I call when life is done -
When its tide has rolled
And its sands have run -
On the angel-shores of the spirit land
To ferry the mystic river.
O Ferryman, Divine Ferryman,
Ferry me over the river.

Here is some prose from a journal of a trip in the mountains.

Monday. Rebs fed before dawn, and saddle and chapel bags packed. Mass at dawn, then boots and saddle and the rising sun shadows us riding south for the trail of Doe when it breaks through the Holston range of the Great Smokies. Noon finds us lunching by Tiger Creek. Rebs is busy with his "turkey" of oats. At twilight the Catholic families of Elk Park greet the soggarth, thirty miles done with horse and man prime. The peaks have been topped and the rivers forded. A long evening and a pleasant one at the home of John Bateman. But the altar must be arranged on the parlor bureau, catechism given, confessions heard, rosary and night prayers recited. The rule must be, early mass and an early saddle.

Tuesday. What a pleasure, morning after morning, to see every Catholic of the hamlet approach Holy Communion. As the mists break and fade before the opening day, Rebel and I are breasting the Smokies, traveling up through cloudland. As the smoky trail winds to the summit land, up from the sea of vapor comes a rim of fairy golden fire, and the sea becomes a vista of dancing light and color painted by the rising sun. In the distance the peaks of Grandfather and the Twin Blacks lift their hoary heads above the rising sun. We make Pianola early. After supper the non-Catholics come to see the altar and hear an explanation of the Catholic Lord's Supper.

> *Wednesday*. Mass over, adieus said, we are off, on the downtrail to the Falls of Linville. Dinner is a thing to be remembered, Linville trout, corn pone, honey-dew. Then down the slope. Here journeying along afoot with some sturdy mountain man, explaining the faith or the Bible, while Rebel meanders by our side.....

Thus it goes, a real slice of the missionary life — but with the Callahan romantic touch. He also wrote some apologetic literature, and for a time ran a little Catholic magazine explaining the Church to the interested.

But most of Father Callahan's days and works were devoted to building churches, from helping out himself with hammer and saw to writing begging letters to the Catholic Church Extension Society and other benefactors. Extension and his brother George, a Knoxville businessman, largely paid for the church in Harriman. When Callahan stayed in Harriman he usually slept on one of the church pew-benches. He also built the churches at LaFollette and Deer Lodge. To the church in Johnson City he contributed his patrimony from his father's estate, around $25,000, plus years of his own salary. Of course he was simply the most picturesque of dozens of splendid priests who also worked in the East Tennessee missions through the years, but Callahan was the premier apostle there.

It's not surprising that he eventually fell ill. On the advice of his physician he went to the Bahamas, where he also, irresistibly, worked as a missionary, finding the people and their environs almost as fascinating as his beloved Smokies. But he never recovered the pristine energy of his youth. He died in Nashville in 1944.

Long before this, in 1916, Bishop Byrne had the good fortune to attract the Dominican Fathers to East Tennessee. The first Dominican pastor was the able and energetic Father S. R. Brockbank. The present church was built in Johnson City in 1932 by Father George Carpentier, who ranks with Marron in influence and effectiveness. The missions of that area, all with some echoes of the presence of Callahan, Elizabethton, Rogersville, Erwin, and Kingsport, fell into zero state in the 1920s, but revived a little in the 1930s, and have undergone an infusion of new life with migration into the East Tennessee area during and since World War II.

Almost as interesting as the Callahan story is the very different one of Winchester, in southeast Tennessee. Flanigen notes in his history, that there were Catholics in this area before the Civil War, many of French origin, who built a church in 1868, but for thirty years there was no parish priest. Missionaries said Mass when they came through the town in little St. Martin's Church.

Then, in 1900, there came a curious turn of events sparked by a Winchesterian named John Marks Handly. He came from a prominent Tennessee family; his uncle, Alfred S. Marks, was Governor of Tennessee and a political power in the state for some years. As a youth John Marks was of a literary bent, and after graduating from Vanderbilt became a New York journalist, and then secretary to the well-known southern novelist and social reformer, George Washington Cable. Cable, whose reformist ideas made him unwelcome in his native New Orleans, had moved to Northampton, Massachusetts. Also in Northampton was a group of Catholic priests of the Congregation of St. Paul the Apostle, which had been founded by the famous convert Isaac Hecker in 1858. Handly himself began inquiring into Catholicism, and was received into the Church in 1895. He then studied for the priesthood as a Paulist and was ordained in 1899.

A few years before this, in 1891, Arthur Handly Marks, a son of the governor, had begun to build a splendid mansion near Winchester which he named "Hundred Oaks". Arthur Marks had lived in England as a member of the American diplomatic corps. He greatly admired the English country houses, especially those of his own time, and designed his own mansion in their flamboyant style. His study was meant to be an exact replica of Walter Scott's famous writing room in his home, "Abbotsford," in the Scottish lowlands.

But Arthur Marks never lived in his grand new house. He and the American heiress he had married in England watched "Hundred Oaks" going up from a rented house in Winchester. But, still a young man, he died before the house was finished, and his widow had no stomach for the project alone. She departed, leaving the mansion unfinished.

Aware of all this, John Marks Handly persuaded his Paulist community to buy the place for a mission center. Bishop Byrne approved, and so, with the help of James F. Shaughnessy of Alabama, the Paulists moved in and finished the building. The unfinished great hall was turned into a chapel, the gift of Martin Condon, of the distinguished Tennessee Catholic family. Father Handly was among the priests who inaugurated the center, which was opened in the spring of 1900. A school was started, staffed by Dominican sisters from Nashville St. Cecilia.

Winchester's Catholicism was added to and confirmed by the Paulists. For a decade or more the Church flourished there, helped along by an interesting Paulist idea, a laymen's association to attract more Catholics to the region. For a while this did bring that rare breed, Catholic farmers, into the area, but their children for the most part did not stay. The leader of the movement was Father John Duffy, who introduced advanced methods of agriculture to the region, and organized the first cooperative creamery in the South.

In 1907 the Paulists built a church in Winchester. At that time the parish was quite large, and it continued to prosper, while "Hundred Oaks" became a popular retreat house, with a staff of four or five priests. The Winchester church burned down in 1936, and was replaced by the Church of the Good Shepherd in adjoining Decherd. Although Franklin County continues to this day to have one of the highest percentages of Catholics of any in the state, its great days go back to the 1900s. The Paulists gave up "Hundred Oaks" in 1953. It is now a popular tourist attraction, with a restaurant and snack bar. But there is still Paulist presence in the diocese at Knoxville, where the old downtown church and the University Catholic Center are in Paulist hands.

The story of Father Callahan is fascinating. The story of "Hundred Oaks" is touching and romantic, not too unlike those legendary settlements, Nashoba and Rugby. But the third story of this chapter is nothing like these. It is a layman's story, a story of quiet dedication to duty and high professional standards. If Thomas Farrell and Michael Burns are outstanding Catholic laymen of the diocese's early years, Charles Patrick Joseph Mooney is a good candidate for the same honor during the Byrne era.

Mooney was not an outstanding Catholic layman in the accepted sense of the term. He was not a Knight of Malta, or even of Columbus, nor president of the Catholic Club, or the confidant of the Memphis clergy. He was simply a devoted Catholic who, as long-time editor of the Memphis newspaper, *The Commercial Appeal*, made an admirable and responsible career by living up to his Christian beliefs.

Mooney was no ordinary editor. Although he owned scarcely any stock in his paper, he alone ran the news side of the *Appeal*. He never went to the owners for approval of any stand he took, and, though constantly accused of doing so, never took a stand to please them. Few editors have such complete freedom, but even fewer earn it by integrity like Mooney's. And, since the paper made money under Mooney's guidance, the owners had nothing to complain about on the financial side.

The solid success of the newspaper is startling in view of its — Mooney's — tireless, resolute and carefully researched attacks on the famous Memphis boss, Edward Hull Crump. When Mooney took over the paper in 1908 Crump was just beginning his career. Mooney stayed neutral, waiting to see what the young Crump, who preached reform, would do as mayor. Actually he did pretty well in many important ways, giving the city then and for fifty years thereafter efficient government. Mooney never gave Crump enough credit for this. But Crump did not crack down on gambling, prostitution, and other immoral and illegal activities, and Mooney saw that the alliance with those who profited from these might lead to Crump's building a political machine. This was especially true of the liquor interests. The leading issue in Tennessee politics for the entire period from 1880 to 1920 was prohibition. In 1909 Tennessee passed a state-wide prohibition law which Crump loftily ignored.

Once again, people who think the prohibition of liquor by law unwarranted may not fault Crump. But even the most ardent upholder of man's inherent right to drink whatever he wishes must acknowledge that prohibition, local, state or national, gave rise to unsavory and vicious politicking.

This is what gave Mooney his animus against Crump. He went beyond this, because he believed that bossism is itself evil, and Crump the incarnation of it. Mooney was a brilliant journalist. He had left *The Commercial Appeal* in 1902 to try to make it in the big time. He was an instant success with Hearst papers in New York and Chicago. But he wanted to be his own boss, with

Hearst an impossibility, and he went back to Memphis, where he could combine administration with writing. He was good at both.

Crump did indeed become as successful a city boss as Mooney was a newspaperman. He was not the standard type; he was personally honest and compassionate. The only personal animosity that came between him and Mooney was based on what Crump thought an attack on his integrity, and he took a full-page ad in the *Appeal* to denounce it. Mooney answered to his satisfaction, and then Crump went on his way, smiling blandly at Mooney's utterly unsuccessful attacks. Crump used to drop in at the newspaper office every now and then, where he maintained friendly relations with the staff.

This state of affairs went on until finally Crump and Mooney found an issue on which they could get together. This was the revival of the Ku Klux Klan in the incredible 1920s. Bishop Byrne was dead by this time, although he had predicted the anti-Catholicism and racism on which the Klan throve. Mooney fought the Klan, which was very strong in Memphis, tooth and claw. The newspaper won a Pulitzer Prize for this fight, but even more important perhaps was Mooney's leadership among his fellow editors. In meeting after meeting with them Mooney led the fight against the Klan, and was co-responsible, with Josephus Daniels, for the Southern Publishers Association taking a strong anti-Klan stand.

Dearer than any of this to Mooney was his stand against the single crop farming system so prevalent in much of the South. Mooney was himself a farm boy. Raised on a little farm in Bullitt County, Kentucky, which he inherited and farmed with tenants all his life, he early developed the conviction that the South was a victim of King Cotton. He often said that he came back south to fight for agricultural diversification. Fight for it he did, with that careful preparation that characterized his anti-Klan crusade. Mooney gave his staff enough elbow room to become experts in some one field, and this collective expertise provided his editorials with such in-depth research that the government itself reprinted them from time to time. Mooney hated empty rhetoric. His editorials bristled with carefully researched facts. In his writing, he made every word count. ''*The Commercial Appeal*'', he wrote in 1923, ''has been hammering on diversified business and farming for fifteen years. We have made some progress, but it is the progress of a frog jumping out of a well. Our people jump three feet, then fall back two, but if they keep on jumping they will finally get out''.

Such was C.P.J. Mooney. He was a deeply devoted Catholic, a daily communicant, but he did not wear his religion on his sleeve. He loved his work, and let his work show the kind of man he was. There were thousands of Catholics like him during the Byrne era, but it is hard to think of any other who had and seized such a wonderful opportunity for showing how to live one's religion.

16

Byrne the Builder

Bishop Byrne bought the property for the new cathedral group in Nashville in 1902 for $18,416. The land originally was part of the 640 areas awarded to John Cockrill, one of the Donelson party which settled Nashville. Cockrill married the widowed sister of James Robertson, Anne Robertson Johnston, Nashville's first school teacher, the one who taught the children on the boat coming to Nashville. It's a pleasant coincidence that Vanderbilt, Peabody, Scarritt, and the cathedral, teachers all, are all on this tract.

Vanderbilt in particular was a source of strength to Byrne's shrewd choice of site. Other locations were considered, and one on Sixteenth and Division Street bought. But West End Avenue was an inspired choice. Vanderbilt University lent the right tone, and the hope of some stability, to the neighborhood. That hope was fulfilled. It's remarkable that the north side of West End Avenue, across from Vanderbilt, continued for some thirty years to be an elegant residence area for Nashville. Twenty-first Avenue also kept its dignity, except for a small stretch where it intersects with Broad Street. But for Vanderbilt it's unlikely that the cathedral parish would be, after nearly seventy-five years, a viable and lively parish in a city which has during that time grown so remarkably.

Byrne had a clear plan. The first building to go up was the rectory, from which the bishop could supervise the building of the pro-cathedral and the school, which were in the second building to be built, to the west of the church site. The pro-cathedral, on the ground floor of the school, was the parish church until the big church itself was built. The entire process took seven years, 1907-1914. Byrne built as he could afford, and with the available funds. He left very few debts when he died. Christian Asmus, who had a large architectural practice in Nashville for many years, was the local architect. A Roman architect, Aristide Leonard, made some drawings for Byrne, who was the main architect.

Just how much Byrne's designs owe in detail to particular buildings in Rome is hard to determine. It is clear that the interior of the church is copied from San Martino on the Esquiline Hill, a very old Roman church which was renovated in 1650 to be the church Byrne knew. Yet the Nashville cathedral is not an exact copy; it had to be considerably modified, if only to suit the needs of the twentieth rather than the seventeenth century. Older Roman churches don't have pews, for one thing, and they rarely use their main altars, for another. And there was the matter of money. The bishop wanted the marble so lavishly used in the Roman model, but it was just too expensive. So were many other details. The facade isn't modelled after any known specific church, but there are dozens similar to it, with the entrances straight off the city sidewalk. It used to be said that the residence is modelled after the Farnese Palace in Rome, but the comparison is farfetched. The Farnese, with its Michelangelo windows and spacious courtyard, is one of the most beautiful buildings in the world. The bishop's residence is a handsome and elegant small building, but hardly in that class.

It also used to be said that the bell tower was copied from the Church of San Damascus in Rome, but Monsignor Flanigen, who studied the history of the Church in Tennessee more thoroughly than anyone else, failed to find any such church or tower in Rome. There are similar towers all over Italy. Flanigen thought the model may have been Santa Maria in Cosmedin, an ancient church in Rome, whose tower is quite similar to the cathedral's.

Leonard's drawings are still in the cathedral archives, but none exist for the residence, which was begun in 1907. Byrne and his household moved into their new home in March of 1908, so the building went up pretty rapidly. It is a spacious house, a good house for the hot Nashville summers. The ceilings are very high and the walls very thick, and the original floor plans airy and open, though Byrne, who had a mania for privacy, was probably not prone to leave the doors to his second-floor private apartments open. Like most multi-purpose buildings, the house, which has had no major change since it was built, is not completely satisfactory either as residence or office. There are touches

Thomas Sebastian Byrne at the time of his consecration in 1893 as the fifth Bishop of Nashville.

In the picture below, Bishop Byrne pauses in procession to the cathedral on (probably) Holy Thursday of 1917 or 1918. Father P.J. Gleeson is on his right; Fathers T.C. Abbott and A.A. Siener are in front. The elaborate vestments were a gift from the Pope, Pius X.

In this photo, made about 1912, Bishop Byrne watches his cathedral take shape. On page opposite, the Cathedral of the Incarnation is viewed from across West End Avenue; facade and bell tower are unchanged since they were built. Photo of interior shows installation of Byrne's successor in 1924.

of Roman decoration inside, but mainly the interior is simple and commodious. The exterior is also simple, but it has an elegance that comes partly from the proportions, partly from the beautiful window pediments echoed in the simple and dignified classical entrance, and much from the red tile roof, an effective decorative feature of all three buildings in the cathedral complex.

The next building to be constructed housed the pro-cathedral on the ground floor and the school on the upper two floors. Its exterior is like the residence's, but with more windows. The interior had offices just inside the entrance. The second floor school rooms were the usual boxes. The pro-cathedral, on the other hand, was fairly ornate. It was to serve as the parish church for five years, and as a daily Mass chapel for another fifty. Byrne had the idea of converting it to a school auditorium once the cathedral proper was built, but the expense of opening and heating the big church for so few for daily Mass was too much for him and his two immediate successors.

The pro-cathedral was a miniature of the cathedral-to-come. The main altar was identical to the one in the big church. The columns, rather too big for the space, were also similar to the ones in the church. There were no side altars. A much used confessional was on the Gospel side of the recessed main altar. The daily Mass was said to an obbligato of school children dashing in intermittently with a clatter of lunch boxes and satchels. The school, conducted by the Sisters of Mercy from St. Bernard's, was a success from the day it opened in the fall of 1909 until the neighborhood ceased to be residential. Byrne had studiously refrained from providing it with enough play space — school was NOT for play, was his view — but the children made do somehow.

With the two auxiliary buildings completed, Byrne set to work in earnest on the central building, the new cathedral. The lovely bell tower went up first in 1909-10; the tradition is that Byrne had the services of a skilled bricklayer at just this time. In the 1980s the cathedral staff found another good reason for doing the tower first. If any tiles fell off the roof they fell harmlessly to the ground without damaging the cathedral roof, as frequently happened when the two roofs were re-tiled in the 1980s.

From the beginning Bishop Byrne had thought of this as a bell-tower, though no bells were installed until 1937, long after he died. But as a purely decorative feature it is superb. The lovely little Romanesque arches rise in a crescendo from the two plain larger ones, which modulate into a row of three, then into three more rows of three whose pillars are of stone. This gives an almost musical effect which the bells would eventually complement. The tower looked westward across to another fine one atop Vanderbilt's main building, Kirkland Hall, and later to the lovely Gothic one atop Scarritt College, a beautiful skyline effect now spoiled by the unfortunate Baker Building on Twenty-first Avenue.

While the tower was settling in 1910 the foundations for the cathedral were laid. The church went up slowly, partly because the bishop frequently changed his mind about some detail, partly because he insisted on supervising everything, and partly because of money. Whatever the reasons, the effects were worthwhile. It is a stylish, elegant, and thoroughly satisfying ecclesiastical structure, individual but not eccentric, expressive of the Church universal in its Italian charm, yet not unsuited to the warm skies of the mid-south.

The facade is a typical Italian ecclesiastical style, in general design like Santa Maria Novella in Florence, which goes back to the early fifteenth century. The central rectangle reflects the basic style of the church, the long nave flanked by side aisles of less than half the nave's height. The rectangle is surmounted by a pediment containing a round stone entablature, with the Byrne coat-of-arms in it and a simple bronze cross on it. This fine summit is enclosed in the charming little triangles with curved hypotenuses joining the big rectangle to the smaller one-story ones for the side aisles. Three simple entrances pierce the facade with pediments like those of the residence and pro-cathedral. The elegant simplicity of all this is beautifully lightened by the flower-like Corinthian capitals of the pilasters. Four shallow niches decorate the main triangle, two above and two flanking the entrance. A fifth over the entrance is a stained glass window, seldom seen inside the church because of the organ loft.

Inside, the church is anything but plain. It is a riot of richly decorated coffered ceiling and sanctuary apse. The basic design is plain, as all basilicas are — basilica simply means a church like the cathedral, with a big unobstructed nave flanked by pillars holding up a clerestory level which contain lots of windows for light — the side aisles may or may not have windows. At the far end of the basilica is the altar. A true basilica has the bishop's throne directly behind the altar, but is impractical in modern churches, so the throne is to the right or left of the altar as convenience suggests, although some recent cathedrals restore it behind the altar.

The plans for the church still exist in the Cathedral archives and the Tennessee State Archives. Plans for the decoration, designed by Daprato of Chicago, are also in the cathedral archives. The ceiling is effective, the columns less so. Byrne wanted marble, of course, for the columns, but couldn't afford it, so settled for scagliola, a cement plaster which gives a marble-like surface appearance. The same material was used in the main altar, the altar railings, and the pilasters. Simple limestone or granite would have been cheaper and more effective, but Byrne was entranced by the Roman use of marble.

The apse is curved to make an emphatic relief from basilica boxiness and stress the importance of the central feature of every Catholic church, the main altar. The proscenium for this emphasis is superb. The entire interior evolves into the apse, with bas-reliefs above and below flanking the curves, and splendid angels in rounded triangles flanking the big arch. Signor B. Mellerio did the original paintings in the apse, copies of old masters, but the general effect is somewhat disappointing. The big stained glass window behind the altar rather diminished it. The miniature domed baldichino is lovely in itself, but is too small to create a dramatic effect. It's likely that Byrne wanted a regular baldichino rising to twenty or so feet covering the entire altar space; he later was instrumental in getting one for the chapel of the Cincinnati sisters at Mount Saint Joseph's. But once again, not enough money.

Byrne and Daprato were equally careful about such lesser appointments as candlesticks, altar rail, pulpit (which originally was just behind the altar rail on the Epistle side), holy water fonts, and such like. A beautiful baptismal font was the gift of Mr. and Mrs. Pat Timothy. The Stations of the Cross are particularly fine. Terracotta bas-relief and full figures alternate in ornate Renaissance framing, creating just the right amount of decoration on the interior walls between pilasters.

The clerestory windows flood the church with the frequent Tennessee sunlight. They were made of plain prism glass. They are also the subject of much controversy. Many think they ought to be replaced by conventional stained glass. The other stained glass windows, the two now in the sacristy which used to be in the church and the one in the choir loft, plus the one now in the baptistery at St. Henry's, do not suggest much excellence in that way of decoration. It was not a good time for stained glass.

The effect of the whole, however, is wonderful. It is grand on a small scale. Excellent taste has kept the decoration in check. The original floor, of wood, gave endless trouble, but was not out of key with the whole. The bishop had every reason to be satisfied when his church was dedicated on July 26, 1914. The Catholics of Nashville and the diocese have been rightly proud of their cathedral ever since. The architecture of the Catholic Church in the United States in its great period of building, 1900-1940, is very conventional. The cathedral of the Diocese of Nashville is a shining and exquisite exception.

Not so the spin-off churches in roughly the same style. The simpler ones, Blessed Sacrament in Memphis and Holy Name in Nashville, both combination church-schools, modeled after the pro-cathedral, are not too bad, serviceable, with a touch of style. The two larger ones in Memphis fare worse. St. Patrick's is almost grandiose, its imitation of the cathedral style rather inept. Since it was built before the cathedral, Byrne may have learned from it. Immaculate Conception is somewhat better, but the mark of elegance is missing. For all of these, there were professional architects, but the Byrne taste is dominant.

A building Byrne did entirely by himself was the "new" St. Mary's Orphanage. He had early become increasingly dissatisfied with the orphanage in south Nashville. The handsome old building was in constant need of repair. The property was too small for the farming Byrne thought essential to an orphanage, not just to cut costs by raising its own food, but also to teach the children the facts of economic life. So, he began to search around for a suitable place for a new orphanage.

The land he bought in 1901 was another instance of Byrne luck and shrewdness, a tract of fifty acres on the corner of present-day Harding and Bosley Springs roads. It was indeed then farmland, but the inexorable drive of the city westward turned it eventually into valuable business property. Meanwhile, it was a good place for an orphanage. The building Byrne designed and built was undistinguished. Of cut limestone, the mortar was faulty, and continually crumbled thereafter. Like the cathedral group, the new orphanage had a red tile roof, its effect somewhat diminished by a mansard story. Situated on a little rise about a quarter of a mile off Bosley Springs Road to the west, overlooking the main line of the Nashville, Chattanooga and St. Louis Railroad to the south, it was well known to two generations of Nashville Catholics to whom the Orphans' Picnic on the Fourth of July was as fixed an engagement as Santa's visit at Christmas.

The bishop himself frequently joined in the construction work as he did with the cathedral, and so may have cut his building teeth on the orphanage. Despite the problem with the mortar, and other difficulties, it lasted as long as there was a need for an orphanage, until the 1960s. Its capacity was around eighty children, but during the Depression more than one hundred were crowded in it.

With most of the building during his long episcopate Bishop Byrne had to be, or chose to be, less involved. At about the same time the orphanage was going up, the Sisters of Mercy built their present building on Twenty-first Avenue, South. Christian Asmus again was the architect for this convent. The property was and is an excellent location. It consists of nine acres on the Hillsboro Pike just a few yards toward town from the old toll gate #1 on the corner of present Ashwood Avenue. Built on a pleasant rise well back from the road, the convent and later on the academy building are very much of their time, typical plain red brick, but with some interesting brick patterning, no doubt the work of the imaginative Asmus. The land had been purchased some time earlier by Bishop Byrne and Father Gleeson, who sold it to the sisters on very advantageous terms. Although the Sisters of Mercy were a pontifical and not a diocesan order, their tradition was close cooperation with the bishops. Byrne was devoted to them.

He dedicated the new building June 30, 1905. The sisters were especially proud of the chapel, which was entirely furnished by "memorials" to various deceased Nashville Catholics given by their relations. Although never very large, the academy carried over, from its earlier days downtown and on Green Street, a panache of piety and the cultivation of womanliness. It was a lovely retreat at the day's end for the sisters who taught in the city schools, and a welcome home for those in schools elsewhere in the diocese. The Mercies succeeded the Sisters of the Precious Blood at Loretto, and staffed the new Holy Ghost Parish School in Knoxville. Then came the Nashville Cathedral School, and then, in 1912, Blessed Sacrament in Memphis.

The Mercies were old hands in Nashville, of course; the bishop lived for ten years in their old convent at 607 Capitol Boulevard. New hands were the Daughters of Charity of Saint Vincent de Paul. This famous and world-wide religious community, whose eastern headquarters were in Emmitsburg, Maryland, came to Nashville at the invitation of Bishop Byrne in 1898 to start a hospital. Catholic Nashville had a history of hospitals that failed to take root, but this was largely because of the way medicine was practiced in the late nineteenth century. Hospitals then were mostly small private institutions run by popular doctors — the Barr Infirmary in Nashville at Eighteenth and Division, and the Dozier Hospital on Monroe Street in north Nashville, are good examples. Such infirmaries were not expected to last beyond the careers of their founding doctors, and were often set up only for his convenience. Thus there was something ephemeral about the very nature of hospitals. The vast sprawling institutions of the present were just beginning to be built throughout the country.

The bishop was lucky to get the Vincentian Sisters for his hospital. At first they went along on the small scale of the past. They bought a lot on Hayes Street only a block away from the site of the new cathedral; it included a big house which was both home and hospital. They named the hospital St. Thomas, after the bishop's patron saint. The scale of operation was slight; around ten admissions a month was the norm. But as the new century came around doctors began to request a larger new building. The ground for this was broken in 1900 and the new building dedicated in 1902. But 1905 was the pivotal year. The first class of nurses was graduated in January, 1905, but the decisive event, the one which foreshadowed the development of the modern hospital, was when Doctor William D. Haggard, Jr., closed his private infirmary and transferred his practice largely to St. Thomas. Dr. Haggard and his father, both celebrated surgeons, were, in turn, both presidents of the American Medical Association. The patronage of the younger doctor gave St. Thomas the momentum it needed, and it went on growing and improving. Its success was a great thing for the city. Nursing the sick back to health was a charity as plain as an orphanage and a good deal closer to most normal people. It was wise of Bishop Byrne to concentrate on these two great charities in Nashville, wise and good. Associating the diocese with the Daughters of Charity was also a good thing. These devoted women caught the imagination of Nashville's most influential people. Mary Morris, the sister of Father, later Bishop, Morris of the cathedral, joined them and made a distinguished career in the community, ending as Soeur Madeline, their American secretary, in the famous motherhouse in the Rue du Bac in Paris.

The story of St. Joseph's Hospital in Memphis is like that of St. Thomas. The distinguished Christian Brother Maurelian took part in the early discussions with Doctor E. M. Willett in 1887, but the sparkplug was the lively and energetic pastor of St. Mary's, Franciscan Father Francis Moening. Finding Bishop Rademacher cooperative, he wrote the Superior of the Franciscan Sisters at Lafayette, Indiana. The Superior hesitated, so he visited the convent in person, and got results. Father Francis then went after property, which he soon found, on Jackson Street. It must have been a good site, for the hospital stayed there until 1969 — again, the pattern in Nashville. The hospital opened on a shoestring in 1889, but by 1901 there were two wings, the original one of three stories, and a new one of four, dedicated by Bishop Byrne in 1902. There were additions in 1908 and 1910. Memphis was growing fast, and the hospital and grew with it.

Especially in the early part of this century, when medical science and medical care were beginning to be really scientific and effective, nothing gripped the imagination of Catholics and non-Catholics alike as much as hospitals. Chattanooga, too, caught the fever, and the part Father Moening played in Memphis was taken there by Father William Walsh, the enthusiastic and talented priest who had established Camp Father Mathew for the yellow fever victims of Memphis, and, as pastor in Chattanooga, built a magnificent church, started and edited the best premodern Catholic newspaper the diocese boasted, and started a hospital as well. What a man! He might have been one of the great legends of the diocese, but he didn't get along with Bishop Byrne, and he was a majestic spendthrift. Still, he was full of zeal. Unfortunately, his hospital did not last, and the present fine medical facility in Chattanooga is a modern enterprize. The Catholic hospital in Knoxville dates only from 1929.

The Catholic Church has always firmly believed in good works — helping the poor, the sick, the unfortunate. Until the modern welfare states began to appear, sparked by Bismarck's Germany of the 1880s, the Church was often the only agency for such charities. It was officially so in the Spanish-speaking countries and in Italy, as it was everywhere in Europe in medieval times. It was only when the western world began to be industrialized that people gradually began to see that the new wealth thus created must be used in part to help those uprooted from the farms and struggling to master industrial society. The Church often was opposed to the new idea that government must do what it had been doing. Many churchmen feared, not without reason, that "welfare" would come to mean secularism. Bishop Byrne was one of these. He was eager for the Church in Tennessee to develop all sorts of charitable institutions, independent of governments. Early in his episcopate, in 1900, he requested the Little Sisters of the Poor to establish a Home for the Aged in Nashville. When the old orphanage fell vacant by the move to the new one, the Little Sisters took it over in 1903 for a home for the aged.

This unusual community was founded by an unusual woman, Jeanne Jugan, later Sister Mary of the Cross, in Brittany, France, in 1839. Sister Mary was nearly fifty years old when she founded her community, and worked as its premier beggar-lady for only twelve years. She was the product of as hard a life as may be imagined in a free country. Left fatherless at three, at sixteen she began to work as a domestic, then gradually, with a few pious friends, moved toward the Little Sisters system, which consisted of begging from door to door and person to person for the day's needs. She and her disciples lived as poor as those they befriended. Their community grew swiftly, and spread wide — they came to the United States in 1868.

Their growth in Nashville was phenomenal. The south Nashville orphanage soon proved too old and ill-arranged for their purposes, but how that old building did cling to existence. It lasted till 1942, when it finally burned down; the main building of Trevecca College stands just about on its site. After a year in it, the Little Sisters built a fine new building across Main Street from St. Columba's Church. Even more than did the Vincentian Sisters they caught the imagination of the City of Nashville. They were everywhere begging — "Something for the poor, please, in God's Name", they'd say, often with a little accent, for many of the Nashville sisters were from French Canada. They called on families only a little better off than those they sought to help, and usually got a quarter or a half-dollar, often also with a glass of lemonade or a cup of tea. They also went from officer to clerk to cook in the big insurance companies, the banks, everywhere. People who wouldn't give a dime to a church gave something to the Little Sisters. When their east Nashville building went up in the great East Nashville fire of 1916, they had little trouble mobilizing support for a larger one on Belmont Hill on the other side of town. There was the usual neighborhood protest, which Bishop Byrne brushed off. The new building accommodated nearly two hundred old people, and, at one time, had one hundred and sixty. The building may well have been designed by the Little Sisters. It wears a somewhat minatory look, and, with its high walls and rounded top windows, looks more like Brittany than Rome.

In all his building, Bishop Byrne had the strong helping hand of Father Thomas J. Plunkett, a Josephite priest who had a natural aptitude for the building trades. Of Irish birth, and from a famous Irish family, Plunkett spoke with the fruitiest of Irish brogues, an ironic circumstance in that he came to Nashville to speak largely to blacks. His brogue and their dialect must have made for some interesting listening.

The Josephite Congregation, officially St. Joseph's Society of the Sacred Heart (SSJ), was founded by Father, later Cardinal, Herbert Vaughan of England as a missionary society in 1866. The bishops of the United States in their Second Plenary Council in 1866 asked for missionary help to work with the four million recently-freed blacks. The Josephite fathers accepted this challenge as a primary mission. They arrived in Baltimore in 1871 and at once began their difficult apostolate. Father Plunkett was ordained there in 1898 and came to Nashville in 1900.

Nothing was nearer to Bishop Byrne's heart's desire than the apostolate to the blacks. He was convinced, and said so with simple and eloquent sincerity, that only religion could ameliorate their sad condition in the United States, especially in the South. As the events of the black revolution proved, he was prophetic on this point. Of course, the religious leadership was not Catholic. It couldn't be. There were simply too few black Catholics.

When Father Plunkett came to Nashville he found there just one black Catholic. There had been more in Bishop Miles' time; Miles, too, was keenly interested in the black apostolate. He ran a Sunday school for blacks from 1844 on, although after his little seminary closed in 1848 the Sunday school faded because the seminarians had been its teachers, and teachers were hard to find. But blacks were still of concern at the cathedral, and during the war Fathers Jarboe and James Keane, later briefly at Knoxville, did what they could to instruct them. In 1867 the Sisters of Mercy started a school for blacks at the cathedral, which attracted twenty-five pupils.

Yet the period from the end of the Civil War until Father Plunkett's arrival on the scene is a bleak one for developing Catholicism among the blacks. The terrible dislocations of the war's aftermath, the fearful plagues, the poignant poverty all contributed, but the main cause was the loss of the paternalism slavery inspired and the absence of anything to take its place.

Byrne and Plunkett changed all that. The latter set to work at once to make a church for the black people of Nashville. He first secured the beautiful old Second Presbyterian Church at Third and Gay, which was built in 1846, and is often attributed to Strickland. Plunkett fixed it up and began services in it almost at once. He and the bishop named it Holy Family Church. No photograph of the interior survives, but it served the growing Nashville black congregation for nearly twenty years.

Meanwhile the bishop had been cultivating the founder of the Sisters of the Blessed Sacrament, Mother Katharine Drexel, a most remarkable woman. She came from the well-known and very wealthy Philadelphia Drexels, one of the half-dozen richest Catholic families in the United States. Katharine made her novitiate with the Sisters of Mercy, but gradually decided to form her own congregation, and use her fortune to finance work for the conversion of the blacks and Indians. Her first mission was to the Indians of the southwest at Santa Fe, but she had sent Bishop Byrne a check for $2,667 to help pay for Holy Family. Early in 1900, Byrne invited her to start a school for black girls in Nashville, but she felt she did not have the personnel.

However, Providence took a hand, as so often happens. Let a letter of Mother Katharine's tell the story:

> . . .At St. Louis [in the fall of 1900] I had to stop off at a convent on business, and whom should I meet there by the decree of Providence but Right Reverend Bishop Byrne, who happened to be visiting the same convent. As you know, he is the Bishop of Nashville, who wrote that very zealous appeal for the Colored and Indian collection which I read to you last spring. He is also the Bishop who has asked our sisters to teach a Colored School in Nashville when he establishes one.
>
> "Why Bishop Byrne", I said, "how did you get here?" I discovered he was on his way to Santa Fe for his health.
>
> "Mother", he said, "I want to have a talk with you, but I'll see you in Sante Fe."
>
> I told him I would not be there for two weeks and he said, "I'll be away from there by that time, but I can come up to see you at St. Michael's if you invite me." Which, of coure, I did on the spot, provided His Lordship promised to be satisfied with missionary fare and a thirty mile drive in a market wagon, to which he agreed. [St. Michael's was her Indian mission in the desert].

From Santa Fe Bishop Byrne wrote her:

> October 8, 1904
>
> . . .Last Sunday afternoon Archbishop Bourgade [of Sante Fe] and I went for a walk and called at St. Catherine's [another school for Indians established in Sante Fe by Mother Katharine]. I was a little surprised at seeing your school there, . . . and I rejoiced to meet your sisters. . . . The thought that came to mind and which I expressed to them was that they would surely some day, not very distant either, be in Nashville. It seemed an inspiration and I hope it is prophetic.
>
> There is a beautiful property in a desirable part of the city [Nashville], but in the opposite direction from the present Church of the Holy Family, and within a short distance of a large Negro settle-

> ment, containing possibly some three or four acres and a splendid house that could be had on easy terms and at a moderate price, say $18,000. It would be an admirable place for an industrial school . . . there is no place like Nashville for beginning such a work and for a centre of operation . . .

After Mother Katharine and a companion came to Nashville and inspected the property, she and her council agreed, and the bishop instructed his attorney, Thomas J. Tyne, to buy the property and convey it on the same day to the Sisters of the Blessed Sacrament. When the former owner learned, from a newspaper story, that the place was to be used to build a school for blacks, he hit the ceiling, and did all he could to undo the sale. Failing that, he tried to get the city council to run a street through the property and wreck the bishop's plans. Neighbors were aghast, and even black ministers thundered against the Catholics. But nothing deterred the bishop, Father Plunkett, or Mother Katharine. This was then white residential property, located on Seventh Avenue South near Lea Avenue. It is now the site of a Sears Roebuck store. The school, Immaculate Mother Academy, was opened in the "splendid house" with the nuns living on the upper floors. It was an instant success. Two years later Father Plunkett began construction of a new school building with an auditorium, which was used as a church. A fine convent soon followed, then a residence for Plunkett. And finally, in 1919, a new church went up to replace the old one on Third Avenue North, since that area had now become mostly commercial and industrial. It is interesting to note changes in attitudes: there is now a street near this property named Drexel Street.

All these buildings made a splendid complex for the education of black children. At first only girls were accepted as students, then young boys were added. Eventually there was a parochial grade school as well as the Immaculate Mother Academy. Father Plunkett oversaw all this construction, as well as helping Bishop Byrne with his orphanage, his cathedral project, and other construction. He was quite a man. He left after Bishop Byrne died to go to Toledo, Ohio, where he had been invited by that city's new Bishop, Samuel A. Stritch, to work among the blacks there, so many of whom had migrated to Ohio during World War I. Plunkett followed Stritch to Milwaukee when he was made archbishop of that city in 1930, and also went with him to Chicago. But Father Plunkett barely survived that move, and returned to die in a Milwaukee hospital in February 1941. Cardinal Stritch had served Father Plunkett as a Nashville altar boy, and loved him for his spiritual advice and deep faith. "He was comfort and strength to me," said the cardinal in his funeral sermon. He was that to many, from the simple blacks he loved to serve to the highest ranks in the Church.

Meanwhile, Memphis had much less trouble in setting up its St. Anthony of Padua church for blacks on Hill and Concord streets in 1909. This was a combination church and school building, also run by the Josephites. Father Joseph Dube was the first pastor, and Bishop Byrne's favorite sisters in Cincinnati, the Sisters of Charity of Mount Saint Joseph, came to run the school. Monsignor Flanigen reported that they served with little or no compensation, so they must have been indeed devoted to the bishop. The parish became a gratifying success from the start.

A third Josephite parish for blacks was started in Jackson. It's a fascinating story. A white Catholic, Dennis Donovan, willed his farm to help establish a Catholic mission for blacks. Father Joseph J. Kelly was the first Josephite to take hold. He wrote,

> I came to Jackson in October 1913 and found eight acres of land, a diocesan property in care of our Society . . . I built a frame building . . . Here I gathered thirty non-Catholics meeting on Sunday afternoons and Wednesday nights for catechetical instructions and devotions. With the exception of aged Louis Norman, there were no colored Catholics in Jackson. Wherefore my labors were of the pioneer kind for eleven months. I toiled and sweated trying to get these thirty souls ready for Baptism and I had them prepared for this sacrament when I was transferred . . . The bishop sold the Donovan land to the city for $8,000. With this fund, ere I departed, I purchased the site on South Market Street . . . a most desirable site. My sucessor moved the frame building I had erected on the Donovan property to the Market Street lot."

This successor was Father Lawrence Schaefer, who followed the example of Father Plunkett in Jackson, doing most of the work himself in building a rectory, whose nucleus was the old building, and a church-school building. Kelly's candidates were duly baptized, and Schaefer also persuaded two graduates of Mother Katharine Drexel's Virginia institution to open a school for black children in Jackson. Tuition proved too much for these poor people, however, and the school lasted only a few months. But the church persisted until integration made it, along with most churches and schools especially for blacks, obsolete.

The Jackson story is in some ways the purest example of the dedication and frustrating labors of the Josephites in the diocese. As Flanigen put it of one of the Jackson Josephites, "He came, he saw, but he did not conquer". And there is, perhaps, more nobility of soul in trying the impossible for God than doing the agreeable possible. The Jackson story is in tiny miniature the story of the White Fathers in Africa, who have tried so hard for so long and so fruitlessly to convert the Mohammedans in that part of the world.

Bishop Byrne the builder had much to look back on in 1916, as he began the twenty-second year of his episcopate. But now, for the first time, he was faced with rebuilding a church which was destroyed in a tremendous and tragic fire.

This was the east Nashville church, whose history is full of disasters. Edgefield, as east Nashville was originally called, might well have been the cradle of the Church in Tennessee. Three railroads terminated there, and spawned the usual Irish work force. Clearly here was a nascent parish, and Bishop Miles agreed with the Edgefielders who petitioned him for one on Christmas night 1854. But not until 1857 did Father Schacht, it will be recalled, finally build a church there at Bass and Fifth, and named it in honor of St. John the Evangelist. But Schacht had no clear title to the land, and Thomas Farrell had to bail him out. Trouble from the word go.

But a new period of Catholic life followed when, in 1871, Father Michael Meagher laid the cornerstone of a new church, named by its Irish-born pastor in honor of St. Columba. The parchment in the cornerstone read:

> This cornerstone of a church, to be dedicated to God under the invocation of St. Columba, has been laid on the solemn Feast of the Resurrection, on the 9th of April, A.D. 1871, by the Most Reverend P. A. Feehan, Bishop, in the City of Edgefield, of which W.A. Glenn is Mayor, in the State of Tennessee, of which D.W.C. Senter is Governor, toward the close of the 25th year of the pontificate of Pius IX,

happily governing the Holy Roman Church and now bravely suffering martyrdom in defense of its liberty.

Jesuit Father Michael Meagher raised much of the cost of the church and rectory lecturing around the country. The school, in the former church, was staffed by lay teachers until 1877, when the sisters from St. Cecilia took it over. As recounted in the yellow fever chapter, tragedy again struck when Meagher went to St. Brigid's in Memphis to help his brother priest, and died of the dreadful yellow jack in 1878.

The man forever associated with east Nashville Catholicism came in 1879. This was Father Eugene Gazzo, of a distinguished Italian family, who volunteered for the Tennessee missions. He was to spend thirty-one of his fifty-five years in the priesthood in east Nashville, to the joy and satisfaction of his parishioners and colleagues. Twice he was sent to Memphis to settle problems among the Italians of St. Joseph's parish there. Once he settled them, and on one occasion that took fourteen years, he begged to return to east Nashville. It was a curious situation. The quarrelsome Memphis Italians became peaceful only under an Italian priest, but the quarrelsome Irish of Edgefield, who had a reputation for breeding some very tough customers indeed, were happily contented with an Italian pastor — so long as it was Eugene Gazzo.

As Father Gazzo settled into his new work, there were portents of what was to come. In 1881 the school burned. A new school went up at once, on Main Street, and it also burned down, in 1882. Plainly, St. Columba's was accident prone. But there ensued twenty years of peace and progress. Most of these years were spent under the pastorate of Father Daniel Ellard while Father Gazzo was in Memphis. He returned in 1915. But he had scarcely got settled before the whole plant was destroyed in Nashville's most disastrous fire in 1916.

March 22 was a windy spring day when a pile of wood shavings in one of the riverside lumber yards caught fire. Fanned by the wind, it spread rapidly eastward, burning throughout the whole day.

On the flyleaf of his baptismal register Father Gazzo made this entry: "March 22, 1916, Church, school and residence with all contents reduced to ashes, in the great conflagration. Sic transit gloria mundi. Dominus dedit, Dominus abstulit. Sit nomen Dominus benedictum. Miseracordia Domini quia non sumus consumpti''. (Thus passes the glory of the world. The Lord has given, the Lord has taken away; blessed be the name of the Lord. It is the mercy of the Lord that we are not consumed.)

Young Father John M. Mogan, destined to be as beloved as Father Gazzo, who was in his first post as assistant, did heroic work in helping people to evacuate. He also removed the Blessed Sacrament before the Church burned. He gave the sacred vessels to Mary Carton, who took them across the bridge to St. Mary's in undertaker Will Martin's car. He also rescued the parish records.

The Little Sisters of the Poor's home for the aged went up in flames. One sister carried an old woman out of the house on her back.

But east Nashville came back. The day after the fire Father Gazzo rented a room over the postoffice on Woodland Street which served as a temporary church. Woodland had by now supplanted Main as East Nashville's principal street, owing largely to the proposed fine new bridge, and it was decided to locate the new church on this street. The church-school building was to be Byrne Renaissance, a cathedral spin-off. Harry Frahan was the architect of record, but it was a Byrne building through and through. It is one of the bishop's better efforts. Old St. Columba's was not a handsome edifice, but the new building had some style and elegance. It still does.

Malignant destiny was not through with east Nashville. In March 1933 a fierce tornado swept through the area in a much greater swath than the fire had made. The church buildings were not damaged, but more than eight hundred east Nashville homes were wrecked. There were also deaths and injuries.

There is no doubt that Bishop Byrne created the visible Church of the Diocese of Nashville. The churches that were built before his episcopate are now, where they survive, shrines rather than churches. Bishop Smith did little church building, other than complete some plans of Byrne's. Bishop Adrian's long episcopate saw many new churches built, some of them very fine indeed, but there was no Adrian trademark on them. They were architects' churches, mostly, no doubt a good thing after the Roman imitations of Byrne. None has the charm of the Nashville cathedral, Byrne's masterpiece. But it was definitely a good thing that Byrne's plans for the boys' high school in Nashville, which were on his desk when he died, were aborted. West End Avenue was a fine place for a church in 1907. It still is, surprisingly, in 1987. But at no time was it a good place for a school. Neither are the streets of Rome.

Byrne was a strong man, and devoted to the Church. Yet he was no organizer, or, rather, he saw little need for organization. He followed with great particularity the rules of the Church for the liturgical seasons, for the sacraments, and for Church discipline. But the present system of consultors, the distribution of duties and responsibilities, the development of societies and organizations, above all the encouragement of lay participation, were disdained by him. It was left to Bishop Smith to bring the Nashville diocese up to date in such matters. Smith was a good organizer. He kept good records and distributed authority widely. Moreover, he encouraged his appointees to exercise their own judgment and discretion.

Byrne did not. Nor did he aspire to; the word "modern" probably would have sounded nasty to him. Yet he was not without a touch of greatness. Of all the bishops of Nashville he was probably the most learned, probably the most gifted, and probably the most tasteful. He was certainly the most arrogant and the least tender. His times were those of the great American robber barons. He would have despised them, too, for their greed. But he probably understood them, and they him.

17

With Emphasis on the Laity, 1880-1920

A fascinating phenomenon in American Catholicism at the turn of the twentieth century was the rise of the Knights of Columbus. Catholic lay organizations were nothing new. They came naturally in parishes, as women gathered in one another's homes or the school to plan lawn parties, to sew layettes for orphans, or merely to play cards and drink tea and chat. Men and women got together to sing both in the church choir and at festive gatherings, to present amateur theatricals, to dance and to pray, especially at wakes. Men without women organized in all sorts of lodges, especially those with insurance features. Nashville had already spawned the national organization of the Catholic Knights of America and formed a local chapter of the Knights of St. John. Nothing could be more natural.

But none of these, nor all of them taken together, had as much impact on American Catholicism as the Knights of Columbus. There are lots of reasons for this, even though they do not entirely explain the attraction of this new organization. American Catholics had always been on the defensive, even where they were in a majority. They elected mayors in several New England cities, including Boston, in the 1880s, yet still felt unaccepted by the Yankees and the Congregationalists of eastern Massachusetts. The same sort of uneasiness prevailed elsewhere, whether there were many Catholics, as in Philadelphia or Milwaukee, or only a few, as in Vermont or Tennessee.

More than any other single force the Knights of Columbus helped to change all this. They boldly proclaimed that Catholics were indeed first-class American citizens with all the rights and privileges appertaining thereto. The Knights of Columbus shared many of the same goals as did other lodges, the Knights of Pythias, the Oddfellows, the Woodmen of the World, and the

Masons: good citizenship, service to the community, help for the unfortunate, fraternity, and above all, patriotism. But the Knights had a special mission. They wanted to make clear to their fellow Americans what the Catholic Church was, to convince them that American democracy was congenial to Roman Catholicism, to expose bigotry and promote truth. The Knights were not primarily founded to defend the faith, but they did steady and effective service for one hundred years in telling the American world that the Church was a domestic, not a foreign growth, and that it flourished, like other American institutions, under the sun of freedom and tolerance.

The organization was founded in 1882, at just the right time. Anti-Catholic feeling once again was on the rise; the Know-Nothings of the 1840s were succeeded by the American Protective Association. The APA did not try to form a separate political party, perhaps learning from the experience of the Know-Nothings, but they tried to influence both the major American parties, especially the Republicans, who had fewer Catholics in their ranks than the Democrats did outside the South. The Columbians, in their publications, speeches, and discussions, stressed that anti-Catholic bigotry was un-American. In their own ceremonials they emphasized the Catholic heritage in America and the pride the new member should feel in his American character. They insisted that Catholics were not monolithic in civic affairs. One of them, Thomas H. Cummings, wrote in an early Columbian publication,

> Much as their adversaries may storm and rave about the Catholic vote, and the political power of Rome in America, Catholics know that in political, material and social affairs they are really more divided than their Protestant neighbors. . . . It can be safely asserted that not until Catholic men have learned the lessons of fraternity and mutual sympathy, will die the misrepresentations, abuse, contempt and caricature to which all Catholics are now subject. There is full need and place for an intelligent organism such as the Knights of Columbus to step to the front, to work for the advancement of Catholic social and material interests, and in its own name and in that of justice, reason and humanity, to cry out to the opposing forces — Halt!

This is the way the organization saw itself, this is the way it impressed its membership, and the way it acted in its best moments. It was a healthy force in the Church.

But it had a time getting to be any force at all. Although the growth of the organization was phenomenal, its growing pains were large and racking. The early promoters knew instant success, but they also knew hostility from some bishops and priests, indifference and suspicion from many of the laity, and uncertainty and frustration in internal affairs. There were many other Catholic insurance bodies soliciting members. Most of these were local, working mainly only in a single city or a region. Although some aimed at national membership, none ever came close to the broad appeal of the Columbians.

''Columbianism was particularly appealing to Southern Catholics'', writes the official historian of the organization, Christopher Kauffman. However, expansion in the South was delayed because the region was considered too high a risk for insurance. Many insurance companies refused to do business in the South because of the epidemics of yellow fever, cholera, and the like, which were such tragic features of life there. But, since the organization had always admitted associate, or non-insurance members, the southern councils were set up on this basis. Associate membership usually outnumbered insurance membership the country over, and international membership, for example in Mexico, perforce had nothing but associates, so this was not Jim Crow treatment. In any case, the insurance ban was soon lifted, in 1909.

Nashville heard about the Knights of Columbus from Louisville. A group of Nashville men traveled to Louisville with organization in mind, only to learn of the ban on Southern councils. They joined with the Louisville group to persuade the National Supreme Council to allow southern associate membership councils, and Nashville then established its Council #544, created December 30, 1900. On that day Knights from the organization's headquarters in New Haven, and from Cincinnati, Cleveland, Toledo, Indianapolis, and Chicago showed up to grace the occasion. Louisville sent nearly a hundred Knights to celebrate its joining with Nashville to bring Columbianism to the South.

Ferdinand E. Kuhn, one of Nashville's foremost Catholic laymen, became Tennessee's first state deputy. He also became a master ceremonialist, presiding over the ceremonies founding councils in Florida, Alabama, Louisiana, and Georgia. Other leading members of the original Nashville council were H.J. Grimes, W.J. Varley, William Smith, and M.M. McCormack. The first Grand Knight was Albert D. Marks. Meetings were held in Watkins Hall, the Catholic Club (across Seventh Avenue from Assumption Church), and finally in the splendid old Ransom home at 1800 West End Avenue. Here the Knights headquartered until World War II. They then had a succession of temporary quarters until 1945 when they purchased the old Drouillard home at 810 Demonbreun Street. By 1962 they were in their excellent new quarters on Bosley Springs Road where there is a fine clubhouse, a swimming pool, and playing fields for parochial league games.

The other early Tennessee Councils followed soon after Nashville. Chattanooga organized in October 1901. John Carroll and John Stagmaier recruited five other men to go to Nashville to be initiated. They then returned to Chattanooga and recruited fifty more. The Chattanooga Columbians soon were strong enough to buy their own clubhouse, and soon outgrew that one. A new one went up in 1914. The Chattanooga council was very active and popular, and its club house a center for Catholic activities of all kinds.

Memphis came next, although actually Knoxville, Memphis, and Chattanooga were all founded at just about the same time, late 1901. The Memphis council might have come earlier, except that there were several competing active Catholic organizations there. But the Columbians established themselves for good in November 1901. In 1916 the Council joined hands with the Catholic Club and other Catholic organizations to build a fine clubhouse, the center for Catholic activities for many years, on Adams Street.

Knoxville got into Columbianism in February 1902 after a group of Knoxville men visited the Chattanooga set-up. The council flourished in rented meeting rooms, and got its own home just after World War I.

Jackson got its council in 1906. A delegation came from Nashville to honor the occasion, but the real godfathers were from Memphis. Several hundred came by special train to give the Jackson Council a real send-off. It worked, for the Jackson Council has been vigorously active ever since.

Many other councils were formed in the state after the Byrne era. Columbianism was indeed appealing to the southerners. All the virtues which made the organization effective at combating anti-Catholicism were treasured in the South, where Catholics were usually a small minority, and often true victims of prejudice and discrimination. Much of this discrimination came from ignorance, not malice, and hence the vitality of a strong lay organization was most useful to the cause of the southern Catholic Church. More than elsewhere in the country, bishops and priests in the South joined and encouraged the Columbians. As early as 1909 the national convention was held in the South, in Mobile, Alabama.

One of the greatest services the Columbians rendered the Nashville diocese was to Catholic journalism. The concept of the diocesan newspaper, or a news letter, or the parish bulletin, or any such organ of information or explanation came only gradually to the Catholic Church. Today the first item of business of any institution is its house organ, but the need for this was slow to take hold in the Catholic Church the country over. Although there had been Catholic newspapers in the early nineteenth century, they usually were organs of opinion rather than news. They frequently were independent papers, often at odds with rather than sponsored by the bishops, and usually the mouthpiece of one man. Such was Father Ryan's *Banner of the South,* such was James A. McMaster's *Freeman's Journal,* and such was *The Catholic Telegraph* of Cincinnati, published by the brother of Archbishop Purcell and consequently closer to being "official" than most. The two outstanding converts to the Catholic Church of the mid-nineteenth century, Father Isaac Hecker and Orestes Brownson, were both brilliant journalists; Brownson wrote for a dozen journals and founded two or three. Hecker's *Catholic World* was for many years the leading Catholic journal. Such magazines were often the lengthened shadow of one man. *The Ave Maria,* published from Notre Dame by Father Daniel Hudson, is a good example; so is the *Catholic World*. Both flourished in the latter part of the nineteenth and the early part of the twentieth century. Mathew Carey's *The American Museum* belongs to a period fifty years earlier.

The early days of the Diocese of Nashville were chronicled by *The Catholic Advocate,* Ben Webb's remarkable journal published in Bardstown-Louisville, and a pure example of the Catholic journalism of the nineteenth century. Webb owned the paper, as well as the job printing shop that produced it. From these he made a good living, the necessary aim of most of those who founded papers, although not the principal one. Webb managed, without losing any of his own integrity, to avoid offending the official Church, and to maintain cordial relations with most of the clergy. He merited their trust.

Webb thought of his circulation area, in pre-Civil War days, as the entire old Bardstown diocese, which embraced the enormous area stretching from the Alleghenies to the Mississippi, and on the north-south axis from Detroit to Natchez. He merged his paper with the *Cincinnati Catholic Telegraph* in 1849, but revived it after the Civil War. By that time the Bardstown diocese had shrunk to Kentucky, and the new dioceses were left without a paper.

Tennessee responded by trying to found one. Its search of trial and re-trial is the history of Catholic journalism in the state until the founding of the *Tennessee Register* in 1937 stabilized the hit-or-miss journalism it replaced. Parenthetically, it is worth noting that the new Diocese of Memphis had a newspaper almost as soon as it had a bishop, so keenly was the need for one felt in 1971.

The earliest trial was made in Memphis. This was *The Southern Catholic,* founded in 1876. Little is known of this paper; no issue of it seems to have survived. It was managed by Messrs. Harrington and Powell. The editor, Mr. Powell, fell a victim to yellow fever in 1878 and the paper ceased publication.

The next paper was probably meant to be a continuation of *The Southern Catholic,* since it begins with Volume Three. But it was named *Adam,* for reasons not clear — the nineteenth century was fond of fanciful titles for papers, like the Nashville *Orthopolitan,* a tradition continued in Nashville by *The Cresset* in 1927. *Adam* was masterminded by Father William Walsh, one of the authentic heroes of the Memphis yellow fever epidemics, and a journalist to the bone. It was described by a Memphis historian as a "Catholic journal of a literary and religious type." Like *The Southern Catholic* it was a weekly. *Adam* expired when Father Walsh was transferred to Chattanooga in 1887. A search failed to turn up a copy of it in Tennessee.

It took Father Walsh a few years to get settled in Chattanooga before his journalistic talents began to flower again. His new venture was entitled *Facts*, published between 1891 and 1895. Ample copies of *Facts* are still available. It was an excellent newspaper. Its format was similar to that of its contemporary journals, both Catholic and non-Catholic. These papers were mostly large tabloids, usually eight pages, each measuring 16 x 22 inches. Page 1 was usually mixed — a column of home news, all sorts of interesting happenings from around the country. Then came ecclesiastical notes, church news. Then a long article on some topic of the day — from Rome, or Germany, or Washington. But there was nothing rigid about this format; it varied greatly. Page 2 was usually given to poetry and fiction, often the continued novels of which newspaper readers of the day were so fond. The ads began to appear on pages 2 and 3, but disappeared on 4 and 5, the editorial pages filled with Catholic apologetics, Catholic historical sketches, and church news from all over — new churches dedicated, obituaries, and so on. *Facts* played with its name. Columns were called "Facts and Fancies," "Facts about the Monastic Life," etc. Nor did *Facts* ignore its home base. There were long articles on the glories of Chattanooga and its big new church, and local institutions. But *Facts* was interesting because it was well-edited and well-written. Father Walsh knew his business.

The circulation was only about half of what the Memphis Catholic papers achieved, despite the editor's intention of selling the paper and its advertisements in north Georgia, Alabama, and other areas close to Chattanooga. There just weren't enough Catholics in these parts to build a respectable circulation. But *Facts* was a lively feature of the Catholic scene in Tennessee until its editor ran afoul of Nashville's new Bishop Byrne, who tried to insist that Father Walsh pay his debts, and attend to the bishop's leadership. Despite Walsh's resistance, Byrne transferred him to Jackson. Without Walsh, *Facts* soon died; there was no one to take his place. Walsh went from Jackson very briefly to Knoxville, but his health was failing and he died still quite young in 1901.

The Catholic paper most like it in its time was *The Catholic Herald*, published in Nashville "with episcopal approval" from April 30, 1898 to June 17, 1899, a brief run indeed. It was more nearly the model Catholic paper, for, though it had episcopal approval, it did not have episcopal backing. It was run by two laymen, J. M. Hussey, editor, and G. F. Connor, business manager, and backed by some lay stockholders. P. G. Breen, Jr. was secretary-treasurer, and P. J. Flanigen, president. Toward the end of its existence, these appealed for more stockholders at $25 a share, but few apparently were forthcoming, since the paper ceased publication shortly thereafter. The final issue announced the hope it would reappear as a bi-weekly, but it did not. Nor did the reduction in price from five cents to two cents make any difference.

The Nashville paper was much like the Chattanooga one in format, but it was less well edited, and is less interesting. The main theme of its short life was the insistence that Catholics supported the United States in the Spanish-American War, even though Spain was Catholic. One article maintained that Spain was not really Catholic, merely nominally so. The very first issue reprinted Bishop Byrne's sermon rallying Catholics to the support of the American cause. "We are true Americans," wrote Byrne. "And we are loyal to our country and to its flag, and obedient to the highest degree to the supreme authority of our nation." This sermon was distributed throughout the country by the American Catholic archbishops.

Other features followed familiar patterns. There was a social column, a church directory, reports of meetings of Catholic organizations, announcements of frequent parish and other picnics at Centennial Park, dances at Glendale, and the like. The editorials ran to themes later popularized by the Knights of Columbus: "Catholics do sometimes enter politics, but they do so as individuals and not through any command, expressed or implied, of the Church," said one. Early on, long articles began to appear by James T. Lorigan, mostly about Ireland, who supplanted Hussey as editor in February 1899. Editor Lorigan became Father Lorigan later on, and was well-known as a journalist. He wrote the article on the diocese for the first *Catholic Encyclopedia,* and he also wrote several short historical accounts of the diocese.

The confused history of Catholic journalism in Memphis continued with a new publication begun in 1888 called *The Catholic Journal of the New South*. That is, the title is new; the publication itself purported to be a continuation of *Adam,* for like *Adam* it continued to number its issues as if all were continuous from 1876.

Indeed, continuity is once again teased with this journal, for its dates read 1888-1935. But actually it ceased being a Memphis publication in 1912, when it was bought by the Milwaukee Catholic paper, and from then on it had only one page of Memphis news and one correspondent providing it.

CJS was from its beginning a pretty substantial enterprise. It was published by a corporation, of which M. Gavin was president, W. Horgan, vice-president, W. Fitzgerald, secretary, and J.S. Sullivan, treasurer. Fitzgerald was the guiding spirit. He was a lawyer of charm and cultivation, president of a Memphis chapter of the Catholic Knights of America, and altogether a person of standing in the Catholic community. In 1903 or 1904 he sold the paper to John J. Shea, a capable journalist. Shea published the paper until his death in 1910, and his wife and daughter continued it. They offered to sell the paper to Bishop Byrne, with whom they were on good if distant terms, but he refused.

Humphrey J. Desmond was the owner and guiding spirit of the Milwaukee Catholic paper. He was one of the most distinguished Catholic laymen of his era, a man of superior talents and education, thoughtful and original. He was an excellent business man, and developed one of the earliest chains of Catholic papers, very different in tone from those developed later out of Fort Wayne and Denver. Like them, Desmond gave a page to local news. The other pages were the same as the Milwaukee ones, but these were filled with thoughtful and interesting articles about the welfare of the Church and its policies. Desmond was against what he thought was an unwholesome preoccupation with Catholic grade and high schools. He felt that the state should provide educational services for its citizens, and that Catholics should use their resources for such things as temperance societies, young people's clubs and homes, employment bureaus, settlement houses, and services which now would be called psychological — what he called "half-way" houses rather than the "end" houses like hospitals, asylums, and schools. Needless to say, his views got nowhere, but they indicate the strength and originality of his mind.

They fell mostly on deaf ears in Memphis, too. The circulation of the early *CJS* was good, around 3,500, but toward the end of its time in Memphis it fell to under 1,000. Miss Mary Fitzgerald was both correspondent and circulation solicitor from 1912 till 1935, the year of her death, and the end of the *CJS*. It did not make much stir in Memphis. Bishop Byrne seems to have taken toward it the same attitude he took toward the Nashville *Catholic Herald*, neither help nor hate, strictly hands-off. However, once again, that was the story of most Catholic journalism at the turn of the century.

This was where the Knights of Columbus enter the picture. Sensing a need for some medium to give their group a stronger feeling of brotherhood, the Nashville Council began publishing a magazine in 1915, named after the national paper, *The Columbian*. Father T.A. Giblin was editor, and Charles J. Lord business manager. Father Giblin was a Precious Blood Father of a roving disposition; he lasted only a brief while at the helm. Charles Lord lasted many years, until 1931.

Lord came to Nashville from his native Canada. He was a convert to Catholicism, and had, like so many such, deep devotion to the Church and its works. He had a natural talent for writing, though he never became the skilled craftsman that the word "journalist" implies. But he was a bear for work. He married a Nashville girl, and worked all his days at the courthouse. What spare time he had went to the Knights of Columbus and its journalism. *The Columbian* and its successor, *The Cresset*, were a success largely because of him — to a greater extent than most people realize, journalistic success, especially at the outset of an enterprise, depends on the talent and leadership of one man.

The contents formula for *The Columbian* was much the same as in the earlier papers, although naturally with more pictures and with magazine, rather than news, treatment. And, of course, with heavy emphasis on Columbian news. *The Columbian* became the official organ of the K of C of all Tennessee in 1926, but in the following year it enlarged its scope and became the semi-official organ of the Diocese of Nashville. It also changed its name to *The Cresset*. A change of name was essential, since *Columbian* implied mainly and primarily the interests of the Knights of Columbus, but *Cresset*, meaning a container or holder for lights, was probably an unfortunate choice, a little far-out for the general public. Lord continued as editor until 1931 when the diocese took it over and Bishop Smith made it the official organ. But the Great Depression proved too much for the new venture, and it ceased publication in 1933.

The editor for those two years was Father, later Monsignor, George Flanigen, one of the ablest and most lovable priests the diocese ever had. Of an old and prominent Nashville Irish family, Flanigen was at home in Nashville and the world. He had the natural poise and ease of manner which comes of knowing who and what and where you are. A natural journalist, he got some training by spending six months learning the ropes in the Denver *Register* system before establishing the lasting venture of diocesan journalism, *The Tennessee Register,* in 1937. He stayed on as editor till 1942 swept him into the war.

Flanigen did everything in Nashville. A natural journalist, he was also a natural teacher, a good administrator as principal of Father Ryan High School, and a devoted pastor. He was perhaps the most versatile priest in the history of the diocese. The *Register,* fifty years old this year, is a testimony to his ability.

One of the tensions in the press, which has deepened since Flanigen's time, as in the Church itself, is how far to go in taking stands in civil affairs. The Catholic press in the United States has so far been pretty neutral. It has not been Republican or Democrat, left wing or right wing. When it has followed the Church, or some part of it, into taking a stand, as in its pro-Franco sympathies of the 1930s, or its handling of the Mexican Revolution in the 1920s, it has not much influenced public opinion outside the Church. But many people think it should become more political, even as the Church itself in the United States moves in that direction, following the much-publicized statements of the bishops on nuclear weapons and the economy.

These are big issues indeed. Most Tennessee Catholics are more concerned about state and local politics. In his excellent book on Nashville in the first quarter of the twentieth century, Professor Don Doyle notes that the Irish vote in Nashville must have been a factor in city elections. No study has been made of it. Catholics were dominant in four wards, the fourth, sixth, ninth, and eleventh, and these usually elected Catholics to the city council. How much influence they had would make an excellent subject for scholarly research. Knoxville's mayors were elected by the council, and hence Catholic councilmen had a better chance of impressing a small group of their colleagues than the whole electorate. This is shown in Knoxville's three Catholic mayors. The third, John O'Connor, was twice elected mayor, 1931-1935, but his bid for Congress was unsuccessful. However, his eloquent campaign answer to the snide attack on his religion by the fatuous incumbent, J. Will Taylor, is dearer to Catholic hearts than his election would have been. But there is no doubt that the Catholic politician in Tennessee finds his path filled with obstructions caused by anti-Catholic prejudice. In 1895 pressure from the American Protective Association forced a Catholic candidate off the ticket in Memphis. Today's prejudice would come from different quarters, and might be less effective, but it would come in ample chorus of ignorance and meanness.

The politics of Memphis were chaotic until Crump took over, and Crump did not achieve total power until 1927. Before him the Catholics formed no clear political base, not even in opposition to the political power of the APA. After Crump they were mostly in his camp, and he rewarded them. Catholic Frank Monteverde was elected mayor of Memphis in 1918. He was then on good terms with Crump. But as mayor he went against Crump's policies, and, his own failing of support, did not run for re-election. Another Catholic of Italian descent, Joseph Montedonico, was elected to the state legislature.

Memphis is the most Catholic part of the state, so it is not surprising to learn that of the twenty-two Catholics in Tennessee history who have been elected to the state legislature, fourteen are from Shelby County. Five are from Davidson County, two from Knox. This probably reflects fairly the distribution of Catholics in the state. It will be interesting to see what future patterns are. They may be as surprising as some past ones, among them the career of the White family. James White (1749-1809) represented Tennessee in the North Carolina legislature before Tennessee was a state. Born in Philadelphia, White attended a French Jesuit college. When he returned to the United States he studied both law and medicine. In 1799 he moved to Louisiana, where his descendants flourished. His son, Edward Douglas White, was in turn a judge, a United States Congressman, and finally Governor of Louisiana. His grandson, Edward Douglas White, Jr., after a term as United States Senator, became first Justice of the Supreme

Court and then its Chief Justice.

But success in politics is no measure of the status of Tennessee Catholics during the Byrne era. Just as population patterns made Catholics in Boston and Chicago more visible on the political scene than they deserved, so the Tennessee patterns limited Catholic public careers. But Catholics were rising on the social scene. And just as Thomas Farrell and Michael Burns were typical of the success of Catholics in the Miles era, let Thomas W. Wrenne be typical of their success during the Byrne episcopate.

Thomas Wrenne was given a job as clerk in the chancery court shortly after he graduated from the city's high school in 1870. He was the third son of Irish parents who came to Nashville from Rockbridge County, Virginia. By 1882 he was master and clerk of the chancery court and a receiver for the Bank of Tennessee. In 1899 he set up the Thomas W. Wrenne & Co., "for the conduct of banking business." He also worked for several of the city's transportation systems. He was superintendent of the South Nashville Street Railroad from 1875 to 1882. In 1888 he was named president of the McGavock and Mt. Vernon Streetcar line in North Nashville, and is given credit for electrifying the line, consolidating it with other road companies, and inaugurating the passenger transfer system. In 1899 he was also named manager of the loan agency for the Massachusetts Mutual Life Insurance Co., a firm which financed St. Joseph's construction.

He was a member of the city council in 1872. He became a member of the board of education in 1879 and stayed on the board until 1891. He was named a director of the Tennessee Centennial Exposition in 1896. Like Burns, he stayed in close touch with the governors of the state, serving on the staffs of the Patterson, Rye, Roberts, and Alf Taylor administrations. His brother, M.J.C. Wrenne, who also served on the council, was the General Superintendent of the Nashville, Chattanooga, and St. Louis Railroad.

Why were there so few Catholics like Wrenne? It's hard to say. In north-east United States, anti-Catholicism is associated with the influx of immigrants lasting all the way up to the 1920s. But there has been no sizeable immigration into the South, and especially Tennessee, since the turn of the century, when Italians in diminishing numbers still came to Memphis. In the rest of the state, the dominant Irish and Germans were undisturbed by smaller groups of Italians in the cities, and small settlements of other nationalities here and there — a few Poles in Lawrence County, refugees from the great Chicago fire of 1871, some Swiss in Hohenwald and on Paradise Ridge, some Lebanese in Nashville, Memphis, Chattanooga, and at Copper Hill, some Poles in Deer Lodge. Not many, and readily absorbed into the life of the Church and the state. It would seem that the native anti-Catholicism of the migration into southern cities from the hill country was even more adamant than that of the native New Englanders.

If the influence of Catholics in politics and business is hard to trace, that of the women's organizations is far more difficult. Ladies love to organize, and their numerous clubs and sodalities flourished and sent off good works like showers of sparks, but, like the sparks, they died instantly. Of the Christian Mothers, the orphans' auxiliaries, the groups that organized picnics and bazaars and fairs and theatricals and all the normal activities of folks, let it only be said that the Catholic ladies were very active. And let the story of just one of the women's organizations, the Ladies of Charity, since it is the oldest, stand surrogate for all the wonderful works of charity and kindness the women of the state have always performed.

Prior to 1910, a small group of Nashville ladies organized the St. Francis de Sales Mission Group to help support Father Callahan's mission work in East Tennessee. They worked closely with Sister Scholastica, the first Superior of St. Thomas Hospital in Nashville, and a leader of commanding ability and energy. So, it was only natural that under Sister's influence this group metamorphosed into the Ladies of Charity. The first group was organized in 1910 in Nashville.

This international organization, the first of the foundations of St. Vincent de Paul, began in 1617 in France, in the saint's parish in Chatillon, near Lyons. Vincent, who inspired charity as others inspire conversation, was overwhelmed by the parish women with food, clothing, and other help for the poor, but this was disorganized, sporadic, more than wanted at one time and less at another. So the future saint formed the Ladies of Charity to stabilize their good-hearted work. The first American association started on December 8, 1857, in St. Louis. It gradually spread throughout the United States. Finally, a national linkage was made: the Association of the Ladies of Charity of the United States, set up in 1960.

In the early days, the Nashville Ladies financed their operations through membership dues, and through tag days, luncheons, card parties, rummage sales, bakery sales, and from their own pockets. In 1922, at the request of Bishop Byrne, Mrs. P. A. Murray represented the Ladies at the first Community Chest of Nashville meeting. Since that date, the organization has received an annual allocation ranging from $2,517.48 in 1922 to $109,000 in 1985.

In 1940, in order to supplement the increasing demands on the welfare budget, a "Thrift Shop" was inaugurated to operate for five weeks in the spring and fall to sell "nearly new" clothing for all the family. This has grown enormously, to be the best-known project of the Ladies of Charity, with hundreds waiting in line to enter on opening days.

Until 1962, the meetings of the Ladies were held at St. Thomas Hospital, but in that year, under the patronage of the seventh Bishop of Nashville, William Adrian, the Ladies bought a splendid building of their own not far from the Cathedral. The growth of their activities demanding additional space, a fine building, designed for their specific needs, was built and dedicated in 1976.

The most striking and most daring of all the Catholic lay ventures of the Byrne era was the Catholic Club of Memphis. The Byrne era was also the era of the downtown club. Athletic clubs, literary clubs, eating clubs, riding (both horse and motor) clubs, university clubs, all flourished. There were also a few Catholic clubs scattered around the country, mostly made possible by the backing and support of the Knights of Columbus's local councils.

Such was the case with Memphis. Or, rather, such came to be the case. For the roots of the Memphis Catholic Club were in the Young Men's Institute. The YMI was a national Catholic movement, and its Memphis chapter was popular. The members needed a larger meeting place than a church basement, one with facilities young people like, game rooms, a swimming pool, and a good dance floor. In 1911 they took the first step toward their ambitious project by buying, for $22,275, the southeast corner of Third and Adams.

At about the same time the Knights of Columbus were looking for a home. The natural combination followed, and in 1922 the handsome clubhouse went up. It was a six-story building done in Louis Sullivan Romanesque style with all the facilities the young Memphians wanted: swimming pool, bowling alleys, billiard rooms, a dining-ball room that could accommodate 500, two floors of rental bedrooms, a gymnasium, and plenty of meeting space. Memphis Catholics loved it and were justifiably proud of it.

For six years it flourished, and then the 1930's Depression struck. In those dismal times the Knights of Columbus took over the building, but sealed off much of it, using only a small part for their purposes. But World War II revived the place, and by 1946 there was plenty of money in the till.

After the war, however, the club's solid base of support, the Knights, now grown to ten chapters in the Memphis areas, wanted more convenient meeting places in their parishes. That did it. The building was sold and repossessed, and sold and repossessed again. Now in the hands of a group of developers, it is just one more vacant downtown property.

It won't come back in the foreseeable future. Downtowns everywhere are fading. Like other former downtown projects, the Knights of Columbus are erecting their clubhouses in the suburbs. And note the plural. The newest idea in parishes is a parish center large and varied enough to accommodate the Ladies of Charity and the Knights of Columbus and all the many other Catholic groups that are the natural product of vitality and confidence.

18

Bishop Smith and His Times

Bishop Byrne was the last of the nineteenth century bishops of Nashville. Although William L. Adrian, the seventh bishop, was in office a little longer (1936-69), and temperamentally was very conservative, the dynamics of diocesan growth made it impossible for him to be a Byrne. Adrian could only slow or decry what he did not like in the new modernism. Byrne would have destroyed any obstacle, or tried to. He was an autocrat, an absolute ruler.

Was Byrne happy, or satisfied, in Nashville? It was an open secret that the ambition of his life was to be Archbishop of Cincinnati, which he somehow felt to be his right. When Archbishop Elder became too ill to function in 1903, fellow bishops wrote Byrne they soon expected to see him in Cincinnati. The congratulations were premature. Ironically, another Cincinnati priest, Henry Moeller, Bishop of Columbus, Ohio, was chosen — ironically because Byrne had for some time been advising Moeller by mail on how to be a bishop, like a watchful father to a biddable child. That was Byrne's only chance at Cincinnati, of course; Moeller lived longer than Byrne did, till 1925.

Byrne himself slowed down a good deal toward the end of his episcopate. His young friend and protege, Samuel Stritch, who was consecrated Bishop of Toledo, Ohio, in 1921, often came to help him. Stritch confirmed the larger classes for him, in Nashville and in Memphis, and helped his old friend and patron, who turned eighty in 1921, in many other ways. From then on, Byrne was frequently ill — his health was never remarkably good despite his tremendous energy; he was arthritic, and subject to colds and bronchial infection. He died during such an attack, on September 4, 1923. Bishop Morris came from Little Rock to preach his funeral eulogy in the cathedral Byrne had built, but his body was shipped to Cincinnati for burial at Mount Saint Joseph's Convent cemetery.

Unlike several priests who came to Nashville from above Mason and Dixon's Line to serve under him, Byrne never became "southernized". His close personal lay friends were Ohioans and easterners. His closest associates among the diocesan priests were two native Tennesseans who became bishops, John B. Morris at the beginning of the Byrne era, and Samuel Stritch at the end. Both these were southerners to the bone. Stritch, who left Tennessee at the age of thirty-four to preside over mid-western sees, retained his Nashville drawl and his Nashville manners to the end of his days. But Byrne, all through his episcopate, was more legate than resident, come to create order and good administration, like the Roman governor of some remote province in the empire. Indeed, Byrne had many of the virtues of the Roman soldier, devotion to duty above all, and some of the vices as well, hauteur to the natives markedly. Yet he accomplished much. Bishop Morris, in his centenary sermon of 1937, said of him, "He gave an impetus to diocesan work which astonished us all, and which vivified and strengthened the cause of religion in Tennessee." This was a noble tribute, and a genuine one.

Byrne was plainly the end of an era. Not only did his authoritarianism go out of favor as an episcopal style, but just about everything else he lived by went with the wind. He was probably the last Bishop of Nashville who knew how to handle a horse, and his papers are filled with receipted bills from livery stables ("Feed, February 1908, $1.50"). Although he rode in automobiles at the end of his days, he did not foresee the automobile era. He could scarcely foresee that it would bring a new sense of freedom to the lower middle classes, both white and black — the automobile, more than anything else, broke open the ghettos. And, more than anything else, the automobile was at the bottom of the frenzied prosperity of the 1920s, in so many ways a false prosperity, excluding the farmer and therefore most of the South, and built on booms.

It was a peculiar time. The World War I song ran, "How ya gonna keep 'em down on the farm, after they've seen Paree?" But either not enough saw Paree, or seeing it made no difference, for the nation, during the 1920s, turned its back on Paree. It

Bishop Alphonse J. Smith

turned down the League of Nations. It enacted legislation restricting immigration and creating preferential quotas for those admitted. It raised high tariff walls. It spawned the revival of the Ku Klux Klan. The clock was running forward, but the mentality of the country tried to turn it back, to an imaginary United States that never existed, a country of happy independent farmers and mechanics going to grandma's for Thanksgiving.

Meanwhile, technology was going the other way, creating a new world. The radio broke down the barriers of isolated rurality and urban ghettos almost as much as the automobile did. More and better education quietly expanded. Cities exploded into suburbs. But the group mentality lagged. Mass labor organization was everywhere suspect, and made little progress during the decade. Old-fashioned bossism was still admired, although more and more people wouldn't put up with it — Byrne would have had a much harder time of it in the 1920s, and, of course, wouldn't have lasted a month in the 1950s. All this made a fascinating contrast with the greatly different atmosphere which followed World War II.

Bishop Byrne was succeeded by a priest as unlike him as can be imagined, one much better suited to the new informalities of the 1920s. To use comparisons that would please both, Byrne's models of sainthood were men like St. Charles Borromeo or St. Alphonsus Liguori, both bishops, both able administrators, both deeply religious, but conventionally so. Byrne's successor, Bishop Alphonse J. Smith, was cast more in the mold of St. John Baptist Vianney — except that Smith was much more intelligent and learned. But you didn't think of Smith as scholarly; indeed, you were surprised to discover that he was generally thought so by his contemporaries in the seminary. What impressed you was not his mind, but his heart. As with the Cure of Ars, you were overwhelmed with his zeal for God and goodness, his ardent desire for grace and God's presence, his devotion to bringing men and women, especially the young, to God. As Cardinal Stritch said of him in his funeral eulogy, Bishop Smith could not understand how anyone could commit a sin. Sin of the sort that ordinary Catholics are daily guilty of was simply incomprehensible to him. He was a loving and compassionate confessor, but if you went to his confessional regularly (and he was there as regularly as the sun rose), you felt this wonder, this child-like astonishment at the thought and fact of sin, and you were embarrassed to own up to such villainies, and resolved more firmly than ever not to cause your confessor — and God — such embarrassment in the future.

Like a proper Roman prelate, Bishop Byrne had a chapel in his house where he used to say Mass and pray. Bishop Smith used the church. When he was in Nashville, he was a familiar figure in the church, always saying Mass there, usually at six o'clock in the morning, then in and out of the confessional and distributing Holy Communion till 8:30 or so. On weekdays this was in the chapel of the school, the former pro-cathedral, but on Sundays and feast days, in the cathedral. Afternoons saw him back in the church around three for rosary and prayer. He lived very simply.

His devotion to the Blessed Sacrament was legendary. When he came to Nashville he found only one Mass being said each morning, and only a few receiving communion. At once he began to preach frequent, daily where possible, communion, exhorting everyone in all the ways he could. His priests found his enthusiasm contagious, and they, too, became imbued with devotion to the Blessed Sacrament. The bishop's success was marvelous. In a few years he had, in a parish of three thousand people, three to four hundred communions a day, and during Lent a fantastic average of a thousand per day.

Bishop Smith inherited his devotion to Holy Communion from his own Bishop of Indianapolis, Joseph Chartrand, who led the Diocese of Indianapolis from 1918 to 1933. A young man at the time, Chartrand had been greatly encouraged in his devotion to Holy Communion by Pope Saint Pius X, whose teaching eventually turned Holy Communion from a twice-a-year special event to a once-a-day ordinary event for lay Catholics. In Indianapolis, Chartrand lived in much the same way Smith did in Nashville, except that his personality was less intense and more detached. As was the personality of Chartrand's other well-known disciple in devotion to the Blessed Sacrament, John F. O'Hara, C.S.C., who, as Prefect of Religion at Notre Dame, turned the university into the "City of the Blessed Sacrament," with hundreds of college boys receiving daily. O'Hara, who went on to become an efficient President of Notre Dame, and a champion of Catholic education there and as Cardinal Archbishop of Philadelphia, spent all morning hearing confessions and distributing Holy Communion, and the rest of his day giving wise advice to adolescents who dearly needed it. He had somehow developed, perhaps from adolescent years spent in South America, the necessary sense of detachment from the hundreds of problems he dealt with. Psychologists and doctors know how essential this is. Smith and O'Hara knew one another well, and corresponded occasionally. Indianapolis was their common point of reference: O'Hara had been born and raised there, and Smith spent most of the years between his ordination and consecration at the cathedral there.

It is a pity that O'Hara could not have taught Smith how to be detached, for the bishop never learned it. Tense, intense, single-minded, Smith never learned to relax. No one who knew him could be surprised at his nervous breakdown late in 1929. He exuded an air of go-go-go, be consumed for Christ's sake, "the zeal of your house has eaten me up", as the psalmist put it. He was an able preacher because this intensity gave a forceful emotion to what he was saying. Even in conversation, his clipped, strong phrasing gave many of his messages power — he was easy to mimic, and inspired some memorable private parodies. This is worth noting, for he never inspired fear. Unlike Byrne, whose bite was as bad as his bark, Smith was as kind and considerate a superior as could be imagined. He was as modest as he was devoted; there was never a hint of condescension in his most vigorous exhortations. Many cathedral parishioners thought him a saint, and the few oldsters who remember him may still pray to rather than for him.

Smith came from a deeply religious family. He was the youngest of ten children, eight of them girls. The future bishop was raised by his older sisters when his mother died shortly after his birth. Three of his sisters became nuns, and the bishop's much-loved older brother, George, also became a priest. So did two of his nephews. The Smith family, German in origin, joined their numerous fellow countrymen in settling along the north bank of the Ohio River in the state of Indiana. Young Alphonse was brought up in the beautiful old river town of Madison, and was schooled there, in nearby Jasper, and at St. Mary's College in Kansas. He then went to St. Gregory's Preparatory Seminary in

Cincinnati, and there was chosen for the North American College in Rome. He was ordained in 1908 in the cathedral Church of Rome, St. John Lateran. ''Cathedral'' was a key theme of Smith's life. Except for a brief stay in a parish, his entire career was spent in the cathedral rectories of Indianapolis and Nashville. He was consecrated a bishop at the Cathedral of Sts. Peter and Paul in Indianapolis on March 25, 1924, after thirteen years of priestly service there.

When Smith came to live at 2001 West End Avenue in Nashville, the file for the new high school for boys was on his desk, where Bishop Byrne had left it. Almost as if on this signal, Smith plunged into developing high schools in the diocese. This was characteristic of his pastoral episcopate: first the parish, with its intensified life. Then the schools, themselves deeply spiritual, nurturing the native vocations to the priesthood so dear to Smith's priestly heart. And then, of course, the sprawling diocese. Smith was, perhaps, the bishop most attentive to the needs of Memphis in the history of the diocese up to his time. Of course, he was also the first to travel everywhere by automobile. Tennessee railroads were notoriously bad. Tennessee highways during Smith's time became much preferable, and mission stations that had been infrequently visited became much more accessible.

School, parish, diocese — these were Smith's parameters. As an intelligent and knowledgeable person, he probably took more interest in national and local civil life than he showed publicly. So far as can be discovered, he never said a public word about three events during his episcopate that rocked the nation, of special interest to Catholics.

The first of these was the trial of John T. Scopes in 1925. This affair, which attracted nation-wide attention in the press, was comic opera from the word go. To begin with, it was cooked up by a few folks in Dayton, Tennessee, to ''put Dayton back on the map,'' as they said. Dayton, in southeast Tennessee, had been a place of some importance till its mining and smelting industries were displaced by better ores in north Alabama. Scopes, a teacher in the local high school, was persuaded to test a Tennessee state law which prohibited ''teaching evolution contrary to the Book of Genesis.'' Although he later claimed that he never taught the theory of evolution, Scopes went along with the scheme, and his trial was a tragic-comic debate of Darwin vs. Genesis, with advocates on both sides quite ignorant of the issues, which were in any case irrelevant to the legal question of whether the state had the right to make such a law. The courts decided that it did, but the Tennessee Supreme Court voided Scopes' fine of $100 levied by the lower court, on technical grounds.

The atmosphere in Dayton that hot summer was like a county fair. To some, like journalist H. L. Mencken, it was hilarious, more fun than the roller-coaster. The American Civil Liberties Union had offered to pay the legal fees for Scopes' defense, and a covey of legal eagles, led by Clarence Darrow, swooped in for the publicity — and perhaps for the cause, it's hard to say. The prosecution was certainly serious. It was led by William Jennings Bryan, thrice the Democratic nominee for President, who provided the tragedy. Bryan, old beyond his years at sixty-eight, made a sad spectacle of himself on the witness stand, and died in Dayton a few days after the trial.

Fundamentalists of the Protestant sects also took the trial seriously. It was they who had put the foolish law on the statute books, they who fought to preserve the purity of the words of the Bible. The Catholic position, which had been threshed out earlier, not without difficulty, was that evolution can be viewed as consonant with God's creation. Bishop Smith was invited to speak to this by the Nashville papers, but declined to do so. It was a wise decision. He would have further outraged the fundamentalists, and Catholics who needed to be enlightened could be informed more privately. It's a pity the diocese had then no official Catholic newspaper. An intelligent and sensible statement of the Catholic position would have made an interesting contrast to the ignorant pronouncements of many of those fundamentalist sects. The evolution-in-the-schools fight is still going on in the South. Although there is scarcely a physical scientist of any standing in the whole United States who does not believe in some form of biological evolution, the fundamentalists are still trying to keep the school children of the South from knowing about it.

The second event that shook the country, and especially the Catholics, was the revival of the Ku Klux Klan, also still with us but in a greatly diminished form. The twentieth century Klan, too, was comic opera stuff. Revived in 1915 by a shrewd Atlantan who wanted to make some money selling the new Klansmen their regalia, the Klan struck a responsive chord in the simple hearts of thousands of simple Americans. Why, is a mystery. The silliness of grown-up men dressing up in sheets and mumbling a ritual which would have embarrassed Tom Sawyer's circle remains, in spite of all the efforts to explain it, inexplicable. Even more inexplicable is the fact that it has refused for so long to die. With leader after leader recanting, one jailed for murder, a long history of money-swindling, and scarcely anything on the credit side, the Klan still kept on and on.

The Klan did some damage politically. It ruined politicians of genuine courage and principle, like Oscar Underwood, the distinguished senator from Alabama, and John K. Shields, his equally distinguished colleague from Tennessee, both of whom stood up to it. Those who didn't, who joined or kept silent out of prudence, may have been more nearly right. That lengthy list includes Hugo Black, the Alabama Senator who spent so many years on the United States Supreme Court bench, and the revered 1920s Governor of Tennessee, Austin Peay. Few avowed Klan candidates made it anywhere. Tennessee was never much of a Klan state. The Klan made a big push to elect mayors of both Memphis and Chattanooga in 1923, and lost both efforts. It was never strong in Nashville.

Never strong, yet it did lots of psychological damage everywhere. It frightened the Nashville Catholics, as it did Catholics over the state. The Klan of the 1920s and 1930s was by no means a southern phenomenon. It was very strong in New England, Indiana, and Ohio, as well as in Texas, Louisiana, and Georgia. It put Catholics everywhere on their guard. Catholics were usually on the Klan hate list, but their place on it varied considerably. The anti-Catholic bias hit a new high or low, depending on the point of view, in 1939, when Imperial Wizard Hiram Evans accepted the invitation of the Catholic Bishop of Atlanta, Gerald O'Hara, to attend the dedication of the new Catholic cathedral there. Evans was photographed with O'Hara and Cardinal Dennis Dougherty of Philadelphia, to the astonishment of everybody. Evans ceased to be Imperial Wizard a few months later.

Although acutely conscious of the hatred of the Klan, Bishop

Smith said nothing about it for public consumption. Once again, he was probably wise to have kept silent. What was needed were more outspoken laymen, like Memphis's C.P.J. Mooney, and a Catholic press.

The third event of the 1920s that shook the Catholic community was, of course, the presidential campaign of 1928. Oceans of ink have been used up trying to decide whether the Catholicism of Alfred E. Smith caused his defeat. Tennessee went Republican, voting against Smith, but that was nothing new. The state had gone Republican eight years before, voting for Harding for President and Alf Taylor for Governor — in that election, the most famous Tennessee politician of the century, Cordell Hull, lost his seat in Congress. And this without a Catholic in sight.

Since the main theme of Tennessee politics had been the prohibition of alcoholic beverages for more than half a century, it's possible that Smith's anti-prohibition stand alone might have defeated him. And, since Tennessee was even more conservative politically than the rest of the country in the 1920s, it is also possible that Smith's stand on the government ownership and supervision of utilities could have defeated him, although this was not much of a campaign issue. To this day people forget that Smith was frequently dubbed a state socialist for his handling of the utilities as Governor of New York. Many others thought him just a good Democrat, like the two senators from Arkansas, Joseph T. Robinson and Thaddeus Caraway, Senator Alben Barkley of Kentucky, Boss Ed Crump of Memphis, and Montague Ross, an official of the Ku Klux Klan in Chattanooga, who left the Klan to vote for Smith.

The Klan officially was, of course, indomitably opposed to Smith, but most of the best newspapers in the state supported him. The *Chattanooga Times*, in the area where the Klan was strongest, discounted its strength. Many thought, then and now, that no Democrat could have defeated Hoover in 1928. But still, as a recent Catholic historian, James Hennesey, says, "the fact remains that the New York governor's candidacies became for his co-religionists one more reminder, and on the highest level of their political sensibility, that they and their church were an object of mistrust and suspicion to an uncomfortably large number of their fellow citizens".

Bishop Smith and his clergy were certainly wise to remain publicly silent during the presidential campaign, although such an abject admission comes hard. Why should Catholics be silent when Protestants were screaming their heads off to beat Smith? Tennessee Methodist Bishop Herman DuBose said repeatedly that the Smith nomination and election would wreck the Democratic Party in the South and bring on a partisan strife the like of which had yet to be seen. DuBose led the Methodist Conference to go on record as officially opposing Smith. The other large Protestant denomination, the Baptists, did not officially do so, but their individual attacks on Smith were probably more harmful. Klansman Ross said the Church should stay out of politics. The Catholic Church in the South did, but the Protestant churches mostly did not. But the Catholic Church in the South was a tiny and fragile minority.

Catholics hoped that the election of John F. Kennedy in 1960 would put a stop to fear of Catholics holding public office, and nothing so formidable as the 1920s Klan or the earlier American Protective Association has recently appeared on the horizon. But there are still some strains of ignorant prejudice left, as the idiocies of the Alamo faction demonstrate. Perhaps Catholics are themselves somewhat to blame for sticking too close to themselves. However innocent, introversion of this sort usually causes suspicion in the United States, and the best way to allay the suspicion is a sensible and generous ecumenism, both individual and official.

No ecumenical spirit was forthcoming in the Byrne-Smith era on the intellectual side. Vanderbilt University was just one city block up West End Avenue from the Catholic cathedral, but it might as well have been in California as far as contact between the two institutions went. In the cathedral archives there is no single peep or beep about Vanderbilt or what was going on there. During the period before World War I this was understandable. Vanderbilt began as a Methodist institution of higher learning, with emphasis on its divinity school. Catholics were welcome as students in other academic departments, and there was an occasional Catholic professor, but the Vanderbilt ambience was not very hospitable to Catholic thought. Official Vanderbilt was itself not very hospitable to the University's most significant intellectual contribution to the humanities. This was the Fugitive and Agrarian movements of the 1920s and 1930s. Among the Catholic clergy of Tennessee were some men whose intellectual formation in Catholic philosophy and theology might have led them to fellowship with the Vanderbilt Agrarians. It was clear almost from the beginning that the implications of this agrarianism were religious, and could be Catholic. Perhaps the most perceptive essay in the famous manifesto of the Agrarians, the book called *I'll Take My Stand*, was the one on religion by Allen Tate. In it Tate suggested that the South, early and late, had failed to find that bedrock of religious belief necessary to genuine culture. There had been Catholicism in Tate's family; he was connected on his mother's side with the Neale family, which produced several remarkable priests in the early nineteenth century. Tate and his wife, the distinguished novelist and critic, Caroline Gordon, both eventually became Catholics, converts of the great Catholic philosopher Jacques Maritain. The story of that conversion is partially and fictionally told in Gordon's novel, *The Malefactors*.

Other members of the celebrated band were also sympathetic to Catholicism. Donald Davidson, the firmest of them all philosphically, came to the threshold of Catholicism without making the final step, but his daughter did make it. Herbert Agar, the distinguished author and editor of the *Louisville Courier-Journal* in the 1930s, and intellectually very close to the Agrarians group, was a cradle Catholic. And, of course, Vanderbilt itself has meanwhile become more tolerant. Today several distinguished professors are Catholic, some converts of recent times. And heaven only knows what Bishop Byrne or Chancellor James H. Kirkland of Vanderbilt would have thought — and said — had they known that several Catholic priests, including the new President of the University of Notre Dame, would take their doctorates in theology at the Vanderbilt Divinity School in recent years.

What a far cry all this is from the naivete of the serious anti-evolutionists and the venomous Smith-baiters. But it does suggest that a higher level of religious discussion and exploration may come through educational institutions. The high-school level is way below that of the Agrarians, but Bishop Smith was eager to start there. Almost his first act was to implement the plans for a boys' high school that Bishop Byrne had bequeathed him. Byrne had made many attempts throughout his episcopate to interest religious orders of men to come to Nashville to establish a boys' high school. In 1916 he bought the imposing home west of the pro-cathedral as a possible residence for the faculty of the high school, and in 1919 the next house to it, for the school itself. But he could never persuade a religious community of men to run the school. Beginning around 1910 the Jesuits bought some property adjoining the present Montgomery Bell Academy, which they sold in 1913 in favor of what they thought was a better site in Belle Meade, about where the Westgate Shopping Center now is. They added to this original purchase, but never made a foundation there, and finally, two bishops later, in 1937, sold the property to Huldah and Leslie Cheek, Jr. But Bishop Byrne favored the Brothers of Mary, whose headquarters were in Dayton, Ohio. He negotiated with them for years, and finally thought he had them sewed up. They consented to staff his high school beginning in 1924, when it would be ready. But by the fall of 1923, the bishop was dead, and the opening of the school had to be postponed.

Why all the agitation for a boys' school? In a letter strongly supporting the new Father Ryan School in 1928, Bishop Morris of Little Rock, with his sturdy good sense, put the matter very well in a letter to Bishop Smith:

> After twenty-two years [elapsed since he established his own school] . . . I am satisfied it has done much for the Catholic youth of this state and diocese, and that it has done a great deal to promote both the temporal and spiritual welfare of our Catholics. So far, my school has produced twelve priests for the diocese, among them the first native of the city to be so ordained. Four young men who are now leading physicians in the city received their degrees from the school. We have graduated several lawyers, one of whom was elected to the state senate over tremendous opposition. . . . Twenty-two years ago Catholics had practically no representation either in the professions or in financial circles. . . . More acute is the question of an educated Catholic laity. It is my firm conviction that the conflict between religion and the world will be fought out by the laity, and if our Catholic men and women are not prepared to meet the issues, then we are doomed to fail . . . The priesthood and the hierarchy must be backed by an intelligent, loyal and educated laity.

What Bishop Morris said in 1928 is even more true today.

The new Nashville high school fulfilled the most optimistic hopes of its backers. It had lots of luck. To begin with, it had the starting boost of good fortune in that the Byrne plans were scrapped. Byrne had no idea that a school needed space. What he meant to do was to round off the cathedral group with a school that looked like the pro-cathedral and rectory, tearing down the two houses west of the pro-cathedral on West End Avenue for the purpose. He engaged a New York architect to plan the high school building. But Smith saw at once that this wouldn't do. He started his school in the houses that Byrne meant to scrap. Under the able leadership of Dan Leary, its first and only lay principal, it got off to a good start, and its founding students developed a love for it that set the tone for its later and grander state.

For Bishop Smith had, for his next stroke of luck, a good site. In 1928, he acquired its location on Elliston Place. Although cramped later, in 1928 its space seemed ample, especially with the stretch of Centennial Park at its rear. The first graduating class to spend four years in the school and who had to use old St. Mary's across Seventh Avenue from the Capitol as its basketball gym, got a taste of the future when their graduation exercises were held in the gym of the new school, in June 1929. Classes in the handsome new building began the following fall.

And then came the final stroke of luck. Most everybody felt that the "Nashville Catholic High School for Boys" was an awkward and uninviting name for the school. The bishop and his advisers worried about a good new name, until Monsignor John Mogan, one of Nashville's most beloved priests and long-time chancellor of the diocese, came up with "Father Ryan". With Ku Kluxers menacing the Catholics, the bishop and his councillors saw at once that naming the school for the famous poet-priest of the Confederacy, a name venerated by Nashvillians and Tennesseans of all faiths, would be a subtle and telling reminder that Catholicism had a much longer and infinitely nobler tradition than the Kluxers and what they stood for.

The name caught on. Non-Catholics sent in contributions to the building fund, in appreciation of the honor done to Father Ryan. Many more non-Catholics, who weren't opposed to Catholicism but who just never even thought of it, now started being aware of it. They usually liked what they saw. Another stroke of luck was the acquisition of the able director of athletics, Leo Long. Young people, males especially, really began to take notice when Father Ryan joined the top athletic teams of the area. The principals of the school, from first to last good choices, became spokesmen for Catholicism in the area. Academically the school was respectable from the start. Its graduates became welcome in good universities, both Catholic and non-Catholic. It is really not too much to say that Father Ryan High School did more than any other single agency of its time to make Catholicism favorably known in the Nashville area.

But best of all was its effect within the Church. A cascade of vocations to the priesthood poured out of it, fourteen in its first twenty years. Its graduates strengthened parish life all around Nashville. As time went on, it evolved and developed with the rest of the community, sometimes, as with racial integration, leading the way. Very much part of the contemporary picture was its admission of girls in 1970. Nothing melds a community as much as a good schoool, and Father Ryan remains a fine example. Nashville Catholics are confident its future will be as bright as its past in its new Franklin Road location.

Just the same sort of thing had been going on in Memphis for over a hundred years. The Christian Brothers High School for Boys has done immeasurable good for the Church in the Memphis area. But the boys' education picture in Memphis has been different from that anywhere else in the state. The Christian Brothers College began when high school and college were just about indistinguishable, in 1871. The two were on the same campus until 1965, and in the Memphis area "CBC", not "CBHS" was the logo in everybody's awareness. Yet under any logo the high school was a magnet for Memphis boys. Graduates of both high school and college became prominent in the public life of Memphis; two of them, Frank L. Monteverde (1918) and Frank Tobey (1953) became mayors of Memphis, and CBC graduates became prominent in banking and the professions. It is impossible to rate too highly the contribution of the Christian Brothers to the Catholic life of Memphis. As Cardinal Stritch said, "Christian Brothers College is a Temple of Tolerance, and has done more than any one factor I know of to break down religious prejudice in

Memphis''.

However, Christian Brothers High School, and its much smaller opposite number for girls, the Dominican St. Agnes Academy, were both elitist, high-tuition schools. It was Bishop Byrne's fondest, and one of his most generous, dreams to have the Nashville high school tuition free, and so it was, till 1956, when rising costs began to make plain what has become more abundantly so since: that good education costs and costs. The Memphis priests plus the bishops had for years wanted alternatives to CBC and St. Agnes. But the local clergy notoriously could not agree about anything, and further secondary education remained a dream, until the new parish of the Immaculate Conception, on Central Avenue at Rozelle, was created. The school was the first building erected, in 1922. It was staffed by the Sisters of Mercy, who lived in the nearby convent built at the same time. The school was an immediate success. The grammar school gradually built up to an enrollment of five hundred, and the co-educational high school to over three hundred. The building, of course, was bursting at the seams, since church services were held in it as well while the church itself was going up. Finally the crypt of the church was completed in 1927, releasing the school auditorium for better service to the school, but still the situation was unsatisfactory. Grammar and high schools in the same building — often plus college — were common enough in the nineteenth century, but by this time the educational world had outgrown these ''colleges''.

One central concern did trouble Memphis priests deeply, and that was the lack of vocations. Nashville far outran much larger Memphis in winning young high school students to the priesthood. Partially to remedy this, ''Catholic High'', as the Immaculate Conception set-up was known, was converted into a boys' only school in 1945. In 1950 the boys moved into their new building on McLean, and the old Catholic High was converted into a girls' school, Immaculate Conception High School for Girls.

Both these schools have prospered to this day. The girls' school added a new wing in 1962, and continued to thrive despite the boys' school following the national trend into co-education. In 1965, still another Catholic high school was built in South Memphis, named for Bishop Byrne.

Nashville and Memphis are key instances of what gradually became diocesan policy: any city with more than one parish should foster a city-wide central high school. This policy has been very successfully followed in Chattanooga and Knoxville. Chattanooga's combined grade and high school became co-educational quite early, in 1898, and so, when the Catholic population expanded and prospered, a co-educational high school came naturally. The same thing happened in Knoxville, and the two fine plants of these high schools show the significant support their cities gave them.

The future of Catholic secondary education, whose foundations were so well laid by Bishop Smith, is difficult to estimate. Much depends on whether the so-called ''southern rim'' will continue to grow as it has since World War II. Schooling in contemporary United States is both complex and costly. The old saw about the best education consisting of Mark Hopkins (a celebrated nineteenth century teacher at Williams College) on one end of a log and the student on the other was always an exaggeration, and today is totally obsolete. You don't go to a one-room ungraded elementary school any more, you go to a sprawling million-dollar school ''complex''. You don't read law with a wise old lawyer, as Thomas Jefferson did with Mr. Wythe, you go to an expensive law school.

But what Bishop Morris said about Catholic schooling is still very true. The Catholic Church needs her schools. Other denominations are following her example. The public schools, not too many years ago the most successful of all American democratic institutions, have fallen on difficult times. Good private schools may help to restore our public schools to health.

The hospitals face a very different situation. The four great Catholic medical centers in the diocese, St. Thomas in Nashville (1898), St. Joseph's in Memphis (1899), Memorial in Chattanooga (1952), and St. Mary's in Knoxville (1930), are now more part of medical care as a national and state concern than they are of a Catholic apostolate. Until recently this was not so. Catholic hospitals, managed by Catholic nuns, where they were established, did as much as schools to promote the cause of Christian charity and the Church, from the Civil War to the recent past. But hospitals have been absorbed into a national pattern, for good or ill, and their future is out of the hands of the religious orders who own them, except as they may influence the way things are done, particularly in medical ethics.

Not Catholic except in inspiration is St. Jude's Children's Research Hospital in Memphis. Its origin is story-book. At a low ebb in his early career, Danny Thomas, the well-known entertainer, and a Catholic of Lebanese ancestry, dropped into a church to ask for divine guidance. He was in such straits that he was considering dropping his acting career and trying something else. He pledged to build a shrine if his prayer was answered.

Very soon afterwards his fortunes took a turn for the better, and Thomas never looked back. In a few years he was among America's best known and best loved television stars. And he did not forget his promise. Raised in Toledo, Ohio, during the episcopate of Samuel Stritch, he went to his old bishop for guidance. By this time, 1951, Stritch had become Archbishop of Chicago and a cardinal, but he had not forgotten his beloved Memphis, where he got his start as a priest and pastor. He suggested to Thomas that he found a hospital for underprivileged children, and locate it in Memphis.

Danny Thomas was somewhat taken aback by this suggestion, which far transcended his promise. But gradually, in discussions with the cardinal, he became more and more attracted to it. He refined the idea for a research hospital into one for children with leukemia, since Memphis had a world-famous hematology center at its Medical School, that of the University of Tennessee.

Pretty soon Danny's dream transcended even the cardinal's, who died the year ground was broken for the hospital. Meanwhile, Thomas had enlisted the aid of many different sources of help. One was the City of Memphis, whose leaders agreed to back the project. Another was St. Joseph Hospital, which became godfather and godmother to its young neighbor, St. Jude's, sharing facilities and lending expert and experienced leadership. Most important were Danny's own people, Americans of Lebanese and Syrian descent. In 1957 they set up the American Lebanese Syrian Associated Charities, which still runs the hospital. But it was up to Danny to raise the money, which he did in a series of public appearances all over the country, and in broadcast programs —

some will remember his appearance on the Jack Benny show.

It was Thomas's idea to dedicate the hospital to St. Jude Thaddeus, the patron of difficult causes. He was right about the difficulties of staffing and maintaining a free hospital for children with childhood cancers. But the difficulties were overcome, and the hospital remains a tribute to the charity of Danny Thomas and his mentor, Cardinal Stritch.

The focus of the Church in the United States has been for so long the school that it is hard to get used to a shift. As this study has emphasized, from the very earliest councils of the American Church came instructions to build schools. This was harped on and intensified through the years. By the 1880s it was fast becoming the common practice to begin a new parish with the school, and frequently to combine school and church in the same building. St. Joseph's in Nashville is a good example. Often the church would be delayed for many years — Immaculate Conception in Memphis is a good example of this. Many a parish used a disproportionate amount of its income keeping up a school, often for only a few pupils; Assumption in Nashville is a good example of this.

And all this was surely as near right as could be. Despite the intelligent arguments to the contrary, Catholics, even among the bishops, were by no means unanimous in placing schools at the head of the list of needs. A great many were in favor of using the public schools, especially where these were good, as they generally were until World War II. Yet in the context of American life as it was lived, it was the Catholic school, especially the high school, which most helped bring Catholics in smaller cities and towns into the main stream of civic life. That is the meaning of the story of Nashville's Father Ryan and Memphis's CBC.

Much as Bishop Smith loved these two schools, he probably loved best another venture of his. This was the Convent of the Poor Clares at Frayser Station in Memphis. Smith brought a group of these contemplative sisters to the diocese from Evansville, Indiana, where they had a large convent. The idea of a group of pious and selfless women retiring from the world and sending up a ceaseless spiral of prayer toward heaven deeply appealed to Smith. Tennessee Catholics are grateful to them and to the man who brought them to the state.

Also fascinating to Bishop Smith's spiritual nature must have been his investigation into the miracle of Memphis. This miracle was much talked about in church circles in that city, but as everyone knows, the Vatican policy in such matters is, go slow, go carefully. The miracle happened in 1913. In the August of that year a Good Shepherd sister in the Memphis convent had been suddenly and completely cured of cancer after praying to the Foundress of the Good Shepherd community, Mother Euphrasia. Since her cause for canonization was being heard in Rome, the Holy See commissioned Bishop Smith to make a thorough investigation into the "Miracle of Memphis." He did so, and his judgment that the miracle was genuine was accepted by Rome and used in the eventual canonization of Mother Euphrasia. How the Smith heart must have glowed at that, especially when the Good Shepherd sisters celebrated the fiftieth anniversary of their coming to Memphis a few months later.

Alphonse Smith was a good administrator. He re-organized his curia — curia simply means the body of officials to whom the bishop (whether of Nashville, Cologne, or Rome) delegates authority. Byrne had such a group, though he delegated little to them, and little sought their advice. Smith, acting on the stimulus of the new Code of Canon Law promulgated in 1918, but just beginning to be a force in diocesan administration in his time, created a body of advisers and helpers who really functioned, albeit very hesitantly at first. Among these were lay people, including the redoubtable Richard Quick, who virtually ran the business side of the diocese for forty years.

But the small range of these activities is nicely indicated by the fact that the new chancery office, replacing the crumbling old rectory next to the old cathedral, housed in its small area rectory, archives, curia, and most of the apparatus of diocesan administration, until the construction of the new chancery building in 1951. There simply wasn't much administrative machinery. There was no central administration of the schools, no newspaper, no central charities organization, no diocesan-wide organizations of lay people, only a minimum devoted to retirement, cemeteries, insurance, and the rest. In restoring the old cathedral and rebuilding its rectory, Bishop Smith made a brave start, but the times were simply not ripe for sweeping changes.

They were ripening. The Smith administration saw, sadly, the departure of many of the older stalwart priests who had done so much to build up the diocese. Monsigor P. L. Mahoney, Fathers Patrick McGuire, William Shannon, Eugene Gazzo, Alphonse Parker, John Nolan, T. C. Abbott, James O'Connor, James O'Neil, Charles Reid, John Sliemers, Joseph Boehmer, Thomas Giblin, James Rittenhouse, and James Lorigan died, along with the two sisters who had done so much for the two older hospitals of the diocese, Sister Scholastica at St. Thomas, Nashville, and Sister Borromeo at St. Joseph, Memphis. Add two of the outstanding laymen, Ferdinand Kuhn of Nashville, and C.P.J. Mooney of Memphis. Also, Brother Joseph Dutton, who spent the last years of his life assisting the famous Father Damien at the leper colony in Molokai, Hawaii. Brother Joseph became a Catholic while working in Memphis. Both Damien and Brother Joseph were immortalized by the eloquent defense of their noble work by Robert Louis Stevenson.

Few of these names have any resonance in Tennessee Catholic minds today. But the following list of ordinations does: Thomas Nenon, Joseph Leppert, Joseph Wilson Cunningham, John Luke, Aaron Gildea, Howard des Champs, Thomas Duffy, Leo Ringwald, John Elliott, William Graw, Joseph Siener, Samuel Ernest Wiley, William and Robert Wiley, Walter Quest, Walter Bush, Leon Englert, John Welsh, Edward Dolan, Frank Reilly, and John Schelley. The name of Father Eugene Hanafee, who died so young, could go on both lists.

Most of the ordinations Bishop Smith sparked came after his death, of course. His episcopate was not notably long, slightly over eleven years. He died as he had lived. Stricken while preaching at St. Vincent's Church in Nashville, on December 16, 1935, he lived only a few hours more. His successor bishop was fifty-four.

Bishop William L. Adrian

19

The Adrian Years

When William Lawrence Adrian was named Bishop of Nashville early in 1936 he had had little pastoral experience. He had been a priest for twenty-five years, twenty-four of which he spent as an educator in St. Ambrose High School and College at Davenport, Iowa, his native state. St. Ambrose had a reputation of training young men for the priesthood, although the institution was not primarily a seminary. Several young men from Tennessee had gone there to try out their vocations. This was the only link to the diocese when Adrian was appointed bishop. Even that tenuous connection had been snapped a year before, when he became pastor of the church in Victor, Iowa, a few miles north of Davenport.

But during his early years as a bishop one would think he had been one for years. Bing, bang, bong, he punched out decision after decision of great importance to the diocese. It was during this time that the Diocese of Nashville became the one we know. Bishop Smith had made the right start. In 1936 the time was ripe for real modernity.

Things were happening in the American Church. The main focus is indicated by the phrase, American Church. That's what the Church was becoming. Since the turn of the century each bishop had been supreme in his own diocese, and had little to do with any others. The togetherness exemplified in the great councils of the nineteenth century had melted away. The metropolitan provinces ceased to have much meaning. Nashville became a part of the Province of Louisville when that diocese was made a Metropolitan See in 1937, under Nashville native son Archbishop John Floersh. But, although Nashville Catholics rejoiced in the honor which had come to their friend and kinsman, the new province made no difference to the diocese.

However, a younger set of bishops were coming to the fore in the American Church. These were men who had been deeply swayed by the papal social encyclicals, and the teaching of Monsignor John A. Ryan of the Catholic University of America. The Great Depression of the 1930s jolted many of them into seeing that social concerns are also often spiritual concerns as well. Many had enlarged and expanded their diocesan charities to help their people over the Depression's hardships. They began to want to exchange information about their new social institutions, to see how others handled problems of youth and marriage and communications, along with the primary ones of social justice.

Bishop Adrian was no joiner. In certain ways he was just the opposite, a rugged individualist, self-sufficient and self-reliant. He was the first Nashville bishop to live alone much of the time. Early in his episcopate he bought a house, the first of two. It was a handsome residence, high on a ridge overlooking the Cumberland River on Porter Road in east Nashville. Much of the time he lived alone here, and in his second house on Graybar Lane in the Hillsboro area of Nashville, ably looking after himself. He loved to putter around these places, carpenter and to mend things, to garden. Working with his hands was his saving relaxation. There is little doubt that Adrian was the healthiest of all the Nashville bishops. He ruled the longest (thirty-three years), lived the longest (eighty-nine), and was ill the least.

Such a man, you would guess, was unlikely to heed the movement toward collegiality the younger bishops were feeling their way toward. But Bishop Adrian was a bundle of contradictions; of all the Nashville bishops he is the hardest to characterize, the most enigmatic. Although temperamentally individualist — in later years he looked askance, without attending any of its sessions, at Vatican Council II — he started Tennessee in the new movements that were springing up in the American Church. He strongly supported the local chapters of the new National Councils of Catholic Women. In a couple of years the NCCW, under steadily capable leadership, became the dominant Catholic women's organization of the state. He presided over the reorganization of the Ladies of Charity, and became its faithful Nashville moderator. He sponsored chapters of the Catholic Youth Organization, and supported the summer camps for youth that had been started earlier. Perhaps most important of all, he established the first official diocesan newspaper, *The Tennessee Register*, which celebrates its golden anniversary this year and is still going strong, helping to bind the Catholic body of the diocese together.

Adrian was consecrated a bishop at home in Davenport on April 16, 1936. The Apostolic Delegate, Archbishop Amleto Cicognani, presided, assisted by Adrian's Bishop Henry Rohlman and Bishop Moses Kiley of Trenton. The new bishop was installed in Nashville on May 6 by Archbishop John McNicholas of Cincinnati, his Metropolitan.

The most pressing item on the diocesan agenda was the upcoming centenary of the diocese. Adrian decided that the centerpiece of this celebration would be a thorough-going renovation of the cathedral. Although the church was only twenty-three years old in 1937, there were alarming signs of decay. The old chandeliers themselves were rickety, the plaster was curling off the walls and ceiling, the heating system was, when it worked at all, the noisiest steam clanker in the state. Worst of all was the floor, which rotted as readily as apples. No matter how often restored, the wood flooring Bishop Byrne settled for, in place of the marble he so ardently desired, was in constant need of repair.

Bishop Adrian went to work to repair all this soon after his installation. Trenches were dug in the solid rock the church rests on for new heating and ventilating pipes, and the handsome new floor of rubber tile, which still did excellent service after fifty years, was laid over concrete and asphalt. It was a good solution to the worst problem of the old church. Its pleasing pattern is the best substitute for marble in the church. Unlike the old scagliola of the altar and columns, it makes no pretences.

To handle the redecoration, Bishop Adrian engaged the same firm that Bishop Byrne had employed, Daprato of Chicago. Perhaps their best stroke was to eliminate the scagliola of the columns and let the plaster be what it is, painted a pleasant beige. Perhaps the worst stroke was the elimination of the scagliola altar, replacing it with a new one backed by a crucifixion group. The window behind the altar was filled in, and a painted drapery on the new plaster became a background for the crucifixion group. New paintings were done on the ceiling of the apse by Anton P.

Albers and his son, and the new marble altar was flanked by statues of two angels.

The most sweeping renovation, however, was the creation of two chapels on each side of the new altar to house the side altars. This also involved an odd switch of the Blessed Mother and St. Joseph. Our Lady was moved to the Epistle side, perhaps because the new choir space was there, in front of the altar, with a small electric organ. Bishop Adrian meant to have the liturgical music recommended by Pope St. Pius X back in the early part of the century, but only by 1930 were there beginning to be enough choir directors trained in the recommended Gregorian chant and Renaissance polyphony. The new music never caught on at the cathedral in any case. The two chapels were separated from the sanctuary by small pillars and arches, and they connected with iron grill work executed by the Forges of Kerrigan but designed by the architects, Asmus & Clark. Heavy green draperies originally hung behind the ironwork, and the walls of the Lady chapel were painted with scenes of contemporary devotional life. The St. Joseph Chapel walls are decorated with Nativity scenes. The fine statues of Our Lady and St. Joseph are the work of the Tommasi Studios of Italy, as are the altars, the communion rail, and the sanctuary floor.

Fortunately, the beautiful old ceiling of the nave was left untouched, only cleaned. The plain white glass of the clerestory windows was replaced by crystal beveled glass, a happy touch; and, emphasizing the dedication of the church to the Incarnation, the words of the Angelus were printed in blue on a band of gold just beneath them. The most sensible touch of all was creating a vestibule at the main entrance.

The only structural modification of the church was the addition, on the southeast side near the rectory, of a new wing which includes a sacristy, baptistry, and vestibule. This two-story addition also has a choir practice room on the second floor. It blends in neatly with the old building. Asmus was again the architect, and V. L. Nicholson the contractor. All this was done in the space of five months. It made clear that Adrian as a builder was a worthy successor to Byrne. It will be interesting to see how much the Sesquicentennial renovation, based on Vatican II, changes the Adrian concept.

When the three-day centenary celebration came, on Sunday morning, October 3, 1937, all concerned had reason to be proud of their work. Bishop Adrian celebrated the High Mass which began the festivities, and the Blessed Sacrament was exposed from 7:30 A.M. to 3 P.M. in thanksgiving. The second day featured a Requiem Mass for the deceased of the diocese, and on the climactic third day the Mass was celebrated by the Apostolic Delegate, Archbishop Amleto Cicognani. The sermon was delivered by Bishop John B. Morris of Little Rock, Arkansas, the first native Tennessean to be made a bishop, a former chancellor of the diocese, and for twelve years rector of old St. Mary's Cathedral. This sermon was printed, and along with Monsignor George Flanigen's souvenir history of the diocese, is the basis of all subsequent history. The two histories are very different. Only occasionally does Flanigen sound personal; his history derives mainly from questionnaires he sent to each pastor and institutional superior in the diocese. Bishop Morris was highly personal, and his history is delightful to read. However, it must have been anything but that to sit through; no matter how valuable as history, it is far too long for a sermon. Both versions were printed, but only Flanigen's found its way into libraries. Copies of Morris's sermon are rare.

On the spiritual side the new bishop convened a synod of his priests, the first since Byrne's of 1906. He announced it in January 1937, and its decrees were promulgated the following June. The bishop took this occasion to revise his curia, and to discuss the steps he hoped to take in directing the diocese. Among these was one bringing educators in the parochial and high schools together; the first meeting of the Advisory Committee on Schools took place on January 25, 1938. The decrees of the synod make rather dull reading, however. Mostly they confirmed and modulated the regulations of the Universal Church. The abiding results lie in the re-affirmation of loyalty and collegiality among the attending priests.

There was more building to be done. Shortly before Bishop Adrian was consecrated, the church of St. Lawrence at Paradise Ridge near Nashville was completely destroyed by fire, and no sooner was work begun on a new church there than the church of the Good Shepherd at Winchester-Decherd, was also badly damaged by fire. By the time the Paradise Ridge new church was going up the bishop bought the land for the imposing new church of Christ the King in Nashville. On the same scale — big church, big school, lively and active parishioners — Our Lady of Perpetual Help was made into a parish in Chattanooga. The Nashville church was in the charge of Father Joseph Leppert, one of the most dynamic young priests of the diocese, and the new Chattanooga church — at last a second parish in Chattanooga — was pastored by another outstanding young priest, Father Harold Shea. Catholic life was thriving and spreading in Tennessee in the late 1930s. And in a third big parish, perhaps the largest in the diocese at the time, Immaculate Conception of Memphis, the church, so long a-building, was finally dedicated by Bishop Adrian in 1938. Its pastor, Monsignor D. J. Murphy, was a Byrne stalwart, and his church the last of the Byrne churches, Roman to the core. Though not without style, it is not quite so happy in its details as the Nashville Cathedral of the Incarnation. But it is a handsome church, and a worthy cathedral for the new Diocese of Memphis.

As the country crept slowly and quietly into World War II, church building took on a new purpose, to minister to the growing number of military and para-military establishments. Those at Shelbyville, Tullahoma, and Oak Ridge were sparked by war preparations. So were, to some extent, the churches at Pulaski and Kingsport. The Gatlinburg church was not; it was the consequence of the growing tourist industry of the Great Smoky Mountains — shades of Father Callahan. And in West Tennessee, the churches at Dyersburg and Union City also reflected the movement of people and military establishments into the South.

What was happening to the Diocese of Nashville as the first years of William Adrian slid into the war years, could flower only after the war. Church building, like civilian building, came to a virtual standstill from 1941 to 1946. War-time prosperity suffused the state, but the only new parish was at Oak Ridge.

Oak Ridge is a fascinating story. In these days of leaks and broken promises, the wall of secrecy surrounding the Oak Ridge atomic plant is almost unbelievable. There was a large number of Catholics among the workers at the plant, and the authorities wanted to keep them in the compound for Mass. Only Bishop

Adrian and the priest he named pastor, Father Joseph Siener, knew anything about the plant, and Father Siener, once there, could not report to the bishop about anything he was doing. For three years Catholic services were held in some building or other appointed by the authorities for the purpose, usually the community center — "St. Mary's parish" meant the Catholic community, not a building. So well kept was the security that Father Siener himself was astonished when the bomb was dropped on Hiroshima. After that, the parish got its church and school.

Only ordinations went on unaffected by the war, except as chaplains departed to work with the armed forces. These were mostly older men — Fathers Flanigen, Reilly, Wiley, Van Beercum, Quest, and Graw. The bishops generally tried to keep the newly ordained priests at home, for obvious reasons. So the stream of new Nashville ordinands found work where they could, dissatisfied as it made many of them. There were a lot: Cleary, Englert, Walker, McRedmond, Rohling, Richardson, Frank Shea, Woodley, Gresham, Tarpy, Baltz, Grannis, Tierney, Henkel, Clunan, Morris Stritch — a long list of good men.

Although the first Tennessee officer to be killed in battle in World War I, Marine Lieutenant Simmons Timothy, was a Catholic, the war itself affected the Tennessee Church scarcely at all. But World War II was in many ways a peculiar experience for American Catholics. As a body they no longer felt they had to show themselves more patriotic than other denominations, as they had during the Mexican War, for example. For war purposes, Catholics were like everybody else (except the blacks), and no doubt, if they had stopped to think about it, they were happy to be so. Yet the fact that Vatican City was a tiny enclave in the heart of enemy country was a sensitive situation for them. Their leading spokesman in the United States, Archbishop Francis Spellman of New York, was also the outstanding friend of the new Pope, Pius XII, elected in 1939. Spellman was always the busy patriot, visiting the troops then and forever after, and he was also the technical head of the Catholic Armed Forces Chaplains. He delegated this job to the able President of Notre Dame, making him a bishop for the purpose, and Bishop John O'Hara was Military Delegate until his transfer to Buffalo just after the end of the war. Yet O'Hara never became a spokesman for the

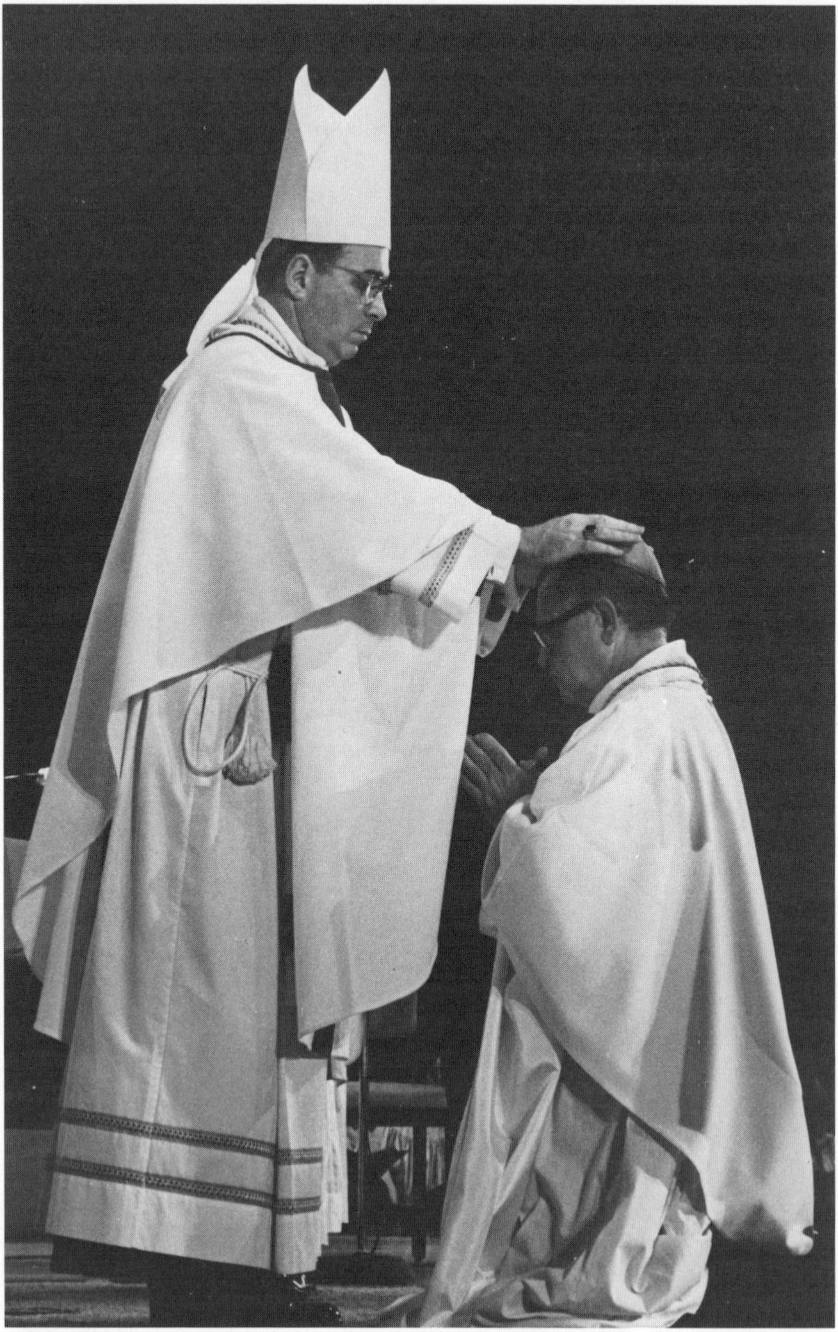

Archbishop Joseph Bernardin of Cincinnati consecrates James D. Niedergeses in 1975 as the ninth Bishop of Nashville.

Francis Shea, Bishop of Evansville.

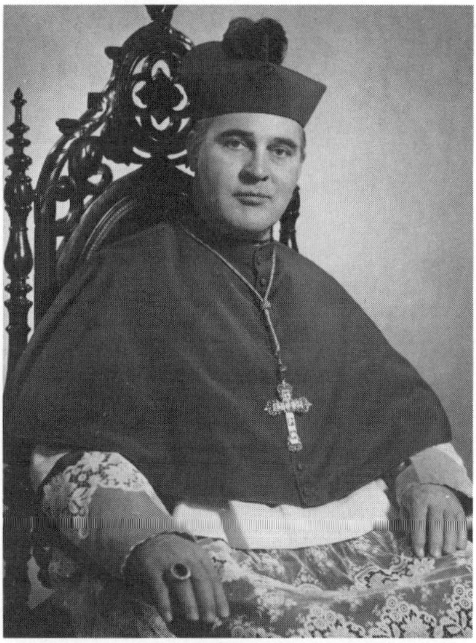

Joseph Durick, born in Dayton, Tenn.

James Niedergeses, Lawrenceburg born.

Bishop Angelo Acerra, O.S.B., native of Memphis, Auxiliary to the Archbishop for the Military Services.

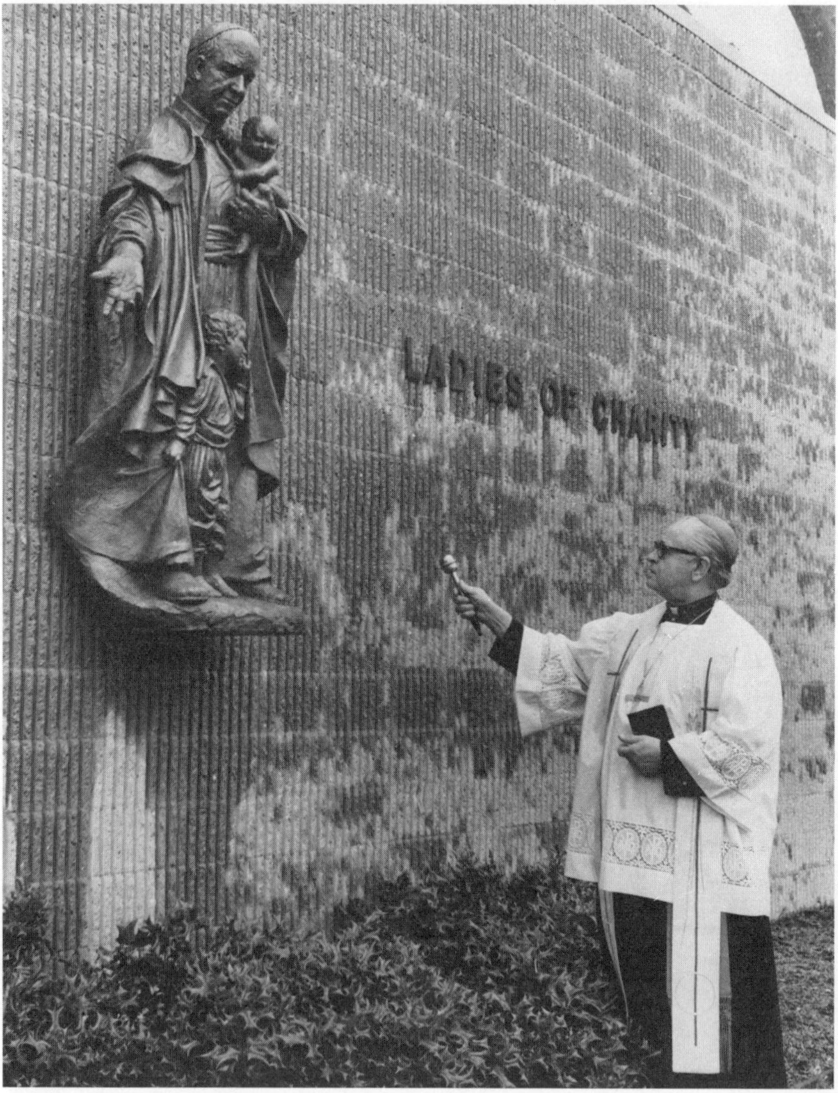

Joe Horton photo from The Tennessee Register.

Bishop Niedergeses blesses the statue of St. Vincent de Paul, founder of the international Ladies of Charity, on wall of their Nashville building.

Bishop Joseph Rademacher of Nashville and, after 1893, Fort Wayne, where he had been a beloved priest.

Father William Walsh survived yellow fever epidemic, edited a newspaper, built Sts. Peter and Paul Church.

These brothers, George and Father Emmanuel Callahan, gave their fortune to build churches in Tennessee.

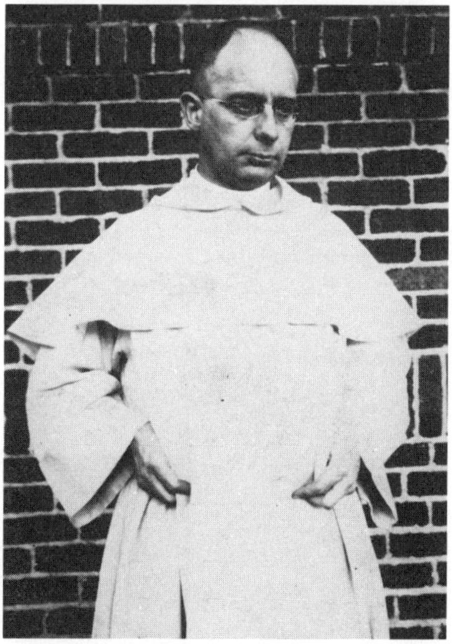

Dominican Father George Carpentier came from France after World War I and served Johnson City valiantly.

Versatile George Flanigen was high school principal, church pastor, and first editor of the diocesan paper.

Organists like Mrs. R.P. Manning of Chattanooga were stalwarts of liturgy from the beginning to Vatican II.

Joseph Leppert was vigorous director of the C.Y.O. and founding pastor of Christ the King Church in Nashville.

Christopher Murray served as priest for nearly fifty years in nearly all parts of the Diocese of Nashville.

Monsignor Albert Siener, Cathedral rector many years, personified the Church in Nashville to many admirers.

Monsignor Joseph Siener, his younger brother, was the founding pastor of St. Henry's Church in Nashville.

Father Owen Campion, on the left, editor of *The Tennessee Register*, engages Cardinal John O'Connor of New York in a lively discussion.

United States Catholics, or for the ethics of the war, or such like. He left the enthusiasm to Spellman, Fulton Sheen, and others. Archbishops Stritch of Chicago, Mooney of Detroit, and McNicholas of Cincinnati drew up some guidelines for the peace negotiations, but they were not much heeded anywhere. Indeed, the ethics of the war, or its conduct, were simply taken for granted until the war's end, when the explosion of the atomic bomb also exploded passionate discussion of its moral implications, and Hitler's genocide policy toward European Jews came gradually to light. Small wonder, then, that Bishop Adrian became just a part of this scenario. Apparently, like most of his people, he simply took the war for granted. We're in it, they implied, let's win it and get it over with.

Of course, the war times were not hardship times for Americans at home. Despite gasoline and meat rationing, and shortages of all sorts of consumer goods, most people were better off than they ever had been, and all were held together by a feeling of friendly and worthy cooperation. World War II was, in the United States, a genuinely popular war. Anybody in a uniform was a hero in embryo. This feeling of togetherness embraced Catholics and Jews and Baptists and everybody. During World War I the Knights of Columbus ran recreation "huts" at 250 centers overseas and 360 in this country — "Everybody welcome, everything free". But in World War II these services were taken over by the United Service Organization (USO), which included the National Catholic Community Service. All the dioceses contributed to this, and also to the immense Catholic Relief Services, which distributed over a billion dollars to refugees, prisoners of war, the homeless and the needy wherever the Church was established. It was a magnificent record of generosity.

It took a long time, however, for this generosity to be extended to those closer to home, the American blacks. Their war experience in the armed services were still those of Jim Crow in uniform. Black civilians had a better time of it, but still were ghetto-ized in the big northern cities they migrated to in search of a better deal. In the South, of course, they were still legally discriminated against.

Their war experience certainly fueled their eventual revolution for equality. In this fight the Catholic Church officially was an ally. In their annual statements of 1943 and 1944 the American bishops urged fair treatment for blacks. "We owe it to these fellow citizens", they said, "to see they have in fact the rights which are given them in our constitution . . . political equality, fair economic and educational opportunites, a just share in public welfare projects, good housing without exploitation." A leading influence in the making of this statement was Archbishop Stritch of Chicago.

But it was still a long time before the inevitable revolt came. The blacks were ready for a leader, and when Martin Luther King blew his freedom trumpet they came a-running. Many Catholics came with them, and most southern Catholic priests were with them in spirit, if not in fact, for the bishops were fearful of riots and demagogues. So, the Catholics who took part in the demonstrations were acting as individuals.

But soon there came the area where the Church must act officially. This was in school integration. It began in a strange and curious way, scarcely where you'd expect it. Who would have planned racial integration as part of the Catholic Students' Mission Crusade? Not a bad idea, come to think of it. But it certainly wasn't planned.

The Crusade was the idea of Jesuit Father Daniel Lord, whose enthusiasm and sense of the times made him the outstanding figure in American Catholic youth work during the 1920s and 1930s. The Crusade, which consisted of teen-aged youngsters of both sexes, was founded to make them aware of and helpful to the missionary endeavors of the Church, and by this means bring them together socially as well. It worked. Lord was a pioneer in seeing that the industrial society required such organizations.

Among the many activities sponsored by CSMC, as it came to be known, was an oratorical contest. In the quickening of the drive to equality of the Negro race in 1945, the students at Nashville's black Immaculate Mother Academy wanted the winner of their local CSMC contest to compete in the city-wide finals at Father Ryan High School. Then came an astonishing turning point in the history of race relations in the diocese, a history filled with surprises. Bishop Adrian approved the request of the Immaculate Mother students.

Adrian is indeed an enigma. In this, and other decisions, he was a hero of integration. There is no question whatever that he made the decisions that mattered, and that he was prudent enough not to overdo. Yet his image, in Nashville and elsewhere, was that of a conservative, opposed to all change. This image came largely from the writings of his later years, especially the columns he did for *The Wanderer*, the arch-conservative privately-owned Catholic paper published in St. Paul, Minnesota. But in the 1950s Adrian was a cautious pioneer in integration.

The diocesan director of the CSMC, Monsignor Charles Williams, accepted the bishop's decision without question, but went in fear and trembling to the contest itself. Anonymous phone calls threatened rocks and rotten tomatoes. But the actual speech-making came off without incident. The black girl from Immaculate Mother made a good speech. She didn't win, which was just as well so far as integration's cause was concerned, but she did attend a party for all the contestants given by the Seigenthaler family, which included a budding orator. The Seigenthalers were strong liberals; their best-known member, John, made a national reputation espousing liberal causes. The attitude of the Seigenthalers was exceptional. Most of the concern, and the opposition, throughout the integration process, came from parents, not their children. Monsignor Williams was even more apprehensive at a later CSMC contest in Chattanooga, a city somewhat rougher in texture than older Nashville. But once again everything went off smoothly.

Of course, a one-night stand like the oratorical contest isn't live-with daily integration. But it did point that way. When, in the spring of 1954, the Supreme Court of the United States ruled that public schools must be integrated "with all deliberate speed", Bishop Adrian was no less decisive. "This is the law of the land", he said, "and it must be obeyed". But his interpretation of "with all deliberate speed" had a touch of genius. He instructed the priests of each of the four deaneries of the diocese to decide how deliberate their compliance with the law would be.

The Nashville deanery convened at once and voted to integrate their schools with non-deliberate speed, in the following autumn. This was in sharp contrast to the Nashville public schools, whose administration, in characteristic bureaucratic fashion, appointed a committee to study the issue and recommend policy.

But black Alfred Kelley, an east Nashville barber, contemplated anew the long distance between his residence and all-black Pearl High School, and filed suit to require nearby white East High to accept his son.

This shook the school board into action. They evolved the famous (or, to many, notorious) "Nashville Plan," which desegrated one grade a year beginning in 1957 — three years after the Catholic schools had welcomed black students. But this gradualism had as many kinks in it as a tax law. It made for token desegregation, not the real thing. Even this was challenged by many groups of Nashvillians. It was a troubled time.

But no demagogue arose in Nashville to turn opposition into violence and bring in the National Guard, as happened in other southern states. Some violence did erupt in the fall of 1957, but it was clear that the collective heart and mind of Nashville could not stomach that. As Catholic city Judge Andrew Doyle told an agitator from outside the city, "If any blood is shed on the streets of Nashville, it will be you and your kind that are responsible. We do not care for your presence here. We hope we may never see you or your likes again."

Catholic leaders could not help feeling a great collective sigh of relief at this. They had made their momentous decision years before. Since then they had quietly and apprehensively lived with it. The faculty of Father Ryan expected trouble there, if any place, and one or two minor incidents did occur. But the capable faculty knew how to handle them. When Father James Hitchcock fielded a question from a white boy about the congenital intellectual inferiority of blacks, he answered calmly, but a few days later gave an assignment which made it clear to the questioner that his own heritage was no great shakes. Ryan lost only two students because of resentment against integration, and one of these returned in a few weeks. Father Hitchcock later became superintendent of all the Catholic schools, but he never again felt as touchy as he did during that period. All the faculty kept looking over their shoulders. The white public schools didn't help. The Father Ryan faculty were told in no uncertain terms that, while they might have black students in their classes, they could not put them on their athletic teams, else Ryan would be barred from the Nashville Interscholastic Athletic Association. But such needling could not last long after Mayor Ben West integrated the street cars and restaurants. West had earned the faith the Nashville blacks placed in him by his wise and forceful leadership.

And the Catholics had good reason to bless him. Until full integration came to Nashville in the early 1960s, they were out on a limb. Looking back, it's easy to say that such integration was inevitable, but that was by no means clear in the unrest of the turbulent decade from 1954 to 1964. Catholic integration went on very quietly. Another wise decision by Bishop Adrian and his advisers was to proceed under the yellow light of caution. There was no boasting, although the Columbia Broadcasting System in 1958 featured Ryan in a network show. But the diocesan paper kept mum. After all, it was circulated in the other deaneries as well as Nashville, and the black Catholics of Memphis and Chattanooga, already restive over their Jim Crow status, could justly demand for themselves what the Catholic blacks of Nashville had. There were a couple of demonstrations for integration in Memphis, but desegregation did not come there till the early 1960s.

Of course, the Catholic situation was far from being the staggering problem facing the general public. The Catholic population was small, the proportion of Catholic blacks minuscule. Moreover, the Catholic blacks tended to come from the upper ranks of black society. The boy Hitchcock shielded at Ryan was the son of a physician. Such youngsters easily fitted into predominantly white society. Reavis Mitchell, a professor at Fisk University in Nashville, who was integrated into Ryan when the black high school was closed, says he never felt discriminated against. "I know I was supposed to," he says, "but I simply didn't. I was not an athlete nor a dance-goer. I went to Ryan for an education, and never felt excluded there."

But the fact that Mitchell's black high school was closed indicates another decision the bishop had to make, one made difficult by history. For many years the diocese had poured money and men and women into schools for blacks. Now, with integration, these schools were superfluous. But, would their closing hurt the cause of Catholicity among the black race? Wisely again — and this decision was not only Bishop Adrian's, but that of his successors — it was decided to keep the grade schools where they throve, but close the high schools, which were so expensive. Closing any school is a traumatic experience for those children in it, and those grown-ups who used to be, but the dynamics of city growth require it frequently these days. What was a comfort was the knowledge that closing a black school did not freeze the children out of a Catholic school.

The story of the integration of the Catholic schools of Tennessee would make an interesting book, a work that would be a useful contribution to Tennessee history. The story is not widely known. The scholar can search and search in the journalism of integration without finding a single reference to what the Catholics were doing. Only Don Doyle, in his book *Nashville Since the 1920s* notes that Father Ryan integrated in 1955 (actually, it was 1954). And, of course, the story of integration is far from finished. But whatever its stage, the wise and Christian course the Catholics of Nashville followed should be better known, and that because it is not a tale of agony or dislocation. Nashville's history of racial integration is one of the bright spots in the whole story, and the Catholics of Nashville the brightest part of it.

Of course, this is the rosy picture of the hind-sight generalization. Integration wasn't all that easy. Monsignor Albert Siener, the cathedral pastor in the 1950s, had some hard and sorrowful times with indignant parishioners. The smaller grade schools of Nashville parishes integrated much more slowly than Father Ryan and the Cathedral schools. Moreover, city growth forced change. When Lafayette Street was widened, the south Nashville black church property became valuable, and was sold to Sears-Roebuck for their store. However, the black population was moving from south to north Nashville anyhow, as the new black Catholic center on Heiman Street demonstrates. The Nashville changes were painful but peaceful.

This was not the case elsewhere. Memphis, with its much larger percentage of blacks, had a harder row to hoe, and the Catholics marched to the same slow tempo as the rest of the city. This isn't to blame them; it was to be expected. Indeed, if Memphis had had a Catholic bishop of its own in 1954 probably the wisest course would have been to do little more than what was done. Chattanooga was in much the same dilemma. In Knoxville, of course, the integration process involved so few blacks that protest was symbolic only, with little danger of spreading disorder.

Meanwhile, segregation and desegregation are changeable themes in Tennessee history. Many blacks are opposed to much desegregation, believing it to threaten what is special and worthwhile in black culture, and fearing it may erode their own institutions of churches and schools, especially universities. This is indeed history in the making, and no sensible person would do more than guess at the long-range outcome. Only one thing is now clear, and that is the basic freedom to integrate. Whether the means chosen by the judicial arm of the government, busing, will work, or continue to be tried, remains to be seen. The integration of Catholic schools has so far proceeded without benefit of busing; Professor Richard Pride's recent book on busing in Nashville does not mention Catholics. A spin-off from school integration in the South is the remarkable proliferation of private schools, an ironic reversion to the state of education in the South before the Civil War, when "academies" were the dominant feature of elite education. So far these private schools have not generated any political pressure.

The Eisenhower Era

The enormous growth of the American Catholic community just after World War II was staggering. Of course, growth of all kinds was in the air, after the restrictions of war-time. The baby-boom was beginning, consumer goods were snapped up in the swirling prosperity, colleges and universities were bursting with former GI's, and inflation was a measly two percent. But the Catholics outdid practically everybody. From 1940 to 1960 the Catholic population of the United States doubled, from twenty-one million to forty-two million, a dizzying increase.

The general opinion about the Eisenhower years, then and now, is that they were years of unbridled materialism. Many Catholic critics championed this view, like the *Integrity* magazine group, the Grailville group, and the steady continuation of *The Catholic Worker* group. On the surface, however, and often well beneath it, there was a strong religious revival in the post-war era. Church membership was up everywhere. Many of the phenomena seemed superficial, although it's hard to tell. No one knows how lasting religious experiences are. It's easy now to smile at the showmanship of Fulton J. Sheen on television, forgetting his genuine intellectual credentials, but Catholics should remember that his was also the era of Frank and Maisie Sheed. The multitude of Catholics going to college on the GI Bill of Rights were not mainly looking for job training. They wanted, above all, a Catholic philosophy of life, the sort of thing Sheed & Ward were publishing and promoting.

College students aside, the religious revival stirred Catholics perhaps less than it did Protestants and especially Jews, shocked into new religious life by the horrors of Adolf Hitler. Indeed, in a highly influential book published in 1955, Will Herberg argued that American Protestants, Catholics, and Jews tended to forget the issues that separated them, and were together creating "the American religion". Herberg's argument implied that the post-war spirit of tolerance and openness derived from this unconscious collaboration of the three religions. After World War I there was also prosperity, though nothing like that of the second post-war era. But there was no opening-out of generous toleration, but a closing in. The Ku Klux Klan was revived, the new immigration laws discriminated against Catholic Europeans, the League of Nations was defeated. After World War II there was a slight similar reaction: the McCarthy communist chase resembled the Mitchell witch-hunt of the 1920s. Partially because he was a Catholic, Joe McCarthy inspired a good deal of Catholic support, but not nearly as much as might have been supposed. Catholics were indeed anti-communist. They still are, at least they are opposed to the Russian variety. But more of them were beginning to follow the path the Kennedys eventually took. John Fitzgerald Kennedy, not Joseph McCarthy, was the symbol of the status of Catholics in the post-World-War II period. And among the clergy there was John Courtney Murray, the prescient Jesuit who at first was suspect, then, in Vatican II, triumphant. Murray was joined in this symbolism by another man whose name began with M: Thomas Merton, the convert who became a Trappist monk, and as influential in pointing the way to a richer inner spiritual life as Murray was in framing the secular life of the Church.

In Tennessee, the 1950s followed the national trend. It was a time of quiet, but almost torrential growth. The war time prosperity of the state increased rather than diminished. Many soldiers who had trained in Tennessee stayed on or came back to live. As industries moved into the state, migration from the north increased. Many a Catholic parish was infused with new vitality by Catholic migration from the north and east. New churches and schools appeared as if by magic. In 1936 the Diocese of Nashville had just thirty-six churches with resident pastors. In 1986 there were sixty-six, excluding West Tennessee. Many of the 1936 churches were, moreover, little structures, roasting in summer, freezing in winter, unheeded save on Sundays. They were looked after by long-suffering priests driving fifty to a hundred miles in those breakfastless days between missions. It wasn't quite like Father Callahan on his horse Rebel, but it was a far cry from today's comparative ease and comfort.

It was on the whole a sunny time for Catholics. Anti-Catholicism did not disappear, especially in Tennessee, but it certainly did lessen — one could say it became more polite. Catholics themselves became more assured. Catholic churches sprouted up in the shadows of the new state university campuses, handsome ones at Cookeville and Murfreesboro, and a beautiful new Catholic Center on the main University of Tennessee campus at Knoxville. When Bishop Adrian bought property for a new church or school, as it sometime seemed he was doing every day — Elizabethton, Kingsport, Brownsville, Norris, Whitehaven, Alcoa, Copper Hill, Columbia, Humboldt, Ripley, Morristown, to name some in the smaller towns — there was no rumble of distress and repulsion from the neighbors, as so often in the past. At the synod of 1957, the third of Adrian's episcopate, the assembled priests could thankfully join him in satisfaction at the progress the diocese had made.

There were plenty of them. Along with the new churches and schools there were new priests being ordained every year. The peak years of growth were 1961 and 1962. In 1961 ten churches were either started or completed, five new schools opened, and seven priests ordained. In 1962 a total of thirteen buildings were opened, including six churches, two rectories, two Newman Club centers, and a hospital. Five priests were ordained. Those two years alone saw enough new building and new personnel to make a small diocese.

The new priests joined a remarkable band of older ones. The

elders of the clergy during the Smith-Adrian episcopates were frequently men of exceptional cultivation and religious spirit. Monsignor John Mogan, who died much too young at forty-five, left behind him a trail of affection and good feeling wherever he went. For most of his career he was chancellor of the diocese and rector of St. Mary's. He had as well a variety of other jobs, such as director of Calvary Cemetery, which he modernized and landscaped, and during Smith's frequent illnesses he was the unofficial administrator of the diocese. Mogan's friend, Monsignor George Flanigen, shared with him an interest in the history of the Church of Tennessee; the papers of both are among the best sources of this book. Monsignor Francis T. Sullivan was the first monsignor Chattanooga had known. He became pastor of its parish in 1911 and stayed there till his death in 1946. Everyone thought of Chattanooga as Sullivan country. The monsignor set his stamp on Chattanooga Catholic life until the new post-World-War II prosperity came to the valley of the Tennessee River and brought wide expansion to the area. Flanigen succeeded Sullivan, adding one more to the number of distinguished priests who left their mark on the city — Fathers Brown, Walsh, and Tobin are memorable predecessors.

Knoxville, too, had fixed stars in the Catholic firmament. Father Francis Marron was for many years the representative of the Church there and to the many missions in East Tennessee. An eventual successor was Father Francis D. Grady, who performed the same functions for many years. Memphis, too, had its luminaries. Monsignor Dennis J. Murphy was pastor first of St. Patrick's and then founding pastor of Memphis' largest church, now its cathedral, Immaculate Conception. He was also for long vicar-general of the diocese. Monsignor James P. Whitfield spent almost all of his priestly career in Memphis, first at St. Patrick's, then at St. Brigid's, finally at Little Flower, which he founded. Also prominent on the Memphis scene was Monsignor Louis Kemphues. Monsignor Merlin Kearney, who was pastor at Blessed Sacrament before coming to Immaculate Conception, was Father Memphis as well as Father Christmas and Father Mirthful for many years.

But the best-known of all was the Siener dynasty. The Sieners are a Chattanooga family who contributed four priests to the Diocese of Nashville. The dean of the family clergy was Father Albert, who lived at, and for most of the time, ran the cathedral of Nashville from 1918 till his resignation in 1962. Priest to the bone, Monsignor Albert kept his charm and his cultivated intelligence under sharp control; he was a most loyal and strict son of the Church. His brother Joseph, also at the cathedral for years, founded St. Henry's parish in Nashville. More open and easy than his brother, Monsignor Joe is a great favorite with everyone. Their nephews, Monsignor Leo and Father Albert Siener II, keep the dynasty going.

A smaller dynasty was that of the Sheas. This was a remarkable Knoxville family, who contributed two priests to the diocese, Father Harold, who held several high posts in the Adrian ministry, and Father Frank, who became the Bishop of Evansville, Indiana. Two of their sisters became nuns. All of them are eminently intelligent and sensible people who have done great service for the Church. And there were other dynasties — the Wileys, three priests and two nuns, the Lynch twins, the two Kirks, the two Cunninghams, uncle and nephew, and the two McMurrays.

There were many more of the senior clergy who were stalwart servants of the Lord and His Church. There was Monsignor John Hardeman, a convert of Bishop Morris, who rivaled Father Gazzo in his tenure at Holy Name, Nashville. There was the cultivated and elegant Father Edward Desmond, who did so many things so well. There were Fathers Nenon and Wilson Cunningham, able and versatile, and yeasty Father Maurath. There were the admirable order priests, Dominican Father George Carpentier at Johnson City, who was a fountain of charity and helpfulness, and who was awarded the Croix de Guerre while serving with the French Army in World War I. There were the admirable Josephites who ministered with such touching charity to the blacks, Fathers Michael Neary, James Crowe, Charles Brown, John Coyne, and others who helped. There were the Franciscans and the Paulist Fathers. The Franciscan Fathers, who came so early to Memphis, and then to Lawrenceburg and Nashville, have a long tradition of service in the diocese, a tradition still kept up at St. Vincent's in Nashville. The Paulists are long gone from Winchester, but still are in the diocese in Knoxville and Memphis. Newer communities of priests are the Oblates of Mary Immaculate, the Glenmary Fathers, the Benedictines, and the Fathers of the Society of the Divine Savior.

The religious orders of women paralleled the growth of men's ordinations in the 1950s. The position of women in the Church, and in Tennessee, has from the first been of paramount importance. One of the few ways in which women of great ability could fulfill their potential in the nineteenth and early twentieth centuries was by careers in the Church. The American Church developed a large number of these splendid executives who took great risks and managed great enterprises for the Church from the beginning. Women like Catherine Spalding, Elizabeth Seton, and Katherine Drexel have their clones by the hundreds in the many religious orders that have flourished in the United States, some of foreign origin and some native to the American soil. In the Diocese of Nashville the Sisters of St. Dominic, the Sisters of Mercy, and the Sisters of Charity of Nazareth have been continuously active for more than a hundred years. The Franciscan Sisters have been in the Dioceses of Nashville and Memphis almost as long, as have the Sisters of the Good Shepherd in Memphis. And there are the Precious Blood Sisters, the Little Sisters of the Poor, the Daughters of Charity of St. Vincent de Paul, the Blessed Sacrament Sisters, the Poor Clares, and, more recently, the Sisters of Charity of the Blessed Virgin Mary, the Glenmary Sisters, and the Sisters of St. Joseph of Carondelet.

Many of the older communities reached their peaks in numbers in those same vintage years of 1961 and 1962. They inundated the campuses of Catholic colleges which had summer sessions, and many state university ones, in their search for higher degrees and teaching certificates. This is in itself a mark of their progress. The number of distinguished master's essays and doctoral dissertations done by them, including not a few used for this book, is astonishing. It is too seldom noted that the schools and colleges run by religious orders of women were, during the period from 1930 to 1960, streets ahead of most of those managed by religious orders of men. And the contribution of these women to the education of Catholic youth is immeasurable in its nobility of purpose and idealism of vision. Of course, there were foolish and silly nuns, as there were indolent and slipshod brothers and priests. But in the main their accomplishments, often in the face of indifference, if not downright opposition, by the clergy, are awesome.

They still are, but in new ways. Time was when the first thing sisters did was establish an academy for young ladies, usually a boarding-and-day school. These flourished all over the country, but were especially strong in the South, where feminine charm and virtue were prized. In many places these schools made Catholicism known and admired among non-Catholics, but nearly always among the elite. Nothing could be further from the ambitions of most of the young religious today. The "Academies for Young Ladies" are everywhere dwindling, in number of students and influence. So, of course, are the number of sisters who ran them and taught in them. Sisters who still teach nowadays are more likely to belong to a mixed faculty, mostly lay, part of a little group who live in a house or an apartment, not a convent, and who wear civilian clothes. This last is a reversion to the early Church in the United States, where sisters usually wore civilian clothes in public, reserving their cherished habits for the convent.

Since Vatican II the position of women in the Church has been unsettled. Much else in the Church has been. This seeking, this restlessness, this tension, is a sign of life, unsatisfying as it may be to those involved. One has only to read Christopher Kauffman's history of the Alexian Brothers entitled *Tamers of Death*, to realize how many changes a community can undergo. The Alexian Brothers established their eminently successful convalescent hospital near Chattanooga in 1938, when they acquired the old Signal Mountain Hotel as a rest home for men. Since then the plant has grown to include facilities for women as well, and a novitiate for the community. It is disquieting to report the enmity the Brothers encountered at first in the Chattanooga area, the old anti-Catholic prejudice continuing as late as 1938. But the charity and usefulness of the work of the brothers soon won the area to their side, and the convalescent homes there are among the nation's finest. These, the Christian Brothers of Memphis, the Brothers of Mary, the Glenmary Brothers, and the oldest community of brothers in the United States, the Holy Cross Brothers, have worked in the dioceses of Nashville and Memphis.

Most of the religious in the diocese were in school work, but hospitals continued to attract the charity of the religious orders of women. The old established ones, St. Thomas in Nashville and

Chattanooga quarters of the Knights of Columbus, 1914, and Model T Ford.

Castle-like "Hundred Oaks" mansion, near Winchester, was home for the Paulist Fathers in Tennessee from 1900 to 1953.

In Gatlinburg, Father Paul Clunan greets American Indian parishioner.

Dominican sisters stationed in Chattanooga entertain other sisters of the area at luncheon in their Notre Dame High School cafeteria.

Tennessean Staff photo.

Some staffers of the Ladies of Charity Thrift Shop in Nashville prepare for the usual rush of buyers. Below, leaders of the Diocesan Councils of Catholic Women, photographed while attending a convention in Memphis.

Joe Horton photo, collection of Elizabeth Baltz.

Fourth Degree Knights of Columbus in full regalia meet with their chaplains. The Catholic Center, on Twenty-first at Linden, houses offices of the Bishop, the Vicar General, Chancellor, Ministry Formation, and *The Tennessee Register*.

St. Joseph's in Memphis, grew and developed in the Smith-Adrian regimes. Both of them abandoned old plants for new and modern ones. The Franciscans who operate St. Joseph's opened another hospital, St. Francis, so successful was the first. But the surprising thing is the new hospitals built by religious.

The Mercy Sisters added to their commitment to schools that of a hospital in Knoxville, St. Mary's. This was started in the depression year of 1931, and under the firm hand of Sister Annunciata Dannaher, administrator till she died in 1963, the hospital went from an opening seventy-five-bed operation to one of four hundred in 1963. The Nashville Sisters of Mercy showed an unsuspected talent for hospital work, and their Knoxville enterprise racked up many firsts in medical care in East Tennessee.

There were likewise some praiseworthy abortive efforts. During the 1890s the Franciscan Sisters operated short-lived St. Margaret's Hospital in Nashville. The Sisters of Charity began St. Vincent's Infirmary in Chattanooga, but this too was forced to close after a few years. However, in 1951 the SCN's came back to Chattanooga to operate Memorial Hospital. This was in response to an acute need for a hospital in the city. Doctors and nurses and other interested citizens had been clamoring for one for some time. The doctors led the way for the new facilities by pledging $100,000 themselves as a nucleus for the new building. By 1950 nearly two million dollars had been raised. The usual anti-Catholic prejudice manifested itself, but a new breed of enlightened Protestant ministers led the way to acceptance. And the acceptance was emphatic. Several expansions have enlarged the hospital, and Administrator Sister Thomas de Sales Bailey was awarded the Dorothy Patten Award in 1983 for "adding to the richness of life in Chattanooga." In recent years sisters and brothers have been coming to the diocese as individuals, or in pairs, rather than as convent-size enclaves, and doing social rather than educational work. This interesting development is as much a part of today's Church as the academies for young ladies were in the nineteenth century. Among the religious communities pioneering in this work are Sisters of St. Joseph of Carondelet, Brothers of Mary, Holy Cross Brothers, and Glenmary Home Missioners. No one can tell what shapes this new direction will take in the future.

Remarkable too, during the 1950s was the growth of lay organizations. The Serra Club was launched in Memphis in 1949 and chapters were begun in Nashville in 1954 and in Chattanooga in 1958. This organization of Catholic men holds up the hands of the bishop in many ways. The older organizations flourished. The Knights of Columbus followed the American pattern by sensibly moving to the suburbs, where their new facilities are better used than in the old downtown clubhouses. The twenty-first Tennessee chapter was organized in Knoxville in 1961. The Ladies of Charity built a splendid new facility in Nashville in 1976, and got going in Chattanooga in 1960.

Aquinas Junior College was opened by the Dominican Sisters in Nashville in 1961. Earlier that year the largest ordination in the history of the diocese was held when seven new priests were made by Bishop Adrian. The Catholic world was moving slowly to a climax. Pope John XXIII, who had been elected in 1958 to the highest office in the Catholic Church, convened the Second Vatican Council in October of 1962. For American Catholics, this overshadowed even the election of Catholic John Fitzgerald Kennedy as President of the United States in 1960. Kennedy's election meant that Catholics were generally accepted as full-size American citizens. But Vatican Council II meant that the Church in America was to become a people's church, turning the Mass from Latin into the vernacular language and de-formalizing ritual. The years 1960 to 1962 — these were the great climactic years for the American Church.

And for the Church in Tennessee also.

A New Diocese

Just about the first thing taught in grade school geography in Tennessee is that the state is really three states, all quite different: East, Middle, and West Tennessee. Fifty years ago this was profoundly true, but since World War II the differences between Middle and East Tennessee are less marked. Along with the rest of the "Southern Rim", Tennessee has prospered since the great war, but nowhere has that prosperity been so remarkable as in East Tennessee. There is still plenty of mountain-style poverty and illiteracy there, but the growth of better living and brighter prospects, for the Church as well as everybody else, in the area stretching north-easterly from Oak Ridge to Bristol, is a showpiece of southern development. From Oak Ridge southward to Chattanooga prospects are also fair, but not so spectacular as those of the northeast.

Something like this has also happened to Middle Tennessee. The southward migration of so many people and so much capital, much of it from the Federal government, has sparked a prosperity not glimpsed in the area since the 1850s. And, as with East Tennessee, lively optimism and big plans for the future.

Memphis, too, enjoyed war-time prosperity and considerable growth in the 1950s through the 1970s. But the well-springs of the Memphis economy are still those of the headquarters of the north delta of the Mississippi: cotton, lumber, and the industries supplied by these and other agricultural products. Memphis is more like northern Louisiana and Mississippi than it is like the rest of Tennessee. Its historical roots run to plantation economy, unlike those of the rest of the state. But proud Memphis has been the largest city in the state since the Civil War, and has a history of dominating the politics of the state since 1900, largely because of deals made by its Boss Ed Crump with East Tennessee, and the great influence of Crump ally long-time Senator Kenneth McKellar. Since the decline of Crump-McKellar power in the state, Memphis has moved uncertainly; it is possible that the Crump legacy has atrophied civic initiative. Memphians do not think so, of course, and feel that their size entitles them to more leadership in the state than other Tennesseans are ready to admit, especially in view of the way the Crump machine had for so many years railroaded its candidates into state office.

This background may help to understand why Memphis Catholics wanted their own diocese. For many years they had resented Nashville's leadership as the see city of the diocese, and the feeling grew more acute during the post-World War II period. Precisely why is difficult to say. Both Bishop Adrian and his successor, Bishop Joseph Durick, paid a great deal of attention to the problems of Memphis.

Perhaps both felt what so many outside Shelby County felt, that Memphis was a thousand miles away. Actually, it is pretty far — 225 miles from Nashville, 600 from the North Carolina-Virginia line. And farther than that in feeling. A group of Memphis priests in 1968 petitioned the Apostolic Delegate in

Washington to make Memphis the see city of a new diocese whose territory would be West Tennessee. The petition at first was tabled, but the delegation began to inquire into the matter. It found official opinion agreeable to division. Then the Washington office wanted information about everything, and asked that everything be kept quiet. It was. Only Bishop Durick and the comptroller of the Diocese, Richard Quick, who put the information together, knew about it. And they were startled when Rome said, upon receiving the documents forwarded from Washington, go to it.

Then, of course, the real work began. Delegations from Nashville and Memphis got together to work out the details. The geography was easy, dictated by the map. The Tennessee River is a natural dividing line just about where all wanted the division. Assets were a different matter, but the division was worked out because all concerned wanted it done swiftly. Naturally, both sides felt they had been short-changed, the Memphis side more keenly. But both sides rejoiced. The new diocese was created with widespread satisfaction. Memphis got what it wanted most, autonomy. It remains for them to work out that special character which all dioceses need eventually to attain. It takes time.

Besides time, it takes leadership. In new Bishop Joseph Aloysius Durick Nashville had in 1970 a progressive young leader attuned to change. Moreover, he was a southerner, born in Dayton, Tennessee — his family gave their home there as a site for a church. After schooling at Cullman, Alabama, and Rome, he returned to north Alabama as head of the Diocese of Mobile Mission Board. He knew the temper of the South.

And, as Bishop Adrian's auxiliary from 1964 on, he came to know Tennessee. In 1966 he was given complete control of the diocese, with the title of Apostolic Administrator; Bishop Adrian was then in his eighties, living in St. Thomas Hospital. Four years more, and Memphis became a new diocese. Its first bishop was another southerner, Carroll T. Dozier, a Virginian, also Rome-educated. Dozier was nearly sixty years old when he was made a bishop. Perhaps he was chosen in some part because he was thought to be into the age of discretion. Neither Dozier nor Durick, however, was concerned with discretion. Both were outspoken and innovative partisans of the black revolution, and almost radical exponents of the "new" Church of the 1970s. Together they helped to make a history of emphasis on racial equality and ecumenical approaches. New efforts, like the Baptist-Catholic-Jewish Trilogue, and association with the divinity schools of Vanderbilt and the University of the South, opened up a new world of Christian fellowship in Tennessee. So 1970, the year Memphis was made a diocese, is a good date for the beginning of the next history of Catholicism in Tennessee. But there are other good dates, as well. April 16, 1961, may be a better one.

On April 16, 1961, Bishop Adrian celebrated a remarkable triple jubilee: his seventy-eighth birthday, his fiftieth year as a priest, and his twenty-fifth as a bishop. It is rare indeed that ordination and consecration fall on the same date, and that the birthday of the celebrant, but this almost happened to Bishop Adrian. His ordination was a day earlier, on April 15, and both his ordination and consecration were a little out of the ordinary. Since there was a conflict between the normal ordination day and some examinations the future bishop had to take, his ordination was advanced two months. And since April 16 is not the Feast of an Apostle, the customary day for consecrating a bishop, Adrian had to get a special permission, one easily forthcoming, to be consecrated on his birthday.

Jubilee Day was celebrated almost entirely as an in-house occasion. That was fitting. For his twenty-five years as Bishop of Nashville were years of steady growth. In Memphis, nine new parishes were established, in Chattanooga a phenomenal four, in Nashville three. Thirteen new parishes were established in smaller places. Ten missions were raised to the status of parishes. Sixty-seven churches were renovated — nearly all there were in the diocese. Five new high schools were established. And much more. It is quite possible that this day saw the diocese at the heights of its estate. The future may see more, but it is doubtful if it will see more in relation to the total Catholic population of the state, about 77,000 in 1961, now nearly 120,000.

Bishop Adrian resigned in 1969, and died in 1972.

Epilogue

The Old and the New

Despite the implicit claims of magazines bearing titles like "Recent History", or "Contemporary History", there really isn't any such thing. History requires some perspective. You have to get a little distance from events before you can relate and judge them. Ask anyone who was in a fighting unit during a war. Like the hero of Tolstoy's *War and Peace,* he rarely had any notion of how a given day's fighting was going in his own little corner of it, let alone how the battle was progressing on a wide front.

So, this book is not going to try to bring the history of the Diocese of Nashville up to last week's happenings. That's the job of *The Register*. The aim of this book is to see the past in perspective, to tie what happened in Tennessee to what was happening in this region, the state, the nation, and above all the Catholic world.

The Catholic Church the world over is now going through a period of unsettledness. In the wake of the Second Vatican Council called by Pope John XXIII and finished by Pope Paul VI, changes are reshaping the way Catholics worship and live. A new vitality is coursing through the Church's body. In Latin America everything is moving and changing; nobody knows what the upshot will be. In Africa the Church is one of the powerful new forces that are remaking that continent. Just about everywhere, except for the old uncracked bastions of Mohammedanism and communist Russia, the Church is finding new ways.

America, too, and Tennessee, are a-quiver with change. It is impossible to tell the Church's story of the recent past. Only a little snatch here, a glimpse there, can be managed, and even then the meaning is elusive.

So, no attempt will be made in this book to deal with the last few years of our sesquicentennial. However, some things whose endings are still far off, and whose meanings are still far from clear, need to be mentioned, at least. And so, our book has no ending. In these last three chapters a few ventures into the recent past are made, a few names are spotlighted for a brief moment, a few developments are sketched. But no attempt has been made to unite these into a continuous and shapely narrative. Our story simply drifts into the future like shadows forming in the haze of early morning. The figures and their destinations will come into the clear light of day a generation later.

The aim of this book, then, is to bring the past to life, to try to make some sense of what the Catholic experience in the state has been. This is, on the one hand, a matter of perspective, of seeing events and trends in relation to their own time, not ours. Slavery is a good example of this. To most Americans today it seems an unthinkable horror. In 1860 it was, for most Americans, a simple fact of life, like automobiles today. On the other hand, history must reduce legend to fact and fill in the blank spaces. An excellent illustration of this is the Catholic history of the period following World War I.

Those who rejoice in Vatican II and its aftermath are sometimes inclined to dismiss all that went before it as provincial and lifeless. Much Catholic life of the 1920s and 1930s was. From the perspective of the 1980s the Legion of Decency, the Christophers, the Catholic Youth Organizations, the Catholic Students' Mission Crusade, and other such, seem inconsequential. Worse was the character of much of the Church. It often was, as Abigail McCarthy notes, dogmatic, defensive, puritanical, and closed. It was also often anti-intellectual and usually authoritarian. It had a substantial quota of priests who were sometimes bullies and nuns who were sometimes silly — many of us are fed up with those unending stories and plays and films about them, creating a legend as false in its different way as the sentimentality of the Bing Crosby movies "Going My Way" or "The Bells of St. Mary's."

But there was another side to the Church of those years between the two World Wars. Along with these sadly dated endeavors there was also a true Catholic Renaissance. Most of the intellectual and artistic explorations and excitements leaked into the United States from Europe, it is true, but the Europeans happily came to this country to stimulate Catholic minds and tastes. Jacques Maritain became a sort of twentieth-century Father of the

Church to the young Americans who read his books and saw and heard him. His compatriot, Etienne Gilson, was scarcely less revered. And it is important to remember that while these savants were respected mainly for their philosophical writing, both also wrote well on art.

European artists themselves were returning to religious subjects after a century of secularism. At Assy, in eastern France, Dominican Father Pierre Couturier master-minded a chapel using the talents of a dozen outstanding artists of the time, Bonnard, Rouault, Braque, Leger, Matisse, Richier, Lipchitz, Chagall, and Lurcat among them. Later Henri Matisse decorated a chapel at Vence in which he did everything, wall painting, vestments, sacred vessels, stained glass, every detail. The most influential architect of the time, LeCorbusier, did his best work in the famous chapel at Ronchamp. In music Igor Stravinsky turned to religious themes, and Francois Poulenc went from the worldly satire of *Les Mamelles de Teresias* to the sacred *Gloria* and *Mass for the Poor*. The French led the way in literature as well as art, with Mauriac and Claudel in the van, but British Evelyn Waugh and Graham Greene were not far behind, along with German Gertrude von le Fort and Scandinavian Sigrid Undset.

The United States felt the force of all this religious resurgence. Maurice Levanoux started *Liturgical Arts Magazine,* which did so much to lift the level of church building and decoration. Writers like Paul Horgan, J.F. Powers, and Helen White celebrated their Catholicity in literature, as did the converts Allen Tate and his wife Caroline Gordon. Tate brings us back to Tennessee, where he was schooled in his most formative years, and influenced other excellent convert literary writers, such as Walter Sullivan and Brainard Cheney. Georgian Flannery O'Connor, a cradle Catholic with the most deliberate religious intent of them all, appeared later on the scene.

To intelligent and intellectual Catholics the time between the wars was a very exciting time, a time when native talent was arising in numbers, meeting as it did so a wave of brilliant converts and another wave of intellectual Catholic refugees from Europe, fleeing the oppressive regimes of Hitler and Mussolini. As with all such new waves, the effects made uneven patterns in Catholic life. Plenty of eager young Catholics were bitterly disappointed when their college professors took them over the same deadening manuals in philosophy and theology they had been using for years, lifeless and obsolete old formulae that squeezed the life out of ideas that once were live and inspiring. But the lucky ones found professors and teachers alert to the new ideas and new life in the Church, and brought these new ways of thinking back to their home places and parishes.

It is impossible to gauge how much of this took root in Tennessee. The Catholics in the state were so few in number and influence as to be beyond measuring. But everyone knew of educated laymen and religious who quickened to the new life that was flooding the Church. Then, too, Tennessee had a little cultural lag. The spirituality that Bishop Smith inspired in the Tennessee Church needed time to be refined into intellectual distinction. But new vigor was backing up in the spiritual reservoirs. In the enormous growth of the southeast that was presaged by Roosevelt's Tennessee Valley development and surged into floodtide during and after World War II, Tennessee Catholicism underwent comparable changes.

The heart and center of all the change was, of course, Vatican II. The center of Catholic life always has been and always will be the Eucharist. But what a difference to have the great act of sacrifice and praise in one's native language. The old Latin gave the Mass an aura of mystery and the supernatural, but the vernacular gives it a feeling of intimacy, of being at home with and close to the communicants. Because Latin could not engender that sense of unity, the pre-Vatican II Church everywhere developed "popular" devotions, novenas, devotions to a wide range of saints, and so on. These devotions, often copied from Italian models, were full of the sentimentality and exaggerated emotionalism of late nineteenth century Italy, a period of depressing bad taste.

Catholics who knew good writing hoped that the new liturgy would be real literature. They were half disappointed. The canon came out fine, but the readings from the Bible are often badly translated. It's a pity that the official Church had, and has, such a tin ear. The greatest translator of classic Greek and Latin of our time, Robert Fitzgerald, was a Catholic, but the Church never gave him a commission.

In the United States the thrust of the effects of Vatican II was to embrace the "people." The phrase, "the people of God," is used so much it's worn thin. And the people of God are slated, by the new liturgists and pastoral theologians, to be as active and busy as fountains. In the South generally, and Tennessee along with it, the drive toward activism seems a little more intense than in the older Catholic centers. Such activism, pushed to extremes, suggests a wholly Catholic culture. This may not work well in the pluralism on which the United States is founded. It is ironic that the nineteenth century saw the American Catholics trying to get out of the ghetto, and at the very moment of their greatest success, 1960-1962, beginning to form one for themselves.

There is no doubt that Catholics are today generally well-received in intellectual circles. In Nashville, a Catholic member of the faculty of Vanderbilt University would have seemed sacrilege to both Methodists and Catholics at the turn of the century. So, in many universities, would a Jew. Now both are plentiful and unremarkable. The same is true to a lesser extent at the Tennessee state universities. There is plenty of prejudice left in the South and in Tennessee, but it is not at the top of the social and intellectual ladder. It hangs around the bottom rungs. It will be very difficult to dispel it, for the bottom rungs of southern Protestantism are as wary of the drive to social justice as they are of Catholicism.

A natural area for Catholic appeal is that of social justice. By no means have all American Catholics followed the teachings of the papal instructions on the rights of labor, the living wage, racial equality, and such like. A man who did command a huge non-Catholic audience speaking on these themes was Father Charles Coughlin, the notorious radio priest of the 1930s. But Couglin's appeal had little to do with spiritual values, and his intellectual foundation was very shaky. His contemporary, Monsignor John A. Ryan, was what Coughlin should have been intellectually, and was very influential in Washington circles. But again, these were elite circles. And Ryan had little to do with the South.

Many southern Catholics were closely involved with the Martin Luther King revolution. Nashville's eighth bishop, Joseph Durick, was a friend of King and deeply committed to his mission, as was the first Bishop of Memphis, Carroll T. Dozier. What King stood for is just about official American Catholic doctrine by this time. But many Catholics, both cleric and lay, had and some still have old southern notions about race equality. The revolution of the blacks in Tennessee, especially in the middle and east sections, was about as peaceful as such things can be. The key issue, as noted earlier, was and is school integration. Integration of restaurants, transportation, and so on was accomplished in Nashville with little trauma. The Catholic churches had long been integrated. Bishop Byrne wrote as early as 1906 that the only solution to racial agony in the South was a religious one. He would have been astonished to find, had he lived this long, that a political solution of sorts had been achieved, but that a religious one has not. The Protestant churches are by and large far behind the Catholics in integrating blacks into their congregations, but this did not mean among Catholics either a large increase in black converts or strong Catholic sentiments of racial equality. These are still in the making.

Here are serious problems without immediate solutions, whose directions and meaning are still not clear. But there is hope for the South and for Tennessee. The South has for long been derisively called "The Bible Belt." That means, at least, that Christianity is alive and kicking there. There are many signs of Christians getting together, too. The history of religion in the South has over-much been a history of separate and defensive Christians. True, Protestants generally have trusted one another more than collectively they have Catholics, but they have also been keen rivals rather than cooperative. One of the most cherished goals of the ninth Bishop of Nashville, James D. Niedergeses, is a deeper spirit of cooperation among all religious people, Christians and non-Christians. His pastoral work in Chattanooga before he was ordained bishop featured a half dozen appointments and honors in civic life, and his episcopate has been equally marked by devotion to ecumenism. He was honored in 1984 by the Nashville Chapter of the Conference of Christians and Jews, and he is frequently to be found at similar efforts to initiate and maintain dialogue with non-Catholics. He is the liaison person of the Catholic Church to the Southern Baptists, and has been instrumental in developing the Roman Catholic-Southern Baptist Scholars' Conference.

Niedergeses is Tennessee-born. He hails from Lawrenceburg,

that most Catholic of Tennessee towns, along with nearby Winchester. His resemblance, even physical, to the man who fostered his vocation, Bishop Smith, is marked. He shares Smith's deep spirituality and love of people, and like Smith is tensely zealous. If pastoral solicitude is the first mark of a good bishop, as many say, Bishop Niedergeses is a nearly perfect specimen of the species.

Problems we have always with us. We need more of Niedergeses' overflowing faith, and abounding love. That unique Catholic southern genius, Flannery O'Connor, put it well at the end of her *Memoir of Mary Ann*:

> The action by which charity grows invisibly among us, entwining the living and the dead, is called by the Church the Communion of Saints. It is a communion built upon imperfection, created from what we make of our grotesque state . . . in us, the good is grotesque, something under construction . . . [our stories] will illuminate the lines that join the most diverse lives and hold them fast in Christ''.

May this story of Catholicism in Tennessee do that a little.

Bibliographical Essay

Three considerations keep this book from being a scholarly work. First, lack of time. Second, lack of resources. And third, lack of intention.

Bishop James D. Niedergeses and his Sesquicentennial Committee did not want a full-dress footnoted scholarly work. They wanted a readable book, one Tennessee Catholics could enjoy in the same way they enjoy hearing about their family ancestors. Nothing discourages this sort of enjoyment more than a litany of footnote references, controversy about matters of small importance from today's point of view, quotations in Latin and Italian from papal documents, and lists of pastors, superiors of religious communities, and purchasers of cemetery lots. In any case, the documents for these are few and mingy. From 1937 on, the diocesan archives are good; the files of the diocesan newspaper, *The Tennessee Register,* alone are ample evidence of this. But behind this, stretching back into the entire nineteenth century, there is little. Little, but still enough for a popular history such as this to feed on.

General

A major resource for this book are three pamphlet-histories. The first one was for the golden jubilee of the old Cathedral of Nashville, Daniel Francis Barr's *A Souvenir of St. Mary's Cathedral (1847-1897) Including the Century's Annals.* The second and third were for the centenary of the diocese in 1937: George J. Flanigen, *Catholicity in Tennessee,* and John B. Morris, *A Sermon Delivered by His Excellency The Most Reverend John B. Morris, D.D., Bishop of Little Rock, On the Occasion of the Centenary of the Diocese of Nashville, Cathedral of the Incarnation, Nashville, Tennessee, October 5, 1937.* Barr's work was useful, that of Morris and Flanigen invaluable, for this book. Flanigen's little book, mostly parish and institution histories compiled from questionnaires answered by pastors and superiors, is in many libraries, but the other two are hard to find. They are in the Diocesan Archives at the Catholic Center, 2400 Twenty-first Avenue, South, in Nashville, along with many other souvenir pamphlets useful to this book. Some of these contain sound history, such as the one Flanigen did for his Chattanooga parish of Saints Peter and Paul, and an anonymous one for St. Patrick's, Memphis, in the Memphis Public Library. But all have some use, however sketchy the history.

Other informal history of great interest is found in the letters of the principal actors of this book. By far the best of these are the letter books of the fifth bishop, Thomas S. Byrne, in the diocesan archives, but there are a good many letters of the first bishop, Richard P. Miles, in the Manuscript Collections of the University of Notre Dame. Notre Dame also has some letters of the other bishops, notably by the fourth bishop, Joseph Rademacher, and many letters of the first priest to be ordained in the United States, Stephen Badin. There are useful letters also in the archives of the Archdiocese of Cincinnati, and the archives of the Congregation of the Propaganda in Rome. I am deeply grateful to the distinguished biographer of Archbishop John Ireland, Father Marvin R. O'Connell, for having some of these Roman documents copied for me — Rome is a resource outside my time and means. The staff of the Notre Dame collections, led by Archivist Wendy Clauson Schlereth, have been immensely helpful. So has Sister Felicitas Powers, the able archivist of the Baltimore Archdiocesan collections, and Father Adrian Wade, the archivist of the Dominican House of Studies in Washington. But the most helpful of all, the Diocesan collections aside, has been Sister Cecilia Lynch, O.P., the custodian of the Flanigen historical collections at Aquinas Junior College in Nashville.

But this is only the beginning. I have also battened off the generosity of the staffs of the State Library and Archives of Tennessee, the Nashville collection of the Nashville Public Library, the Memphis Shelby County Public Library and Information Center, the Chattanooga Public Library, the Filson Society Library of Louisville, the Archives of the Sisters of Charity of Nazareth, Kentucky, the Archives of Georgetown University, the Archives of the Archdiocese of New Orleans, the State Library and Archives of Arkansas at Little Rock, and the Archives of the Congregation of the Mission in New York. Josiah Brady in Memphis, Charles Nolan in New Orleans, and above all Sister Agnes Geraldine McGann in Nazareth, have been helpful far beyond the call of duty.

Moving now to formal history, but not yet to books, I have found somewhat to my surprise and greatly to my satisfaction, unpublished M.A. and Ph.D. essays and dissertations of great help. "Unpublished" is an anomalous word here as applied to Ph.D. dissertations, for some are available from University Microfilms, Ann Arbor, Michigan. This excellent service to scholarship has made available to me such fine studies as J. DeBerry's *Confederate Tennessee* and Sister Mary de Lourdes's *Political Nativism in Tennessee to 1860*. Much farther from publication than these, but in almost daily use as I wrote, are the short biographies of Tennessee priests compiled by Monsignor John Mogan, Chancellor of the Diocese of Nashville in the 1930s. Monsignor Mogan also wrote in longhand a sketch of the early history of the Tennessee Church; had he lived a normal span he might have been the historian the early Church in Tennessee so sadly lacked. Another candidate for that post is Father James T. Lorigan, who wrote the good short history in the first *Catholic Encyclopedia*. His close friend Father John Larkin, also interested in history, is reputed to have written a longer history of the Catholics of Tennessee, now lost, but which we keep hoping will turn up somewhere.

Several M.A. essays have been useful, among them two ethnic ones, James J. Flanagan's *The Irish Element in Nashville* and Joseph

McPherson's *Nashville's German Element,* both in the Vanderbilt Library. Father Owen Campion's undergraduate essay on the history of Tennessee's Catholicism is also worthwhile.

The periodical literature is considerable. In addition to *The Register,* other diocesan publications have been useful. *The Columbian* (1915-1927) and *The Cresset* (1927-1932) help understanding an oddly neglected era in diocesan history, while the short-lived *Catholic Herald, Facts* and *The Catholic Journal of the New South* shed some light on their earlier times. The daily secular newspapers need to be combed further; I have used them mostly as secondary sources. I have gone through some early volumes of Protestant journals, such as *The Tennessee Baptist* and *The Methodist Christian Advocate;* except for material on topics of national concern I doubt further search in these is useful. But I have carefully mined the forty-six volumes of the *Tennessee Historical Quarterly* and its predecessor, the *Tennessee Historical Magazine,* and the yield is high. The occasional papers of the East and West Tennessee historical societies have also deepened and clarified many subjects. The nineteenth century *Catholic Advocate* of Bardstown-Louisville has many articles date-lined Nashville and other Tennessee cities and towns. Catholic historical journals such as *The Catholic Historical Review* and *The U.S. Catholic Historian* have a few articles on southern subjects, as do, much more rarely, the secular historical journals. *The Official Catholic Directory,* an annual, has been a reference work almost as valuable as the dictionary, as have both editions of *The Catholic Encyclopedia,* especially the older one. Another resource of daily use was the diocesan chronology compiled by Monsignor Flanigen for Bishop Adrian's 1961 triple jubilee.

Turning now to books, I have found James Hennesey's *American Catholics* the most useful general reference work, though I have also used two others: John Tracy Ellis' *American Catholicism,* and Andrew Greeley's *The Catholic Experience.* The *History of Tennessee* by Stanley J. Folmsbee, Enoch L. Mitchell, and Robert E. Corlew has also served me as well, as have three books about Memphis, Gerald M. Capers, Jr.'s *Memphis, The Biography of a River Town,* an outstanding book, the older J.M. Keating's *History of the City of Memphis and Shelby County, Tennessee,* and the sketches in Shields McIlwaine's *Memphis Down in Dixie.* Don Doyle's books on modern Nashville, *Nashville in the New South 1880-1930* and *Nashville Since the 1920s* are excellent social history. There is a shoal of books on early Nashville. I have used A.W. Putnam's *The History of Middle Tennessee* (to 1859), J. Woodridge's (ed) *History of Nashville,* and Jesse Burt's *Nashville: Its Life and Times* along with the picture books by Carl Zibart, John Egerton, James Hoobler, and Adams and Christian. Reminiscenses by Jane Thomas recall *Old Days in Nashville,* while Jack Norman and William Waller's capacious memories bring back the turn-of-the-century era. I have paged through much more.

The premier historian of the Chattanooga area is James W. Livingood, and his books are a model for regional historians. They are *Hamilton County, Sequatchie* (with J. Leonard Raulston), and (with Gilbert E. Govan) *The Chattanooga Country*. A well-known early history of East Tennessee is Goodspeed's, who also wrote histories of Hamilton, Knox, and Shelby counties. The most ambitious history of Knoxville is one edited by Lucile Deaderick, *Heart of the Valley,* and there is also a history of early Knoxville by Betsy Creekmore. A souvenir history of Immaculate Conception Church by Lawrence V. Gibney, *The Church on Summit Hill,* is so good a history of Catholicism in the Knoxville area I wish it could be extended to book size and incorporate the neglected Catholic history of northeast Tennessee.

Since so much of the history of Catholicism in Tennessee follows the history of its Irish immigration, William V. Shannon's *The American Irish,* Carl Wittke's *The Irish in America,* and Emmett Larkin's *The Historical Dimension of Irish Catholicism* have helped me to understand Irish racial characteristics. John Lawrence Connelly's *North Nashville and Germantown* gives some insights into the German character, though it is mostly factual. There are several good accounts of the German settlements in Lawrence County in the parish histories, but the subject has yet to get the book it deserves. The Italians, the Poles, the Lebanese and other nationalities also need remembrancers before they are forgotten, like the French in Winchester. Finally, Gerald Shaughnessy's *Have the Immigrants Lost Faith?* raises the right questions about an important and difficult subject.

Topical, Chapter by Chapter

PROLOGUE **(The Spanish and the French).** My best sources for the explorations were two books by Carl Ortwin Sauer, *Sixteenth Century North America* and *Seventeenth Century North America*. The best source on DeMonbreun was an outstanding article in the *Tennesse e Historical Quarterly,* Wirt Armistead Cate's "Timothy DeMonbreun", September, 1957. Harold McCracken's *The American Cowboy* is excellent.

CHAPTER 1 **(Roots of the Present: Maryland and Kentucky).** The best source was Ben J. Webb, *The Centenary of Catholicism in Kentucky*. Invaluable for this chapter as well as the next four was Victor F. O'Daniel's *The Father of the Church in Tennessee,* a life of Nashville's first bishop, Richard Pius Miles. O'Daniel's *The Dominican Province of St. Joseph* was also helpful. J. Herman Schauinger's *Stephen T. Badin* was essential. Filling in some gaps were M. J. Spalding's *Sketches of the Missions of Kentucky,* Anna C. Minogue's *Pages from 100 Years of Dominican History,* Carl Driver's *John Sevier,* and Samuel Cole Williams's *Early Travels in the Tennessee Country*.

CHAPTER 2 **(Richard Pius Miles).** All of the above, plus O'Daniel's *Life of Edward Fenwick*, and Reginald Coffey's *The American Dominicans*.

CHAPTER 3 **(The Bishop of Nashville).** Same as the preceeding two chapters, plus parts of several railroad histories.

CHAPTER 4 **(The 1840s and the Cathedral).** The literature on Strickland, already large, is growing. Among the older studies Agnes Gilchrist's *William Strickland* is a standard, while the account of Strickland's work in James Patrick's *The Architecture of Tennessee*, reviews the career of Adolph Heiman as well as Strickland's. Monsignor Charles Williams' story of St. Mary's in Alfred Leland Crabb, ed., *Seven Early Churches of Nashville* is especially good on the renovations. Ellis Coulter's *William Ganaway Brownlow* has been useful.

CHAPTER 5 **(The Early Church in Memphis).** Francis W. Kervick's *Patrick Charles Keely, Architect*, an unpublished manuscript in the Notre Dame Architectural Library was helpful, as was Bennie Hugh Priddie's unpublished M.A. essay in the Vanderbilt Library, *Nineteenth Century Church Architecture in Memphis*.

CHAPTER 6 **(Taking Care of the Young).** Several histories of religious communities of women form the foundation of much of this chapter, among them Sister Margaret Hamilton's *History of St. Agnes Academy* (Memphis), Sister Rose Marie Masserano's *The Nashville Dominicans*, Sister Loyola Fox' *A Return of Love* (the Nashville Sisters of Mercy), Sister Julia Gilmore's *Come North* (Sisters of Charity of Leavenworth), and Sister Agnes Geraldine McGann's *SCNs Serving Since 1812*. There is a good sketch of Father Schacht in T.H. Kinsella's *The History of Our Cradle Land*, and two good souvenir histories of St. Mary's Orphanage in the Nashville archives.

CHAPTER 7 **(Catholic Life in the Miles Era).** The periodical history of railroading in Tennessee is so wide-ranging as to require a special bibliography. I have been especially helped by two books, Maury Klein's *History of the Louisville & Nashville Railroad*, and Jesse C. Burt Jr.'s *A History of the Nashville, Chattanooga and St. Louis Railroad*.

CHAPTER 8 **(Catholic Attitudes Toward Slavery).** Madeleine Hooke Rice's *American Catholic Opinion on the Slavery Controversy*, Judith Wimmer's unpublished Ph.D. dissertation (Drew University) *American Catholic Interpretations of the Civil War*, Benjamin Blied's *Catholics and the Civil War*, and most of all Michael V. Gannon's *Rebel Bishop: The Life of Augustin Verot*, were of use. I have done more research on Whelan than any other subject of this book, turning up in the process a little-known report he made about his time in Nashville in the Tennessee State Archives. But his episcopate is still a puzzle to me. The best account of him is in Reginald Coffey's *The American Dominicans*. There are revealing glimpses of him in Thomas T. McAvoy's unpublished M.A. essay in the Notre Dame Library, *The War Letters of Peter Paul Cooney, C.S.C.*

CHAPTER 9 **(Civil War Chaplains and Nurses).** On nuns, Ellen Ryan Jolly's *Nuns of the Battlefield,* George Barton's *Angels of the Battlefield,* "A Memorial to Nuns of the Battlefield", an address by Auberon Kennedy of Rhode Island, printed in *The Congressional Record* of 1918, have been useful. For priests, Herman Norton's *Rebel Religion* has proved outstandingly helpful. Peter Meaney's article on Father Bliemel, "Valiant Chaplain of the Bloody Tenth" in the *Tennessee Historical Quarterly,* 1982, fills a need, and Joseph T. Durkin's editing of the journal of Confederate Chaplain James B. Sheerin, C.SS.R. gave useful incidental information. Three other books have been helpful: Ella Lonn, *Foreign ers in the Confederacy,* Walter Durham's *Nashville: The Occupied City,* and James Lee McDonough's *Chattanooga: A Death Grip on the Confederacy.* There is ample material on Father Ryan, including the long essay as a preface to his *Collected Poems* by John Talbot Smith, but the best source is Monsignor Charles C. Boldrick's article, "Father Abram J. Ryan, The Poet-Priest of the Confederacy", in the *Filson Club History Quarterly,* July, 1972 (Louisville, Kentucky). Useful especially for the letters was an unpublished M.A. essay in the Peabody branch of the Vanderbilt Library on Ryan by Robert E. Freidel. There are also some Ryan letters in the Tennessee State Archives in Nashville, and much material in the Nashville diocesan archives. Extremely useful for Ryan's later years is an excellent article by Edward J. Cashin, Jr., "The Banner of the South: A Journal of the Reconstruction Era", in *Richmond County History* Vol. 6, #1, Augusta, Georgia.

CHAPTER 10 **(After the War)** and CHAPTER 11 **(Education and Clerical Growth During the Feehan Era).** The only book-length biography of Archbishop Feehan, by Cornelius J. Kirkfleet, is disappointingly thin. Roger Hart's *Redeemers, Bourbons and Populists* is good for the political background, but the industrial background provided by the expanding railroads' histories are too occupied with financial rather than social history. Vincent L. Naes' *Rounding Out a Century* is a good account of the Catholic Knights of America, and W.J. Battersby's books on Brother Maurelian and the Christian Brothers are at the top of their class. Charles Shanabruck's *Chicago's Catholics* contains a good account of Feehan's episcopate in that city.

CHAPTER 12 **(The Yellow Fever in Memphis).** I have relied heavily on two sources: Gerald Capers Jr.'s article "The Yellow Fever in Memphis in the 1870s" in the *Mississippi Valley Historical Review,* Vol. XXIV, March, 1938, and D.A. Quinn's *Heroes and Heroines of Memphis.* Leo Kalmer's *Stronger Than Death* has also been useful. Dr. Rudolph Kampmeier of the Vanderbilt University School of Medicine has kindly supplied me with useful medical information.

CHAPTER 13 **(The Rademacher Interlude).** There is useful information in the Manuscript Collection of the University of Notre Dame.

CHAPTER 14 **(Four Catholic Bishops from Tennessee).** This is a rewrite of my article, "Three Catholic Bishops from Tennessee", in the *Tennessee Historical Quarterly* for Spring 1978, which is carefully documented. The new material on Archbishop Floersh came largely from the archives of the Archdiocese of Louisville.

CHAPTER 15 **(The Legendary Bishop Byrne and Some Other Legends)** and CHAPTER 16 **(Byrne the Builder).** The Byrne era is the first to be amply documented in the archives of the diocese and in the religious and secular press. Besides these M. Edward Hussey's *A History of the Seminaries of the Archdiocese of Cincinnati* and Michael J. Kelly and James M. Kieran's *History of St. Mary's Seminary of the West* have been helpful on Byrne's priestly schooling. Special aspects of Byrne's career are noted in Katherine Burton's *The Golden Door: The Life of Katherine Drexel,* and John Tracy Ellis' *The Formative Years of the Catholic University of America,* Thomas H. Baker's *The Memphis Commercial Appeal* was helpful on C.P.J. Mooney. The Nashville background is nicely described in William Waller's two books of reminiscence, *Nashville in the 1890s* and *Nashville in the 1900s,* and the social and political history are admirably done in Don H. Doyle's *Nashville in the New South*. The Memphis background is well done in William H. Miller's *Mr. Crump of Memphis*.

CHAPTER 17 **(With Emphasis on the Laity).** The material on the Knights of Columbus is based on Walter Kauffman's superb history of that organization, *Faith and Fraternalism*. Files of the Catholic journals are scattered throughout the archives of the state. The political material comes in part from Dan M. Robison's *Biographical Directory of the Tennessee General Assembly,* Two Vols.

CHAPTER 18 **(Bishop Smith and His Times).** Charles C. O'Donnell's *A Short Life of Alphonse J. Smith, Sixth Bishop of Nashville,* an unpublished M.A. thesis at St. Mary's Seminary, Baltimore, was useful for material on Smith's early life. A Vanderbilt M.A. thesis, Leslie M. Gower's *The Election of 1928 in Tennessee,* provided useful background, as did David M. Chalmer's *Hooded America,* a history of the Ku Klux Klan, and a University of Minnesota unpublished Ph.D. dissertation, Clayton R. Robinson's *The Impact of the City on Rural Immigration to Memphis, 1880-1940.* With this chapter my own memory comes into play; I knew many of the Vanderbilt agrarians and their biographer, Louise Cowan, personally. I also knew many others mentioned from here on, and heard much from my elders.

CHAPTER 19 **(The Adrian Years).** My thanks to Professor David L.

Rowe of Middle Tennessee State University, who has helped me with Christian Asmus, the architect who did so much work for the Nashville diocese. Professor Reavis Mitchell, of Fisk University, wrote his M.A. essay on *The Black Man and the Catholic Church in Nashville,* also for MTSU. Robert Holton's *In The Beginning* is about the founding of the Memphis diocese. Useful for backgrounding was Don H. Doyle's *Nashville Since the 1920s*. The Diocesan Council of Catholic Women has published a volume about their activities, *Catholic Women in Tennessee,* with several supplements. But my main source in this long chapter has been the telephone. So many of the actors of the Adrian years are alive and cooperative still; my warmest thanks to them.

THE EPILOGUE, of course, expresses my own personal speculations; it is no more history than the predictions of the scores of football games. It does, however, suggest better than any other notation, reading not mentioned in this essay, where I have confined myself to little known and controversial matters.

INDEX

C

D

I

J

Mc

Index compiled by Christine Benagh

Production Notes

The Catholic Center transcribed the author's original typewritten text to a Lanier word processor, which was used to incorporate his subsequent revisions.

The disks from the word processor were converted directly to type-set pages by Ambrose Printing Company, of Nashville, using a Compugraphic 8400 Quadex typesetting computer.

The typeface throughout the book is Palatino, eleven point for the main text, larger sizes for the title page and chapter headings, and smaller sizes for long quotations, picture captions, bibliographical notes, and index.

Ambrose printed the book in twelve signatures of thirty-two pages on a Heidelberg Speedmaster perfecting offset press.

The paper is Warren's Olde Style, acid free and long lasting.

The printed sheets were folded, gathered, sewed, trimmed, and bound in durable cloth covers by the Nicholstone Book Bindery, of Nashville.

Robert A. McGaw designed the book and dust-jacket, and saw to the successive phases of production.

ESTABLISHED 1865

Ambrose Printing Co.